THOMAS GARDNER

THOMAS GARDNER

The True, The Fictive, And The Real

The Historical Dictionary Of Architecture

Of

Quatremère de Quincy

Laguiche del.

A. Simonet sculp

THE TRUE, THE FICTIVE, AND THE REAL

THE HISTORICAL DICTIONARY OF ARCHITECTURE

OF

QUATREMÈRE DE QUINCY

INTRODUCTORY ESSAYS AND SELECTED TRANSLATIONS

BY

SAMIR YOUNÉS

ANDREAS PAPADAKIS PUBLISHER

ACKNOWLEDGMENTS

The collective work of Léon Krier, Demetri Porphyrios, Carroll William Westfall, and David Watkin has greatly influenced the ways in which I think about architecture, and to them I have incurred an intellectual debt. I have benefited considerably from discussions with D. Porphyrios, C.W. Westfall, David Lovekin and Joseph Rykwert. They provided a valuable exchange of ideas on various phases of the manuscript.
Teaching at The University of Notre Dame's School of Architecture with colleagues who share and build a sense in common regarding Nature, the Good City and Architecture has been and continues to be a joyful endeavour. The School's leading and reformatory role in the teaching of traditional architecture shows the powerful instrumentality of ideas such as those examined in this book. Norman Crowe was always a wise counsel and unwaveringly willing to exchange ideas on a daily basis. Michael Lykoudis and Richard Economakis were unfailingly supportive and encouraging in their esprit de corps. Both have provided valuable advice on the etymology of Greek terms. I also wish to acknowledge my students' keen inquiry regarding many of the themes in this book, as they were considered in graduate and undergraduate seminars and studio projects.
I am grateful to the Graham Foundation for Advanced Studies in the Fine Arts for providing the necessary travel grant, without which much of the research would not have been possible, to my publisher Andreas Papadakis for his encouragement and support, and to Sheila de Vallée for her editorial work.
The amiable hospitality of many libraries and their staff in Europe and the United States greatly facilitated my research. Of these I am particularly grateful to the Bibliothèque de l'Académie de France à Rome, Villa Medici, especially to Sra. Maria-Teresa de Bellis for her cheerful and kind assistance. Mme. Mireille Pastoureau and M. Christian Förstel made my stay at the Bibliothèque de l'Institut de France in Paris most fruitful. I am equally appreciative of the staff of the Biblioteca Hertziana in Rome, the Avery Library at Columbia University, and the University of Notre Dame Libraries, in particular Mrs. Linda Messerschmidt and Mrs. Debby Webb who provided valuable help in finding sources. Special thanks are also due to Mrs. Susan Lesko for proof reading parts of the manuscript.
Finally, I am especially thankful to my wife Maria Luisa, and my children John-Paul and Maya Christina for their unconditional support, patience, and humour.

Samir Younés
Notre Dame, 1999

A ma mère et à la mémoire de mon père

FRONT COVER: Un rêve d'architecte à Bordeaux. Carl Laubin.
Oil on canvas, 105cm x 153cm, 1989

FRONTIS: A.C. Quatremère de Quincy,
Membre de l'Académie des inscriptions et belles-lettres,
Secrétaire perpétuel de l'Académie des Beaux-Arts.
Engraving

BACK COVER: A.C. Quatremère de Quincy,
Le Jupiter Olympien, 1815

First published in Great Britain in 1999 by
ANDREAS PAPADAKIS PUBLISHER
An imprint of NEW ARCHITECTURE GROUP LTD.
107 Park Street, London W1Y 3FB
Tel. +44 (0)20 7499 0444 Fax +44 (0)20 7499 0222

ISBN 1 901092 17 8

Printed and bound in Singapore

CONTENTS

Accordance, Allegory, Antique, Aptness, Architect, Architecture, Authority, Art, Bizarre, Boldness, Building (art of), Caprice, Changing of proportions, Character, Colour, Combination, Composite, Composition, Conception, Construction, Contractura, Contrast, Convention, Conventional, Copy, Corinthian, Correction, Decorator, Decoration, Diminution, Disposition, Distribution, Doric, Effect, Elegance, Enlargement (of column), Eurythmy, Exaggeration, Execution, Genius, Grandeur, Harmony, Hut, Idea, Illusion, Imagination, Imitation, Ingenious, Invention, Ionic, Irregular, Licence, Manner, Misuse, Optics, Order, Ordonnance, Ornament, Painting, Perspective, Practice, Principle, Proportion, Propriety, Public Edifices, Restitution, Restoration, Ruin, Rule, Sculpture, Simple, Style, Symmetry, System, Taste, Theory, Tree, Tuscan, Type, Uniformity, Unity, Visual Angle, Wood.

LIST OF ILLUSTRATIONS

INTRODUCTION

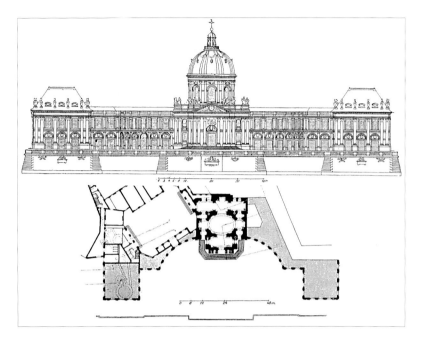

Fig. 2. The Institut de France, Paris.
From: Julien Guadet, *Éléments et théorie de l'architecture*,
Librairie de la construction moderne, Paris, 1909

Until the middle of the eighteenth century in France, the ancient division of the arts, between those that please and those that are useful, still applied. In this view, architecture was classified as an art that served utility rather than a liberal or fine art. It was in the abbé Charles Batteux's *Les beaux-arts réduits à un même principe* of 1747, that appeared the first categorical division of the arts into fine and mechanical.[1] To these he added another category, one that had been defined as early as the Sophists, those arts that partake in both the pleasurable – *l'agréable* – and the useful – *l'utile* – namely, rhetoric and architecture. Batteux had not included architecture and rhetoric directly among the fine arts, because he did not consider these two arts to be imitative of nature; a quality which – he believed – characterized poetry, music, dance, painting and sculpture.[2] Since Claude Perrault's scepticism about architecture as an imitative art, or as an art imitative of nature, many architectural thinkers had provided but indecisive and fragmentary propositions about their acceptance or rejection of such an idea.

Their propositions lacked the comprehensiveness of a general theory of the fine arts, and the role played therein by architecture. Such a theory, as we shall see, was provided by Antoine Chrysostôme Quatremère de Quincy, who disagreed with Batteux's contention that architecture was non-imitative of nature and developed an architectural theory where imitation played a central role. Batteux's classification gained prominence, although in the amended form of fine and mechanical arts, by including architecture and rhetoric among the seven fine arts.[3] Grouping architecture and rhetoric within the fine arts meant that architectural form and verbal form were instruments for the mind's ordering of the world and for its own aesthetic appreciation of this order. This is perhaps at the root of the contemporary contention that architecture and language shared the same dialectical structure.

The study of architectural theory and its terminology necessarily passes through the architectural treatise, the philosophico-aesthetic treatise, the *précis*, the *parallèle*, the *recueil*, the *cours*, the *dictionnaire*, and the classification of their respective discourses into a theory of art in architecture, a theory of beauty in architecture, tectonics, stereotomy, etc.[4] Thus, within the French context for example, a study of aesthetics necessitates the consultation of Cl. Perrault's preface to the *Ordonnance*, Diderot's *Traité du beau*, Briseux's *Traité du beau essentiel*, and Quatremère's *De l'imitation*. For a perspective on the pedagogical role of the architectural treatise, one must cover Cl. Perrault's *Vitruve*, F. Blondel's *Cours*, Laugier's *Essai*, and J-N-L. Durand's *Précis des leçons*. Quatremère's *Dictionnaire historique d'architecture* offers a Platonic discourse on the idea of type, whereas Durand's *Parallèle* provides an operative understanding of typology. Desgodetz's *Edifices antiques de Rome*, Cl. Perrault's *Ordonnance* and Fréart de Chambray's *Parallèle*, provide operative and theoretical discourses on the orders.

The dictionary, however, has had a shorter history than the treatise. Earlier dictionaries provided little more than limited definitions of some technical terms, whereas later ones grew in accuracy on technical issues and in erudition with respect to historical and theoretical matters. These works had little in common with our contemporary dictionaries, which provide a short definition of terms, followed by a limited example of their uses. Rather, they were veritable encyclopaedias, where each article is an essay on etymological, theoretical, historical and practical concerns.

To establish the doctrines they were expounding, educators such as Quatremère de Quincy, A-L. Millin,[5] and E-E. Viollet-le-Duc,[6] used the dictionary form because of its accessibility. This form, however, is not conducive to the systematic sequence of ideas that qualifies the treatise. From here derives the difficulty facing the dictionary in its attempts at framing the largest area possible of architectural knowledge, of laying its epistemological foundations and engaging in the current architectural debates, all in an alphabetical order which bears no relation to the subjects at hand. In these selected translations I have kept the alphabetical order while providing suggestions for grouping various articles in a note to the reader which follows these introductory chapters.

According to Louis Hautecœur,[7] the Italians may have brought the architectural treatise to France perhaps as early as 1500, when Fra Giocondo gave a lecture on Vitruvius in Paris.[8] More than a century later, Bernardino Baldi composed, in Latin, three lexicons which were to have an influence in France. The first two, *De verborum Vitruvianum* and *Scamilli impares*, were published in 1612, and the *Lexicon Vitruvianorum* in 1648. In 1676 André Félibien published his *Des principes de l'architecture, de la sculpture, de la peinture et des autres arts qui en dépendent, avec un dictionnaire des termes propres à chacun de ces arts,* which was overseen and approved by the architects of the Académie Royale. His appended dictionary was a pioneering work in France, superseding the modest circulation of Baldi's books.[9] Strongly influenced by Félibien, Charles Daviler published his *Cours d'architecture* in 1691, which also contained a dictionary as a second volume. The numerous editions of this *cours*[10] occasionally included or omitted the dictionary. Daviler still saw architecture as a utilitarian art, and he divided it into two parts: civil and hydraulic. He saw three components to civil architecture: the art of building, the art of distribution, and the art of decoration. Félibien also advised Thomas Corneille – the brother of the dramatist Pierre Corneille – on the latter's 1694 *Dictionnaire des arts et des sciences,* whose importance lies in its etymological sources and its compilation of the varied meanings assigned to artistic terms. In 1714 the abbé Jean-Louis de Cordemoy published a version of his 1706 *Nouveau traité de toute architecture,* augmented with a *Dictionnaire de tous les termes d'architecture dont on s'est servi dans ce traité.* This dictionary is more valuable for its historical material than for its limited terminology in theoretical and technical matters. In 1737-39, Amédée-François Frézier published *La théorie et la pratique de la coupe des pierres et des bois pour la construction des voûtes...* an important work on stereotomy, in three volumes, the first volume of which ends with an *Explication des termes.*

The latter half of the eighteenth century displays a marked interest in theory and technical knowledge. From 1751 to 1780, Jacques-François

Blondel composed the articles pertaining to architecture for Diderot's *Encyclopédie*,[11] while in 1770 Charles-François Roland de Virloys published his three-volume *Dictionnaire d'architecture civile, militaire et navale, antique, ancienne et moderne*.

Keeping to the eighteenth century classification of the arts between fine and mechanical, Charles J. Panckoucke commissioned Quatremère and Jacques Lacombe for his *Encyclopédie Méthodique*.[12] The former, to compose the *Dictionnaire d'architecture* – in three volumes – and the latter to compose the volumes consecrated to the *Arts et métiers mécaniques*.[13] Quatremère's influential *Dictionnaire* for the *Encyclopédie Méthodique* was the most thorough work to date in the French language – be it a treatise or a dictionary – to frame the widest theoretical scope for architecture and the fine arts. This helped to establish his role as an architect,[14] archaeologist, and theorist, despite this *Encyclopédie*'s erratic pace of publication.[15]

In 1832, Quatremère recast and condensed the dictionary into the two-volume *Dictionnaire historique d'architecture, comprenant dans son plan les notions historiques, descriptives, archéologiques, biographiques, théoriques, didactiques et pratiques de cet art*, which is the subject of the present translation. In this task, he was seconded by J.-B. Rondelet who composed the articles on technical matters.[16] The 1832 publication occurred at the height of a long career in scholarship, pedagogy, and considerable political influence – from his transformation of Ste. Geneviève into the French Panthéon in 1791, to his succession of J. Lebreton in the post of *secrétaire perpétuel* of the *Académie des Beaux-Arts* in 1816. By then, Quatremère was the scholar whose additive achievements counted: the *Mémoire* on Egyptian architecture, his bold proposal to reform art education and the academy in the *Considérations sur les arts du dessin en France*, his contribution to the *Encyclopédie Méthodique*, and his denunciation of Bonaparte's plunder of Italian art in the famous letters to General Miranda. To these he added his massive archaeological dissertation on material polychromy, *Le Jupiter Olympien*; his enormously influential essay *De l'imitation*; and his archaeological restitutions of ancient monuments, the *Monuments et ouvrages d'art antiques*. He was the respected erudite of Parisian intellectual circles, whose essays appeared in the *Journal de Paris*, the *Mercure de France*, and the *Moniteur Universel*. Yet it is for his twenty-three year tenure – 1816 to 1839 – as *secrétaire perpétuel* of the *Académie des Beaux-Arts* that he is most remembered. During these years, Quatremère strongly influenced French art by instituting an official aesthetic to the academy, a project whose realization he had probably coveted since his *Considérations* of 1791, and by exerting disproportionate power over the membership of various commissions of the *Bâtiments civils*.

But the authority of the *Dictionnaire* stemmed more from Quatremère's profound reflections on the nature and ends of architecture, on the principles which are at the source of her rules, and on the roles of imitation and invention within tradition. For these reasons, the *Dictionnaire* became the measure to which other thinkers referred and against which they gauged their positions, whether in agreement or in opposition.[17]

In the *Dictionnaire*, Quatremère distinguished between three kinds of architectural theory:[18] the metaphysical,[19] which designates the essence of the art, the source of its rules; the didactic, which includes most treatises, *parallèles* and *précis*; and the practical, which refers to the pragmatic aspects of construction. The first can be seen to include L.B. Alberti's *De re aedificatoria*, as well as Quatremère's *Dictionnaire*. The second can be seen to include A. Palladio's *Quattro Libri*, while the third may include J.B. Rondelet's *Traité théorique et pratique de l'art de bâtir*.[20]

Quatremère's theory does not materially or factually demonstrate how to compose and build good works; for this aspect had been skilfully covered by various didactic treatises. He held that

"the object of all theory is to teach. One can only teach what can be proved. One proves only to the reason and understanding. If, therefore, it is required that sentiment should be convinced by reasoning, sentiment will require an explanation of every explanation, a proof of every proof. There is, on every subject, a limit to all reasoning, which limit theory is bound to respect, and which it would be imprudent to go beyond. There commences the unsolvable. Farther we cannot go. It is the mathematical line. It is the region of the imaginary, where reason quits us, and whither none can follow us. It is also that of Icarus, where the wings of the mind too frequently abandon him..."[21]

In scope, Quatremère's theory can be characterized as being at once a polemic and a system. It is a polemic in that it distinguishes itself by opposing or corroborating other doctrines. For example, Quatremère's polemic can partially be seen as an intervention to steer architecture away from the scientific and Cartesian direction within which Cl. Perrault began to situate it in the seventeenth century, and which Durand and the polytechnicians began to concretize in the early nineteenth. It is a system for two reasons: first, because it is mainly concerned with what he termed "metaphysical" theory, which designated the realm of ideas that constitutes the very source of rules, conventions and practice. Secondly, it aims at providing a broad conception of architecture and the fine arts, in relation to aesthetics.

In this *Dictionnaire*, Quatremère established the framework for an aesthetic system where architecture, as the highest imitative art, is never confined solely to the factual, the real, or the immanent, but remained necessarily open to the paradigmatic, the true, and the transcendent. The True, here, can be defined as an Idea through which the Good is known, whilst Idea designates that universal aspect that makes the visible comprehensible, as in the relationship between *eidos* and *idéa*. Artistic truth, then, is a congruence between the nature of an art, and that art's ends and means. The word transcendent here refers to a meaning that strongly influences a work of art or architecture while remaining outside it. This, of course, depends on the extent to which an art can absorb external meaning; a notion that is strongly tied to propriety. Within this framework, architecture, the word, the image, the symbol and

the tool, assured the mediation between nature, society and history within clearly defined realms.

By upholding nature as a paradigm, and considering the man-made paradigm as *natural*, as in the idea of the hut, and justifying type, character and style based on social propriety, Quatremère's word-concepts such as principle, rule, imitation, invention, type, and character, clearly framed the milieu of ideas that architects ought to refer to, in relation to the boundaries of the art where they stood. And in this endeavour, the word of architectural theory played a crucial role, as Quatremère subtly defined and etymologized.

The critic may wonder why the role of the word in architectural theory seems to be so highly privileged here, if in the end, it is the building that matters. The answer is twofold. First, if the contention that the word helps the mind to order the world is true, then the word plays a major role in delimiting the scope of a field and in helping to lay its epistemological foundations. The word occupies a capital role as the instrument upon which the mind depends for its operations and expressions. More specifically, the word of architectural theory demonstrates how the mind orders the ideas that are manifest in architectural form. Such is the aim of terminology in Quatremère's *Dictionnaire,* in the sense that this very terminology stands as a symbol for architectural knowledge. Indeed, Quatremère's *Dictionnaire* associates two major epistemological projects: the encyclopaedic aim of framing a theory of the arts of design (*les arts du dessin*), side by side with the aims of the architectural treatise, especially in theoretical and historical matters. Doubtless, Quatremère's interest in terminology stemmed from the encyclopaedic breadth of his project, in a manner reminiscent of Diderot and D'Alembert's understanding of the role of language in their own *Encyclopédie*. The *Dictionnaire* aims at organizing, defining and orienting architectural knowledge through the use of the word. This task is truly ancient. The reader will recall Vitruvius's alliance of architectural terminology with the terminology of aesthetics and philosophy that qualified Hellenistic thought, and the fervent wish of Renaissance authors of *trattati* to compose *the* great theoretical treatise which could synthesize a universal theory of art and a theory of beauty. In this sense, Quatremère's terminology brings a much needed reform and clarity to the symbolic poverty of contemporary architectural theory and its terminology.

But the universality to which Quatremère aims does not necessarily entail that his *Dictionnaire* be regarded as a prescriptive treatise. Some of his detractors have focused on the determined and unyielding aspects of his personality,[22] on what they considered to be his domineering approach to education, especially during his tenure as *secrétaire perpétuel*. In fact, he once referred to himself, half seriously, as a "dictator in the republic of the arts." These detractors err, however, when they

terminology of rhetoric permitted architectural theory to flourish.[23] Vitruvius suggests that the architect's knowledge comprises two aspects: the one having to do with practice (*fabrica*), the other theoretical, discursive and serving to explain buildings (*ratiocinatio*).[24] Put differently, architecture has to be built and explained. In 1,1,3, he writes: "In all matters, but particularly in architecture, there are these two points: the thing signified (*quod significatur*) and that which gives it its significance (*quod significat*)."[25] These two inseparable points can be seen to suggest a linguistic bridge assuring the links and boundaries between the artistically "true" of architecture (*quod significat*) and the "real" of construction (*quod significatur*).[26] Vitruvius's definitions of

Fig. 4. Socrates defending himself before his Judges, A. Canova.
Engraving by H. Moses. From Henry Moses, The Works of Antonio Canova,
Septimius Prowett, London, 1887

concentrate on this aspect of his personality in order to dismiss the ideas he promulgated and defended. For, to deduce a prescriptive or proscriptive theory from an unyielding personality is a hasty syllogism; one that tends to overlook the depth of Quatremère's thought and its applicability to the circumstances of contemporary practice, for his time and ours.

The second reason for the importance of the word of architectural theory, is that rhetoric has been the intellectual region, *par excellence*, which joined the terminology of such a theory, to that of philosophy and aesthetics. Vitruvius's *De Archi-tectura*, and Quatremère's *Dictionnaire* accrue a distinctive value for their convergence of the arts of rhetoric and architecture, in the sense that the

ordinatio, *dispositio*, *eurythmia*, *symmetria*, *decor* and *distributio*,[27] and Quatremère's *ordre, symétrie, unité, variété, beauté, harmonie, imitation, invention,* and *génie,* strongly parallel the classifications of rhetoric, which include content, order, composition, disposition, propriety, cadence and style. Both rhetoric and architecture seek to delight through proportion, harmony and rhythm, as well as convince through usefulness, propriety and legibility. Architectural legibility is tied to character and propriety (*convenance*) as part of a system of values which is at once external, for example social mores and sense-based observation mediated by language, and internal, for example, architectural composition as language. Herein lies an important analogy for the recovery of the word of architectural theory and of its role in the intellectual edifice of the current reconstruction project in architecture.[29] And further, therein lies the vital contemporary relevance of Quatremère de Quincy's *magnum opus*: the encyclopaedic project of a dictionary of architecture; a task on which he laboured for more than forty years, and which gained him the reputation of the "grammarian of the arts." Part II of this book, provides the first English translation of the theoretical articles from the *Dictionnaire*.[30] Given the strong similarities between legibility and translation, in the sense that both have an aesthetic role and seek a transparency to meaning, I have adopted an approach that has kept faithful to the character of Quatremère's academic discourse and his literary style.

In presenting this translated selection, two criteria were adopted. First, this translation aims at covering the articles related to architectural theory for the importance that they hold for the understanding of classical architectural thought in general, and its contemporary instrumentality in particular. Second, the articles that concern factual material such as the history of archaeological sites, architects' biographies, and architectural details, have been omitted because this material has been superseded by subsequent historical scholarship. Thus, articles such as allegory, architecture, authority, character, composition, Doric, harmony, hut, imitation, invention, licence, proportion, propriety, principles, rules, restitution, restoration, and type, have been translated. Articles such as abacus, Antinopolis, scotia and lime have not been translated because such information is readily available in history books, treatises and construction manuals with greater detail and accuracy. For, as attested by Quatremère himself, his *Dictionnaire* is to be read as a treatise on architectural theory, and studied less for its factual details than for the principles it expounds.

*   *   *

Against the conjugated effects of empiricism, romanticism, and a techno-scientific view which was indiscriminately applied to the arts and the sciences, Quatremère's *œuvre* is that of a Platonic dialectician whose foremost aim is to rescue enduring principles from being eclipsed by the relativism of historical contingencies. For this reason, he dedicated the better part of a long life to reforming the very ways in which the arts and architecture are to be thought (see my biographical chapter). In this sense, one reads Quatremère in the same way that one reads Alberti, because both these thinkers were primarily concerned with how architecture is to be thought. Accordingly, his metaphysical theory aimed at basing architecture on essentialist foundations, admonishing architects never to lose sight of the dual origin of principles in Nature – understood more in her laws, and less in her products – and in conventions. He greatly clarified what the *anciens* had only partially explained and what the *modernes* had only superficially treated, regarding the instrumentality of conventions in contemporary practice. First, he elucidated the manner in which architecture was an art imitative of Nature and conventions, distinguishing between the type and the model, the imitation and the copy. Underlying this distinction were three notions that one may term: the true, the fictive, and the real, seen in the following relationship. The enduring principle – the realm of the true – transcends but stands indissociable from what is historically contingent – the realm of the real – while the fictive bridged the distance. Quatremère affirmed a view of making as a poetic order, understood here in the Greek sense of making (*poein*: to make). Secondly, he asserted that while imitation and invention were ontologically linked to the human character, this did not necessarily imply that invention operated in the same way in the arts as in the sciences; indeed he distinguished between discovery in the sciences and invention in the arts. Invention is not independent from rules and clearly defined artistic genres; otherwise, there would be no epistemological grounds for judging invention. Invention steers a difficult and necessary path between the needs of an individual's artistic freedom, the *sensus communis* of larger artistic conventions, and propriety within the boundaries of each art. The ideas comprised in the concepts of imitation and invention are discussed in Chapter I.

Chapter II discusses the parallels drawn by Quatremère between theories of origin and language, evident in his positions on type, character and style. Architecture and language are discussed against the system of codification, signs and analyses posited by the *Encyclopédie*, as well as the notion of *l'architecture parlante*. Discussing Quatremère's ambivalence vis-à-vis analogical and literal relationships between architecture and language, this chapter concludes in favour of keeping these relationships on the level of analogy.

Chapter III is chiefly concerned with the idea of poetic order, seeing Quatremère's *Historical Dictionary of Architecture* as one way to access this order. This chapter proposes that the word of architectural theory is instrumental in establishing the idea of poetic making, through a reconciliation between the true, the fictive and the real. Re-constructing architecture therefore implies

re-visioning the ways in which it is thought, by re-visioning the very ways in which its theory is written. This chapter cautions that a contemporary approach to such great theoretical texts should be cognizant of another order, namely the technological, which is to be categorically distinguished from the poetic.

This book does not aim at placing Quatremère's ideas within a compartment of historiography; on the contrary, it is based on a firm conviction of their contemporary instrumentality, and not their past value alone. Quatremère stood in the middle of the modern era as a Janus figure. He prophetically saw architecture and art's descent in the direction of whole immanence, and away from any transcendence. For this purpose, he deployed Herculean measures to delay this development throughout a long career as a scholar, educator and politician. If the arts were the seven horses, then Quatremère was the charioteer who was desperately pulling the reins in order to prevent their fall into the precipice of immanence.

NOTES

1 See, pp. 5-7.

2 For a historical survey of artistic classification, see Tatarkiewicz, W. *A History of Six Ideas*. Martinus Nijhoff, The Hague, Boston, London. PWN, Polish scientific publishers, 1980. See also Kristeller, P.O. "The Modern System of the Arts: A study in the history of aesthetics" I and II, in *Essays on the History of Aesthetics*, ed. P. Kivy, Library of the History of Ideas, University of Rochester Press, 1992.

3 In the preliminary discourse to the *Encyclopédie*, D'Alembert had included architecture among the fine arts.

4 A comprehensive history of the co-evolution of architectural terminology and theory remains to be written. For a recent survey of the terminology of architectural theory in the French context from the sixteenth until the nineteenth centuries, see Szambien, W. *Symétrie, Goût, Caractère*. Paris, Picard, 1986.

5 *Dictionnaire des Beaux-Arts*. 3 vols., Paris, 1838.

6 *Dictionnaire raisonné de l'architecture française du XIe au XVIe siècle*. Paris, Morel, 1854-1868.

7 Hautecœur, L. *Histoire de l'architecture classique en France*. Paris, A. Picard, 1943-57.

8 Hautecœur, *Ibid*, Vol. 1, Chapter III, Les leçons de l'antiquité. p. 193. For a general survey of the fortunes of the Vitruvian manuscripts, see P. Fleury's introduction to *Vitruve, De l'architecture*. Livre I. Paris, Les Belles Lettres, 1990. It was not until 1547 that Jean Martin and Jean Goujon's *Vitruve* was published.

9 For a bibliography of treatises and dictionaries in the French context, see Szambien, *Ibid*.

10 In 1693, 1694, 1710, 1720, 1738 and 1755, respectively.

11 See T. M. Russell's *Architecture in the Encyclopédie of Diderot and D'Alembert: the letterpress articles and selected engravings*. Aldershot, Scholar Press, 1993.

12 For a history of this encyclopaedia, see Darnton, R. *The Business of Enlightenment*. Cambridge, Belknap Press, 1979, especially Chapter VII. See also Appendix C in Lavin, S. *Quatremère de Quincy and the Invention of a New Language in Architecture*. Cambridge, Mass., M.I.T. Press, 1992.

13 Earlier, in 1752, Lacombe had composed an amateur's dictionary of the fine arts: *Le Dictionnaire portatif des Beaux-Arts*..

14 His reputation had begun to rise when he wrote in 1784-85 his *Mémoire sur l'architecture égyptienne*, for which he received a prize from the *Académie des Inscriptions et Belles-lettres*. Only on two occasions was Quatremère involved in construction: the first was his supervision of the transformation of Ste. Geneviève into the French Panthéon in 1791-93, the second - and only built work - was a pulpit in Saint Germain-des-Près, which he constructed in 1829. See the biographical and bibliographical chronology.

15 The first volume - "Abajour" to "Coloris des Fleurs" - was published in 1788. J-B. Rondelet assisted in the endeavour by writing the technical articles: *stéréotomie* and *construction des voûtes*. The second volume was issued in two parts: the first, "Colossal" to "Escalier" was published in 1801, and the other, "Escalier" to "Mutules" in 1820. J-N. Huyot and A.L. Castellan assisted Quatremère by writing several articles for the third volume, which was published in 1825.

16 In association with a group of renowned scholars, which included Visconti, Castellan, Dufourny, Huyot, Chaudet, Le Sueur and Raoul-Rochette, Quatremère was to collaborate on yet another dictionary: the *Dictionnaire de l'Académie des Beaux-Arts*. This dictionary was published in an incomplete form - letters A to G in six volumes - from 1858 to 1896.

17 Most notable among these thinkers was E-E. Viollet-le-Duc, whose massive *Dictionnaire raisonné* stood in opposition to Quatremère's imitative theory and his denigration of the Gothic in favour of the Classic as a modern practice. This opposition notwithstanding, Viollet-le-Duc was still explicit in his referral to Quatremère's *Dictionnaire* in order to polemically distinguish himself from it. See especially Viollet-le-Duc's articles *Style* and *Unité*. For a recent commentary on Quatremère and Viollet-le-Duc's dictionaries, see Barry Bergdoll's "The *Dictionnaire Raisonné*, Viollet-le-Duc's Encyclopaedic Structure of Architecture" in *The Foundations of Architecture, Selections from the Dictionnaire Raisonné*, Trans. by K. D. Whitehead, New York, G. Brazilier, 1990.

18 See the articles: *Principle* and *Rule*.

19 "The word metaphysics... applied to the science of the nature of things, and of souls, intelligences and origins." See Acton, H. B. "The Philosophy of Language in Revolutionary France" in *Studies in Philosophy*, British Academy Lectures, New York, Oxford Univ. Press, 1966, p. 145.

20 In 7 vols., 1802-1817.

21 *Essai sur la nature, le but et les moyens de l'imitation dans les beaux-arts.* Paris, 1823. Introductions by L. Krier and D. Porphyrios. Archives d'Architecture Moderne, Brussels, 1980, p. 254 (p. 284-285 Engl. Tr.) This book will be henceforth referred to as *De l'imitation*, and the following quotes in English are from J.C. Kent's translation of 1837. I have listed the pagination from both the French original and the English translation.

22 The only comprehensive biography remains René Schneider's *Quatremère de Quincy et son intervention dans les arts*, and his *L' Esthétique classique chez Quatremère de Quincy*. Paris, Hachette, 1910.

23 For a discussion on the art of rhetoric and *De Architectura*, see Callebat, L. "Rhétorique et Architecture dans le *De Architectura* de Vitruve" in *Le Projet de Vitruve*. Actes du colloque international organisé par l'Ecole Française de Rome, Palais Farnèse, 1994.

24 "*Architecti est scientia pluribus disciplinis et uariis eruditionibus ornata cuius iudicio probantur omnia quae ab ceteris artibus perficiuntur opera. Ea nascitur ex* **fabrica** *et* **ratiocinatione.** *Fabrica est continuata ac trita usus meditatio quae manibus perficitur e materia cuiuscumsque generis opus est ad propositum deformationis. Ratiocinatio autem est quae re fabricatas sollertiae ac rationis pro portione demonstrare atque explicare potest.*" Vitruvius, *De Architectura*, 1,1. *(Emphasis added.)* See P.H. Schrijvers, *Vitruve I, 1,1: Explication de texte*, In the *Proceedings* of the *International Symposium on Vitruvius' De Architectura and the Hellenistic and Republican Architecture*, Leiden, 1987, p. 50.

25 Morris H. Morgan trans., New York, Dover Publications, 1960, p. 5.

26 The notion of links and boundaries is developed in Chapter II.

27 Morgan, p. 13.

28 These comments imply only a mediatory function to the linguistic analogy, and do not suggest that language and architecture share the same dialectical structure. See Chapter III.

29 The word reconstruction is used here in the sense given to it by Léon Krier. See, for example, his "La reconstruction de la ville." in *Architecture Rationelle*. Brussels, Archives d'Architecture Moderne, 1978; and *Houses, Palaces, Cities*. D. Porphyrios ed. London, Academy Editions, 1984. For an historical and theoretical context of this reconstruction, see A. Barey, *La déclaration de Bruxelles*, Brussels, Archives d'Architecture Moderne,1980; and Culot, M. & Lefèbvre P. "The State of Defiance," in *On the Methodology of Architectural History*. D. Porphyrios ed., London, Architectural Design, 1981. See also Demetri Porphyrios's *Classical Architecture*, London, Academy Editions, 1992; and C.W. Westfall's discourse in Van-Pelt, R. and Westfall, C.W. *Architectural Principles in the Age of Historicism*, New Haven and London, Yale University Press, 1991. More recent works include *Building Classical*, R. Economakis. ed., London, Academy Editions, 1993; *Rinascimento Urbano*, G. Tagliaventi ed., Bologna, Grafis Edizioni, 1995; and *Building Cities*, N. Crowe, R. Economakis, M. Lykoudis eds., Artmedia, London, 1999.

30 A selection of articles from Quatremère's first dictionary: the *Dictionnaire d'architecture*, 1788-1825, has been translated by Tanis Hinchcliffe. "Extracts from the *Encyclopédie méthodique d'architecture*." London, 9H, 1985. See also the *Dizionario Storico di Architettura*, Marsilio, Venezia, 1985, with introduction and annotations by Georges Teyssot and Valeria Farinati.

I

QUATREMÈRE DE QUINCY'S THEORY

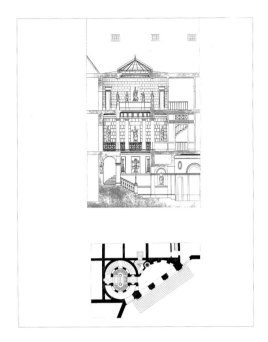

Fig. 4. Stair, Bibliothèque Mazarine, L.M.D. Biet.
From: Gourlier, *Choix d'edifices publics...*,
Paris, 1845-50

The sound theory of art consists in freeing the true – a matter that can be easily travestied – from a double bias that emanates from a single source, and which consists in the denial of that which cannot be demonstrated physically, or its depreciation to the most material level possible." A.C. Quatremère de Quincy.[1]

Throughout his life, Quatremère de Quincy was deeply concerned with an artistic knowledge that endures beyond the historically contingent, as well as a sense-based apprehension of the world. In this, he is part of a lineage of Platonic thinkers, who, while understanding the inevitability of Heraclitean change, endeavoured to find and affirm that which persists, that which is essential and beyond contingent change, albeit without excluding change.[2] This need not necessarily entail – as some have suggested – that as a Platonist thinker, Quatremère disregarded the contingent, or that he regarded the enduring and the contingent as mutually exclusive. For as we shall see, his artistic theory rests on a dialectic that grouped imitation, invention, and genius; the

artist's intellectual freedom and the clear boundaries between the arts; and the instrumentality of history in the renewal within tradition.

By the time Quatremère reached his third decade, his compatriot *philosophes* had been heralding the primacy of sense-based experience and systematic observation as the privileged approach to knowledge, and the only way to deduce truth in the sciences and the arts. Early in the eighteenth century, Du Bos was expressing Lockean sensate theory in order to link artistic genius to man's physiological constitution on the one hand, and attain the factual immediacy of aesthetic experience on the other.[3] He announced the relativity of aesthetic appeal of subjects which by their very natures were susceptible of universal or individual interest, but strongly emphasized the sources of individual – subjective – aesthetics. To these propositions Condillac added his contention that the senses were qualified by an exclusively inward directionality, and that the formation of ideas followed logically and solely from the sensuous perception of physical objects.[4] The often repeated assertion that what is in the mind must have first passed through the senses, was wholeheartedly shared by D'Alembert in his preliminary discourse to the *Encyclopédie*. Le Camus de Mézières, while claiming to write the first discourse on the relationship between that which is arduously perceived in architecture, namely architectural proportions and their relationship to the senses, hoped that his treatise would acquire for architects the same importance that Condillac's treatise had for the *philosophes*.[5] In holding this sense-based psychology as the privileged key to knowledge, the *philosophes* came to see the notion of a transcendent, understood as the knowledge of a truth beyond the senses, as contrary to reality. Knowledge had to be qualified by an immediacy with physical reality, which was defined as the realm of empirical experience. In this view, sight was a universal guarantor that things will be perceived as they *are*, and not as they *could* or *should* be, and sight looked at the world through this image.[6] In other words, meaning was associated with the visible, and less with an invisible causal realm. In such a manner, reality and the perceived image came to be synonymously identified.[7] Diderot's claim that "metaphysics proves nothing" signalled a decided shift towards factual experience, or the context of immediacy between subject and object: the sensuously evident was the locus of the true and the real.

Against these assertions, and for the better part of a career that spanned the last two decades of the eighteenth century until the fourth decade of the nineteenth, Quatremère affirmed a view of art based on Platonic metaphysics. In such a view, there are things that are seen and thought, there are things that are seen but not thought, and more importantly there are things that are thought but not seen. The latter category are the Platonic Forms, in the sense given to them in the *Republic*, *Cratylus* and *Phaedo*. Forms exist in nature and occupy a causal role *vis-à-vis* phenomena, prior to any constituent subjectivity. For example, to know if an act is just, one looks to the Form of justice. A Form is a paradigm that sensible objects imitate, although they do so imperfectly and incompletely. Forms or types exist as an ontolog-

ical essence that covers the particular partially because only parts of the essential are able to manifest in the particular.[8] For Plato, there is a Form of Forms, the ultimate measure of the good, the true and the beautiful, which for Quatremère is nature considered in her laws or *natura naturans*. This view explains what is the same in all cases of these Forms, and Quatremère agrees, hence the importance that the idea of type accrued in his thought.[9] Nature – considered in her laws – for Quatremère is that highest realm that permeates the phenomenal world, and exists as much in her invisible aspects as in her visible manifestations. This view also concerns the kind of presuppositions that the mind assumes in its quest for and in its construction of knowledge; a realm where the word plays a formative role.

A close reading of Quatremère's two most important texts – *An Essay on the Nature, the End, and the Means of Imitation*, and the present *Historical Dictionary of Architecture* – would be greatly aided if accompanied by keen attention to the role of the word in Quatremère's system of art, as his definitions build his concepts and his concepts in turn build his theory. Undoubtedly, the word is not an infallible guarantee against the ambiguities of usage, and the reader will recall how Plato's dissatisfaction with the word as an imitation of nature and as a result of convention, led him to distinguish between the name giver, the dialectician, and the teacher.[10] The name giver is closest to nature and therefore invents the first names based on a direct imitation of nature. The dialectician possesses the best knowledge of all three, because he uses both the natural and the conventional and emends the possible failures of both in deviating from a truth or a reality, even if usage makes this divergence inevitable; while the teacher uses and propagates what the first two have already established. The following discussion will make evident the manner in which Quatremère is the Platonic dialectician – a characteristic permeating the *Historical Dictionary of Architecture*. His terminology stands as a beacon of clarity among the bewildering semantic variations that have contributed to the crisis of definition in architecture since the late eighteenth century.

The Idea of Imitation

A unifying aspect to Quatremère's thought is its metaphysical character, which he defined as "the science of the operations of the mind."[11] It is this aspect that distinguished his thought and that of Cousin and Lamennais in France[12] – including his colleagues Portalis, Jacobi and de Stolberg, during their common exile in the Holstein – from empiricism, the proliferation of sense-based theories, as well as rising romanticism. Quatremère's Platonism made him inclined to see each art as a different manner of seizing and representing one aspect of what he called the "universal model in nature,"[13] which he understood as *natura naturans*. This is the realm of

Fig. 5. Terpsichore, A. Canova. Engraving by H. Moses. From: Henry Moses, *The Works of Antonio Canova*, Septimius Prowett, London, 1887

Forms or essences, which are necessarily archetypal. This study of nature,

"...does not consist so much in the special investigation of an individual and barren reality, as in the observation of the fertile principles of an ideal and generalized model. ... What is individual and particular may be everywhere found, and may always be evidenced by the senses; but that which is universal and general, can only be grasped by thought or the action of the mind. This *general*, as regards imitation, can only be defined by the understanding, and genius alone can imitate it."[14]

Through extensive observation, a grasp of causes, organizing systems, general traits and relations, the imitating artist distills nature into a system; hence the notion of the ideal.

"Now this system is nothing else than the ideal type of imitation, a type formed not on this or that isolated work of nature, but on the generality of the laws and motives manifested in the universal whole of her works. It was therefore no longer the particular work, but the general motive of the supreme Worker, that became the true regulator of the operations of art, and here we see why ideal imitation must be accounted pre-eminently the imitation of nature. If we consider that we are imitating her when we are ruled only by one of those partial productions which are frequently but deviations from her plan, do we not imitate much more and much better, when we appropriate the very principle of her laws, and study the collective whole of the universal order of nature on which those laws are imprinted?"[15]

Here, the Platonism of Winckelmann and Quatremère concur, in that *idealische schönheit*, *le beau idéal*, and *la belle nature*, are Forms, but not necessarily the form of any existing object. However, while both agree that this ideal achieved its most perfect manifestations in Periclean Greece, Quatremère placed a stronger emphasis on the realizability of this ideal as a modern project. He saw reason and sentiment as the guides to understand the laws that nature has adopted in the manifestations of manifold individuals. But the fact that nature is this enveloping milieu within which everything is comprised, does not necessarily mean that *natura naturans* is manifest in every art and in every object of imitation to the same degree.[16] Accordingly, a single work of art is never the complete manifestation of the artist's imitation of nature, for the same reason that an individual by itself cannot gather all the perfections found in nature. Only, nature and art have different ends, and the perfection to which nature aims is not necessarily that to which art aims, even if art imitates the order, harmony and proportions found in nature.[17] It is through a purposive finality that art's aims parallel nature's ends. And here, Quatremère drew on the Aristotelian similarity between art and nature which states that had nature been involved in producing houses, then they would have the appearance that architecture ought to bestow upon them, and conversely, had architecture been involved in producing trees, then they would have the appearance given them by nature.[18] As a poetic form of making that has an efficient cause which is distinctly other than itself, art – fine and mechanical – can only operate based on a clear knowledge of its nature, ends and means. Therefore, one may ask, in what wise does art imitate nature according to Quatremère? And more specifically, in what wise is architecture imitative of nature, and what are the particular characteristics of this imitation? To the first question, Quatremère replies that

"...since there are two ways of considering nature, the one in the details of her works, the other in their collective whole; the one in the partial instance of the individual, the other in the type of the species,... There is the model affording the imitation of a *man*, and that affording the imitation of *man*. The difference between these two models, and their imitations, is the same as that which our minds distinguish between genus and species, between species and the individual. It is then a fact, and a philosophically evident one, that the idea of nature, in so far as it embraces generalities, corresponds with the idea attached to the genus, or species and not with that of the individual."[19]

Drawing on this analogical correspondence between nature and the arts, Quatremère concluded that each art has in nature two models, the one general and the other particular.[20] By selecting and assembling nature's disparate beauties, the artist recognizes and produces parts of the ideal[21] by representing *man* and not one man, architecture and not one building. Although this pursuit

of the ideal involves separating the contingent from the essential, in order to reveal the essential, this need not necessarily imply a categorical rejection of the idea of contingency. For how could one negate the circumstantial and transient outcomes that inevitably accompany every human endeavour? Suffice it to say that since the rise of relativism, the idea of the enduring has been eclipsed or denied by those who herald the supremacy of contingency. This explains the inability or unwillingness of some, in this age of historicism, to see art, architecture and the city from the Aristotelian perspective of what *ought* to be; for they can only see what *is*. This phenomenon, perhaps more than any other, contributed to the eclipse of commonly held principles, within one

Fig. 6. Helen, A. Canova. Engraving by H. Moses.
From: Henry Moses, *The Works of Antonio Canova*,
Septimius Prowett, London, 1887

culture or pan-culturally. Quatremère prophetically foresaw these developments, against which many of his writings are aimed.

As to the second question regarding architecture and her imitation of nature, Quatremère maintained that this imitation does not necessarily depend on the physical tangibility of that model in order for the model to be considered real, as the empiricists contend. Architecture, as distinguished from other arts, has no direct model in nature that can be concretely considered an origin.[22]

Here, it is useful to distinguish fundamentally between an origin and a beginning, a distinction that Quatremère does not explicitly make. For as constitutive elements of the classical tradition, theories of origin – since Vitruvius – have emphasized empirical experiments leading to a beginning or beginnings, to the *archi* in architecture. This shows that the hut is a beginning and not an origin, for a certain distance had to be traversed to arrive at it. The locus of the origin was somewhere between a natural shelter and the first interpretations of constructive elements devoid of purely natural connotations. Thus the first construction was neither the hut nor the temple, for these buildings converge many experiences, and their details imply a sophisticated way of ad-dressing the built work from the exterior. The hut for Quatremère is a fictive type, and its influence should not be seen in a material sense but in a metaphorical one. For if the hut were regarded only in a material sense, then humanity would have continued building the

The success of the hut, and later carpentry, resides precisely in the fictive or metaphorical transformation from wood into stone. It is through this fictive aspect that the hut came to occupy the role of a natural model for architecture. In this acceptance of a fictive model, architecture appropriates the Aristotelian artistic truth, in contradistinction to the factual or cognitive truth of a historical genealogy. Architecture's imitation of nature is analogical and not similitudinal;[26] and here, Quatremère is removed from Plato's understanding of truth.

Two other models combined to make architecture an art of imitation: the analogical imitation of the human body, and the abstract imitation of nature. First, the observation of the proportions

Fig. 7. The Primitive Hut,
M.A. Laugier.
From: Essai sur l'architecture, 1753

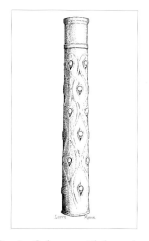

Fig. 8. Column with branches.
From: Josef Durm, *Die Baukunst der Etrusker und Römer*,
A Kröner Verlag, Stuttgart, 1905

same hut *ad infinitum*, and the column would have always remained a tree.

Nature, according to Quatremère, offers three kinds of materials: earth, wood and stone.[23] Earth, when formed into brick or dried in the sun, will rank among stones; and stone, he contended, on account of its material difficulties, was only adopted after centuries of development in wooden construction. Stone projections, cornices, dentils, could only have received their forms from the imitation of another material, namely wood. For if stone were to copy itself, he believed, then it would be condemned to a constant repetition of the same constructional members.[24] Wood, however, offered the imitative mind a vast array of "analogies, inductions, and free assimilations."[25]

of the human body directly and through sculpture, revealed reciprocal and necessary relations between the parts and the whole. These relations, in their variety, implied general laws of order, and explained diverse qualities of strength, elegance, opulence, etc. Architecture appropriated and transposed the system of proportions and various characters of the human body, to the set of necessary relations that various modes of carpentry established between architectural members. The resulting rules and proportions in sculpture and architecture, were seen by Quatremère – as they had been by the Greeks – as "rules of varying flexibility." These laws of proportion are "always constant as to their principle and always variable as to their applications,"[27] and not a set of proscriptive dictates. Quatremère also considered such an imitation of the body as analogical and far from any direct physical resemblance or transposition. Accordingly, he found Vitruvius's consideration of the Doric, Ionic, and Corinthian columnar types as imitations of the male and female bodies, to be a reasonable proposition if kept on an analogical level. Only Vitruvius's acceptance of literal parallels between the baseless Doric column and a man's naked foot, or the ornate base of the Ionic column and the elegant footwear of women; or their head-dress and the volute; or the folds of their robes and fluting; all were considered by Quatremère to be the results of a flawed reasoning based on an abuse of the idea of imitation.

the idea behind the individual appearance of a building, a Platonic Form pregnant with infinite potentialities from which many dissimilar buildings may derive. This he distinguished from the model as a specific object that can be copied identically.[28] The higher form of the type allows the understanding of essences in architecture: the realm of the true; while the form of the model becomes a means for individuating particular buildings: the realm of the real. It can be said that, in matters of imitation, the idea of the true is of an intellectual evidence, while the idea of the real depends on a sensuous evidence.[29] Even if the type is imitated and the model copied, they are inseparable entities, for the model can physically complete what the type – or archetype – *per se* cannot.

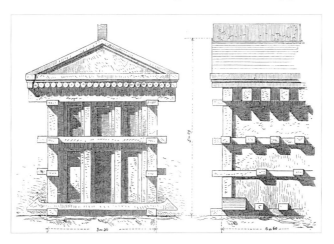

Fig. 9. Lykian Tomb.
From: Josef Durm, *Die Baukunst der Grieschen*,
A. Kröner Verlag, Leipzig, 1910

Second, the transposition of the idea of order in nature provided architecture with the most ideal form of imitation; one that imitates nature in her laws, for example, unity through variety, the general and the particular, symmetry and proportion. Here, the architect is at once the artificer and the philosopher, endowing architecture with a purposive finality analogous to the one that qualifies nature. This form of making, modelled on nature, was based on a theory of essences, evidenced in Quatremère's appropriation of Platonic and Aristotelian theories of universals for the purposes of art and architecture; hence his theory of type which accrues in truth in proportion to its universality. Thus, for Quatremère, the type was an evidence of nature's order; the type was natural. It is

The importance of Quatremère's contribution to imitative theory in architecture, resides in his synthesis of four ideas. First, he proposed that the hut, as a model, had a fictive aspect to it, and was not to be understood literally or materially. Second, he introduced a lucid – and new – clarification between two dualities: the type and the model, the imitation and the copy.[30] Third, he indicated that architecture's imitation of the human body through proportions was analogical and not literal. Fourth, he outlined how architecture's imitation of nature was an abstraction of a perceived natural order. Quatremère's demonstration that architecture was indeed an art imitative of nature answered Batteux's earlier unexplained contention that architecture – and rhetoric – was not imitative of nature. Quatre-mère concludes

"... that with respect to her *essential nature*, architecture is an *art* based on necessity, and whose imitation, being purely ideal, is not material or factual; that she draws some imitative analogies from nature and from the arts which are her evident imitation; but that she imitates no reality; that her form is for the mind, only a combination of relations, proportions, and reasons which please inasmuch as they are simply expressed."[31]

Quatremère's Platonic inclinations made him consider *idea* and *image* in themselves – as Forms – to be synonymous concepts; while his knowledge of artistic practice and his reflections on perception, made him realize that *idea* and *image* become distinct entities only with respect to the percipient who applies the first to the objects of the mind, and the second to material objects which address the senses.[32] This implied that there are two qualities in works of imitation which in turn divide these works into two classes. The first class of works is mostly the result of the mind which perceives beyond empirical reality, reaching toward the world of ideas or principles, and toward the production of images, in view of an equilibrium between both.[33] This is the realm of the true, or what he termed ideal imitation, affording the highest intellectual pleasure, which is the aim of imitation in the fine arts.[34] The second class is mostly the products of the senses and involves the imitation of reality in its most positivist and material level.[35] Accordingly, the imitative image does not reproduce the reality of an idea or object, but one of its many possible appearances. Thus, between the *idea* and the *image* lies the same distance as between what we termed the true and the real. This distance is measured at once intellectually and materially, for the material image is needed to represent that which is most immaterial, namely, the idea. Imitation in the fine arts produces the resemblance of an object in another object that becomes its image. Such an imitation is to be decisively distinguished from the illusion of the copy which repeats the reality of an object. Put differently, the copy produces a "similarity by means of identity," as in the mechanical repetition of the same model. This repetition or sameness, does not afford the kind of intellectual pleasure that results from imitation, for it primarily lacks the distance needed by "resemblance by means of an image."[36] Accordingly, Quatremère saw similarity by means of identity as befitting the mechanical arts, and resemblance by means of an image as characterizing the fine arts. For this reason, he agreed with the eighteenth-century principal division of the arts into fine and mechanical. Concomitantly, he held that the objects of intellectual imitation correspond to the faculties of the soul or the intellect, in as much as physical properties of objects correspond to the senses, and that these two reasons stood behind the various divisions in the fine arts. For example, he contended that the idea of imitative unity derived from the fact that the soul or the mind is a unity, and that each sense is also a unity, evident in the fact that no two senses are simultaneoulsy engaged in two different actions to the same degree of intensity. He therefore concluded that it was nature herself that fixed the division between the arts, and their correlative relationships to the faculties of the soul or the mind.[37] Every work of art must embody a unity of object and a unity of subject[38] within its proper boundaries, for to rupture the division between the arts is an affront to nature.

Quatremère's re-affirmation of the sharp distinction between the causality of the true, which is deduced by the mind, and various classes of sensory contents, indirectly addressed one of the capital epistemological questions that faced eighteenth-century *philosophes* without actually naming it, to wit Molyneux's problem. Molyneux's inquiry regarded whether the perceptual content of one kind of sensuous experience, for example, sight, could in any way construct the perceptual content of another,[39] for example, touch, through the mediation of the mind. Could a person born blind who was familiar with a spherical object through touch, and who recovers sight after an operation, recognize a sphere upon seeing it without the mediation of touch? The empirical answer to this question was provided as early as 1728 when after such an operation a formerly blind boy was unable to visually recognize the objects that he knew from touch. Indeed he had to construct his visual ability to distinguish objects with great difficulty. Thus if the visual and the tactile appear to be indissociable, this was so only after repetitive experiences and habit, for there was no way of constructing the perceptual content accessed through one sense from the experience of another.

That the lessons of empirical experience concurred with Quatremère's insistence on the separate qualities of each sense, need not imply his adoption of an epistemological view that reduced perception to the senses alone,[40] for his concerns resided in a transcendent order that gives coherence to the objective world. By strongly associating the untransgressable boundaries between the arts to the untransgressable boundaries between the senses, he was advancing the view that the confusion between artistic genres had its roots in a crisis of perception. Implicit in such a position, was a concern about the rupture between the conceptual and perceptual realms that invaded artistic thought as a result of the crises in scientific epistemology since the late seventeenth century.

Similarly to Batteux, Quatremère attempted his own classification of the arts, which featured poetry in the first place, then music, painting, sculpture and architecture, followed by dance and pantomime, the latter two addressing more particularly the senses.[41] In this scheme, the arts are ranked according to the kind of pleasure they provide, namely, intellectual and sensuous pleasure; and the degree of intellectual pleasure increased in proportion to the intellectual distance between an individual work of art and its model. Clearly, this distance has its limits; if it is too close the model and the individual work of art may be "in actual contact,"[42] and if it is too far then the relationship of genre is ruptured. Architecture,

"which does not imitate anything real or positive, is always classed in its due place

on this imitative scale, its office being to employ matter, its forms, and the relationship of their proportions to express moral qualities, at least those that nature shadows forth in her works, and which produce in us the ideas and their correlative emotions of order, harmony, grandeur, wealth, unity, variety, durability, eternity, etc.; in such a manner that the material of the art, which with the generality of persons, is the object of a sensual admiration, may be only a means employed by the artist, of leading our minds to intellectual enjoyments."[43]

Every imitative resemblance has something incomplete and something fictive, and

"Each of the fine arts finds in the perfection of its own means, a corrective for the pretended imperfections of its nature, a compensation for what is necessarily fictious [fictive], and a substitute for what is incomplete. But it must be confessed that genius alone can discover that substitute, and sentiment alone can enjoy it. Mediocrity finds it a shorter way to plunder what it cannot acquire, and ignorance more easy to give itself up to the reality of gross and sensual emotions."[44]

As the task of artistic imitation is not the production of sameness, it is apparent how in the change of material and materials that accompanies the production of the image, more aspects become important in an imitation than were in an original. It is in this sense that the distance involved in stone's imitation of a wooden origin in architecture should be approached.[45] Such a distance is at once intellectual and material, and is "wholly different in kind from that which, for instance, is discoverable between a badly executed portrait and its original."[46] A depiction of a historical setting can rely on factual truth as in Canaletto's views of Venice and London, or distance itself drastically from factual truth while still appearing real. Consider, for example, Canaletto's *capriccio* where three Palladian buildings –

the Basilica and the Palazzo Chiericati of Vicenza, and a proposal for the Ponte Rialto in Venice – were brought together in a characteristically Venetian composition. In fact, his depiction appeared so true that, according to Francesco Algarotti, many Venetians asked about the location of such an area of the city which they had not seen before. The same distancing applies to the following four situations: compare the above-mentioned Palladian *capriccio* with other paintings by Canaletto that factually depict the same bridge as built by Antonio da Ponte; with a photograph of the same *veduta*; and with standing physically in the same place. Similarly, to observe a landscape painting and an actual landscape produce two different pleasures, for the intellectual and physical distances are different. Quatremère considered the sort of man-made landscape that appears as if made by nature –for example, English landscape, *le genre irrégulier* – to be a lesser art, in despite the skill required to realize it,[47] because in this form of landscape, the materials used and the truth or reality they are supposed to represent are the same. Such an artistic practice he considered anti-imitative, for it fosters sensuous illusion by collapsing the distance between the true and the real. Here, Quatremère differed sharply from Kant's classification of the man-made landscape – whether geometric or irregular – as a form of painting. For Kant, the interest in the forms of art resided primarily in their mutual relationships as well as the mind's reflection – and therefore aesthetic appreciation – on these relationships, and less so in their intrinsic natures as objects.[48] Thus, Kant could see the garden as the painterly disposition of natural forms. But in opposing the forms of irregular gardening that proliferated in the latter part of the eighteenth century, Quatremère aimed at combating what he considered to be erroneous beliefs regarding the idea of imitation and its relationship to nature. Many thinkers, artists and *gens de goût*, fused their belief in the perfection of nature, with a literal application of Horace's *ut pictura poesis*.[49] This confluence gave rise to a syllogism which implied that since nature does not produce regular geometries, and since art attempts to imitate a perfect nature, then an irregular garden could be considered an imitation of nature, while a geometric garden could not. Such a syllogism was untenable for Quatremère, for he saw that nature also comprised regularities and symmetries, and their abstraction by art was but an evidence of a perceived order in nature.[50] But more importantly, he saw in this syllogism the collapse of the distinction between the imitation and the copy, which in turn caused the collapse of that fortunate distance between a general model – or the type held as the true – and a work of art which provided at once unity, in the universal applications of the model, and variety in the manifold expressions made possible by this very distance.

No art form alone is capable of manifesting in its images the artistically true in its entirety. Therefore, as a mediation between the true and the real, imitation requires a set of means in order to bridge their distance. This explains the rise of conventions as the means of imitation. Their effect is "to *prevent us from perceiving* the imperfection arising from what is wanting in imitation in order for it to be complete, and also to *prevent its impression* from being too much weakened."[51] For these two reasons, Quatremère distinguished between two classes of conventions, namely, the intellectual and the practical, depending on the degrees of ideal or material imitation. Parts of this quote are italicized in order to link the two classes of conventions with the two qualities of works of imitation mentioned above. The practical class of conventions concerns execution and provides the necessary means for the existence of an art. For example, in the superposition of orders such conventions concern the pragmatic matters of load bearing, load borne, and spanning. The second class constitutes a set of intellectual means, a class of theoretical conventions "given the artist to be at once the ministers of his thoughts, and the guides to the instruments he has to employ."[52] In drama, for example, the unities of action, place and time elevate a simple narrative to the level of theatrical art. In architecure, this class of convention includes the superposition of columnar types, diminution as part of eurythmic adjustments, or Laugier's recommendation that a pediment, as an idealization of a roof, ought to occur only at the crowning of a building and not be repeated at every storey or in the interior where no roof occurs. A further example might be how the simple details of construction in wood of vernacular buildings are transformed into a commemorative representation – whether in wood or masonry – drawing on the cumulative experience of generations in matters of taste, proportions, symmetries. In such a manner details in wood are transformed into the abacus, the torus, the triglyph, the dentil, etc. This second class of intellectual means leads to the ends of imitation by reminding the artist that the ends of art are not to be confused with its means, and that the ideal depends on conventions for its attainment.

Quatremère distinguished yet a third class of conventions which he named poetical conventions. He used the word poetical as a synonym of the fictive or metaphorical[53] which he believed to be notions common to all the arts. While practical conventions demand close attention to the details of execution, and intellectual conventions guide the artist's compositions, poetical conventions allow a transformation or recomposition of the model itself. This recomposition consists of two principal steps: the act of generalizing and that of transposing.[54] Generalizing, according to Quatremère, belongs in the realm of metaphysics and depends on a choice of form in the selection of the most universal aspects, for example the type. While transposing occurs on the level of composition and involves analogous changes to scattered characteristics found in various models, which are in turn unified within one work. This implies knowledge of the universal principle upon which the particular is based; the character of a genus as it impresses the individual species with various qualities. Choice and union also require a discerning judgment which is formed by the long observation of the laws of nature – for example the organization of the human body – and the corroboration of this knowledge by various minds over generations. Thus, choice and union are not arbitrary, for they have the authority of

experience. In the final analysis, whereas practical conventions are a means of applying and modifying the reality of the model, poetical conventions are a means of applying and transforming the model itself on the level of the true. Poetical conventions further "another kind of truth:"[55] the fictive. It is this fictive aspect that elevates the real in the direction of the true: *ex ficto verum*. Poetical conventions transformed the simple wooden hut in such a way that it came to occupy for architecture the role that natural models themselves played for the other arts. It is also in this sense that poetical conventions transposed the systems of carpentry into the systems of building in stone. It is significant here, to note the reciprocity between architecture, construction and building on the one hand, and poetical, intellectual and practical – or prosaic – conventions on the other.[56]

Architecture	Poetical conventions	(Metaphysical theory)
Construction	Intellectual conventions	(Didactic theory)
Building	Practical conventions	(Practical theory)

It is also important to note the remarkable degree of flexibility exhibited in Quatremère's theory, a point that is often overlooked by his critics who erroneously think of his work as a rigid monolith. Far from opposing any artistic change, this theory accepts transformation and change on the very level of poetic conventions and the principles that inform them. In other words, this theory accepts transformation even in the most enduring aspects of an artistic tradition, namely, its principles. What Quatremère's theory rejects is the indiscriminate acceptance of any change simply because it occurred.

Quatremère warned about three abuses of conventions.[57] First he saw how sense-based theories or what he called the "materialist spirit"[58] caused a loss in the intellectual nature of imitation, by considering the senses as the sole determinant in the apprehension of the world, thereby privileging practical conventions, and making artists forget that "imitation itself is but a convention the highest degree of which is the ideal."[59] Second, he warned against the proscriptive application of conventions, for this abuse profoundly injures architecture when its adherents cloak themselves with the disguise of the authority of the antique, thereby violating even the examples of the ancients who applied conventions much more liberally. This abuse also attains architecture by reducing it to mere construction, or that which is pragmatically necessary. Third, he cautioned against those who reject conventions entirely, by denying all rules and by falling into the capricious and the arbitrary.

Concluding this section on Quatremère's theory of imitation, we recapitulate its nine principal points. First, one may say that, for Quatremère, the domain of imitation is twofold: those arts that have in nature a direct tangible model, for example, painting, sculpture, and those arts that hold in nature a moral or intellectual model, for example, architecture, rhetoric. Second, resemblance by means of an image partakes in the very nature of imitation. It reveals an object within another, in varying degrees of completeness, using a model as a measure. Third, the image gives an incomplete resemblance of an object. It is rather a selection of qualities from that object, hence the notion of the fictive which serves another kind of truth: artistic truth. Fourth, the image as such, produces resemblances that are materially distinct from the model. Fifth, having no direct model in nature, architecture imitates three models which come to occupy the role of natural models. They are the idea of type exemplified by the hut, the analogical imitation of the human body, and the abstract imitation of order in nature. Sixth, for Quatremère art does not present a reality through sameness, for that would be counterfeit or mimicry. Rather, art pleases by taking reality's place.[60] Thus, the imitation and the copy are to be clearly differentiated. Seventh, the ends of imitation in the fine arts reside in the pursuit of the ideal. Eighth, conventions are the means of imitation, and Quatremère distinguished between two classes of conventions or means: the practical and the intellectual, while he discerned a more ideal form of intellectual convention, namely the poetic.

Ninth, in matters of imitation, the idea of the true depends more on an intellectual evidence, while the idea of the real depends more on a sensuous evidence.[61] In the final analysis, imitation is not simply located between *verum* and *factum*, it mediates both.

Invention, Propriety, and the Boundaries between the Arts

"There ought to be an antecedent to everything; nothing whatsoever comes from nothing, and this cannot but apply to all human inventions."
A.C. Quatremère de Quincy

Nature, remarked Quatremère, offers no tangible models for the poet and the architect – unlike the painter and sculptor who have direct models in nature – and yet, this does not prevent them from finding an intellectual model based on an observation of nature's "harmonizing concord of relations. The same may be said of every invention, and it is perhaps the best that can be made between the words *invent* and *find*. What exists may be found. That can only be invented which does not exist."[62] This statement should not be interpreted as Quatremère's espousal of the idea of creation *ex nihilo*, for as a Platonist thinker, he carefully stressed that "man creates nothing in the elementary sense of the word, and that he only finds new combinations of pre-existing elements; the same also applies to the inventor who finds these combinations."[63] Indeed, he later affirms that what the architect finds "... not only does not exceed the laws of nature, but is, on the contrary, its very spirit and epitome, since what is commonly taken for nature is very far from answering to the name, seeing that we should understand by it, not all that is, but whatever is as it might or ought to be."[64] In this quote from *De l'imitation*, we encounter two important ideas: the distinction between inventing and finding, and the Aristotelian *ought*. Quatremère returned to the first idea in the *Historical Dictionary of Architecture*, and distinguished between discovery in the sciences and invention in the arts, affirming that one discovers what already exists, while one invents what does not exist in physical reality. Following the steps initiated by Cl. Perrault in the seventeenth century, Durand and other polytechnicians were methodically inducting architecture into the new views on scientific epistemology derived from the theories of Newton, Bacon, and Descartes. But like François Blondel before him, Quatremère did not integrate architecture into these views, and he cautioned against the error of applying the same considerations of progress in the sciences to the "works of genius and invention in the fine arts." If the moderns are superior in the realm of science, the same does not apply to the arts, for there is an opposition between the very natures of the arts and the sciences, reflected in the differences in their *modus operandi*.[65] Scientific experiments rely on direct repeatability. Anyone mixing certain chemical components under the same conditions will find the same results. It is also in the nature of sciences that every experiment is the result of a preceding one and connected to the next. Thus, sequentiality is part and parcel of this development. Contrariwise, the analysis of the inventiveness in an architect's or artist's work is no guarantee that one can appropriate it to one's advantage, not to mention the difficulty of penetrating the inner thoughts which animate the architect's mind. One may use the same materials employed by Raphael, Michelangelo or Palladio after a thorough analysis of their works, but this does not necessarily guarantee the same results if one were to build by combining the same materials, for nature bestows genial qualities on some individuals which most do not possess.[66] Put differently, the geologist and the painter do not look at a landscape in the same way; the physician and the sculptor look for different laws governing the human body; and the botanist and the architect extract different lessons from the organization of a tree.

Since the Perrault brothers' leading role on the side of the moderns in the *Querelle*, the idea that all knowledge is qualified by a decidedly future orientation was transposed from science into art and architecture, resulting in the notions of progressivity and the superiority of the modern.[67] Later, eighteenth century thinkers linked techno-

scientific experimentation and free inquiry with an aporetic discourse without closure, in the Cartesian belief that they will lead to freeing humanity from nature's determinism, thus throwing their lot behind utopian progressivity. Therefore, if Quatremère's position seems anti-progressive, it is so only for believers in teleological determinism: the true historicists. This belief necessarily blinds them to Quatremère's concerns about the undermining effects of techno-scientific progress on the nature, ends, and means of architecture and art. More than a mere call for the separation between the methodologies of the arts and sciences, Quatremère's argument should be seen as a position against the monistic conclusions reached by scientists – and appropriated by art theorists – in their heralding of a single prescriptive ideology applicable to all knowledge. Equally monistic was the application of this ideology to the arts and sciences regardless of their different intentionalities and values; and the hasty adoption of such conclusions precipitated a major crisis of identity in the arts, as they became absorbed into a techno-scientific teleological realm which announced a future perfection with high certainty, even if such a contention remained to be proven. This ideology saw its early development in the late seventeenth century, albeit in a state where science and technology were undifferentiated. It reached a widespread development in industrialization, and received its epistemological legitimation when the *Encyclopédie* subjected all areas of knowledge to this ideology's constant scrutiny.[68] The article on "Art" in the *Encyclopédie* stated that following the examination of nature and her creations in their qualities, purposes and symbols, the appellations science or art were given to common points of observation which could form a system and a set of rules.[69] The same article asserted that mechanical objects were comparable to natural organisms, and that art or the machine were equally an imitation of nature. This view claimed that the *Encyclopédie* had unraveled an epistemological *"système général"* equally applicable to the sciences and the arts. The distinction between liberal and mechanical arts, and between the beautiful and the useful was eliminated, while the rational and the efficient were considered to have a validity equal to the speculative. An inventor of the steam engine could be called *un artiste*, and a painter could be called *un artisan*.

Part of this immensely self-expanding techno-scientific monism was the notion of infinity, as it stretched over the whole of human endeavour. Applied particularly to artistic invention, this notion ignored the fact that whereas the maker's inventiveness and freedom are potentially infinite, this does not necessarily imply that the arts and their materials are infinite in potentialities to the same degree. Indeed, they have definable limits which are indissociable from the nature, ends and means of every art. In other words, if invention – or the laws governing the maker – manifests in potentially infinite combinations of form – under the laws governing the made – these combinations themselves may be potentially infinite only within the art's own limits, propriety or *convenance*. When the means of art tend toward an infinity, as has happened since the late eighteenth century and especially in the twentieth, then art's nature and ends are eclipsed, and the artistically true and real collapse into each other. This gave rise to the great modernist fallacy that a change in means necessarily entails a change in ends. In other words, the *means* for individuating a work of art have come to be confused with the *reasons* and the *purpose* for individuating it. But whereas the pursuit of the infinite (the explosion of limits) grew immensely in the twentieth century, one must not lose sight of its rise in the eighteenth. Indeed the whole of the enlightenment project may be seen as a pursuit whose goal is the experience of limits,[70] and to a certain extent their rupture. One effect of the cumulative reflections of Pascal, Newton, Leibniz and D'Alembert on infinitesimal calculations, is that the infinite came to be regarded as the limit of the finite, or *that* toward which the finite tends continuously without ever arriving there: what Hegel called the spurious infinity.[71] This is not to deny the import or usefulness of mathematical reflections on the infinite or the infinitesimal in their proper realms.

Indeed, by their immense philosophical scope, these reflections intersect the idea of unlimited creativity; and the move toward an infinite may very well be an integral part of the human character. For example, it may be said that idealism tends towards an infinity of a transcendental nature, while positivism tends towards an infinity of an immanent nature. Likewise, it may be said that the sublime arises when aesthetics tends toward the infinite. Only the very idea of beauty – even in its reduced form of aesthetics – implies a finiteness, a limit, while the idea of the sublime implies an unattainable presentation of ideas, as Kant pointed out.[72] This is why the infinite and the indeterminate should not be confused.

When mathematical reflection was inseparable from philosophy, philosophy determined the realms of the infinitesimal and the infinite. But as mathematical reflection detached itself from philosophical values, since the late seventeenth century, it came to be applied to any area of endeavour, eventually reaching our contemporary situation where it serves an abstract technological order. This understanding of infinity as developed by the sciences and an abstract technological will, invaded the fine arts and exploded the clear boundaries between them, to the point where their very identity was put in question. This precipitated the most pervasive fracture in the very idea of making in art, because that which characterizes the maker – invention and genius – came to be considered as the logical opposite of that which governs the made – imitation, rules, conventions. Thus, invention came to be classified within the exalted realm of the infinite – and by extension, unlimited artistic freedom – while imitation and rules were classified within the realm of the finite, and came to be seen as confining to invention and artistic freedom.

Quatremère prophetically understood the dangerous implications of these developments on the future unfolding of architecture and art. For this purpose, he repeatedly clarified that while invention grouped the creativity and the intellectual freedom of the artist in the combination of pre-existing elements, these elements must have among themselves a kinship, a relationship of genre; hence the importance of propriety. Therefore, to say that invention is an *ars combinatoria* with infinite possibilities is a vague platitude, for invention is not made of any possible combination without regard to larger conventions. Invention knows many regulators, two of which are reason and propriety. Reason keeps imagination and taste in check, as a guarantee from falling into the abuses of conventions. For example, while licences are exceptions to rules, they do not necessarily imply the rejection of rules. Indeed as individual interpretations, some licences reinforce rules by accepting them as larger collective meanings.[73] However, when individual taste eclipses reason and becomes the only determining guide, it comes to legitimize individual meanings, the private *doxa*, at the expense of collective meanings. Indeed, they come to be seen as logical opposites. From here derive what Quatremère called the *caprice* and *bizarre*, and what some artists of the later twentieth century proudly called the self-referential sign.[74]

The second regulator, propriety and aptness – *convenance* and *bienséance* – corresponds to the Vitruvian *decor*.[75] After Vitruvius, Quatremère distinguished between three kinds of *bienséance*. The first is part of a theory of character, and involves aptness in the nature of buildings, aptness with respect to the user, in the temples relative to the deity, and in civic buildings. The second involves *accord et harmonie* or agreement and harmony between the different parts of a building.[76] Thirdly, there is aptness as a result of custom.

The nuance between *bienséance*, aptness, and *convenance*, propriety, did not escape the keen intellect of Quatremère, and he remarked that "…the idea of aptness relates more to morals, and that of propriety to manners and customs. Thus the figure of a dance will offend aptness by the obscenity of the postures whereas another will shock propriety by the unfaithfulness of costumes."[77] By describing the difference between propriety and aptness in theatre, and implying a wider applicability to the fine arts, Quatremère emphasized the strong relationship between the intrinsic meaning of art and the extrinsic significance assigned to it by society. Transposing this analogy to architecture, a building may be said to have propriety when its type and character befit its destined purpose.

Invention then, cannot arbitrarily derive from any imaginable provenance, for as a new combination of pre-existing elements, it must relate to the propriety of the art in question, and be regulated by reason. Accordingly, when balancing the laws of the maker and those of the made, reason alerts the imagination that it *ought* not to transgress the clear boundaries of the art in question. For this reason, Quatremère cautioned the artist against falling into two errors. The first "consists in *stepping beyond* his own art to seek, in the resources of another, an increase of imitative resemblance."[78] The second "consists in seeking the truth *short of the limits* of every art, by a system of servile copy, which deprives the imitation of the image of that fictious part which constitutes at once its essence and its character."[79] Parts of the above quotes have been italicized in order to emphasize Quatremère's insistence on circumscribing artistic boundaries. The first error implies the borrowing of effects or means that are foreign to the art in question, and Quatremère illustrates this point by discussing the means proper to sculpture and painting. If sculpture renders form through relief, and painting renders depth by varying hues and shadows, then it will be improper for a sculptor who intends to paint a statue, to use the means of the painter in order to render the idea of depth or variations of the skin. In other words, the sculptor should not paint the effect of depth, even if the statue is polychromatic.[80] Thus, artists must ever be mindful that while the means circumscribe the physical limits of an art, they must clearly distinguish between what an art can and should represent. The second error implies the confusion of a work of art with its model, resulting in the production of sameness.

Building upon Quatremère's advice regarding the two errors, it is useful to distinguish between links and boundaries. A link connects at least two distinct entities, anchoring them to a place or a tradition, without commingling them, thereby assuring their identities. A boundary guarantees identity through closure and containment in time and space, separating at least two distinct entities, without excluding the possibility of their informing each other, thus guaranteeing at once passage and distinction. Such a dialectic allows various arts to inform each other, without eroding the boundaries that assure for each its proper character, thereby maintaining intrinsic content – immanent meaning – and extrinsic significance – transcendent meaning. For example, a close examination of the notion of allegory – for example, in architecture and painting – instantly raises the question of the links and boundaries characteristic of each art, *vis-à-vis* the object of the allegory.[81] Needless to say, the clarity sought in distinguishing or dissociating links from boundaries is not achieved through an exacting mathematical specificity, which is a value only for a technical mentality. Rather, this clarity is part of a larger dialectic which does not exclude tensions resulting from perceptual interpretations in determining where one art begins and where another ends.

The issue of links and boundaries, also has a direct bearing on the question of perception in empirical experience. For example, while observing the painted polychromy – as opposed to a material polychromy – of a marble building, or a statue; or when music and dance are performed together, one could reach either of two conclusions. Either one is beholding two separate arts at once, or the division of the arts is merely empirical, while their aesthetic experience tends toward a unity – perhaps an *a priori* unity, furnished by the artist's mind and that of the observer. But while the unity of aesthetic experience depends on a compositional unity of the arts, it does not imply a (con)fusion of their proper ends and modes of representation. This is not to dismiss the whimsy of, say, a *trompe l'oeil*, which despite its fictitiousness, still respects the clarity of links and boundaries. But when the boundaries of architecture, sculpture and painting are confused, in favour of privileging optical and psychological illusions, the ensuing collapse of boundaries implies that the empirical experience of an art can be confused with that which communicates the

art's own aesthetic character. Thus, the clear definition of links and boundaries plays a constitutive part in a clear understanding of the nature, ends and means of each art, without which there is a confusion of genres.

But what of the relationship between artistic genres and the artist's intellectual freedom? For example, how is an architect to depict a naval victory in a monument dedicated to it? And, more precisely, how free is an architect to commemorate such an event within the limits of architecture? Comparatively, how could a painter or sculptor approach the same subject? Both the painter and the sculptor can depict in a painting or a bas-relief the factual happenings, the number of ships, and the intensity of the combat. The painter and the sculptor can also use allegorical figures of war, pity, pain, magnanimity or ruthlessness; for their arts allow for this kind of analogy. But such is not the case in architecture. The architect may have the rare luxury of choosing the location for the monument. The architect may also combine motifs which have historically been associated with victories and armies, such as the triumphal arch, or perhaps a temple front. Bas-reliefs and even allusions to a ship's prow in some detail may be used. Still, to achieve this commemoration, the architect can only attenuate the boundaries of architecture to a certain extent, beyond which the limits of architecture will be eroded. For instance, it would be totally indecorous to erect a building in the shape of a ship. For buildings are not ships, and unlike ships, they are static objects. In the final analysis, artistic freedom can be said to be indissociable from the links and boundaries which are suitable to each art. Thus, a universal application of the axiom: *ut pictura poesis*, should be taken *cum grano salis*. For what is available to poetry's modes of fiction is not to painting or landscape, and there is still less of it available to architecture.

Following this discussion, one may ask: if the architect's intellectual freedom is indissociably linked to the boundaries of the art, then what are the inward parameters influencing this freedom? First, as a thinker and maker, the architect is free through reason but is constrained by the causes and effects of the material world. For example, a pure aesthetic judgment is the more free in so far as it is less dependent on sensory perceptions. Second, the mind can be seen as having constructed and apprehended the phenomenal world in accordance with its own structures. Thus, the confluence of the empirical experience of sensory perception, as well as the mind's own ordering systems, are then projected onto a part of the phenomenal world. Observe, for instance, how the *a priori* unity and aptness with regard to sensory material are inherent in the mind while it reflects upon itself and while it connects present experiences with earlier ones, and with the material at hand. As in a Herbartian scheme, the architect's intellectual freedom is influenced by the way the mind associates present and past ideas, perceptions, models and motifs in an *ars combinatoria* which includes collocation, composition, disposition and distribution. These words and others infer that the architect reflects on three relationships at once. First is the building's internal order: the Vitruvian *ordinatio*, (order); *dispositio*, (disposition); and *distributio*, (distribution).[82] Second are the aesthetic qualities of architecture: the Vitruvian *symmetria*, (symmetry); *eurythmia*, (eurythmy); and *decor*, (propriety or aptness.) Third is the building's aptness, the Vitruvian *decor*, in the sense of its external relationship with a tradition or with the cultural context at large. Thus, the architect works at once with the material of a tradition and within it. The scope of this freedom is evidenced in the distance between a type or a model, a tectonic allusion to a theory of origins, the faithfulness or departure from propriety, the selectiveness and mastery of the composition of elements, experience, introspection and self-criticism, and, of course, the architect's own genius.

Freedom is in art's ends, and less so in its means, which have to conform to these ends. The means of this artistic freedom – to be distinguished from political freedom[83] – is in the thematic, compositional and allegorical methods of the arts in general, while there is another order of freedom still, which is proper to the essence, ends and means of each art. This propriety extends to national characteristics, social mores, climatic parameters, regional customs and tastes as well as individual taste.

In the final analysis, what characterizes invention in the fine arts, affirmed Quatremère, "...is not the independence from any restraint, but liberty within rules.... Far from rules being injurious to invention, it must be said that invention does not exist outside rules; we would add that the value of invention would be worthless if it were possible not to have rules; for there would be no way to judge invention."[84] Accordingly, it would be an error to consider invention and rules as logical opposites, and the mark of genius resides in overcoming this illusory division. However, when for the sake of originality – that quality which has been so zealously sought since the Enlightenment – the production of novelty becomes an end in itself – for example the phenomenon of making-different, or rupture and transgression of conventions as ends in themselves – invention becomes confused with innovation, and the artist's individual freedom divorces itself from the realm of artistic boundaries. For this reason Quatremère opposed what he called "*l'école de modèle*," later known as Romanticism;[85] first on the ground that this view of art privileged individual expression at the expense of collective meanings and conventions, leading to the erroneous corollary that individual invention or genius works in opposition to the artistic rules of a tradition, which were regarded with scepticism. Second, he saw the confluence of constant change and individual expression based on a sense-based view of the world, as aimed toward negating universal principles or the theory of essences that he held so highly. He saw that by tending towards a spurious infinity, the accelerating flux of frantic change would come to hinder the very apprehension of knowledge. These first two reasons led him to consider such a position to be inadequate to build a system of art, since it was based on a negation, namely that of artistic rules.[86] Third, he considered Romanticism's literal adoption of Horace's *ut pictura poesis*, to be the cause of the confusion between artistic genres.[87] These forces, Quatremère feared, would combine and contribute to the dissolution of the arts, injuring especially the notion of invention.

True invention steers a delicate path between the degrees of constraint and freedom needed by the mind, and the meanings, rules, conventions and proprieties of art. Artistic making – or the laws that apply to the maker and those that apply to the made – results from a confluence between the invention of the maker, the con-straints found in the practice of an artistic tradition, the power and freedom to realize forms, tempered as they are by artistic and social propriety, and the characteristics of the pre-existing material. Imitation and invention for Quatremère, are both ontologically linked to the nature of the mind and its close association with the body, as both intellectual and physical needs move alternatively from action to rest in relation to societal and individual parameters.

NOTES

1   See the entry *Imitation*.
2   The reader will recall Socrates's statement about knowledge pertaining to that which endures rather than that which is in a state of flux. " For if Knowledge itself does not change from being Knowledge then Knowledge would always remain and be Knowledge. But if even the Form of Knowledge changed then at the very moment of the change into another Form of Knowledge there would be no Knowledge, and if it is always changing then there would always be no Knowledge. The consequence is that there would be neither knowing nor known." *Cratylus* §§439C-440B. Furthermore, adds Aristotle in his summary of Plato's Forms, "there is no knowledge of things that are in a state of flux." *Metaphysics* 1078 B13-45.
3   Du Bos, Jean-Baptiste *Réflexions critiques sur la poésie, la peinture et la musique*. Paris, 1719. II, 2, pp. 14-17, and I, 1, pp. 75-80.
4   Etienne Bonnot de Condillac *Traité des sensations*. Paris, 1754. I, XI, p. 8.
5   *Le Génie de l'architecture ou l'analogie de cet art avec nos sensations*. Benoit Morin, 1780. See the recent translation by D. Britt, with an introduction by R. Middleton, *The genius of architecture, or, the analogy of that art with our sensations*. Santa Monica, CA, The Getty Center for the History of Art and the Humanities, 1992.
6   The view that associates the image with the real has been associated with Western culture for at least two millenia. Only, it was given a special formulation in the eighteenth century, when the symbolic meaning of perspective inherited from the Renaissance was changed, and came to designate an equality between the image and the object it represents. Later still, and under the full impact of technological determinism, this phenomenon accrued the immanent and exacting specificity of isometric drawing, leaving no place for any transcendent meaning.
7   See C-F. Volney's *Les Ruines*, 1791. *A new translation of Volney's ruins*. New York, Garland, 1979.
8   "We - said Socrates- have regularly assumed a Form for all the manys to which we apply the same name, one form for each many."*Republic*, §596A.
9   Quatremère read M. Ficino's translation and commentary of Plato: the *Divini Platonis Opera quae exstant....*1590, as well as V. Cousin's commentary: the *Procli philosophi Platonici Opera e codd....commentaris illustravit V. Cousin*. Firmin Didot, 1827. See Merlin, R. *Bibliothèque de M. Quatremère de Quincy, de l'Académie des inscriptions et belles-lettres, secrétaire honoraire de l'Académie des Beaux-Arts; Collection d'ouvrages relatifs aux beaux-arts et à l'archéologie; dont la vente aura lieu le lundi 27 Mai 1850*. Paris, Adrien Le Clère, 1850.
10   *Thaetetus* pp.160-168.
11   *De l'imitation*, p. 288; (p. 321 Engl. Tr.)
12   See Cousin, V. *Cours de philosophie professé à la Faculté des Lettres pendant l'année 1818 sur le fondement des idées absolues du vrai, du beau et du bien*. Paris, 1836. And Lammenais, F. *Esquisse d'une philosophie*, Paris, 1840-46.
13   *De l'imitation*, p. 103; (p. 121 Engl. Tr.)
14   *Ibid*, p. 180; (pp. 204-5 Engl Tr.)
15   *Ibid*, p. 196-7; (pp. 223-4 Engl Tr.)
16   *Ibid*, p. 200-1; (p. 227 Engl. Tr.)
17   *Ibid*, p. 203; (p. 230 Engl Tr.)
18   Aristotle, *Physica*, II 8, 199.
19   *De l'imitation*, pp. 218-9; (pp. 246-7 Engl Tr.)
20   See the entry *Imitation*.
21   This ideal is only partially present, for no work of art can contain it in its entirety.
22   See the entry *Imitation*.
23   See the entry *Architecture*.
24   *Ibid*.
25   *Ibid*.
26   See the entry *Principle*.
27   *Ibid*.
28   On this distinction, see the entry *Type*.
29   *De l'Imitation* pp. 30-31; (pp. 41-42 Engl. Tr.)
30   Quatremère published his distinction between the type and the model in the third volume of the *Dictionnaire d'architecture* in the *Encyclopédie Méthodique* (1825). This distinction accrues great historical significance, when compared to the collapse of the difference between the imitation and the copy brought about by industrial production. The proliferation of this production came to gradually absorb artistic production from the middle of the eighteenth century.
31   See the entry *Art*.
32   *De l'imitation*, p. 186; (p. 212 Engl. Tr.)
33   *Ibid*, pp. 115-6; (pp. 134-5 Engl. Tr.)
34   Quatremère adopted Plautus's ideal of poetry and Cicero's ideal of oratory. In *De l'imitation*, he quotes the latter: "I lay it down as a principle that there is nothing of whatever kind so beautiful, but there is something more beautiful above and

beyond it, which may be imitated as an original, inaccessible to our senses, and which mind and thought alone can embrace." *Ibid*, (p. 274 Engl Tr.)

35 *Ibid*, pp. 184-90; (pp. 210-216 Engl. Tr.)

36 *Ibid*, pp. 21-8; (pp. 31-9, Engl. Tr.)

37 *Ibid*, pp. 29-48; (pp. 40-60 Engl. Tr.)

38 *Ibid*, p. 48; (pp. 59-60, Engl. Tr.)

39 See the entry *Harmony*. Such an epistemological problem fervently occupied the minds of Berkeley, Voltaire, Condillac, Diderot and Mérian. See the following sources: William Molyneux *Dioptrica nova, A treatise of dioptricks*. London, 1692; Etienne Bonnot de Condillac *Traité des sensations*. 1754. Paris, Librairie Hatier, 1930; Denis Diderot, *Lettre sur les aveugles*. Ed. critique par Robert Niklaus. Geneva, E. Droz, 1963; Jean-Bernard Mérian *Sur le problème de Molyneux*. Paris, Flammarion, 1984. Various recent studies have enlarged the discussion of perceptual theories based on Molyneux's inquiry since the eighteenth century. See especially: Francine Markovitz *Diderot, Mérian et l'aveugle*. Flammarion, 1984. Also Degenaar, Marjolein *Molyneux's problem: three centuries of discussion on the perception of forms*. Dordrecht, Netherlands; Boston, Kluwer Academic Publishers, 1996.

40 Indeed, on occasion he expressed his opposition to the materialism of the senses by such vociferate emotions: "Quoi!, N'y aurait-il rien que du physique?"

41 *De l' imitation*, pp. 145-7; (pp. 166-8 Engl Tr.)

42 *Ibid*, p. 146; (p. 167 Engl Tr.)

43 *Ibid*, p. 147; (p. 168 Engl. Tr.)

44 *Ibid*, p. 112; (p. 131 Engl .Tr.)

45 *Ibid*, pp. 125-6; (pp. 144-5 Engl. Tr.)

46 *Ibid*, p. 152; p. 173 Engl. Tr.)

47 *Ibid*, pp. 149-50; (pp. 170-1 Engl. Tr.)

48 See Kant's *Critique de la faculté de juger*. A. Philonenko Tr. Paris, Librairie Philosophique J. Vrin, 1993. §51 "De la division des Beaux-Arts," pp. 222-8. It is unclear whether Quatremère knew Kant's *Critique of Judgement,* which was first published in Berlin in 1790. However, he may have known Kant's philosophy in greater detail from J.M. Portalis's opposition to it, during their common exile in the Holstein from 1797-1800. See my biographical chapter. The catalogue from Quatremère's estate sale shows that he owned a French translation of Kant's *Observations of the Feeling of the Beautiful and the Sublime*. (Originally published in 1764 in Königsberg) H. Payer Imhoff Tr. Paris, 1796. See Merlin, R. *Bibliothèque de M. Quatremère de Quincy, de l'Académie des inscriptions et belles-lettres, secrétaire honoraire de l'Académie des Beaux-Arts; Collection d'ouvrages relatifs aux beaux-arts et à l'archéologie; dont la vente aura lieu le lundi 27 Mai 1850*. Paris, Adrien Le Clère, 1850.

49 At least four decades before Rousseau's *La Nouvelle Héloïse*, 1762, the ideas presented by Addison in *The Spectator*, 1711-12, were known in France. Other notable works on gardens were C-H. Watelet's *Essai sur les jardins*, Paris, 1774; R.-L. de Girardin's De la composition des paysages, Paris, 1777; G.-L. Buffon's *Epoques de la nature*, Paris, 1778; D. d'Argenville's *Voyage pittoresque des environs de Paris*, Paris, 1779; W. Masons's *Le jardin anglais*, Paris, 1788, (The English Garden, 1772), and J.-A. Cerutti's *Les jardins de Retz*, Paris, 1792. For an anthological survey of garden literature, see D. Wiebenson's *The Picturesque Garden in France*. Princeton Univ. Press, 1978; B. Saint Girons's *Esthétiques de XVIIIe siècle*, Paris, P. Sers ed., 1990; and M. Mosser and G. Teyssot's *Architecture of Western Gardens*, M.I.T., 1991.

50 See the entries *Jardin, Jardins chinois* and *Jardinage* in his *Dictionnaire d'architecture* in the *Encyclopédie Méthodique*, Vol. 2, Paris, 1820.

51 *De l'imitation*, p. 262; (p. 294 Engl. Tr.) Author's italics.

52 *Ibid*, p. 258; (p. 289 Engl .Tr.)

53 *Ibid*, p. 268; (p. 300 Engl. Tr.)

54 *Ibid*, p. 274; (p. 306 Engl. Tr.) See Chapters 3 through 6.

55 *Ibid*, p. 271; (p. 303 Engl. Tr.)

56 See the entries *Building (art of)* and *Construction*.

57 See the entry *Convention*.

58 For example the work of Dubos and Le Camus de Mézières.

59 *De l'imitation*, p. 260; (pp. 291-2 Engl. Tr.)

60 *Ibid*, pp. 117-136; (pp. 136-55 Engl. Tr.)

61 *Ibid*, pp. 30-1; (p. 42 Engl. Tr.)

62 *Ibid*, p. 178; (pp. 202-3 Engl Tr.)

63 See the entry *Invention*.

64 *De l'imitation*, pp. 179-80; (p. 204 Engl. Tr.)

65 See the entry *Antique*.

66 This does not necessarily imply the denial of the idea of sequentiality or precedence in the unfoldment of art and architecture.

67 See W. Hermann's *The Theory of Claude Perrault*, London, Zwemmer, 1973. A. Pérez-Gómez has painstakingly analyzed this scientific and philosophical context, see his *Architecture and the Crisis of Modern Science*. Cambridge, M.I.T. Press, 1983, and his introduction to Perrault's *Ordonnance for the Five Kinds of Columns after the Method of the Ancients*. I. Kagis McEwen Trans. Santa Monica, CA, The Getty Center for the History of Arts and the Humanities, 1993. For a detailed account of Perrault's scientific role, see A. Picon's *Claude Perrault ou la curiosité d'un classique*, Paris, Picard, 1989. Quatremère's biographical entries on architects, in the *Historical Dictionary of Architecture*, which he published in 1830 as *Histoire de la vie et des ouvrages des plus célèbres architectes du XIème siècle jusqu'à la fin du XVIIIème*, are silent on the *Querelle*. See especially the entries: *Perrault* and *Blondel* of the *Histoire*.

68 This phenomenon, which Jacques Ellul called *la technique*, attained its most diffused and saturated stage in the decades following the second World War. Far from being a simple array of means, this phenomenon integrated all areas of *episteme* into its world which is exclusively determined by rationality, efficiency and quantity. The contemporary crisis regarding the natures, ends and means of art and architecture may be greatly clarified through a proper understanding of the phenomenon of *technique*. Ellul's most seminal works in this area are: *La technique ou l'enjeu du siècle*. Paris, A. Colin, 1954; *Propagandes*. Paris, A.Colin, 1962; *Le système technicien*. Paris, Calmann- Lévy, 1977; *L'empire du non sens*. Paris, Presses Universitaires de France, 1980.

69 *Art* in *Encyclopédie, ou Dictionnaire raisonné des sciences, des arts et des métiers...* Paris, 1751-65. Vol. 1, pp 713-4.

70 See the study by Chouillet, J. *L'esthétique des lumières*. Paris, Presses Universitaires de France, 1974.

71 See *Hegel's Science of Logic*. A.W. Miller Tr. London, Allen & Unwin, 1969. Book One, Chap. 2, pp. 137-50. I am indebted to David Lovekin for this reference, see his *Technique, Discourse and Consciousness*, London and Toronto, Associated Univ. Presses, 1991.

72 Kant, *Ibid*, Philonenko's tr. p. 84 and p. 105.

73 See the entries *Licence* and *Misuse*.

74 Quatremère saw taste as an instrument of the mind rather than genius and distinguished three ways of understanding taste: 1) taste in the sense of *decor*, of *convenance*, propriety; 2) taste in the way one understands and imitates nature; 3) taste in providing the notion of distinct character to architecture. Taste does not provide rules for design, but it provides justification for the application of rules or deviation from them. See the entry *Taste*.

75 Vitruvius distinguishes three parts to *decor*. First, there is *decor*

following rules, as in the adaptation of the character of Doric, Ionic and Corinthian temples to the character of divinities. Second, there is *decor* following custom, for example the propriety of the character of interiors, and the impropriety of dentils in Doric architecture. Third, there is *decor* following nature in the choice of *locus* for various temples, and in the choice of building orientation. In the concept of *decor*, the *aspectus*, appearance of a building, achieves propriety through the authority of tradition; *probatio* , approval, and *auctoritas*, the authority of general acceptance.

76 This agreement is in turn constituted by another triplicity: 1) disposition in plan; 2) distribution of ornaments; 3) unity of character and style. There are two kinds of agreements: agreement in composition, plan, elevation, relationships of dimension, interior and exterior decoration; and an agreement of taste and style, in the union of construction and decoration, of other arts and of architecture. See the entry *Accord*.

77 See the entries *Aptness* and *Propriety*.

78 *De l'imitation*, p. 68; (p. 81 Engl. Tr.) Author's italics.

79 *Ibid*, p. 86; (p. 102 Engl. Tr.) Author's italics.

80 *Ibid*, pp. 11-14; (pp. 19-23 Engl Tr.) In this passage, Quatremère is not necessarily arguing against polychromy. He is simply pointing out that relief and not paint is the proper way for sculpture to show depth. Quatremère held opposing views on the issue of colour in architecture. Compare, for example, his writings in *De l'imitation*, with the entry *Colour* in the present book. René Schneider, his biographer, suggests that while Quatremère held an official position against polychromy in sculpture, he was secretly encouraging his close friend, the great Canova, to experiment with colour. On the various debates and controversies regarding Quatremère's favouring of material polychromy over painted polychromy, see David Van Zanten *The architectural polychromy of the 1830s*. New York, Garland Publishing, 1977. And Robin Middleton ed. *The Beaux-Arts and nineteenth-century French Architecture*. Cambridge, MIT Press, 1982.

81 See the entry *Allegory*.

82 Vitruvius, *De Architectura*, II, 1,2 and II, 2, 1.

83 On these two freedoms, see Younés, S. "Of Two Freedoms: the Political and the Artistic" *The American Arts Quarterly*, Summer 1996.

84 See the entry *Invention*.

85 Early in the nineteenth century, Mme de Staël and August-Wilhem Schlegel delineated the ideological conflict between Classic and Romantic. There was, however, a brief alliance between Quatremère and such later figures of Romanticism as Charles Nodier and Victor Hugo.

86 See his, "*De l'universalité du beau, et de la manière de l'entendre. Extrait d'un essai de théorie sur le Beau dans les Beaux-Arts.*" Séance publique annuelle des Quatre Académies. Le mardi 24 Avril, 1827.

87 Many pages of *De l'imitation* are dedicated to opposing Romanticism. See also his "*Dissertation sur la diversité du génie et des moyens poétiques des différents arts.*" Extraite d'un essai de théorie sur le système imitatif des arts et le génie poétique de chacun d'eux." Séance publique de l'Institut. Le 7 Vendémiaire, an XIII. Le 29 Septembre 1804.

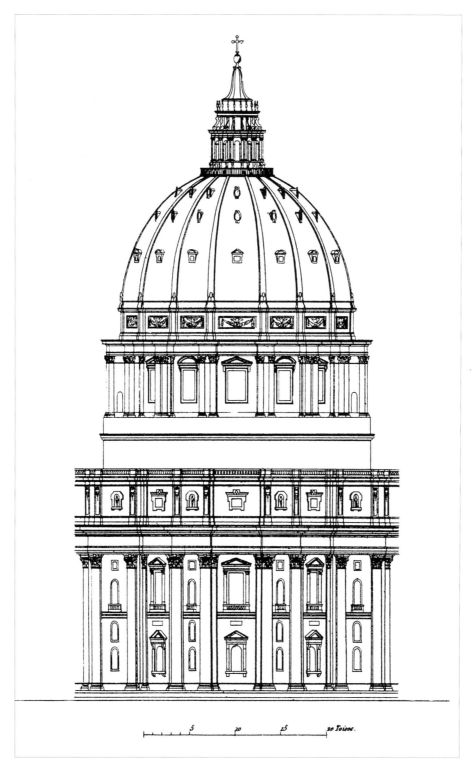

Fig. 10. St. Peter's Dome, M. Buonarotti.
From: A.C. Quatremère de Quincy, *Histoire de la vie et des ouvrages des plus célèbres architectes*,
Jules Renouard, Paris, 1830

II

ARCHITECTURE AND LANGUAGE

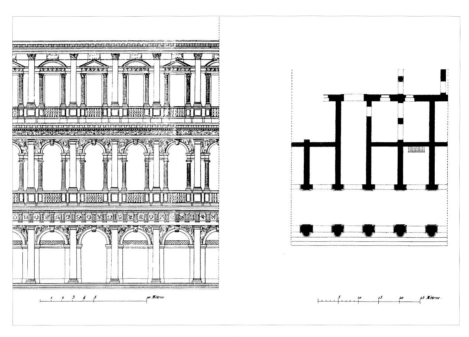

Fig. 11. Procuratie Nuove, V. Scamozzi.
From: A.C. Quatremère de Quincy, *Histoire de la vie et des ouvrages des plus célèbres architectes*,
J. Renouard, Paris, 1830

"...of all the arts of design, architecture while ostensibly having the least in common with what is known as the art of writing or literature, has nonetheless adopted the sort of metonymy which once associated the intellectual expression of ideas, with the notion of the instrument that was initially only intended to trace their signs." A.C. Quatremère de Quincy.

Type, character and style

Theories of origin played a normative role for the eighteenth century *philosophes* and architects. It involved speculations on the ontological essence of architecture, the materiality of its historical developments, and its relation to other fields. Two of Quatremère's early publications were dedicated to such concerns, and helped to establish his reputation as a theorist: his 1785 *Mémoire sur l'architecture égyptienne*, for which he was awarded a prize from l'Académie des Inscriptions et Belles-lettres, and the first volume of the *Dictionnaire d'architecture*,[1] in Panckoucke's *Encyclopédie Méthodique*. In a discourse which combined notions of need, social, geographic and climatic determinants, Quatremère proposed three original architectural types: the cave, the tent and the hut which developed, respectively, with societies of hunters, shepherds and farmers. Light could be shed on historical developments by emphasizing the genealogical lineage from each of these types, especially with regard to the expression of character. Accordingly, he saw the excessive solidity of Egyptian religious architecture with its dark and cavernous interiors, as evidence of its derivation from the cave;[2] by contrast, the lightness of Chinese architecture in wood could be explained in comparison with the tent; while the wooden hut, the type for Greek architecture, occupied a just and temperate middle, and was the only principled type. Following Vitruvius, he identified the interconnectedness between societal, architectural, and linguistic origins, and asserted that "the invention of architecture should be considered as aligned with that of language, in the sense that both inventions cannot be attributed to one individual, but are rather attributes of humanity."[3] In his *Mémoire*, Quatremère elaborated his belief in a universal grammar, which, he cautioned, must be distinguished from the "rules of syntax which are proper to an individual language."[4] He also pointedly emphasized that no necessary genealogical connection between two languages needed to be drawn simply because both had a syntax. This view, which he transposed into architecture, served two of his aims. First, he opposed those who saw in Egyptian architecture an origin or at least a major influence on the Greek, by positing separate origins to both.[5] He also sought to justify the primacy of the Greek paradigm in architecture based on climatic, political and artistic grounds. Second, he advanced the idea that there are principles to the art of building that are common to all architectures, and that these should not be confused with those particular to individual architectures. Such a proposition regarding a set of principles of an art of building common to all stemmed from the Cartesian belief in the universality of reason – the essential cross-cultural unity of the human mind.[6] Thus, type, character and style could bear an analogical correspondence to universal grammar, while columns, lintels, arches, cornices, walls and roofs correspond to the syntax of a particular language.

Quatremère drew on etymological studies in order to emphasize that type, character and style shared a common origin in writing. Type "derives from the Greek word *typos*, whose general acceptance applies to many nuances and varieties of the same idea, and expresses what is understood by model, matrix, imprint, mould, figure in relief or *bas-relief*.[7] Character, from "...the Greek word *characteer*, derives from the verb *charassein*, and it signifies, in the proper meaning of the word, a mark, a particular object's distinctive sign."[8] As for style, "the etymology of this word, whose use in French has deviated from its original meaning, is the Latin word *stylus*, or the Greek word *stylos*. In each of these two languages, the word designated either a round body such as a column, or an engraver's point, round like a pencil, sharp on one end and flattened on the other, which was utilized to write on wax-coated sheets."[9]

Thus, as the ontological essence of architecture, the type is a principle which informs manifold objects, presenting "... less the *image* of a thing to copy or completely imitate, and more the *idea* of an element which serves as a rule for the model."[10] The words image and idea are italicized to indicate that the etymology of type, character and style implied a metaphorical relationship between a figurative character, and an idea having its own image(s) in architecture. Hence the association between the hieroglyph as a kind of *bas-relief* or ornament, and the hieroglyphic writing on the walls as an open book, a "public library," where a nation recorded its cultural accomplishments.[11] In this view, the hieroglyph could be seen as the concrete form where the word and the image converged.

Those in the eighteenth century who understood type as a classificatory device, likewise saw character as explaining a species or an object's belonging to a larger family, according to major distinctive traits. But the larger implication was that character and type gained their value precisely from the qualities that they shared with other buildings. Character was distinguished from type in that character implied something more expressive, especially for that century which privileged the senses so highly. Indeed, Le Camus de Mézières saw character as a *genre expressif*, which related architecture to social mores and sensations within a social hierarchy, for example, the character of a house for a magistrate and a house for a soldier.[12] Ledoux's *Architecture considérée...* associated character with national mores and laws.[13] His prison at Aix presented, in its massing ensemble and details, the most severe physiognomy, and his house for the inspector of the waters of the Loue river for the Saline de Chaux was in the shape of a sectioned water conduit. The architectural character of the public monument also became a constant preoccupation. Consider Piranesi's Rome, Brongniart's Pyramide de Mauperthuis, Boullée's Cenotaphs and the projects for the French Pantheon. Within this *architecture parlante*, the notion of character implied that the image of a building bore an intimate association between the mind, the sensations, and social mores. Hence the importance of *convenance* or propriety as a social contract between architectural character and the meanings attributed to it by society. Only the late eighteenth century gave a higher emphasis to propriety as a system of valuation outside architecture over the aptness internal to it. And in so doing allowed for a mind set which gradually transformed the relationship between architectural character – including stylistic symbolism – and social significance from one of metaphorical association to one of near equivalency. The leap to an equivalency between architecture and language was not too far.

But Quatremère saw a much wider application of the concept of character than his contemporaries. In one of the lengthiest articles of the *Dictionnaire d'architecture* of 1788, Quatremère distinguished three meanings to architectural character: the essential, the distinctive and the relative, the latter two being an outcome of socio-political forces.[14] Essential character is a "natural" character, the very thingness of a thing. It

> "... partakes in the very essence of things, and usually derives from the expression of qualities inherent to their nature, or because it is the most important and occupies the first place among the different characters. This is also the reason *par excellence*, for which it is called *character*. And what other character can aspire to this appellation, save the one which comprises the meaning and the assertion of the ideas of force and grandeur?"[15]

By partaking in the "very essence of things," in this case architecture, essential character bears a strong parallel to type, in the sense that both refer to that internal constitution of architecture, beyond which it cannot be reduced. On this level, character and type show no categorical difference. He saw distinctive character as a particular application of essential character, and considered it "accidental" because it is subject to the contingencies of history, to mores, climate and habits. It refers to a building's dominant quality. For example, Quatremère considered solidity and massiveness to be the qualities of Egyptian architecture; light-

ness to be that of the Chinese; grace and harmony to be those of the Greek; and opulent luxury and vanity to be that of the Roman. Within relative character, Quatremère distinguished two regions – the ideal and the imitative – each of which pointed either to the intellectual or the physical realms, in a manner similar to the distinction drawn in painting and sculpture between ideal beauty and imitative beauty.[16] The first, or ideal character, pertains to the art of architecture "metaphysically considered." It reaches to the level of principle, and occupies for architecture, a rapport akin to that which poetry plays for language.[17]

The second, or imitative character, is synonymous with propriety and depends on rules in the sense that it allows for a sensuous apprehension of ideas through the manipulation of forms.

> "Every edifice, whatever it be, is destined for a particular usage. It is the manifest expression of this usage which constitutes *relative character*. This expression, depending on the nature of buildings, may be rendered either though the gradation of richness and dimensions which are proportionate to their nature, required by social decorum; or by indicating the moral qualities inherent to every building, the feeling of which was independent from rules; or by the general and particular forms of architecture; or by the kind of construction that it may utilize; or by the resources of decoration; or finally, by the choice of attributes which partake in it."[18]

The concept of style, according to Quatremère, was transposed into architecture from the literary arts. And whereas he saw in style a synonym to manner, in that they both refer to drawing and composition, he nevertheless distinguished between the two. Illustrating his meaning in a discourse reminiscent of Winckelmann's discussion of the Apollo of the Belvedere and the Laöcoon, he compared the drawing styles of Michelangelo and Raphael; and concluded that Michelangelo had a better *manner* in execution, technique and *chiaroscuro*, but as far as *style* was concerned, he favoured Raphael for the congruity between his compositions and his choice of moral and intellectual subjects.[19]

"Architects use also the word style to designate the issue of taste in the arrangement of all the parts which constitute the whole of architecture. They recognize a style of forms and proportions, a style of profile and details, a style of decoration and ornament. Thus, of all the arts of design, architecture, while ostensibly having the least in common with what is known as the *art of writing* or literature, has nonetheless adopted the sort of metonymy which once associated the intellectual expression of ideas, with the notion of the instrument that was initially only intended to trace their signs. And why should this metaphor not justly apply to architecture, if it is true that this art, in accordance with the spirit which constitutes its genre of imitation, through this or that choice of forms and proportions, renders intelligible to the eye this or that abstract conception, this or that intellectual combination; if it is true that this art, through the diversely modified use of parts, members, details and ornaments, awakens in us resolute ideas and positive judgments of the objects it creates, as do the signs of writing; if it is true that through the modulated harmonies that it produces, it knows how to arouse in us the impressions of all the moral qualities which belong to its imitative domain."[20]

Quatremère's validation of type, character and style based on their etymological parallels, and especially his three divisions of character, point to two deductions. First, architectural character and language represented a culture's character, influenced as it is by geographic, climatic, historical, ethical and aesthetic qualities. Second, by drawing from and returning meaning back to nature and society, architectural character and language commonly share their adoption of nature and society as paradigms against which to measure

form and meaning. Naming through character designated the building in its essence, its use, and its decoration. In this sense, architectural character returned the gaze of society and its mores, in a discourse qualified by two directions, the one oriented toward architecture, the other toward society, taking architecture as its departure point.

Like many of his contemporary intellectuals, especially the encyclopaedists, Quatremère considered architecture to be a language. Indeed, in some statements he expresses a literal relationship between architecture and language, for both convey ideas and impressions. Architecture could be seen as "...an ocular language, a kind of hieroglyphic writing," in form, for example type and character, and detail, for example the allegories of

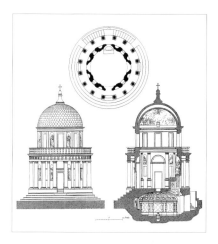

Fig. 12. San Pietro in Montorio, D. Bramante.
From: A.C. Quatremère de Quincy, *Histoire de la vie et des ouvrages des plus célèbres architectes*, J. Renouard, Paris, 1830

decoration and ornament. Decoration and ornament were integral parts of a building's character, and were not arbitrary accoutrements that could be added or removed without any consequence. But while accepting the normativeness of allegorical means because they qualified early man's "...figurative manner of speaking and writing,"[21] and addressed the intellect and the imagination, Quatremère remarked on the limited applicability of allegory in architecture. He spoke approvingly of the Roman temples to Virtue and Honour, which were disposed in such a fashion, that one had to pass through the first to access the second.[22] But he disapproved of the strained allegorical interpretations of some of his contemporaries – for example Viel de St. Maux – who saw mystical meanings in pediments, columns and votive stones. Clearly, Quatremère was interested in issues of putative meaning, and especially in regard to delineating the limits of what could be transposed into architecture from language or other fields. For he observed with alarming concern, the rising confusion of artistic genres among his contemporaries, especially after the Revolution, which he feared would lead to the demise of the arts. Hence his linking of artistic boundaries with the signifier and the signified. Curiously, he did not extend this clear distinction to the relationship between such different fields as architecture and language. Indeed, as we saw, he sometimes spoke of an analogy between architecture and language, while in other instances he spoke more of a literal relationship. It is rather paradoxical that this brilliant theorist who perspicaciously drew distinctions between the limits proper to each art, and between universal and particular grammars, would admit the possibility of a literal relationship between two autonomous fields.

Architecture's linguistic analogy

From *l'architecture parlante* of the late eighteenth century, to the structuralist codes of the late twentieth, the assimilation of architecture into language or its structures, has oscillated between an analogical, a literal relationship, thus necessitating the question: if architecture and language exhibit order, does this imply that both share the same dialectical structure?

Much of the philosophical discourse in late-eighteenth-century France occurred in an ideological region which gave language a privileged position as a phenomenon upon which thought depended for its expressions and operations. Inquiry into the arts and the sciences was inextricable from rationally organized linguistic signs. The *Encyclopédie* and institutions such as the *Institut National des Sciences et Arts*, worked toward developing a language devoid of ambiguity, where reading between the lines was out of the question. Through an excessive elevation of the sign, they sought to materialize that one rational and efficient method was valid for all scientific areas, and by extension all knowledge. In other words, the more exactitude a sign attained *vis-à-vis* its referent, the better the state of knowledge, while the reverse implied the opposite conclusion.[23] This was but a manifestation of the monism spoken of in the last chapter, which reduced architecture and construction to a system of signs decipherable through grammatical analysis, later giving rise, under the names of structuralism and codification, to the confusion between what can be dismantled with what can be made. Such a system contributed to privileging an outside legitimizing meaning to architecture at the expense of architecture's internal aptness, while assimilating this art into a realm where its limits are dissolved.

Fig. 13. Church of the Sorbonne, Le Mercier.
From: A.C. Quatremère de Quincy, *Histoire de la vie et des ouvrages des plus célèbres architecte*s, J. Renouard, Paris, 1830

Propriety, as already stated, governed architecture's relationship within a larger social context, while aptness governed its internal legibility as a field. Architectural legibility depends on a congruence between type, character and style. But by privileging sensuous appearance as *the* criterion for social legibility, the eighteenth century placed a higher emphasis on architecture's sensuous appearance, for example, style, than on its essential nature, for example, type and character. In this way architectural legibility was strongly tied to style and its syntactic forms. Social meaning began to be associated more with style, and less with type, reaching a point where the separation of architectural meaning and type became a common occurrence. This phenomenon was used by the eclecticists who delighted in stylistic proliferation, and by the positivists, who in their pursuit of an essence to architecture solely within the functional and the structural, found style to be a superfluous accoutrement.

An *architecture parlante* became an architecture solely accessible through a provided narrative. Now, whereas architectural theory since Vitruvius has helped to access meaning in architecture through language, and whereas architecture *has* a language that can allegorically relate internal and external meanings, there is no transparent equivalent, no identical dialectical structure between architecture and language. For as autonomous formal entities and distinct experiences, the linguistic

(the word) and the visual (the image) are irreducible to each other. A reduction occurs only if architecture and language are absorbed into a uniform flux of signs that dissolves their boundaries. If language, through its mediation, helps the mind to construct the world, then language is at once indissociable but irreducible to this construction. Similarly, whereas the building cannot be dissociated from the materials that compose it, neither can it be reduced to these materials. Indeed, it is by transcending and idealizing construction that building can aspire to be architecture. In the final analysis, the extent of the usefulness of the linguistic analogy in architecture depends precisely on it remaining on the level of analogy.

NOTES

1   Quatremère republished an amended version of the *mémoire*, in 1803, under the title, *De l'architecture égyptienne considérée dans son origine, ses principes et son goût, et comparée sous les mêmes rapports à l'architecture grecque. Dissertation qui a remporté, en 1785, le prix proposé par l'Académie des Inscriptions et Belles-lettres*. For a discourse on the historical context of *De l'architecture égyptienne*, see S. Lavin, *Ibid.*

2   Quatremère did accept that the Egyptians eventually developed huts; however, he still maintained that it was the cave which remained the principle that gave character to Egyptian architecture.

3   *De l'architecture égyptienne*, p. 12, author's translation.

4   *Ibid.*, p .13.

5   Paradoxically, even though Quatremère espoused the idea of autochthonous architecture (which had been advanced earlier by Winckelmann in his *Histoire de l'art*), he still judged Egyptian architecture by the standards of the Greek. In 1777, J.G. Herder criticized this approach in the context of Winckelmann's thought.

6   This belief permeated the works of the *philosophes* who authored the *Encyclopédie* where the mind is referred to as being "... of the same species, of the same nature... the germ of the same talents, the same spirit..." *Encyclopédie, Langue* Vol. IX, p. 256.

7   See the entry TYPE.

8   See the entry CHARACTER.

9   See the entry STYLE.

10 See the entry TYPE. Emphasis added. For the concept of idea, see E. Panofsky *Idea: A Concept in Art Theory*. Columbia, University of South Carolina Press, 1968. It was in the third volume of the *Encyclopédie Méthodique* of 1825, that appeared the full Platonic meaning of Quatremère's distinction between type and model.

11 *De l'architecture égyptienne*, p. 59. See also the articles *Allégorie* and *Egyptienne* in the *Dictionnaire historique d'architecture*. For a wider discussion on the hieroglyph, see Lavin, "The Transformation of Type," *Ibid.*, pp. 86-100.

12 *Le génie de l'architecture, ou l'analogie de cet art avec nos sensations*. Paris, Benoit Morin, 1780, p. 56.

13 L' *Architecture considérée sous le rapport de l'art, des mœurs et de la législation*. Paris, 1804.

14 *Dictionnaire d'architecture*. 3 vols. *Encyclopédie Méthodique*, C.J. Panckoucke, Paris, 1788-1825. pp. 477- 521. By contrast, the article character in the *Dictionnaire historique d'architecture* of 1832, was considerably abbreviated and lacks the thoroughness and clarity of the earlier one. However, the division into three characters was still maintained, while they were respectively associated to the terms: grandeur, originality and physiognomy.

15 *Dictionnaire d'architecture, Encyclopédie Méthodique*, p. 500.

16 *Ibid.*, p. 503.

17 *Ibid.*, pp. 502-6.

18 *Ibid.*, p. 506.

19 See the entry STYLE.

20 *Ibid.*

21 See the entry ALLEGORY.

22 *Ibid.*

23 "The competition brief held in the year V by the Institut National des Sciences et Arts, read as follows:

"1. Is it really the case that sensations can only be transformed into ideas by means of signs? Or what comes to the same thing, do our earliest ideas essentially depend on the help of signs?

2. Would the art of thought be perfect if the art of signs were brought to perfection?

3. In those sciences where there is general agreement as to what is true, is the result of the perfection of the signs used in them?

4. In those branches of knowledge which are a constant source of disputes, is not this division of views a necessary result of the inexactitude of the signs employed?

5. Is there any means of correcting signs that are badly made, and of rendering all sciences equally susceptible of demonstration?" From the *Mémoires de l'Institut National des Sciences et Arts. Sciences morales et politiques*, i, pp. i-ii. Quoted by Acton, H. B. "The Philosophy of Language in Revolutionary France" in *Studies in Philosophy*, British Academy Lectures, New York, Toronto, Oxford University Press, 1966, p. 152.

III

POETIC ORDER

Fig. 14. Polymnia, A. Canova. Engraving by H. Moses.
From: Henry Moses, *The Works of Antonio Canova*,
Septimius Prowett, London, 1887

"We must agree that the authority of the antique does not prevail over the authority of reason."[1]
A.C. Quatremère de Quincy

In his third division of architectural theory – the metaphysical – Quatremère distinguished a causal realm, which is the source of rules, namely, principles.[2] He considered principles to be simple truths from which derive many lesser truths or rules. Unity for example, is an elementary principle shared by all the arts, from which derives symmetry or the concordance and harmony between the parts and the whole. In this sense, symmetry[3] is not an ordinary dimensional relationship between objects, it is a system of correlative measures aiming towards unity.[4] Principles derive their authority from that universal, rational acceptance known as *sensus communis*, which in turn gives authority to rules. As composite derivatives, rules are more numerous than principles; they are variable in their applications to varying circumstances, and the possibility always exists for the appearance of new ones.

Quatremère distinguished between four classes of rules, the first two of which are based on nature, and the other two are based on conventions. These are: reason, or "the nature of things;" the constitution of soul, mind and senses; the authority of precedents; and even habit and prejudice.[5] By pointing to the dual origin of rules in nature (the realm of the true) and in convention (the realm of the real), he emphasized that although the rules deriving from architectural conventions are paradigmatic, they alone did not constitute a sufficiently comprehensive basis for architecture, because there are manifold rules that the mind does not invent, but rather deduces or discovers after a close observation of nature's laws and products. Paralleling Laugier's advice never to lose sight of the primitive hut, this admonition reminded architects that the contingencies of practice ought not to detract from architecture as a poetic order.

Order is that system of principles and rules which organizes the internal and external relationships of a field of endeavour and its constitutive elements. The idea of nature, and that of social decor, are examples of external relationships. Imitating the order found in nature, amounted to art and architecture analogically appropriating the "...system of laws which governs the organization of all living beings."[6] Order also designates a social contract between a culture and its productions, as in the case of architectural *commoditas* and *decor*. An example of internal relationships is order within the work of art proper, when its constitutive parts are proportionate to the whole. Indeed, Quatremère considered proportion as the very "image of order."[7] When it manifests as an *ordonnance*, order involves the disposition of volumes, solids, voids, and columns on the one hand, and plans, entries and circulation

Fig. 15. Apollo crowning himself. A. Canova. Engraving by H. Moses. From Henry Moses, *The Works of Antonio Canova*, Septimius Prowett, London, 1887

on the other.[8] Therefore, transcending the narrow definition of *ordonnance* as a theory that strictly applies to columnar types, Quatremère saw order as a cause of which an *ordonnance* is but one effect among many.

The systemic character of Quatremère's theory[9] is evident in his framing of the limits of architectural theory within a four-part dialectic. First is a theory of art in architecture, evidenced in such essays as: imitation, invention, principles, rules, types, models, idea and order. Second, is a theory of beauty in architecture, found in the essays: symmetry, eurythmy, proportion, character, style, composition, *ordonnance*, propriety and aptness. Third, is a strategy for the retrieval of traditional

knowledge, and the critical theory necessary for this knowledge to be instrumental in contemporary practice, explained in the entries: antique, authority, restitution and restoration. Fourth, are the theoretical parameters influencing renewal within tradition, for example: the indissociable couples imitation and invention, principles and rules, conventions and genius.

Quatremère's architectural theory sees no necessary schism between tradition and contemporary practice; rather, it incorporates and re-interprets the principles of tradition and requires their comparison with current contingencies; thus maintaining an equilibrium between the enduring and the contingent. This theory contains at once continuity and renewal within tradition, and avoids, on the one hand, the *tabula rasa* suggested by primitivism, and on the other, the *tabula rasa* enforced by those who reject tradition or conventions in an *a priori* fashion. With reason as its guide, this position does not accept a blind faith in an unsurpassable past, nor a blind faith in a teleology that heralds an unknown future ideal which will emerge from the contingencies of history. The authority of reason, here, is not an end in itself, nor has it anything to do with authoritarianism.[10] Reason gains its authority precisely because of its corroboration by many minds in many places and times, reflecting upon similar concerns, and building a sense in common. Therefore, the authority of tradition does not imply its blind repetition, for that would be an affront to reason. In other words, there is an authority to principles and rules because there is an authority to reason.

Tradition is at once about the enduring, the permanent, and about the changing circumstances of the contingent. Permanence concerns enduring principles within one culture or pan-culturally, even if Quatremère heralded only the Greek ideal as the highest source of artistic principles. These principles have formative and normative values which assure continuity, and against which various phenomena or historical contingencies are measured. Finally, it is within the contingency of historical events that the universal is experienced; and belief in the enduring must not necessarily exclude historical change and ruptures, nor must belief in the contingent necessarily negate historical continuity. Thus the enduring concerns posterity, and refers to two regions: the intellectual, in the significant value of the paradigm, and the physical, in the notable value of solidity. Many a theorist committed two catastrophic errors, either in the assignment of a proscriptive primacy of the enduring to the exclusion of the lessons of historical contingency, or the equally proscriptive denial of the enduring in favour of the circumstantial. An example of the first is the upholding of an unsurpassable glorious past. An example of the second is the assumption that a change in means necessarily entails a change in ends. Thus, to see a mutual exclusivity to the enduring and the contingent, entails adverse consequences on *praxis* and the understanding of history, in the broadest senses of these words, and their instrumentality in the contemporary life of the mind.[11]

Foreseeing that these views were to constitute an obstacle to the uses of history, and the participation in its making, Quatremère distinguished between restoration and restitution, in order to differentiate the roles of the archaeologist and the architect, and direct the architect's thoughts away from the material exactitude of the restoration *à l'identique* needed by the archaeologist, toward a more instrumental use of tradition for contemporary practice.[12] In this sense E-E. Viollet-le-Duc's restitution of the city of Carcassone and the Château de Pierrefonds, in a form that did not resemble their supposed *first* historical appearance, should be considered as paradigmatic; for he regarded the Gothic as a reasoned contemporary practice and not a mere historical revival. Despite their widely divergent views on the Classic and the Gothic, Quatremère and Viollet-le-Duc, each in his own separate way, saw them as two forms of contemporary architectural practice: a living tradition. Similarly, the present selection from the *Dictionnaire* is not offered because it once had a value which fitted the context of the early to middle decades of the nineteenth century. Rather, it is offered because it contains many lessons for its applicability in the contemporary

reconstruction of architecture and the writing of its theory. Facing the lack of composure in contemporary artistic practice, *vis-à-vis* learning from history and a reluctance to contribute to it, this text proposes to engage history by fully participating in its very making.

The realm we have been discussing in these introductory chapters, is that of poetic or symbolic order, onto which Quatremère offered one perspective. This poetic order is the means used by the mind as one of many approaches to immanent and transcendent meanings which one could group under the rubric of symbolization as mediation.[13] Such a mediation made possible the relationship between art and a view of nature, art and reality, and art and truth. Thus arose many a discourse on the extent to which art depends on a truth or a reality, and the extent to which art was distinct and autonomous from them. This meant that a dialectic thrived on the symbolic tensions between a universal and a particular, a type and a building, language and speech. This dialectic allowed for that fruitful distance known as the realm of the fictive, in which consciousness reached, appropriated, and returned to a physical reality a certain art form. The fictive then, mediates the distance between the paradigm (the true) and the individual work (the real), thus providing various perspectives on our partial knowledge of the world, as well as that of artistic truths. This knowledge is necessarily partial, because if a truth – artistic or otherwise – were fully known, then it would have no need of a mediatory expression such as representation. Similarly, if we had complete knowledge of what the first building was, or if our knowledge of making was equal to that first precipitate of making, then we would have veritably acquired some of the characteristics of the gods. But since – for most of us – such a complete knowledge is lacking, we require a theory of art to mediate between our consciousness and a truth, a reality, an object. This symbolization as mediation is an access to *a* truth; and is not the truth itself. Poetic or symbolic order then, is that mediation which allows subject and object to remain related yet reciprocally other. This occurs precisely, because the true (the enduring) and the real (the contingent) are related and yet reciprocally other. Such a proposition sheds light on *poesis* and *techné* in the following manner: as a question of making, *poesis* has a *techné*, which is a question of doing, involving *mimesis* for example. Put differently, *techné* as the real, reveals *poesis* as the true.

From here, derive two important deductions about artistic making: first, making is characterized by a purpose, which is distinctly *other* than itself;[14] a purpose that is not enclosed, nor exclusively identified within the limits of processes or techniques. Second, meaning in making is at once transcendent and immanent to the made object; it is never confined to an internal relationship alone. The dialectical space between these two deductions constitutes the *sine qua non* for the very possibility of having an art theory, and the collapse of this dialectic inevitably precipitates the collapse of art.

This is precisely the contemporary predicament of architecture and the arts, facing the daunting presence of a milieu which has eclipsed nature, the city and its architecture, forming a reality *in se*, namely, the technological order. Having become an all-encompassing milieu, this order established a determinism of its own, thus framing the contemporary mind's reality. This monistic and autonomous order refers to itself, replicates and resembles itself, in a causal progression and with an absence of finality.[15] Meaning, here, is a wholly immanent affair, characterized by an opacity toward meanings that are external to this order. Being all means, this order is its own ends. And where the means and the ends are confused, the distance needed for symbolization as mediation is eclipsed; and meaning, being confined to an internal relationship alone, collapses.[16] This resulted in the collapse of any legitimizing meaning to a work of art that is not logical with the dictates of the technological order. By symbolizing itself, this order cannot point beyond itself; thus it is non-dialectical. This is so because making in the technological order is its own ends, its own *other*, a spurious infinity. It is for this reason that invention and innovation within the technological order are an end, whilst in a poetic order, they are a means. Compare the hut and the *maison domino* for example, and consider the differences between generating and replicating. The hut can be considered a paradigm, because the hut – as a type – allows for a distance between itself and the multitude of buildings of varied characters which it generates, as well as an indissociable unity of form and meaning, constituting this art's truth. By contrast, the *maison domino* can only replicate and resemble itself with no distance. In this mentality, structural form is dissociated from character and meaning, which become removable attributes, thus displacing the issue of artistic truth, along with the links and boundaries between technological and artistic representation and production. Put differently, and in connection with painting, Canaletto's analogous Venice cannot be confused with a virtual reality Venice, for this implies a rejection of the categorical distinction between *seeing* and *seeing as*.[17] To confuse seeing with seeing as, means a confusion as to the nature, means and ends of artifice, and ultimately a confusion between the true and the real.

For the reasons outlined above, the major ontological question facing *episteme* in general and architecture in particular today, lies in a categorical distinction between the poetic order whose form of making is qualified by a purpose other than itself; and the technological order, whose form of making is its own ends. The first order is dialectical; it is qualified by a distance between the true and the real, where the true is the measure of the real, and where the means serve the ends. The second order is non-dialectical, it is a world of immanence where the distance between the true and the real is eliminated, causing them to collapse into each other. Put differently, when the real subsumes the true, the means eclipse the ends.

Instrumental in reconstructing this collapse, is that phenomenon which is ontologically linked to the human character, namely, the word, for the following reason. Qualities and values of being are determined by modes of thought. If the subject of being is thinking, and if the object of thinking is the meaning of being, then the word claims a high place in the pursuit of a truth. In the *Phaedo*, Plato suggests that an object takes the name of the Form from which it derives. Naming, therefore, partakes in the Form because linguistic conventions establish a relationship between words and a truth that is outside language.[18] Therefore, the word is a mediation between Form and object, Type and model. For Plato as well as Quatremère, the word is a representation of the true, and not a chimera that lurks behind the linguistically real.

When it is turned toward the object, the word as naming[19] serves to "call forth," and thus to manifest the object. Therefore, in the word's dual functions of meaning and referring, meaning

Thus, if the contention according to which we inhabit the world through the word is true,[22] as well as the parallel claim that language is one of the human activities that demonstrate that the mind's relationship to the world is analogous to that between the architect and the building materials,[23] then the wise use of the word seeks an equilibrium between two things: the word's dual function of meaning and referring, on the one hand, and the image on the other. In the act of designing and building, the image helps the mind to appropriate a part of the world as an object, while the word helps the mind to appropriate the world as a subject. In such a manner, subject and object remain connected, while being reciprocally other. This occurs precisely because

Fig. 16. True Plurality and False Pluralism, Léon Krier.
From: Léon Krier, *Architecture, Choice or Fate*,
A. Papadakis Publisher, London, 1998

Fig. 17. Basilica at Fano, E-E. Viollet-le-Duc.
From: E.-E. Viollet-le-Duc, *Entretiens sur l'architecture*,
A. Morel, Paris, 1863-72

corresponds to the word's relation to a truth, while referring points to the word's relation to a reality. In this perspective, the relationship between Vitruvius's *ratiocinatione*, or theoretical know-ledge, and *fabrica*, or practice, can be understood respectively as the true naming the real as the made.[20] Similarly, the distinction made by Quatremère, between *architecture, construction*, and *building*, indicates to what the reality of construction alludes in the truth of architecture as an art, demonstrating that without the fictive truth to which architecture alludes, for example aspects of tectonics,[21] it will remain subservient to the dictates of necessity, to the reality of construction, to mere contingency. Here, the word of architectural theory links truth and making.

the word and the image remain connected, yet reciprocally other. For the word is in the domain of the true, while the image presents the real and alludes to the true.[24]

Attaining a balanced co-existence between the true and the real is a difficult aim, and it should not be confused with the means used to achieve it. For to restrict the true to the factual, causes the true to collapse into the real, displacing art in its essential nature. Whenever the true is not confined to the real, and whenever meaning is at once transcendent and immanent – as in the recovery of the symbolic function – then the technological order's hegemony has collapsed, and our ability to keep a critical distance from its empire is retrieved. This necessary freedom, from which the word cannot be dissociated, assures *where one stands and what one refers to*; a freedom essential to establish a world which is independent of the dictates of technological deter-minism, while nevertheless possessing techniques.

Far from claiming that the word constructs architecture, this argument however, emphasizes that the recovery of the word of architectural theory is one of the ways with which to liberate architecture from the enclosure of technological determinism and the technicist image, which are at the root of the symbolic poverty that qualifies contemporary architecture, as she stands blind to her essential nature. Here, the *Historical Dictionary of Architecture*, occupies a high instrumental value for contemporary architectural thought for two reasons: it constitutes one enlightened approach to poetic order, and its paths lie outside the framing powers of technological determinism.

Quatremère used the word as a symbol for the aesthetic activity of the mind, allowing involvement in immediate experience, in the real, as well as an independence from this immediacy to serve other objects of the mind, such as engaging in reflection or perception beyond the level of ordinary experience, namely, the realm of the true. Here, the word *theoria* is necessary for the architectural imagination, whether in its Kantian form of a unity between sense data and concepts in ordinary perception or aesthetic judgment, or in the Vichian form of *fantasia* needed for the retrieval of a poetic wisdom answering the tragedy of history, in a manner akin to Quatremère's Platonic understanding of type in architecture.[25] For Quatremère, architectural knowledge does not operate independently of the word, which as we said earlier, links the truth of an art with the making of this art. Herein lies the capital importance of his work, for it opens the way for a theory of art in architecture; a theory of beauty; objectivist and subjectivist concerns in aesthetics; and their relation to an enduring ideal as well as the contingent in culture.

NOTES

1 Quatremère de Quincy, A.C. *Dictionnaire d'architecture*. 3 vols. *Encyclopédie Méthodique*, C.J. Panckoucke, Paris, 1788-1825, p. 458.
2 See the entries *Principle* and *Rule*.
3 See the entries *Symmetry* and *Proportion*.
4 Contrariwise, a numerous repetition of the same architectural elements does not endow a building with unity, but rather with uniformity.
5 See the entry *Rule*. See also S. Younés "The Instrumentality of History or Janus the Architect," in *Building Classical*, London, Academy Editions, 1993.
6 See the entry *Order*.
7 See the entry *Ordonnance*.
8 *Ibid*. For Vitruvius's *ordinatio*, see 1,2,1; 1,2,2.
9 Quatremère's theory did not always exhibit a consistent homogeneity; indeed, his thought occasionally shows some radical shifts. For example, betraying an influence of Y.M. André's *Essai sur le Beau*, Quatremère affirmed the idea of an essential beauty found in architecture in his 1785 *Dictionnaire d'architecture* which was subsequently rejected in the 1832 *Dictionnaire historique d'architecture*. Compare respectively the entries *Beau* of 1785 and *Antique* of 1832.
10 Those who practise the authority of reason or tradition in an absolute sense engender many problems; but the rectification of these problems ought to attain the notion of absoluteness and not that of authority.
11 This is one of the most poignant lessons of the recent writing of history, and is evident in the conflict between those whose practice is rooted in tradition and two other groups. The one group includes those who are unable to see tradition save in a museal sense. This is the revivalist position, characterized by an archaeological search, followed by an identical repetition of past architectural forms, and assuming tradition to be immobile. The second group includes those who indiscriminately herald change as the only constant, thus making the very idea of tradition unrealizable. These two extremes fracture the dialectic between that fateful couple: imitation and invention. The first by reducing imitation to the copy, the second by reducing invention to innovation, and considering the latter to be the aim of art.
12 See these articles. We leave for another study the issue of the adverse effects of the museum and museal attitudes on artistic practice and cultural continuity. On Quatremère's role in the débacle around the *Musée des monuments français*, see R. Schneider's *Quatremère de Quincy et son intervention dans les arts*. Paris, 1910; *L'Esthétique classique chez Quatremère de Quincy*. Paris, Hachette, 1910; "Un ennemi du Musée des monuments français," in *Gazette des Beaux-Arts 2*, 4 (1909). M. Greenhalgh's "Quatremère de Quincy as a Popular Archaeologist," in *Gazette des Beaux-Arts 71*, 6, (1968). B. Foucart's "La fortune critique d'A. Lenoir et du premier Musée des monuments français", in *L'information d'histoire de l'art 14*, 5 (1969). A. Vidler's "Architecture in the Museum," in *The Writing of the Walls*. Princeton, Princeton Architectural Press, 1987.
13 Symbolization here designates myth, language, architecture, aesthetics, or that knowledge which enables an object to acquire meaning beyond its internal parameters; while mediation refers to that which facilitates the passage of ideas between at least two realms.

14 "The business of every art is to bring something into existence, and the practice of an art involves the study of how to bring into existence something which is capable of having such an existence and has its efficient cause in the maker and not in itself." Aristotle, *Ethica Nicomach*. 1140a 9. On this Aristotelian distinction see Nahm, M. "The Theological background of the Theory of the Artist as Creator," in *Essays on the History of Aesthetics*, Ed. P. Kivy, Library of the History of Ideas, Univ. of Rochester Press, 1992.

15 Ellul, J. *Le système technicien*. Paris, Calmann-Lévy, 1977.

16 The interiority spoken of here, refers to an isomorphic relationship with the technological order.

17 This distinction is Wittgenstein's.

18 For Plato, only Forms can be strictly named, just as they are the only things to be known.

19 See Heidegger's discussion of the word of poetic naming in the notions of 'essence of the word' and the 'word of essence,' in *Acheminement vers la parole*. Paris, Gallimard, 1976, p. 185.

20 Vitruvius, *De architectura*, I, 1. Morgan.

21 Tectonics is a poetics of construction. It is that aspect that elevates mere construction to the level of art.

22 See Heidegger, M. "Bâtir Habiter Penser," and "...L'Homme habite en poète...," in *Essais et conférences*. A.Préau Trans. Paris, Gallimard, 1954.

23 See Cassirer, E. *The philosophy of symbolic forms*. New Haven, Yale University Press, 1953-7.

24 On the word and the image, see Ellul, J. *La parole humiliée*. Paris, Seuil, 1981.

25 On I. Kant's imagination, see P.F. Strawson's "Imagination and Perception," in *Experience and Theory*, L. Foster and J.W. Swanson eds. Cambridge, Mass., 1970. On G. Vico's *fantasia*, see D. Verene, "Vico's Philosophy of the Imagination," in *Social Research*, 43, 1976.

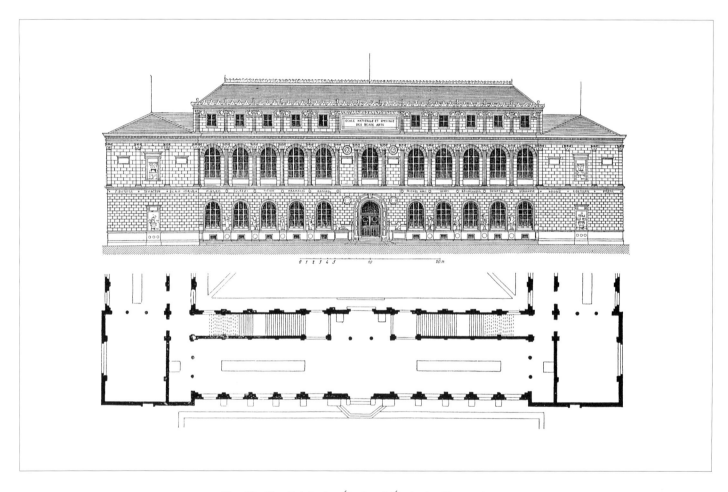

Fig. 18. The Palais des Études, L'École des Beaux-Arts.
From: Julien Guadet, *Éléments et théorie de l'architecture*,
Librairie de la construction moderne, Paris, 1909

IV
A BIOGRAPHICAL AND BIBLIOGRAPHICAL CHRONOLOGY

1755

Antoine Chrysostôme Quatremère de Quincy was born on 28th October, in the rue St. Denis in Paris, of a Parisian bourgeois family of cloth merchants, whose origins were in Burgundy.

1765

The famous sculptor, J.B. Pigalle, a friend of the family, encouraged the youth, after noticing a *bas-relief* that he had moulded in a window. At the Collège Louis-le-Grand, Quatremère covered his school books with drawings.

His father intended that he enter the legal profession, and arranged for his apprenticeship at a lawyer's office. However, Quatremère, who was uninterested in the study of law, spent much time playing backgammon with his permissive tutor.

1772

He learned sculpture at G. Coustou's *atelier*. He studied the monuments of Paris, Versailles and Fontainebleau, and read J.J. Winckelmann, A-C-P. Caylus, B. de Montfaucon and D. Diderot.

1776-80

A small inheritance from his mother assured him modest financial independence. He travelled throughout Italy, where he visited Rome, Naples, Pompeii and Herculaneum, and studied the Greek monuments of Paestum and Sicily. He successfully identified the Temple of Zeus at Agrigento, based on a text by Diodorus and measurements of scant ruined fragments. Later, in 1805, he would present a full restitution of this temple in a lecture at *l'Institut*.

In Italy, he developed a reputation for his passionate debates on art theory, defending the classical with resounding orations against the followers of G.L. Bernini and F. Borromini. An illustration of this reputation is the story told by the baron Desnoyers of *l'Académie des Beaux-Arts*, of a tragi-comical debate between Quatremère and an unfortunate interlocutor, which took place in the vicinity of the Trinità dei Monti. The exchange, which continued with ferocity until an advanced hour of the night, was interrupted only when the interlocutor vacated the premises suffering from pulmonary convulsions which resulted in his coughing blood! Such was the intensity of the debate.

In Rome, Quatremère encountered A.R. Mengs and G.B. Piranesi, and greatly influenced J.L. David's artistic direction during their common visit to the Neapolitan region in 1779.

1780-4

After a brief sojourn in France, he returned to Italy, where he met A. Canova in front of the latter's *Theseus and the Minotaur*. They developed a close friendship that was to last forty years. He also met W. Hamilton, encountered J.L. David again in Rome, and made a second voyage to Sicily.

He was listed as a junior officer (*écuyer*) at the masonic lodge of Thalie, in Paris, from 1782 to 1786. The lodge was founded in 1776 and closed in 1789.

1784-85

He returned to France, and wrote his *Mémoire sur l'architecture égyptienne*, for which he received a prize from *l'Académie des Inscriptions et Belles-lettres*. His *Mémoire* on Egyptian architecture was not based on personal experience, but rather on the scant descriptions and drawings of various travellers. However, the prize attracted the attention of C.J. Panckoucke, the editor of the *Encyclopédie Méthodique*, who later commissioned Quatremère to compose the *Dictionnaire d'architecture*. Quatremère later published, in 1803, an amended and augmented version of this essay: *De l'architecture égyptienne considérée dans son origine, ses principes et son goût, et comparée sous les mêmes rapports à l'architecture grecque. Dissertation qui a remporté, en 1785, le prix proposé par l'Académie des Inscriptions et Belles-lettres.* This essay's importance resided less in the archaeological material presented – the Napoleonic *Description de l'Egypte* had provided a wealth of new archaeological material – and more in Quatremère's theory of origins, the normative role of type, the relationship between architecture and language, and the theory of imitation.[1]

In Paris, his circle of friends included, J.L. David, C. Percier and P.F.L. Fontaine, P. Julien and C.-L. Clérisseau.

1787

Writing for the *Journal de Paris*, he expressed his opposition to the removal of J. Goujon's *Fontaine des Innocents*, and proposed its dismantling and re-erection on another site.

1788

He published the first volume of the *Dictionnaire d'architecture* ("Abajour" to "Coloris des Fleurs") in three volumes, for C.J. Panckouke's *Encyclopédie Méthodique*. (The second volume appeared in two parts: "Colossal" to "Escalier" was published in 1801, and "Escalier" to "Mutules" was published in 1820. J.-B. Rondelet assisted Quatremère by writing the articles on constructional matters. J-N. Huyot and A.L. Castellan helped in writing several articles of the third volume of this *Dictionnaire* , which was published in 1825.)[2] This publication was to firmly establish his authority as a theorist, architect, antiquarian and archaeologist.

He travelled to London to study C. Wren's St. Paul's cathedral.

1789-90

He embraced the Revolution's ideals while greatly favouring France's brief experience with a constitutional monarchy, and was elected representative to the *Commune de Paris*.

He was engaged in projects for the embellishment of Paris, and published a defence of the Italian *Opera Buffa* in Panckoucke's *Mercure de France*, entitled *Dissertation sur les opéras bouffons italiens*. He also began to publish essays in the *Moniteur Universel*.

1790

He published his *Discours sur la liberté des théâtres*, defending artistic freedom and denouncing the political censorship that the *Commune* exerted over theatres. He refused the post of *censeur*.

1791

He was elected member of the *Assemblée législative*, and became a member of the powerful *Comité d'instruction publique* which included, among others, P.C.-M. Talleyrand and G.J. Danton. This was the *comité* that was given the task of reforming public education and that eventually closed the *Collège Mazarin*.

He was commissioned by the *Directoire* to transform the church of *Ste. Geneviève* into the French Pantheon, and was assisted in this task by J.-B. Rondelet in constructional matters, and ironically by the church's architect, J.G. Soufflot, who was named *inspecteur des ornements*. Quatremère suggested a circular plan for the *place* around the Pantheon, worked on disengaging the building from the ruins of the Roman *Thermae*, and closed the fenestration in the drum, in order to admit light only from the dome. He also removed the towers of the former church, as well as Soufflot's Christian sculptures and symbols, rewrote the iconographic programme and selected the sculptors. For the *tympanum*, Quatremère ordered the removal of Coustou's *Triumph of Faith* and its replacement by the *Motherland Crowning the Civic Virtues*, which was to be executed by J.-G. Moitte.

In September, he was elected *député* of the *Département de Paris*, and assumed the task of representing the arts and the rights of artists at the *Assemblée*. As a member of the *Comité d'instruction publique*, he proposed an open *Salon* with an open selection of jury, against the formerly exclusive privileges of *l'Académie Royale de peinture et de sculpture*. Quatremère wanted to reform the *Académie* and its pedagogy, but was opposed to the demands for its elimination. To present his reforms, he published his *Considérations sur les arts du dessin en France suivies d'un plan d'académie, ou d'école publique, et d'un système d'encouragements*, followed by the *Suite aux Considérations sur les arts du dessin, ou réflexions critiques sur le projet de réglemens de la majorité de l'Académie de Peinture et de sculpture*, and ending with the *Seconde suite aux Considérations sur les arts du dessin; ou projet de réglemens pour l'école publique des arts du dessin; et de l'emplacement convenable à l'Institut National des Sciences, Belles-lettres et Arts.* These *considérations* contained a general plan for a full curriculum for a state-directed school of fine arts, much of which came to fruition later. They proposed that the school's faculty be composed not solely of practising artists, but also of theorists, aestheticians, art historians, archaeologists, and men of letters.

Quatremère explored proposals for the *dépot* of the Petits-Augustins, and a project for a monument to J.-J. Rousseau.

He came to the defence of Lafayette. And his subsequent defence of Duport, the former minister of *la marine*, provoked insults followed by an attempt on his person by the Maratistes, an attempt from which he had a narrow escape. His membership of the *Club de la Ste. Chapelle* which was noted for its strong royalist sympathies, was to have ominous consequences.

1792

L'Assemblée Constituante established a museum at the Louvre, and ordered the gathering of nationalized and salvaged works of art at the dépot des Petits-Augustins, under the aegis of Alexandre Lenoir, who had been engaged in this activity since 1790. In 1795, the Musée des monuments français was officially established. (See the notes below, under 1816.)

1793

He published three reports which he delivered to the *Directoire du département de Paris* on the progress of work at the Pantheon.

Marat signed a decree which was directed against state officials who were suspected of royalist sympathies. This decree included the name of Quatremère, who soon went into hiding at Cernay, a small town near Montmorency. His hiding place was known only to Danton. Quatremère's uncle, Marc-Etienne Quatremère (the father of the orientalist, Etienne Quatremère) was executed.

There was a storming of the academic Bastille by the mob in February, followed by the closing of all the academies in August. This period is marked by J.L. David's strong influence in re-organizing France's artistic world.

1794

Quatremère was discovered, arrested, and imprisoned at the Madelonettes. Among the signatories of his arrest warrant was his old friend J.L. David.[3] While incarcerated, Quatremère used the mud in his cell to model a bas-relief to which he gave the title *l' Amour et l'Hymen.* Shortly afterwards, when the fall of Robespierre (during the events of the 9th *thermidor*) and a petition signed by fifty-two artists combined to win his release, he refused to leave prison until his modelling was complete!

1795

On the steps of *St. Roch*, Quatremère incited the populace against the *Convention.* This event was violently interrupted by the *gendarmes* who opened fire into the crowd. Quatremère, however, was able to escape through the back of the church. Later on, the *conseil militaire*, whose headquarters were at the *Théâtre Français*, found him guilty of inciting armed insurrection, condemned him to death, and confiscated his property, including his library. Quatremère initially hid in his own house on the rue Saint-Dominique in Saint-Germain, entering through a concealed door, while the police stood guard outside the front door. Later, he took refuge in his former prison at the Madelonnettes, where he had befriended his jailer!

1796

From the Madelonnettes, Quatremère denounced Bonaparte's spoils of war by writing his *Lettres sur le préjudice qu'occasionneraient aux arts et à la science, le déplacement des monuments de l'art de l'Italie, le démembrement de ses écoles, et la spoliation de ses collections, galeries et musées*, otherwise known as the Letters to General Miranda. In these letters, which were published under the signature "A.Q.," Quatremère spoke of a European "fraternal republic of the arts," where national borders did not exist, but where Italy and especially Rome, that great "integral museum," occupied a capital position. He deplored the fragmentation inflicted on art by the dismemberment of collections, and called for the return of Italian art to Italian soil. He believed that while Italian art had become the universal European paradigm, its masterpieces should nevertheless remain in Italy, as examples of the felicitous effects of Nature and genius.

On *22 thermidor* of that year, he defended himself in his own tribunal and was acquitted. He was later elected *député* at the *Cinq-cents* from the *Département de la Seine*. There, he took part in the reduction of the *Directoire*'s power, in order to pave the way for the return of the monarchy.

His active participation at the famous royalist meeting at Clichy caused him to be sentenced for deportation under the law of *18 fructidor*. However, his friend Talleyrand gave him a timely warning and provided him with funds and a passport, under the name of Quartini, to enable him to flee the country.

1797-1800

He took refuge in the town of Tremsbüttel in the Schleswig-Holstein region of Germany, joining the Comte d'Angiviller and J.E.M. Portalis. It was there that the latter composed much of his *L'esprit philosophique durant le XVIIIème siècle*, including his famous critique of Kantian philosophy. These expatriate Frenchmen formed part of an intimate circle of intellectuals which included F.H. Jacobi and F.L. Stolberg, both of whom were members of the Münster circle of Platonists. In this late-eighteenth-century Tusculum, Quatremère furthered his knowledge of German philosophy, aesthetics and archaeology, and began plans for his archaeological dissertation *Le Jupiter Olympien*, which he published fourteen years later.

1800

As *premier consul*, and as part of his reforms of the French government, Bonaparte signed a law (the 3rd *Nivôse* of the year VIII) allowing those who had been deported without proper legal process to return to France. This law permitted Quatremère's return.

1799-1804

During the *Consulat*, Quatremère tried, in vain, to recover his library. He became a member of the *Conseil général du département de la Seine*, and worked on the embellishment of Paris. Although he had denounced Bonaparte earlier, Quatremère tried but failed to gain his favour by seeing him as the benefactor of Paris.

1804

A very important year in the history of the *Académie des inscriptions et belles-lettres*, for on February 16th, July 20th, and November 23rd, respectively, Quatremère, E.Q. Visconti and A.L. Millin, all came to enrich its ranks.

1805-6

He delivered, at the *Académie*, a series of nine lectures on light in Greek and Roman temples, the *Mémoire sur la manière dont les temples des Grecs et des Romains étaient éclairés*. These lectures were particularly important for the debate about hypethral temples. Answering Emeric-David's *Recherches sur l'art statuaire chez les anciens*, which defended individualistic representation in sculpture, Quatremère published in the *Archives Littéraires* his *Essai sur l'idéal dans les applications pratiques aux œuvres de l'imitation propre aux arts du dessin*, where he argued for ideal representation. He also published in the *Archives Littéraires* the *Réflexions critiques sur les mausolées* .

1806

In association with a group of scholars which included Visconti, Castellan, Dufourny, Huyot, Chaudet, Le Sueur and Raoul-Rochette, Quatremère participated in composing a *Dictionnaire de l'Académie des Beaux-Arts*. This dictionary was published in an incomplete form (letters A to G) between 1858 and 1896.

1807-8

He gave a series of nine lectures on the ideal in sculpture and painting, *L'Emploi du genre idéal*.

1808-9

He took part in the collective work entitled *Descriptions de Paris et de ses édifices...* by writing the section on *Les Palais*.

1810

Knowing the high esteem in which Bonaparte and his entourage held Canova, Quatremère collaborated with the latter, on obtaining a decree which awarded the *Accademia di San Lucca* nearly a million francs for the restoration and excavation of ancient monuments.

He was named honorary foreign member of the academies of Munich and Göttingen.

1812

He proposed a restitution of the two Parthenon fronts, based on the drawings of J. Carrey. Carrey, who was one of the first artists to draw the temple, formed part of the mission of artists and men of letters sent to Greece by Louis XIV, in 1673.

1814

He published, with a dedication to Louis XVIII, *Le Jupiter Olympien ou l'art de la sculpture antique, considéré sous un nouveau point de vue...*, a scholarly and massive archaeological dissertation on material polychromy, (toreutics and chryselephantine sculpture), whose influence quickly extended beyond the borders of France.[4]

1815

He played a role in returning to the allies the art that had been plundered during Bonaparte's military campaigns.

He published the *Considérations morales sur la destination des ouvrages de l'art*. Six years later, H. Thompson's English translation was published in London as *The Destination of Works of Art...*

With the return of the monarchy, Quatremère's honours multiplied. He received the *Légion d'Honneur*, became *Chevalier de St. Michel*, and a member of the *Conseil Royal d'instruction publique*.

An *ordonnance* signed by Louis XVIII appointed him *Intendant des arts et monuments publics*, a post for which he received twenty-five thousand francs.

1816

L. Dufourny, who was unanimously selected to succeed J. Lebreton as *Secrétaire perpétuel de l'Académie des Beaux-Arts*, refused the position, and instead highly recommended his colleague and friend Quatremère de Quincy. Quatremère was to occupy this most influential post for twenty-three years, during which time, he sought to establish an official doctrine in the academy – a project whose realization he had coveted since his *Considérations* of 1791. Quatremère greatly enlarged the role of *secrétaire perpétuel*, which included curricular matters and their *règlements*; public lectures on art and architectural theory; the historical notices on the lives of various artists; the awarding of the *Grand Prix*; control of the *Ecole des Beaux-Arts* and *l'Académie de France à Rome*; and disproportionate power over the membership of various commissions. During these twenty-three years, *l'Académie* held powerful sway over French art, much of it under the direct or indirect influence of Quatremère.

1816 is a significant year for higher education, for V. Cousin, one of France's most important Platonist philosophers of the nineteenth century and a friend of Quatremère, began teaching at the *Ecole Normale*, and later at the *Faculté des Lettres*. The course that was subsequently published in many editions under the title *Du vrai, du beau, du bien*, frequently refers to Quatremère's positions, especially on the artistic ideal.

A. Lenoir's *Musée des monuments Français* (the site of the former *Couvent des Petits-Augustins*) was the subject of bitter debates on art theory and national heritage. These debates were accompanied by a political war between the opponents of the museum – Quatremère and J.B. Deseine – and its enthusiastic supporters – A. Lenoir and E.-David – among others. Quatremère, held a double opposition to the museum. The first, was an ideological opposition of museal institutions as cemeteries where art was dispersed out of its proper context. The second was his inveterate prejudice against Gothic art which this museum housed. Through his considerable political influence, Quatremère obtained two *ordonnances* which effectively closed the museum. The first,

(April 24th) ordered the return to the Church and to private ownership, of the art that had been collected by Lenoir during the Revolution. The second (October 18th) allowed the expropriation of the museum's site and buildings for the use of *l'Ecole des Beaux-Arts*. F. Debret was commissioned to build the school, replacing parts of Lenoir's museum, while preserving the cloister of the old convent.

Quatremère was also a member of the *Comité du Journal des Savants*.

1817

He became a member of the *Conseil honoraire des Musées*.

1818

The contagious enthusiasm aroused by the Elgin marbles, including the commentaries of Visconti, C.R. Cockerell, and especially Canova's descriptions, persuaded Quatremère to undertake his own study. For this purpose, he visited the British Museum, with Cockerell as his guide. It was there that he composed his famous observations in the form of seven letters to Canova. These letters were later published under the title *Lettres écrites de Londres à Rome, et addressées à M. Canova sur les marbres d'Elgin, ou les sculptures du temple de Minerve à Athènes*.

1819

Quatremère appointed J.-N. Huyot, one of his disciples and collaborators on the *Dictionnaire Historique d'Architecture*, to teach architectural history and theory at *l'Ecole*.

He published his *Recueil de dissertations sur différents sujets de l'antiquité*.

1820-1

He was appointed chair of archaeology at the *Bibliothèque Nationale*, and helped write the *règlements* at *l'Académie des Beaux-Arts*.

Another *ordonnance* from Louis XVIII appointed him *Président du collège départemental*, on 4th November.

He gave a lecture entitled *Sur la statue antique de Vénus, découverte dans l'île de Milo en 1820...* at

l'Académie Royale des Beaux-arts. The Venus de Milo had been acquired by the Louvre earlier that same year.

1823

He published a very influential essay on imitation in art the *Essai sur la nature, le but et les moyens de l'imitation dans les beaux-arts*. Also known as *De l'imitation*. This book is a compilation and augmented edition of many articles that he had been publishing in *Les Archives Littéraires* since 1805. [5]

1824

He published the *Collection des lettres de N. Poussin*, and his biography of Raphael *Histoire de la vie et des ouvrages de Raphaël*. An Italian translation of this biography was published five years later by F. Longhena in Milan, the *Istoria della vita e delle opere di Raffaello Sanzio da Urbino....* In 1835, a German translation was published in Leipzig under the title *Geschichte Raphaels und seiner Werke*, followed by W. Hazlitt's English translation, *History of the lives and works of Raffaello by Quatremère de Quincy*. This translation enjoyed such popularity in England that five editions of it were published in the nineteenth century.

1825

He published the *Restitution des deux frontons du temple de Minerve à Athènes*.

1826

K.F. Schinkel visited Quatremère on April 30th. The two men were to meet on two other occasions in May, the most important was at a lecture on Vitruvius's *symmetria* and *eurythmia* which Quatremère delivered at *l'Institut* with Schinkel seated beside him.

Quatremère's social circle included von Humboldt, Percier and Fontaine and Hittorff.

He published the first volume of the *Monuments et ouvrages d'art antiques restitués*.

Students interrupted and protested during Quatremère's eulogy to the memory of the architect Bonnard. This necessitated the intervention of the police to restore order.

1827-8

He published two important essays on aesthetics: *De l'universalité du beau et de la manière de l'entendre*, and *De l'invention et de l'innovation dans les ouvrages des Beaux-Arts*.

1829

Quatremère built a pulpit in *St. Germain-des-Près*, and published the second volume of the *Monuments et ouvrages d'art antiques restitués* .

He opposed much of H. Labrouste's *envoi* of Paestum, even its restrained polychromy, and championed the earlier, less accurate *envoi* of Cl.M. Delagardette. This issue was the subject of a heated debate in correspondence between Quatremère and H. Vernet, who was the *directeur* of *l'Académie de France à Rome*, and had conducted his own measurements at Paestum.

1830 He published a collection of biographical essays on architects, the *Histoire de la vie et des ouvrages des plus célèbres architectes du XIème siècle jusqu'à la fin du XVIIIème*, in two volumes.[6] A German translation was published in 1831, *Ge-schichte der berühmtesten Architekten und ihrer Werke...*

He was wounded during an explosion which occurred at the casting of a statue of King Stanislas, which was destined for Place Stanislas at Nancy, in place of the statue of Louis XV.

1831

The interior minister, Montalivet formed a commission whose mission was to make administrative recommendations regarding the relationship between *l'Académie des Beaux-Arts*, *l'Ecole des Beaux-Arts* and the *Académie de France à Rome*. An event that greatly perturbed the members of *l'Académie* who were fearful for their autonomy and authority. This necessitated the intervention of Quatremère, who, after difficult written exchanges with the interior minister, was able to maintain the organization by which *l'Académie* had controlled *l'Ecole* since 1816.

1832

He published his very influential *Dictionnaire historique d'architecture, comprenant dans son plan les notions historiques, descriptives, archéologiques, biographiques, théoriques, didactiques et pratiques de cet art* in two volumes, the subject of the present translation. In this task, he was seconded by J.-B. Rondelet who wrote articles on technical matters. Two separate translations appeared in Venice in 1835 and Milan in 1838. In 1842 and 1844, respectively, appeared the first and second volume, in Mantua, translated by A. Mainardi, under the title *Dizionario storico di architettura...* In 1877, extracts selected by C. Cervi were published in Novara. In 1985 an annotated edition of the theoretical articles was published in Venice, with introductory essays by G. Teyssot and V. Farinati, and a translation of a biographical essay on Quatremère from R. Schneider's 1910 dissertation, *Quatremère de Quincy et son intervention dans les arts*.

1833

He published the essay *De la marche différente de l'esprit humain dans les sciences naturelles et dans les Beaux-Arts*.

1834

He published a biography of Canova entitled *Canova et ses ouvrages ou mémoires historiques sur la vie et les travaux de ce célèbre artiste*. He also published a collection of his funerary orations for various artists and architects, the *Recueil des notices historiques lues dans les séances publiques de l'Académie Royale des Beaux-Arts à l'Institut*.

1835

He published a biography of Michelangelo, the *Histoire de la vie et des ouvrages de Michelange*.

Amidst much stubborn debate about polychromy, he refused to permit V. Baltard to travel to Greece to conduct restoration studies of ancient monuments, despite the favourable recommendation of J.A.D. Ingres who was then *directeur* of *l'Académie de France à Rome*. Otherwise, Ingres's directorship (1835-40) was marked by a close relationship with *l'Académie* and Quatremère.

Another student protest erupted during one of his lectures.

1836

He published a *Recueil de dissertations archéologiques*, and his letters to Canova and Miranda, *Lettres sur l'enlèvement des ouvrages de l'art antique à Athènes et à Rome, écrites les unes au célèbre Canova, les autres au général Miranda.*

1837

He published the *Essai sur l'idéal dans ses applications pratiques aux œuvres de l'imitation propres des arts du dessin.*

1839

On June 1st, he resigned as *secrétaire perpétuel*. His action aroused deep emotion at the *Académie*, and a committee of friends and former students hastened to visit him to express their gratitude and confer on him the title of *secrétaire perpétuel honoraire*. He continued to attend the *Académie*'s sessions; his last visit was on April 10th, 1840. He was succeeded by his *protégé*, D. Raoul-Rochette.

1842

In a January 14th letter from Naples, King Ferdinand II, named Quatremère correspondent of the *Reale Accademia di belle arti.*

1849

He died in Paris, on December 28th, at the rue de Condé, N° 14.

NOTES

The following sources served to compile this chronology.

Boschot, A. *Le Centenaire d'un esthéticien.* Les usuels de L'Académie des Beaux-Arts, Séance solennelle, tome 110, No. 17, Paris, 1940.

Ecole Nationale Supérieure des Beaux-Arts. *Paris, Rome, Athènes.*, Paris, 1982.

Guigniaut, M. *Notice historique sur la vie et travaux de Quatremère de Quincy.* Mémoires de l'Institut national de France, Académie des inscriptions et belles-lettres, tome 25, première partie. Séance publique, le 5 Aôut 1864. Paris, 1877.

Jouin, H. *A.C. Quatremère de Quincy, deuxième secrétaire perpétuel de l'Académie des Beaux-Arts.* Paris, 1892.

Lapauze, H. *Histoire de l'Académie de France à Rome.* Paris, Plon-Nourrit, 1924.

Le Bihan, A. *Francs-Maçons Parisiens du Grand Orient de France.* Paris, 1966.

Magnin, M. *Funérailles de M. Quatremère de Quincy.* Discours de M. Magnin, Président de l'Académie. Le Dimanche 30 Décembre 1849. Académie des inscriptions et belles lettres.

Middleton, R. ed. *The Beaux-Arts and Nineteenth Century French Architecture.* Thames & Hudson, 1982.

Rochette, D-R. *Discours prononcé aux funérailles de Quatremère de Quincy, le 30 Décembre 1849.* Paris, 1850.

Rowlands, T. *Quatremère de Quincy: The Formative Years, 1785-1795.* Ph.D dissertation, North Western University, 1987.

Schneider, R. *Quatremère de Quincy et son intervention dans les arts.* Paris, Hachette, 1910.

Schneider, R. *L' Esthétique classique chez Quatremère de Quincy.* Hachette, Paris, 1910.

Szambien, W. *Schinkel.* Paris, Hazan, 1989.

Wallon, H. *Centenaire de l'élection de Quatremère de Quincy.* Académie des inscriptions et belles-lettres. Séance publique annuelle. Tome 73, No. 16, Paris, 1903.

Miscellaneous: Papiers d'A.C. Quatremère de Quincy, secrétaire perpétuel de l'Académie... Bibliothèque de l'Institut de France, Manuscrit N° 2555.

Bibliothèque de M. Quatremère de Quincy, Collection d'ouvrages relatifs aux beaux-arts et à l'archéologie; dont la vente aura lieu le Lundi 27 Mai et les jours suivants, à sept heures précises du soir, Rue de Condé, No. 14.

1   In 1992, Silvia Lavin published a study which dealt with the intellectual context of this essay, entitled *Quatremère de Quincy and the Invention of a Modern Language in Architecture.*.

2   In 1977 the article "type" from the *Dictionnaire d'architecture* was translated by Anthony Vidler. This was followed, in 1985, by a translation of various extracts by T. Hinchcliffe.

3   A copy of this warrant still remains in MSS #2555 containing some of his papers at the *Bibliothèque de l'Institut de France.*

4   Three years later, L. Cicognara published extracts from this work in Vicenza: the *Estratto dell'opera intitolata "Il Giove Olympico"...*

5   Among the most noteworthy responses to this work were the three essays published by L. Cicognara in *Antologia, giornale di scienzi e arti di Firenze.* J.C. Kent's English translation of this book was published in 1837 in London as the *Essay on the nature, the end, and the means of imitation in the fine arts.* A facsimile edition was published in 1980 in Brussels, with introductory essays by D. Porphyrios and L. Krier, accompanied by a biographical essay on Quatremère from R. Schneider's 1910 dissertation *Quatremère de Quincy et son intervention dans les arts.*

6   In 1970, a facsimile edition in one volume was published in the United States.

PART II
Selected Translations

Fig. 19. Aux Arts

NOTE TO THE READER

While the dictionary offers the convenience of an alphabetical arrangement of articles, such an arrangement has no relationship with the subjects discussed.

The following groups of entries, could be read together with benefit. [*Trans.*]

I   Principles, Rules, Order, Type, Hut, Art, Idea, Theory, System, Unity, Simplicity, Variety, Uniformity

II   Architecture, Architect, Art, Authority, Antique, Convention, Conventional, Doric, Hut

III   Imitation, Invention, Copy, Antique, Genius, Ingenious.

IV   Character, Propriety, Aptness, Taste, Style, Manner.

V   Type, Character, Style.

VI   Symmetry, Proportion, Accordance, Harmony, Propriety, Aptness, Changing of Proportions, Visual Angle, Correction, Optics.

VII   Building (art of), Construction, Execution, Solidity, Wood, Tree.

VIII   Antique, Ruin, Restoration, Restitution.

IX   Composition, Conception, Combination, Contrast, Distribution, Disposition, Exaggeration, Illusion, Allegory, Imagination, Colour, Perspective.

X   Effect, Elegance, Grandeur, Boldness.

XI   Caprice, Licence, Misuse, Irregular, Bizarre.

XII   Ornament, Decoration, Painting, Sculpture.

XIII   Ordonnance, Diminution, Enlargement of Columns, Doric, Ionic, Corinthian, Tuscan, Composite.

ACCORDANCE Of particular relevance to music, this word applies also metaphorically to the other arts. It pertains to painting on account of the mixing of colours and the effect of light and shadow. Architects use this word either in connection with drawing and shadowing their projects, or on a more essential level still, in relation to the disposition of the plan, the distribution of ornament, the arrangement of parts, and the unity of character and style.

There are two kinds of *accordance* in architecture: the first is one of composition, the other is one of taste and style. The first consists in this wise intelligence which admits nothing that is useless, combines the plan with the elevation, calculates all the proportions and all the dimensions, relates the exterior decoration with interior forms, satisfies the eye by the appearance of solidity, and the mind by the correlation of the parts with the whole. This *accordance* has little influence on the senses at first sight, but the pleasure that it provides is ceaselessly renewed. Indeed, one never beholds edifices where *accordance* is evident without discovering new reasons for the enjoyment experienced; and this enjoyment, which results from satisfied reason, is one of the greatest that architecture can provide. Such is the pleasure that one experiences when beholding the architecture of the Greeks, especially their Doric temples, which are the most beautiful models known of this perfect *accord* that links all the components of architecture, rendering the agreeable necessary, and the necessary agreeable. It is this *accordance* that especially presides over the choice of ornaments, distributing them with economy, and rejecting all these redundant details of a poor ostentatious luxury whose false variety destroys unity, spoils the whole, and ruptures the harmony of edifices.

This *accordance*, one of the first merits of architecture, is rarely found in modern edifices. There is no *accordance* in the plan of an edifice whose interior form follows one manner, and the exterior another. There is no *accordance* in the elevation of a temple that presents several orders on the front, and only one on the inside. There is no *accordance* in the decoration of a palace whose façade is adorned with columns that are often useless, and whose parts and details, through an excess of simplicity, offer a shocking contrast of the greatest opulence and the greatest poverty. This defect in *accordance* is most noticeable in a great number of modern monuments, even the most important ones, where the columns seem to be extraneous to the work, but deliberately placed in order to better portray the nudity of all the rest.

The second *accordance* of which we spoke, and which we called *accordance* of taste and style, derives from the union of both. It demands of the architect a knowledge of practice, and even the exercise of the other arts that contribute to the embellishment of architecture. The result is that individuality of character, that unity of style and manner, which make a monument appear as if it was the work of one man, and leaves it doubtful – because of the cohesion between decoration and construction – if the decorator was the architect, or the architect was the decorator. This value is evident in the most beautiful works of the ancients. And since the arts were then unified, and since almost no art was ever practised to the exclusion of other arts, the architect either executed all the parts of a monument, or entrusted them to an associate; but there was always a single intelligence that presided over the making of the whole work; and since one mind directed the whole, the effect was that of unity, and the impression was not fragmented.

The same does not apply to the moderns, where each art remains isolated from the others in practice. Architecture suffered especially from this isolation. From here derives this disparateness in monuments which are left to the *discordance* between artists who do not work in concert with each other, and often without knowing each other. (*See* HARMONY)

ALLEGORY This word may seem foreign to the art of architecture properly speaking, for even though the monuments of all ages and countries are laden with emblems and allegorical figures, these, in turn, belong to sculpture and ornament and take part in architecture only as accessories that are as independent of her as she is extraneous to them. However, this kind of language that belongs particularly to these arts that directly imitate nature, these arts that find all the shades of thought within the variety of signs, was sometimes adopted by the architecture of the ancients. Only, since the ideas prone to being expressed by architecture are as few as the figures or the signs that may form her language, then the examples that one can cite are not common.

A true *allegory* in architecture was the Temple of Virtue and Honour, built in Rome by Marcellus, whose particular disposition comprised an allegorical meaning as well as a moral lesson. He wanted this temple to house the riches that he had brought from Sicily, but the high priest, whose approval he had sought in advance, forbade him to carry out this enterprise under the pretext that a single temple could not enclose two divinities. Therefore, Marcellus built two temples, the one next to the other, in such a manner that one had to pass through the Temple of Virtue to arrive to that of Honour, thus conveying the idea that it is by treading the path of virtue that one can accede to honour. This temple stood at the Capena Gate.

Other temples, also, owed their form to an allegorical motif, such as the Temple of Vesta built by Romulus, as well as the one at Mantinea, which seemed to owe the figure of their plan to the form of the hearth. A circular temple in Thrace, dedicated to the sun, symbolically designated the disc of this luminary. One finds a symbolic meaning in other edifices of antiquity, such as the portico at Olympia, which was dedicated to the seven liberal arts, and where (according to Plutarch) poets who recited their verses, heard them repeated up to seven times by the echo. One could also rank approximately in the same class, a temple to Mercury, as seen in a medallion from the reign of Aurelian, which, instead of being supported by columns, was actually carried by *Hermes* [1] figures or *Terms*,[2] as they are still called today. The pediment of this temple displays representations of a dog, a rooster and a tongue, which are figures whose meanings are known.

Such are the examples of the kind of *allegory* to which architecture lends itself. The monuments of Egypt, where construction was directed by the priests, may have presented similar symbols with allusions intelligible to all. Their meaning disappeared with the knowledge of figurative writing. This great manner of writing thoughts, and of using these great characters that forever fix these thoughts may very well be the genius of Egypt.

Following these examples, some systematic minds imagined that they could reduce all of architecture to *allegory*, and clothe all her forms with an emblematic veil. According to them, architecture as well as the other arts, having issued from religious cults, partook in these mysterious emblems which they believe had been invented only to hide or conserve the precious trust of all kinds of truths. They no longer see in the pediment the representation of a roof or the roof itself, but through the fortuitous relationship between a form based on necessity and a geometric figure, the roof, in their eyes, is but a mysterious triangle, an emblem of divinity. Columns are no longer the supports created by necessity in order to carry roofs and architraves, they owed their origin to votive stones, to *Hermes* figures and symbols, or the first types of statues of deities. Column pedestals are transformed into altars; and for having been decorated with allegorical accessories, friezes, entablatures, modillions, cornices and capitals themselves, become *allegories*.

Thus, by an absurd transposition of the most simple ideas, and for the lack of distinction between accidental forms, architecture may find herself totally decomposed, and may end up becoming the result of that of which she is the principle. These strange systems, which do not deserve opposition, stem from lack of knowledge and false ideas about *allegory*, of which one must distinguish two kinds. The first is the outcome of early societies and their figurative means of speaking and writing, and have nothing of the mysticism imagined by many people. It is the subsequent loss of their intelligibility and meaning that caused all the mystery. The other kind comes from humanity's taste for fiction, and differs from the first in that while it is the least intelligible, it is nevertheless the more true, for it is the most lively and simple expression of objects, affections and sensations. This second kind, whose key is more readily available to us because it is more modern, is born within cities and the most civilized societies; consequently, *allegory* could have never given birth to architecture. Since the latter is an art of primary necessity, it is well established that the idea of shelter must have preceded all the ideas of symbol and mystery. Later, there were some more or less fortunate applications to the details and ornaments of architecture; first in hieroglyphic writing, and then its continuation and perfection in sculpture.

Thus, it is to sculpture and painting that *allegory* particularly belongs. The architect, however, cannot study enough and penetrate its spirit and its reasons within the ornaments of antiquity, in order to avoid these banal applications, these misplaced, cold and insignificant allusions, that make the decorations of buildings an enigma for ordinary people, and a childish game for those who understand their meaning.

ANTIQUE The grammatical meaning of this word needs no explanation. As a synonym of *ancient* and *old*, it expresses something more *elevated* than the first of these words, and more *noble* than the second.

But the word *antique* in the language of the arts, and especially the arts of design, comprises in many cases the idea of a superlative qualification that ordinarily makes it a word of praise.

It must also be noted, that in their habitual parlance, artists never apply the word *antique*, especially as a laudatory epithet, save to the works of certain ancient nations, or certain centuries, or certain epochs of these nations. Thus, although one recognizes considerable remains – dating from distant times – regarding the monuments or the ruins of edifices in India, Persia or even Egypt for example, the artist, in speaking of them or in citing some separated fragments, will not give them the appellation *antique* alone, taken in its emphatic sense. The same applies, with greater reason, to the fragments of sculpture and other arts that time preserved in the middle of many cities which ceased to exist a long time ago.

In short, we affirm that in the usual language of the arts of design, the word *antique* is used only to praise and to designate the works of those nations and centuries that distinguished themselves by the superiority of genius, talent and judgment in imitation. Furthermore, regarding even the works of these nations, one is to exclude from their reigns the latter days that witnessed the deterioration and the degeneration of the principles and the products of imitation. Thus, the artist, speaking as an artist, will not use the word *antique* to designate the late works of the latter days of the Lower Empire nor those of the Middle Ages.

Consequently, with respect to the study of the arts of design and the imitation of works taken or given as models, the artist will not ordinarily consider as *antique* other products than those of the genius of the Greeks, and the monuments whose style, principles and taste – having been perfected among them – subsequently spread to the Romans, and then, through their conquests, were propagated throughout the different nations of Europe where they prospered until their decadence.

Thus we observe that in matters of art, and in the mouths of artists, the word *antique* has become synonymous, as it were, with *beautiful*, *excellent*, *perfect*.

It is not without importance here, to justify this agreement on the part of modern centuries and peoples, and this almost unanimous accord in recognizing the preeminence of *antique* works in the imitative arts. I said: *almost unanimous*, because in various periods, there has been some uprising against the idea of the superiority of the arts of antiquity, because of the pride of some individuals, and the vanity of some eras. Some found this superiority insulting, others found in it a contradiction to the pretension of an indefinite perfectibility in the sciences of observation as well as the arts of imagination.

THEORETICAL CONSIDERATIONS
ON THE RELATIVE PERFECTIBILITY IN THE
SCIENCES AND THE FINE ARTS

Without entering here into a speculative theory about the nature of the faculties of the human spirit, whose true philosophy shows us at once their extent and limits, we can advance, that the error regarding the object of the present discussion, stems from the ambiguity in which one falls when one presumes to apply to the works of genius and invention in the fine arts the same observations that one sees in the research and works which are proper to the natural sciences.

The seemingly indefinite progress which one observes in these sciences is a necessary effect, so to speak, of their nature. Indeed, regarding the study and knowledge of the material world, everything can be more or less progressive, because it is readily in the nature of one discovery to be the effect of a preceding discovery, and to become the cause of the following one. The word *discovery* is one that designates man's conquests over the secrets of nature, thus correctly expressing the idea. Man effectively succeeds in slowly lifting her veil and, with experience, he forces the discovery of what she has hitherto hidden. Well, one must say, this effect is more the product of time than that of one individual in particular. Where is this progression headed? This point matters little for the present discussion. We are only reflecting here on the nature of the object of the physical sciences, on the kinds of means that man uses in this kind of research, and on the paths that lead him to discovery. Well, these means are time and experience; these paths are the knowledge of all that has been discovered before. But it is evident that the means and the paths of which we speak are not necessarily lost with the one who used them. Others who follow him, heirs to his efforts or his successes, will not only enjoy this heritage but will be able to expand it. Thus, once a path is opened in areas hitherto untravelled, it invites its pursuit; and what has been done facilitates the means to go further. Such is the image of discoveries, where in every kind of positiv[ist] science, generations transmit the result of these works to the following ones, as well as the ambition to further enrich their heirs.

We have compared the succession of discoveries in the domain of science, to the progressive endeavours on a road that can always be prolonged. We shall see that the pace of invention

within the realm of genius and within the non-material world is of a different nature.

But first, let us note that the results of this work are no longer called *discovery*, but rather *invention*. Well, there is a notable difference between the ideas that these two words express. One *discovers* what is hidden, what one knows to be hidden, and what one searches for. What is *invented* is of the nature of things *encountered*, but often without knowing *where*; and often, the more one searches, the less one finds. Hence the word *invention, invenire*; that is to say *encounter*, rather than *find*; and such is the difference, not only in language but also in fact, between the procedures and the results of scientific endeavours in the domain of reality, and those of the fine arts, within the realm of the ideal world, which is that of sentiment and imagination.

Such is indeed the world of the arts, and such is the nature of their model. No matter the rules that theory strives to establish, or the types and principles of imitation to which an artist's work is referred, it is evident that nothing in theories and their principles, or in models and their rules, could ultimately rest, as in the sciences, on material facts which are incontestable by the physical senses. These arts must always remain dependent on the organ of intelligence and of moral sentiment. Well, it is known that the insights into moral vision and its intellectual results sustain enough variety, depending on the individual, for them to never be contested; in fact they would be contested even further if a large number of individuals, in a certain time and by virtue of a certain education, were to be inclined to prefer material knowledge; in other words, when the physical sense holds sway over the moral[3] sense.

It is therefore indubitable that there should be no succession of facts or truths from one generation to the next in the domain of works of genius, nor as a consequence, a progression of experimental knowledge by virtue of which the last to come, being the heir of the knowledge of his predecessors, will further expand the facility to acquire new knowledge for his successors.

Some may say, perhaps, that in the domain of invention there are arts which are subject to the conditions of the non-material world where their models and their imitative means reside; that what is said of poetry or music, for example, whose models and means are more or less outside the material region of the senses, cannot be said of the arts of design whose types and objects of imitation are found in the region of the shapes or organisms of material nature. Without entering into a long discussion about this issue, we shall merely answer that if some arts have material objects as the subjects of their tangible imitation, it is much less the representation of what is material in these objects that makes them arts of genius, than the ideas, the moral impressions, the abstract qualities of their model, the expression of the sensations that they produce, the undefinable charm of the beauty and harmony whose secret they steal from nature. It is in such a manner that architecture – which seems to be made solely of inert matter, and to represent but the utilization of material means – is, of all the arts of design, perhaps the one that owes the most its merit to non-material causes.

The same applies to the arts of design as well as the other arts. That is to say, that their culture or their progress, being much less dependent than it is thought on the physical senses and on matter, depend little on the succession of time and the experience of preceding works. No, there are no real inheritors here, nor any natural heirs to the riches of the past. Progress, or what one may call the steps made by predecessors, leaves no traces, no terms that successors could use as a starting point.

If we have compared the sequential progress of the sciences in their research of the material world to a road carved in the earth by the efforts of those who came first, we could compare the way genius operates in the imitation of the non-material world, to a bird's flight on an aerial path that leaves no trace to indicate its direction.

We shall finally add that the elevated degree achieved by genius in the arts of invention, not only gives to others no means of attaining it, but often places obstacles by sometimes multiplying these servile copyists who aim only to repeat, and other times, these bizarre minds who only endeavour to do things differently rather than accomplish more or better.

We thought it best to place this short theory only in an article whose goal is to establish the superiority, in matters of art, of the genius of the *antique* and its productions; knowing that it will excite the condemnation of those who, confounding the principles of things, by seeing or by wishing to see the superiority of the moderns in the sciences, will necessarily conclude an equal superiority in the arts; that is to say, assume an equal evolution to two faculties whose motives are very different, if not opposed.

If the few considerations that we barely covered could suffice to prove the error of this pretension, it must be acknowledged that the Greeks were perhaps so advanced in the career of genius, precisely because the taste for the sciences – the result of a generalized observation and of a long experience – did not acquire among them the ascendancy that it received among modern nations.

It remains to demonstrate that the facts are entirely in accordance with the preceding theory. It remains to show and prove, if the agreement of all ages and of all nations will not provide sufficient proof to this effect, that there is not one of the fine arts in which Greece did not produce artists and works that the suffrage of all centuries and all countries never ceased to consider as occupying the first places.

Let it be explained then, how it happened that in astronomy, physics, geography, chemistry, natural history, etc., the Greeks will yield to the least of our students in these fields; and how come that in every kind of lyric, epic, and dramatic poetry, in all divisions of the art of writing, rhetoric, history, and in the vast and varied sphere of the arts of design, their works still remain the teachers of the moderns today? How is it that the fragments of their statues, the remnants of their edifices, have remained and continued to be for all the nations of Europe, the models that one despairs of even equalling, and which have acquired the authority of nature in the eyes of their imitators? How is it, finally, that in all its meanings, and in evaluating our artists' works, the word *antique* has come to express the highest order of praise.

We leave it to each individual to answer these questions. Now, having established in this short theory, that what happened must have happened as a result of the nature of things, we shall further try to indicate, in few words, what were the secondary and particular reasons that converged in Greece and among the Ancients, allowing them to carry the arts of design to so high a perfection.

HISTORICAL CONSIDERATIONS
ON THE CAUSES OF THE PERFECTION
OF WHAT IS KNOWN AS THE ANTIQUE OR
THE ARTS OF GREECE

Having developed the effect of the most general cause which seemed to us to assure for the *antique* or for the arts of Greece the privilege that they enjoyed for centuries, we shall briefly consider, following certain historical notions, the principal causes that must have influenced the perfection of all the arts of design.

One such cause seems to us to be the advantage that this people had in not owing to any other people either real examples or material lessons, and in having been what one must call *original*, in the fullest meaning of this word. We shall not consider here the kind of resemblance that can be found between the primitive trials of these arts, and those of some nations like Egypt that always remained in the trial stage. Nothing is more insignificant than the research conducted on the first adumbrations of Greek art, except the system of borrowing that is based on finding certain similitudes. Indeed, all beginnings necessarily resemble each other everywhere without there being communication; like children everywhere, who do the same things without copying each other.

In fact, the history of Greece teaches us that this country passed through many centuries when all endeavours seemed to have been the long apprenticeship towards what it achieved when it attained maturity. Yes, these arts took a very long time before they soared; and as it cannot be ascertained from whom they received their lessons, it is evident that they owed their success to their own advancement. These arts were *autochthonous*; as the Greeks thought of themselves as a people. From here derived the true principle of their original quality, the natural and slow progression that accompanied their development, the depth of roots that the art of imitation threw out, and the long duration of a style which, even when it suffered the general law of decline, never entirely lost that character of grandeur and simplicity which is still evident even in its latter productions. The Greeks then, owed the perfection of their arts to the necessity of being original.

Another cause for the superiority of the *antique* or the art in Greece, is found in the facility exhibited by artists in the study of nature, the laws that organize the human body, and the principles

Fig. 20. Tower of the Winds. Athens.
From: Stuart and Revett's *Antiquities of Athens*,
Reprint, B. Bloom, New York, 1968

of the beauty of form. Climate made nudity acceptable to custom, but it was more especially encouraged through the exercise of the body; hence these gymnasia, these stadia that offered public spectacles, where force, agility, beauty, propriety in proportions, were for the artist the subject of daily study. The spectators also learned to appreciate the models as well as the imitations of artists. Thus, the study of nature within the human body, far from being relegated to the few, and instead of being restricted within the enclosure of a school, or limited to the partial imitation of one individual, necessarily became a universal study, a sort of public teaching that best suited the knowledge and taste for corporeal beauty, beautiful forms, and the best proportions.

This is what made – and still makes today – Greek works that imitate the human body truly fit to replace nature herself in many ways, as examples to all those nations whose climates or customs prevent the generalization of this teaching upon which depends not only the imitation of nature, following an incomplete definition of art, but the most beautiful imitation of the most beautiful nature.

We cannot be exempt from considering – albeit briefly, and especially on account of manifold writings on the subject – the power exerted by religion on the perfecting of the arts of Greece. It is evident that the Greeks, having materialized all their gods in their imagination, soon had to represent them not only in bodily form, but they also tended to ally these material representations with the notion of an ideal perfection which is a necessary attribute of superhuman beings. Well, quite naturally, there must have been here, a reciprocity of action. The moral idea of divinity demanded of the physical image the greatest beauty; and it so happened, that the material perfection of the god-statue portrayed a higher idea of its superhuman existence. Without a doubt also, the diverse means that art possesses to modify physical qualities, must have contributed to the manners of envisaging the same deity. From here derived the incredible variety of idols and the infinite number of different characters, the diversity of age, nature, allegories, and emblems to which the artist was compelled to apply all the resources of his talent, in order to satisfy all the fantastical creations of the imagination of nations.

How, and through what processes did the Greeks arrive at establishing the rules on which these conceptions of genius were based? This is the subject of a theory that has no place here. Suffice it for us, in this article, to ascertain the facts that prove and explain the superiority of their arts. Well, one of these facts, which is substantiated by their most ancient monuments, is once again this facility that they had early on to fix the rules of proportion whose effects were not to restrict genius within servile calculations, but rather to prevent the deviations where too much independence necessarily leads – either short of rules or beyond them – one whose only guide is routine or the accident of an isolated feeling.

APPLICATIONS
OF THE PRECEDING CONSIDERATIONS TO ANTIQUE ARCHITECTURE

We have tried to show that *antique* art, which is the original production of the genius of the Greeks, was the result of causes that have not been reproduced elsewhere since ancient times within the arts that aim at corporeal imitation. We must now explain the common link through which architecture unified and assimilated herself to these arts, thus producing a system whose very excellence served its propagation among all nations.

In many an article (*See* ARCHITECTURE, WOOD, HUT) we developed the original principle of this art's construction as a source of its imitative system. Here, we shall merely indicate the common link between Greek architecture and the arts whose intended purpose is the imitation of the human body; the sort of analogy that is lacking in all other architectures.

It is easy to conceive how, in Greece, the arts that imitate the bodies and the forms of nature, having attained the greatest truth in imitation through the study and observation of the laws of proportion, must have accustomed the eyes and minds of beholders to a harmony of lines, forms, and contours, whose inobservance in other subjects would have naturally revolted the senses. Thus, such a degree of comparison – found everywhere, and visible to all – could not but compel all sorts of works to be commensurate with it.

Linked and associated in many ways to the art of sculpture in a great number of works, and owing to her original principle a preventive measure against the arbitrariness of an ignorant instinct, architecture awaited still the regulative and more fixed laws of proportion. She found these laws in the arts that imitate forms and corporeal beauty, where she learned the causes of the varying impressions that affect our senses and our minds.

As soon as the architect perceived and comprehended the law that nature adopted in her own works, an invincible propensity must have led him to apply the spirit of these laws to the combination of lines, forms, masses, and dimensions that compose the building. The art of architecture became – not directly or materially – an imitator of nature only in an intellectual sense, by appropriating the system, the principles, the rules of proportion, and the pleasure that results from observing them in the organization of the human body. Architecture imitated nature not in the representation of her works, but in the assimilation of their qualities. Architecture imitated nature not by doing what she does, but as she does.

Thus, *antique* architecture owes her superiority to her system of proportion that she preserved over and above any other architecture. And the study and the imitation of the *antique* in architecture are considered and must be considered with good reason, as a sort of equivalent – relative to this art – to the study and imitation of physical nature with respect to the other arts of design.

Nature – those whose limited vision perceives naught but the material side of things will say – created no houses, no edifices or columns; thus architecture has no model in nature. Doubtless, we shall reply, nature, understood in a physical and material sense, did not make edifices and columns. But nature made the laws of solidity, equilibrium, and balance; nature established the laws of ratio, symmetry, proportions, and number; nature gave us organs and faculties which, through their agreeable or painful impressions, teach us what is or is not in accord with her wishes and her laws. Now, the effects of these impressions, are the means through which nature replaces, in architecture, the material model available to the other arts.

Similarly, nature gave no model to music; if by this word is meant written harmonic themes or chanting scores. But within the faculty of hearing, within the propriety of sound ratios and their combinations, which either please or delight us, or annoy our instinct and our taste, nature wrote the laws of harmony or melody. There, the musician finds as tangible a model as the one that governs the anatomical relations and forms of the human body used by the painter and the sculptor.

But then, is there nothing but the physical, the corporeal, and the material in the very works of nature? Is the positive model for the painter or the sculptor nothing but matter, because it is demonstrable to the exterior senses? If this beauty, if this harmony that reveals itself to us, only addressed the physical senses, would there be any discussion, any dissent or diversity of opinion among people? If there was only the physical or the material in the imitation of the human body, then would one not infallibly arrive at perfection, such as the perfection that depends on the ruler and the compass? Yet, how come so few artists are able to reproduce the perfection and the beauty of their supposed positive model? It is because, in truth, all that makes the perfection of the model and of its imitation belongs to the moral realm, the world of sentiment and intelligence.

The same obtains in architecture. Although architecture owes her condition or her visible exterior constitution to some analogies with tangible and material types, her true model for the mind, will always be one that rests on reasons of a superior order, such as the laws of nature applied to the system of proportions and the harmony of forms in relation to our intelligence and our affections. Now, the study of works that have unified and best manifested the relation between these laws of nature with those of our senses and our intelligence, has always been – and will never cease to be – the study of the monuments of *antique* or Greek architecture.

ON THE CHOICE AND THE CRITIQUE
TO BE MADE IN THE STUDY OF WORKS OF ANTIQUE ARCHITECTURE

The study of *antique* monuments demands more discernment and critique than one ordinarily thinks. We shall reduce our recommendations in this regard to two technical or scholastic observations. The first concerns the choice of *antique* works to be taken for models; the second relates to the spirit that must direct their imitation.

Regarding the first point, there are two distinctions to be made: the one is about time, the other is about place. That is to say, one must well discern in the works of the same architecture, the eras that saw their birth, and the peoples or countries that produced them.

The *antique*, or what is known as such in the language of the arts of design, occupied the duration of fifteen hundred years. But the arts also have their eras of growth and decline. It is therefore important to know and fix the history of art by the history of nations, and to distinguish the period of their maturity. Of special importance is to learn to differentiate the characters through which one can recognize either the weakness of their youth, or the decrepitude of their latter days.

Fig. 21. Temple of Vespasian, Roman Forum.
From: Josef Durm, *Die Baukunst der Etrusker und Römer*,
A. Kröner Verlag, Stuttgart, 1905

Indeed, one must consider as useful, the study of monuments that bear the imprint of these first steps where a naïve instinct was the precursor of a bolder sentiment; or that experience which later begat masterpieces. It is no less necessary to guard against the false authorities from the monuments of the centuries of decadence, that some mistook for examples, thereby confusing them with those of the birth of architecture.

One cannot count the errors and prejudices that infiltrated architecture through the effect of this confusion, and how much ignorance or bad faith contributed to accrediting this indiscriminate mixture of works belonging to different eras. Some – the deceived – admitted everything without discernment; others – the deceivers – profited from the confusion in order to justify their capricious inventions.

It is therefore from the monuments of the golden age of Greece that one must demand at once the lessons and the examples of good style and good taste, and the precious traditions of this analogical imitation of nature which, in this respect, made architecture the rival of the other arts. The remains of antiquity, where these lessons and this teaching are written, pertain particularly to the ages of Pericles and Alexander. Subsequent to the monuments of this era, one could indicate the monuments of Greek art that were transplanted in Rome during the time of Augustus, Nero, Trajan, and Hadrian, who employed only Greek architects and artist, who, in turn, were very recommendable continuators of the manner of their predecessors.

If in the succeeding centuries and reigns, architecture, more than the other arts, preserved itself from the preceding traditions and errors, then it is advisable to proceed with caution regarding the trust that is accorded them. It is well known that the era of total decadence can be dated to the reign of Constantine. It is also in the monuments of this age that began the practice of constructions built from the remains and fragments of monuments that were either destroyed or have become useless. Additionally, one observes in these dismembered compositions, some fair details commingled with coarse copies and the most revolting incoherences.

Yet, in some remains of the magnificence of these centuries, as in Rome in the Thermae of Diocletian, or outside Italy, in Spalato in Dalmatia, and Palmyra and Baalbeck in Caleo-Syria, the architect still finds material for instruction, but more in the grandeur of the plans and the richness of the ordonnances than in the purity of style, the correctness of forms, or the refinement of ornaments. The architect shall be content to admire this character of grandeur and nobility that left its mark even in the late enterprises of *antique* art.

The second observation we have announced with respect to the imitation of the *antique* in architecture, aims to explain the spirit that should guide the imitator.

There are two manners of imitating the *antique*. The first, improperly called imitation (*See* this word), consists in reproducing only the appearance through copies. The second consists, on the part of the imitator, in appropriating the principles of the *antique* and consequently its genius or its causes, along with their consequences.

The first manner is naught but a routine aping, which is likely to discredit its own model in the eyes of those who lack discrimination in this respect. Nothing is easier than this so-called imitation. In fact, the architect here, finds a given number of forms, parts, or members – akin to what in rhetoric is known as the parts of the discourse – that are the necessary elements for implementation, only whose value derives from the reason that determines their place, and the genius that employs them toward the proposed goal.

But, particularly in architecture, nothing is easier than this transfer of all the parts of an ordonnance or a composition to another, the ornamental details of an edifice to the project for another, especially if the work of the architect is limited, as often happens, to drawing alone. Nothing then approaches the extravagance of riches that these cold plagiarists amass, able as they are to reproduce, in project form, all the temples of times past, but perhaps inept at making a simple house.

If these so-called imitators were asked to execute a building that has no corresponding antecedent among the ancients, and where they are not to adapt the banal luxury of columns or peristyles, then the poverty of their genius will be discovered, as will their inability to characterize the propriety of each edifice through a choice of forms that befits its use, and through a judicious application of significant ornaments.

The true manner of imitating the *antique* consists, then, in a wise penetration of the spirit and the reasons behind its works; in an understanding of the motives that once caused the artist to employ certain means of execution; and in discovering the veritable causes of the impressions that we receive from such and such a combination of correlations, dimensions, or decorations. The necessary and the useful form the first requirement of works of architecture. From the useful must derive the agreeable, and from their intimate union results the favourable impression received by us. Utility, or need, was the basis and the principal generator – as we shall see elsewhere – of the Greek or the splendid *antique* architecture. It is in following the precious thread –in the study of monuments – that once guided the inventors of this art, that the moderns could learn to be the continuators of the Greeks.

New needs or different uses will oppose on many a point a conforming reproduction of a great number of ancient edifices within modern works. But the imitation is not the copy. Consequently, the difference in customs and in practice in the new compositions of the art of building, could only pose a difficulty for one who has not learned to read the great book of antiquity, or one who understands only material evidence. However, one who is schooled, not in the letter, but rather in the spirit of these teachings, knows that imitating the *antique* is not repeating what the ancients built, but rather as the ancients themselves would have built, were they to answer to the same exigencies of other needs and new conditions, as they themselves did.

This is what actually happened when the art of the Greeks was transposed to Rome. There, artists remained constantly faithful to the types and to the principles observed by their predecessors. They were free under the weight of their rules to transpose in greater dimensions, and adopt to more extensive and varied needs, the same harmonies, the same effects, without stepping outside the original conditions of their art.

The error of modern times in architecture and especially with respect to the *antique,* has very often been to confuse the idea of imitation with that of the copy. This confusion stems from the lack of distinction between what pertains to the essence of the constitution of an art, and what pertains to the infinite variety with which to employ its means.

Regarding the essence of architecture, there is an order of things that rests on the elements of nature and could not change without destroying this art; and there is an order of these elements which is always variable in their use according to the artist's will. The same applies to all the arts, and even to poetry which offers an inexhaustible resource of variety without its means ever having to change. Thus, for the poet and the orator, the forms of discourse, the metaphors, the tropes, the images, the rapprochement or the opposition of ideas, are and have always been the necessary materials of an imitation that everyone's judgment, with a varying degree of propriety, can apply, with varying degrees of success, without ceasing to be original.

For the architect, the types, the forms of order, the relation between proportions and the visual faculties, are the necessary elements of his imitation. Genius does not consist in finding other elements. It consists in the propitious application of their varieties to the purpose of each monument, to the impressions that it must produce, and to the ideas and sentiments of which genius is at once the motive and the interpreter.

Thus, in the sixteenth century, *antique* art was renewed by skilful architects who never ceased being original by imitating the works of the Greeks, nor being their faithful imitators while conforming themselves to the constraints of other needs and of new institutions.

APTNESS This is the term that better explains the meaning of what Vitruvius called *decor*. *Aptness*, according to the Roman writer, was one of the constitutive qualities of architecture. "Aptness (propriety) is that perfection of style which comes when a work is authoritatively constructed on approved principles. It arises from prescription (Greek, *thematismos*), from usage, or from nature. From prescription, in the case of hypaethral edifices, open to the sky, in honour of Jupiter Lightning, the Heaven, the Sun, or the Moon; for these are gods whose semblances and manifestations we behold before our very eyes in the sky when it is cloudless and clear. The temples of Minerva, Mars, and Hercules, will be Doric, since the virile strength of these gods, makes daintiness entirely inappropriate to their houses. In temples to Venus, Flora, Proserpine, Spring-Water, and the Nymphs, the Corinthian order will be found to have peculiar significance,

because these are charming divinities and so its rather slender outlines, its flowers, leaves, and ornamental volutes will lend aptness (propriety) where it is due. The construction of temples of the Ionic order to Juno, Diana, Father Bacchus, and other such gods will be in keeping with the middle position which they hold; for the building will be a befitting combination of the severity of the Doric and the delicacy of the Corinthian.

Aptness (propriety) arises from usage when buildings with magnificent interiors as in the case of all sacred precincts are provided with elegant entrance-courts that correspond; for there will be no aptness (propriety) in the spectacle of an elegant interior approached by a low, mean entrance. Or, if dentils are carved in the cornice of the Doric entablature, or triglyphs represented in the Ionic entablature over the cushion-shaped capitals of the columns, the effect will be spoilt by the transfer of the peculiarities of the one order of the building to the other, the usage in each class having been fixed long ago."[4]

Vitruvius here, indicates three kinds of *aptness*: the first is an *aptness* that refers to the very nature of edifices, and to the qualities of the beings or persons for whom they are built. Elsewhere, he tells us also that *aptness* requires the richness of the habitation to be proportionate to the owners's social positions. Hence, it is apparent that this *aptness*, which in temples consecrates an order proper to the rank and nature of each deity and in domestic buildings proportions the degree of opulence to the owner's social standing, falls under what we call a proper character to each building, relative to its purpose and its essence. (*See* CHARACTER).

The second kind of *aptness* concerns the balance between an edifice and its constitutive parts; in this sense, *aptness* means accordance and harmony.

The third kind of *aptness* is that of usage or custom. It pertains to objects that a long practice has consecrated, and whose forms or disposition should not be permitted to change, because these disarrangements, which offer no advantage to art, would unnecessarily present a new order of things whose strangeness could only prove injurious to sight. (*See* PROPRIETY).

ARCHITECT This word is composed of the two Greek words: *archos* and *tecton*, signifying chief of builders. This is actually, in the material sense of the word, the definition of one who presides over the erection of a building. Architecture, also considered in a material sense, can be defined as the art of building. But this art ranks among the liberal arts only in so far as its practice is based on principles drawn from nature, and according to rules that become the expression of the need and pleasure that our eyes and minds demand of the *architect*.

Still, the etymology of this word clearly implies that the artist who received this appellation in Greece was in fact the supreme organizer of all the work involved in the formation of edifices. Now, this superior function presupposes a rare union of qualities and a very wide range of knowledge on the part of its executor.

Indeed, the extensive knowledge that Vitruvius demands of his *architect*, gives a high idea of the merits and talents that the ancients recognized either in the art itself or in those who practise it.

"In all matters, but particularly in architecture," says the Roman *architect*, whose theory we abbreviate considerably here,[5] "there are these two points: the thing signified, and that which gives it significance. That which is signified is the subject of which we may be speaking; and that which gives it significance is a demonstration on scientific principles. ...knowledge is the child of practice and theory. Practice is the continuous and regular exercise of employment where manual work is done with any necessary material according to the design of the drawing. Theory, on the other hand, is the ability to demonstrate and explain the productions of dexterity on the principles of proportion.

It follows, therefore, that architects who have aimed at acquiring manual skill without scholarship have never been able to reach a position of authority to correspond to their pains, while those who relied only upon theories and scholarship were obviously chasing the shadow, not the substance. But those who have a thorough knowledge of both, like men armed at all points, have the sooner attained their object and carried authority with them.

...He [the architect] ought, therefore to be both naturally gifted and amenable to instruction. Neither natural ability without instruction nor instruction without natural ability can make the perfect artist. Let him be educated, skilful with the pencil, instructed in geometry, know much history, have followed the philosophers with attention, understand music, have some knowledge of medicine, know the opinions of the jurists, and be acquainted with astronomy and the theory of the heavens."

Pytheos, one of the most celebrated *architects* of antiquity, who distinguished himself by building the Temple of Minerva in Priene, demanded of the *architect* in his treatise an even deeper knowledge of each science in particular than is required of those who practise these sciences; but being more judicious, Vitruvius demanded only a fair knowledge of these matters. He said, that it was neither possible nor necessary for the *architect* to become as good a grammarian as Aristarchus or as great a musician as Aristoxenes, or as excellent a painter as Apelles, as skilled a sculptor as Myron and Polyclitus, nor as knowledgeable a physician as Hippocrates. It is sufficient, he adds, that the *architect* not be ignorant of grammar, music, sculpture, medicine, since one mind is not capable of attaining perfection in so many excellent fields.

With these particular or general studies, Vitruvius wants the *architect* to combine bountiful work with a perfect disinterestedness. "There may be some people...who...think that the wise are those who have plenty of money. Hence it is that very many, in pursuit of that end, take upon themselves impudent assurance, and attain notoriety and wealth at the same time.

But for my part, ...I have been taught by my instructors that it is the proper thing to undertake a charge only after being asked, and not to ask for it; since a gentleman will blush with shame at petitioning for a thing that arouses suspicion. It is in fact those who grant favours that are courted, not those who receive them. What are we to think must be the suspicions of a man who is asked to allow his private means to be expended in order to please a petitioner? Must he not believe that the thing is to be done for the profit and advantage of that individual?

Hence it was that the ancients used to entrust their work in the first place to architects of good family, and next inquired whether they had been properly educated, believing that one ought to trust in the honour of a gentleman rather than in the assurance of impudence. And *architects* themselves would teach none but their own sons or kinsmen, and trained them to be good men, who could be trusted without hesitation in matters of such importance."[6]

Considering the wide range of knowledge that entered in the education of the *architect* among the ancients, one is not surprised to learn that Plato advanced that a good *architect* was a rarity in Greece. But today there is another opinion on this subject. If in fact one wishes to compare the studies that were once demanded of the *architect*, with the contemporary manner of teaching and learning architecture, one would conclude that either this art has lost many of the difficulties that it once faced, or that most of those who profess it have eliminated many of the conditions required by this art's perfection.

Yet, if one were to except astronomy and music, whose elements are less necessary today than they once were for the construction of theatres and sundials, it is certain that the art of architecture cannot do without all the other studies prescribed by Vitruvius, that is, if modern needs did not render other studies just as necessary.

And first, is not the knowledge of literature and history more useful still to the contemporary *architect*? Vitruvius wanted his architect to be knowledgeable about all that links his art to historical facts or opinions, such as the origin of caryatids and other similar objects. How much more indispensable then, is this erudition today, since in adopting the art of the ancients, the *architect* employs an infinity of constitutive parts or decorative objects of architecture whose use could become inopportune or often ridiculous if, in ignoring their origin and consequently their

reasons, he uses them in a manner that is misconstrued and contrary to their meaning.

Indeed, in order to explain his projects and their motives, the *architect* is often compelled either to substantiate them in writing or to explain them orally to an educated audience. He must therefore know how to develop them methodically, with clarity, facility, and agreeableness.

The sciences of arithmetic and mathematics are no less necessary for the *architect* today. Only, he must not limit himself to the elements of arith-metic; he is supposed to possess an extensive know-ledge of its practice, either for the execution of his projects, or to avoid the ordinary errors of evaluating expenses that cause problems with the builder.

But the modern *architect* needs the help of geometry and mechanics more than *architects* in antiquity. The kinds of construction used in most modern nations depend on these two sciences. Generally, the nature of materials, the simplicity of installation or assemblage among the ancients, as well as that of the plans and distributions, demanded less artifice than that which is more often required of the moderns, such as the need for complicated curves in vaults, and the necessity to provide varied plans with solid roofs and with materials of reasonable dimensions. Now, the study of geometry facilitates the means of tracing and measuring all the figures and masses by teaching the diverse properties of all kinds of curves. Mechanics teaches the equilibrium between forces that act and those that support or react. Whoever neglects these studies will never find the happy mean, which is necessary at once for the solidity of construction as well as for economy. Through the use of machines that replace manual labour, mechanics is also of great assistance to the modern *architect* in the execution of his projects.

Perspective and optics are also necessary. They serve not only to ascertain the effects of the building's views, but also to find the means to properly light the interior, to enhance certain parts, or to modify them depending on their placement or on the distance from which they are to be seen.

The *architect* must also study physics, at least in a general way. He must know not only the practice, but also the principles of the composition of materials, and their diverse qualities depending on location. He must know the physical or meteorological causes of the qualities of the soil, air, and climate in which he builds, in order to determine the most salubrious orientations for the edifice. This is the knowledge that Vitruvius recommends to his *architect* under the name Medicine.

Drawing – by this name we do not only understand simple delineation, but rather that study of the forms of the human body and nature in general, which is the basis of painting and sculpture – must form an essential part of the practical studies of the *architect*. Some authors have advanced that one can be a good *architect* without being a good painter or sculptor. If one were to consider the state of the arts in antiquity, one could still find – notwithstanding the small amount of information that time and numerous revolutions concealed from the history of the fine arts – a very high number of authorities that favoured these common studies and practice that reigned between these arts and those who practised them.

But it is especially in modern Italy, and in the middle of the most splendid centuries of art, that one finds this union of skill and renown in each of the arts of design combined within one individual. One could compile a very long list of the most acclaimed painters and sculptors recognized as such today, who also brought the knowledge, the taste and the practice of architecture to an elevated degree. There, one would read the famous names of Giotto, Orcagna, Mantegna, Michelangelo, Raphael, Giulio Romano, Polidorus, Vasari, Tibaldi, Daniele di Volterra, Giovanni di Bologna, Domenico [Veneziano?], Cortona, Bernini, Algardi, etc. To this list corresponds another, composed of individuals who were more particularly famous for their works in architecture, and whose talents extended to the other arts. One could cite in this category: Brunelleschi, Alberti, Ammanati, Sansovino, Sangallo, Bramante, Vignola, etc. Thus, there is almost no fair monument in Italy that is not the fruit of the combined knowledge and practice of different arts.

The reason for this union of talents, which was once common but has since become rare in one individual, is that the common point in the teaching of these different arts was the study of nature manifesting in each art, in the direct or indirect relations, in the physical or moral qualities of this great exemplar in which everyone could read and appropriate the laws and effects of unity, variety, the harmony of forms, contours and proportions. Instructed and impregnated with these great principles, each artist, through the special practice of design, could apply them to each of the dialects of the same language, and knew how to pass from one of its forms to another without changing the essence of this language.

Thus, it was often observed, that an artist who was compelled by the chance of circumstances to exercise an art that he had not hitherto practised, was suddenly able to develop an aptitude that today would seem to require an entire lifetime. Architecture in particular exhibits a multitude of examples of this sort. In the *Life of Baccio d'Agnolo*, Vasari remarks that this art, more than the others, was practised by a great number of individuals who had not studied it, and who did not know even its technical terms. This writer, painter and architect adds that one cannot excel in architecture without an accomplished judgment in the knowledge of drawing, or the continual practice of painting and sculpture. *Se non da coloro che hanno ottimo giudizio e buon disegno, o che in pitture o sculture abbiano grandemente operato*. "The cause of this facility (continues Vasari) possessed by painters and sculptors in learning architecture, resides in their study of the relations between statues and buildings, and in the necessity to make and to compose architecture in their paintings. Thus they are compelled to know this art and the areas associated with it."

Obviously, Vasari gives reasons of a very inferior order about this subject. In fact, the reason that compels the painter and the sculptor to instruct themselves in the elements of architecture, is far from being the cause that enables them to produce masterpieces in this art. Thus, in order to explain what happened in this regard, one must refer to analogies of a superior order, deriving from these principles of general harmony, and the effects that evolve from them. Of these, the artist receives the most enlightened lessons in the arts that imitate the perfections of nature, more directly and tangibly. We shall develop this subject in the entry ARCHITECTURE, based on this text from Vitruvius: *Non potest aedes ulla sine symetria atque proportione rationem habere compositionis, nisi uti ad hominis bene figurati membrorum habuerit exactam rationem.*

No matter the authority of examples and theories on this point, as well as the consequences that can be deduced from them, one cannot today make a law of this union in the teaching or practice of the various arts, nor expect it to be applied. The nature of these ideas unites them, and their intellectual elements are drawn together; only the power of material procedures, the habits of modern schools and the methods of practice, have erected among them some nearly insurmountable barriers. Therefore, if one can no longer demand of the *architect* a real practice of painting and sculpture, then at least one should ask him to join the knowledge of the theoretical notions of imitation in these two arts, to some trituration of the art of figure drawing for the purpose of introducing the proper ornaments in the compositions of his projects, or to enable him to direct the manner and the style of the artists in charge of executing his projected decorations.

But what one cannot recommend enough to the aspiring *architect*, is the study of antique monuments. One could say of these works that they are for the student what the sight and the study of the human body are for the painter and the sculptor. For since architecture's model does not reside – as with the other arts, in a formal manner that is understood by the exterior senses – within forms that are physically tangible, then, modern genius, intelligence and reasoning must find their lessons and examples in works where genius, intelligence and reasoning once combined to imprint the harmony of all the perfections of the human body within buildings.

Now instinct, feeling and the experience of centuries, as well as all educated individuals in all countries, never ceased to affirm and proclaim

that in no other country on earth, and in no other time, no other art of building than the one called *antique* was the true imitator of the beauty of nature's physical works, or the faithful interpreter of the laws that she follows in producing her creations. (*See* ANTIQUE).

ARCHITECTURE This word, in its simple sense and most general acceptation, signifies the *art of building*. However, the first of these words, the word *art*, has two meanings, depending on the nature of the objects or matters to which it is applied, or the diverse characteristics comprised in each of these matters. In fact, this word designates either the last of mechanical practices and the most common of crafts, or that which is most elevated in the conceptions of genius; thus one speaks of the *Art of the Potter* and the *Art of the Poet*.

Sometimes, the same kind of work will comprise a more or less mechanical part, known as *craft*, and a second part which is a unique tributary of the faculties of the mind, known as *art*. Thus, the arts of design include the above-mentioned two elements in the scope of their domain and their activity. If common parlance does not always make this distinction, then the first task of theory is to establish this distinction in order to prevent any confusion.

Since the art of building, which is a definition of *architecture* in the most generic sense, comprises this division, we shall exclude from our theory any extraneous art of building that corresponds to the material part, thus limiting our discussion to the art that rests on all matters other than physical need, that is to say, on the combinations of order, intelligence and moral pleasure.

This preliminary explanation enables us to confine the notions that will compose this article to a restricted framework, since it will concern only Greek architecture, the only one to which the conditions that constitute art could apply, according to the definition that we gave.

This article will therefore be divided into two parts, the first theoretical, the other historical. The first will comprise theoretical notions regarding the originating causes of Greek architecture, its imitative system and the principles upon which it is based. In the second part, we shall survey the history of this architecture and of its vicissitudes.

PART ONE
THE THEORETICAL NOTIONS OF GREEK ARCHITECTURE

Architecture does not begin to be an art (in the more or less elevated sense just defined) before a society reaches a certain wealth of moral culture. Before such a time, there is only what one must call *building* [*la bâtisse*] that is to say, one of the necessary crafts for the physical needs of life. Now as the needs themselves are limited at that time, the use of this craft amounts to providing a shelter that covers man from the ravages of time and the inclemency of weather.

However, during this more or less prolonged period of infancy, the art of building in different countries begins to appropriate these customary forms and practices which will mark this art with such remarkable differences of expression. These original differences, among other constraints which may have contributed to their formation, seem to us to derive from two principal causes. The one is the kind of life that nature herself dictates to each primitive society, the other, is the kind of materials available for the early experiments in construction.

Indubitably, all sorts of different conditions concurred to familiarize man with forms of habitation, and consequently with very different forms of construction depending on one or the other of the principal modes of life (that of the hunter, that of the shepherd or that of the farmer) found in various countries and climates during the first ages of societies. Now amongst these primitive societies, there is no doubt that the mode of agricultural life was the one that motivated man to build the most solid shelters and the largest habitations. Agriculture requires both an active and a sedentary life. Living on his field, and enjoying the fruits of his labour, the farmer has provisions to stow away and defend, either against the inclemency of the weather, or against the violations of his property. He therefore needs a habitation that conforms to his needs, that is to

say, solid, healthy, commodious, safe, and spacious. Thus, he will require from nature certain means that are at once economical and easily implemented, that is to say, materials which are appropriate to the necessities of his condition.

If nature offered and still offers, depending on the conditions in each country, some already formed shelters in the hollows of rocks, in underground caves, or some kind of terrain from which it is easy to excavate a haven, one must also admit that these are exceptions upon which one can only establish some rare deviations from the general laws that formed the first societies which arrived at a beginning of civilization. At this point, where through his labour man demands of the earth the means to provide for the needs of the

Fig. 22. Parthenon.
From Stuart and Revett's *Antiquities of Athens*,
Reprint, B. Bloom, New York, 1968

the present and those of the future, not only for himself but also for his family, he must necessarily construct a habitation that suits these conditions.

But which materials will he use? Nature offers – and can only offer – three kinds of materials for construction: stone, earth, and wood.

§ I *The original causes, or the system borrowed from primitive wooden construction, or the hut.*

Stone, to which architecture will one day be indebted for its greatest works in perfected societies and during the infancy of the nation in question here, was the least appropriate material with respect to the available means and instruments. Stone demands laborious quarrying, costly transportation, means of lifting and laying that require machines and numerous painful efforts.

There is no doubt, however, that earth presents a simpler, easier and much more economical use; but it must be realized that before the appearance of an industry that was capable of improving this material, of facilitating its use, and making it solid by firing it, earth alone in its pure natural use, could only form buildings that are fragile, inconsistent, and of a limited expanse.

Wood must have presented itself in the most natural and universal way to the societies of which we speak, and to those that needed to procure enduring shelters at little cost. In fact, it suffices to recall the state of these first gatherings of people known as primitives, found by travellers throughout the world, and the state in which these inhabited countries appeared to their research. What does one read in all their narratives? One sees that the earth is everywhere covered with forests, that early societies first inhabited these forests and slowly emerged out of their rustic shelters, established families, and gathered in huts built at the expense of forests, in such a way that the more these societies increased, the more forests diminished.

Thus, early shelters were formed out of branches of trees. Soon, the tree trunks were cut and were transformed into supports and beams. The property of wood was to lend itself with more or less difficulty to primitive constructions. Also, wood never ceased to be, among the most affluent and industrious nations, one of the materials most abundantly used in the construction of the largest cities. Nowadays, there are still immense regions in Europe whose cities are built uniquely out of wood.

How could this material not have entered as a necessary element in the primitive constructions of an agricultural society? It is difficult to conceive that one could have done without it; and as we saw, it is more difficult still to imagine that cut stone was used, because there was no intention to exclude all materials like pebbles and scattered débris which, when mixed with earth, could form walls, partitions, etc. Nothing but the tree could lend itself more naturally to all the situations required by the simple needs of a people without art and science.

When we speak of the tree as the primary material for habitations, we must refrain from taking this word in a very factual sense, as did some speculative writers who misused this theory by suggesting that, in a simple sense, the column was a copy of the tree. It is not the purpose of this theory to provide *architecture* with models to imitate in a rigorous sense. We shall see that all that concerns architectural imitation rests on analogies, inductions, and free assimilations.

The use of the tree and of wood in the constructions of the time of which we speak, was but the coarse use of the processes of carpentry; and this *symbolic hut*, which is designated as the type of *architecture* in Greece, means nothing else but an adumbration or an attempt at carpentry, that is to say, the mechanical art that consists in properly disposing and assembling pieces of wood in order to form a solid and ordered building. (*See* HUT, WOOD.)

Without a doubt, trees entered the rustic constructions of early times in a more or less rough-hewn fashion; and the memory of this use may have transmitted to the following centuries some ornamental motifs that recalled its idea. But such is not the material system of Greek *architecture*. This is rather found in the use of already shaped wood, so as to form the assemblies which became the prototype for various combinations in a perfected *architecture*.

What do we effectively see in this adumbration? Squared or rounded pieces of wood laid perpendicularly or horizontally, fashioned in such a manner as to receive the superposition of other pieces of wood, and to coordinate ordered intervals between them.

What we are going to relate is neither a history imagined after the fact, nor an imagined system. Being a necessary result of natural causes, this already irrefutable matter is demonstrated by the evident results before our eyes.

Thus, the trees or the beams that were driven into the earth, became the first columns. As trees diminish in thickness from the bottom to the top, so did the columns, especially those of the primitive order (the Doric), where this diminution is the most evident. These beams planted in the earth without any apparent support, are also represented by the same baseless Doric order. When it was realized that this method exposed the wood to decay, substantial blocks or plates of wood of varying thickness were placed under each beam, serving at the same time to give it a base and greater solidity. From these plates of varying continuity and height, derived the foundations, plinths, dies, torii and profiles which occur at the bottom of columns.

The natural consequence of these additions to the lower ends of beams, was the crowning of the higher ends with one or many plates which were also suitable to give a solid support to the transverse beams. Hence the capital, which was at first a simple abacus, to which was later added the echinus in the Doric order.

Who does not recognize in the very appellation of the architrave (*epistylium*), that the use of wood and the labour of carpentry were also its generating principles? The joists necessarily came to be placed on the architrave, while the visible ends of these joists as well as the intervals that separate them, gave birth to the triglyphs and the metopes, whose name signifies a *hole in between.* (*This is the Doric frieze.*)

Continuing the enumeration of all the necessary parts of what we called *the hut* or the rustic habitation whose inventory we are listing, we observe that the inclined joists of the roof that rest on the joist ends of the planking, produce this projection which formed the cornice that juts out of the building to cover the walls from the rain.

The roof, or the gable, necessarily yielded the form of the pediment, which in its varying inclinations must have followed the slope of roofs, depending on countries and climates.

We have briefly surveyed the parts which are at once constitutive of the primitive work of carpentry or wood in early habitations, and the system of imitation proper to Greek architecture in its application to the largest buildings. We shall not treat all the consequences of this imitative system in their application to a large number of details, such as arcades, vaults, and many ornaments.

It suffices for us here, to have proven in a manner that we may call demonstrative, the real identity that exists between a model and its imitation. As we have seen, this identity is such, that the description of the copy serves for that of the original, that is to say, to give an exact idea of the *Greek hut* through the analysis of the *Greek temple*.

Having shown that carpentry, or the assembly work in wood, was the generative principle of Greek architecture that has since become universal, it must be proven that no other element of construction could have provided the art of building with a model that is more complete, more unified, and altogether more varied.

This model must be first sought within some material, and later within the modifications of which this material is capable. But we have seen that nature offers the art of building only wood, earth and stone. Earth, as we said, can only be used when it is converted into brick, or dried in the sun, or baked in the fire; then, it will rank among stones.

What is left then is the concurrence between cut stone and wood. We have seen that the use of cut stone could not have occurred within the nascent industry of early societies; and hence, it could not have influenced habits and tastes, nor found the resources of strength, of expenditure, and the means that only belonged to later centuries. But, assuming that the practice of cut stone was then what it became later, let us consider what this material could have produced if it were left to its own properties; in other words, had it drawn solely from within itself the forms, the members, and the details of architecture. We conclude that to determine the use of stone in the past based on its present use is a fruitless and erroneous exercise. Nowadays, we see this material adapted to all the varieties of form, details, projections, plans and elevations. It is made to be the copy and the repetition of types, forms and combinations made outside its practice, and where its craft could have never suggested or realized these combinations without a model that is foreign to its domain.

However, there are some critics who found it unfortunate that stone could become representative of another material or at least its forms and assemblies. These critics do not want marble to be reduced to a subordinate role, exhibiting forms whose origin derives from poor and wretched huts, or from wooden buildings. They would prefer that each material drew from within itself, and within its own means, either the nature of its form, or the diversity of its manner. But one might ask, what does stone, whether in the quarry or in the field, find to emulate, imitate or feign? Should stone imitate the caves or the mountains and rocks from which it is quarried? This amounts to saying *ex nihilo nihil*. By copying itself, stone copies nothing, offers no form to art, no variety to the eye, and no relations for the mind to compare. This is nearly the case of Egyptian architecture. Stone, having only itself to imitate, or better still, having no representation of combinations to emulate, no projections, no solids and voids, and no correlations or proportions within the massing and its parts, finds nothing else to build but surfaces, and nothing else to express but massiveness.

Stone then, offers no origin to art, no model, no copy; it can only be the representation of uniformity.

On the contrary, the material of carpentry, being at once solid and light, satisfies all the conditions of necessity and all the requirements of taste. Wood, as Algarotti observes, was the most proper material to offer art the greatest variety of *modinatures* [profiles], modifications and ornaments of all sorts. While stone offers only surfaces and suggests no idea of variety, wood or carpentry everywhere provides projections, recesses, masses that overhang or retract, distribution of parts, all in diverse relationships with each other.

The kind of imitative borrowing whose elements and proofs we just developed is without doubt a sort of fiction in the spirit of the system of architecture, since no kind of imitation that one may call material or positive can lay claim to the means of this art; and it is precisely that which is fictitious in the transposition of the work in wood into that of stone that makes its value and its delight.

We shall soon see that such is not the matter upon which rests the morally imitative property of architecture; that such is not the reason to which architecture owes its rank among the arts imitative of nature, rather it was by virtue of a very superior order of imitation. Yet, if this fictitious model, whose authenticity some would like to contest, is not found in nature, it is no less due to her inspirations; if such a model is not her direct work, then it is its copy. Nature did not produce this model, but she suggested it; and to renounce it amounts to throwing oneself into the ways of arbitrariness and chance that have no end nor exit, and lead but to the emptiness of caprice.

Let them reject what one might call this theory's physical truth of fact, since the fact in question has but the consequences of the very fact itself as a proof, the fictitious model of the hut exists no less in the moral order of the matter, as a fortunate element of propriety, order, symmetry and other qualities of which it became the allegorical prototype for architecture.

§ II *On the system borrowed from the organization of the human body and the general order of nature.*

To consider architecture's imitation of wood construction, or what is known as the *hut*, to be a fiction given consistence by an earlier theory whose effects on architecture are impossible to ignore, we affirm that architecture owes all the other properties that make her an art of imitation to this fortunate invention.

Actually, the assimilation of the material model defined in the preceding paragraph, could not have elevated architecture to the rank of the arts truly imitative of nature. To attain this rank, she needed a kind of adumbration which was, so to speak, already prepared, and apt to receive forms and combinations of a superior order. The model in wood that derived from a material imitation was awaiting another vestiture from another kind of model, deriving from another principle of life. This new development came from the perfecting of the arts that imitate the human body.

Every progress in imitation requires the knowledge, the choice and the comparison between many models. But until then, the art of building could not have received the idea of such an amelioration. If restricted to the forms of necessity that were dictated by physical need, this art could have remained at this level, which is that of routine among nearly all peoples where the imitation of the human body was perpetuated in a state of eternal infancy. Now, there is a necessary sympathy between sculpture and architecture for example. All the works of art in all countries reveal to us that where the arts of design, in other words the expression of forms in the imitation of bodies, did not attain truth, so the art of building could not have emerged from the terms of an ignorant practice.

But the fortunate soil of Greece could not have remained unfruitful for art. As soon as sculpture gradually rose above the indication of the most shapeless signs, toward the distinction of the principal correlations of dimension and proportion in the statues to Hermes, in idols, or in the figures of men and gods, it was quite natural that the habitual contact between the works of the sculptor and those of the architect, showed the latter if not a new and effective model, then at least a new analogy of idea and process which enabled him to employ in his works an application of a hitherto unknown kind.

The architect had hitherto known only simple relations of dimension prescribed by necessity, and he did not suspect the existence of a model that is indirect with respect to truth[7], and whose spirit and reality were easily transposable to his work. This model was a system of proportions, imitating the one that nature offered as an example in determining the laws that govern the constitution of the human body. Now proportion in a body implies a disposition of parts placed in a particular rapport with each other, and with respect to a whole, in such a way that the whole determines and makes known the precise measure of each of the parts, and that each part is apt to do the same with respect to the whole.

Architecture, being already constituted and founded on the types of carpentry, and composed of fixed and necessary relations, offered the most favourable field of application for the system of proportions that we just defined. It was realized how in its appropriation of the plan, the facts,

and the combinations that nature follows in the organization of the human body, art was truly rivalling her. It was understood how a building ordered in the same spirit and the same principles as those of nature, shared the same kind of perfection, and produced the same kind of pleasure that she makes us experience. It came to be known that nature disposed the human body in such a fashion, that there is nothing useless, nothing whose purpose and reason cannot be recognized. Hence, the system of architecture only admitted that which could be justified, as in nature, as having a necessary use and being dependent on a general order.

It was on the basis of this plan that the forms dictated by need and by the imitation of carpentry were disposed and regularized; only their use had not yet been refined by reason and the feeling of harmony. For example, this is how the tripartite division, whose first model inspired the use of the principal parts of the orders, was henceforth based on nature herself who consecrated it in her works, and became a principle of proportions applicable to a whole that was already composed of three parts: the column, the entablature and the pediment. Soon, the same principle subdivided each of these three parts, still into three sections. Now, the reason for the use of this division is that it alone could provide the greatest number of relations that the eye could at once hold and observe attentively without much weariness.

In another example also, nature endowed the imitation of the human body with a determined measure of relations, a scale of proportions, which, taking either the human foot or the head, could serve as a module for the imitated figure by establishing a permanent accord between the parts, as well as regulate the whole in a manner independent of the variations between individuals, or of the errors of sight. Likewise, *architecture* created a similar measure, which in the Doric order for example, is the triglyph in the frieze, while in the other orders, it is the diameter of the column.

The effect of the consequences of this imitation was that an edifice became for the mind, a kind of being or organism governed by laws which are the more permanent, the more they find their principle embodied in this very being. A code of proportions followed, in which each part found its measure and its rapport by reason of the modifications prescribed by the character of the whole. The whole and each part, found themselves in a reciprocal dependence from which resulted their inviolable accord.

But a thorough study of natural varieties in the formation of bodies explained to the artist these nuances of age, of qualities, and properties that shaped the diverse modes of form that Polykleitos had fixed in his treatise *On Symmetries*, and whose examples were preserved for us in antique statues. Here, too, *architecture* received from the imitation of bodies and through the arts of design, a new and more fortunate stimulus. To this stimulus, she owed the setting of her diverse modes whose characters, rendered evident in the three orders, became for the eye as for the mind, an expression which is at once material and intellectual, of the varied qualities of power, force, grace, delight, lightness, wealth, luxury and magnificence.

Such then was the progress of architecture. It was by assimilating her work and her processes to a more superior example than her first model, that she was able to reach the rank of the arts that directly imitate the body. In observing the degrees through which this art evolved, there is no need to remark that the imitation in question is not the repetition of that which is material in the model, but rather, this imitation is the one that transposes into the work, the rules and laws of the object that serves as an example. It is never the material aspect of form that this imitation appropriates, but that which is intellectual; it never copies the thing itself, but the reasons for this thing.

Also, when Vitruvius tells us that the Doric order was an imitation of the male body, and the Ionic that of the female body, this imitation should be understood (as common sense indicates), as one of moral analogy, and not of physical resemblance. This is also what he implies by adding that the first order imitates the naked simplicity of the male body, and the Ionic the delicateness and the dress of the female body. But

when he takes this comparison further, and finds a similarity between the baseless column and a man's naked foot; or the ornate base of the Ionic order and the elegant footwear of women; or between the folds of their robes, their head-dress, their bracelets, and the volutes and flutings, what should one make of this theory? That it is based on a flawed reasoning that is bent on banishing reason; or that it is an imagined allegory to veil the truth, but which may also tend to hide this truth by distorting it.

Others have gone farther still. Following false comparisons and flawed interpretations of a misconceived imitation, they took a column's capital to be a man's head, and his body to be the shaft, etc. which is a parallel of absurd and childish consequences. Thus is ridicule cast on a parodied system, and thus is the true destroyed by exaggeration; for truth stands to lose more by being poorly defended than by not being defended at all.

It is no less evident that in order to apply to the coarse adumbration of carpentry the merit and the pleasure of a set of proportions, one finds no model that is more appropriate and within the reach of ordinary intelligence than the human body. This analogy is so natural, that to praise a beautiful body one compares it to a well ordered building; and the comparison applies reciprocally. This is what Vitruvius expressly says. "Without symmetry and proportion there can be no principles in the design of any temple; that is, if there is no precise relation between its members, as in the case of those of a well-formed man. "[8]

Non potest aedes ulla sine symetria atque proportione rationem habere compositionis, nisi, uti ad hominis bene figurati membrorum habuerit exactam rationem.

But soon it was realized, that although fixed and immutable, the proportions of the human body were subject to numerous variations. Sculpture herself had come to regard the calculations of proportions not as chains but as rules of varying flexibility, depending on the needs of the art. It was even more important for the spirit of architecture to free itself from a servitude that would have transformed this art into a routine. The Greeks understood that all the methods of profiling were more or less relative, and that these rules of proportion, although borrowed from the organization of the human body, could also be subordinated to the maxims of a moral and intellectual order which alone could steal the secret of ideal nature.

It is on this path that art embarked in pursuit of the great model, and to obtain the revelation of the means necessary to awaken in us the idea of beauty and the impressions of delight. It was by increasingly generalizing the applications of this model that architecture succeeded in extending indefinitely the sphere of its imitation. It was no longer carpentry, or the wooden hut, or the human body and its proportions; but rather it was nature herself, in her abstract essence, that architecture took as a model. It was order in nature which became, *par excellence*, her archetype and her genius.

The imitation of carpentry, through the necessary relations of parts and dimensions constituted, as it were, the skeleton of architecture.

The analogical imitation of the human body through the fortunate application of the system of proportions, came to invest this skeleton, as it were, with all the rational forms that animate nature as well as her properties and character.

The abstract imitation of nature, studied and considered in her general laws of accord and harmony, in her principle of universal order, and in the means with which she moves and delights us, came to endow *architecture* with a moral principle that rendered her the rival of her own model.

Thus this art, which is apparently subject to material causes more than the other arts, became under the influence of this last issue, the most ideal of them, that is to say, more apt to stimulate our minds. Nature, indeed, offers only intellectual analogies for architecture to reproduce. This art imitates its model less in its material aspects, and more in its abstract ones. This art does not pursue its model, it stands beside it. It does not produce that which it beholds, but rather the manner in which that which it beholds has been produced. It is not attached to the effects but to the causes that produce them.

As an emulator of nature, its efforts aim at studying her means, and the reproduction of her effects on a smaller scale. Thus, when other arts of design imitate already created models, the architect must create his own, without finding it anywhere in reality. In short, his true model resides in the principles of order, intelligence, and harmony, from which derive the feeling for beauty, and the source of pleasure which we experience in the works of nature.

If *architecture*, then, is an art of imitation, it is not for having conserved, and embellished, the coarse forms with which necessity endowed the first habitations of early societies, but because architecture imitates nature in the laws that she prescribed for herself. It is because architecture acts through the same means, and the same processes that she stole from nature. It is because

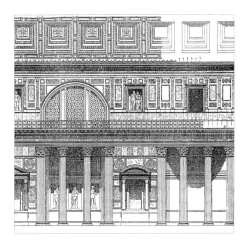

Fig. 23. Pantheon, interior.
From: Josef Durm, *Die Baukunst der Etrusker und Römer*,
A. Kröner Verlag, 1905

architecture appropriated the effects of these mysterious causes that make us experience agreeable or painful sensations at the sight of certain compositions. From here derived the laws of proportion, always constant as to their principle, and always variable as to their applications. (See PROPORTION).

PART TWO
HISTORICAL NOTIONS OF GREEK ARCHITECTURE

The reader will doubtless find it agreeable to follow the history of Greek *architecture* presented in its entirety, from her birth, passing through her full development, until her total decadence; and later, from her renewal until the present period.

But obviously, such an expanded presentation does not fit the organization of a dictionary. These notions must then be subdivided among the particular articles and their corresponding words. We shall complete this article in accordance with our indicated plan and, consequently, also with a befitting brevity. In the first article, we sketched rather than traced the genealogical history of Greek architecture; the following will simply be its chronology.

There is nothing more difficult, even with the help of history and traditions, than to fix the *first beginning* of human inventions. I intentionally use these two seemingly redundant words. Only, the truth is that in many things, the first step or the point of departure if you will, turns out to be a problem. Many arts are born unnoticed, and develop for a long time without any attention being paid to them. When they finally arrive at a point that awakens curiosity about their past, one is very far from their origin to be able to trace it with some certainty.

If there is an art that hides its origin, it is *architecture*. How many centuries did it take for this art, under this name, to succeed in assimilating itself to the other arts that imitate nature? Likewise, how much time elapsed under the simple title of the *art of building* before this art took its place among the inventions useful to the needs of early societies.

However, as we saw in the preceding article, Greek *architecture*, in her ensemble and her details, carries her origins written in too legible a manner for one to be mistaken as to the order that gave birth to her. Thus, the Doric order is for us the unimpeachable witness that testifies as to the primitive state of this art before it accomplished all the trials through which it must have passed to reach its aim.

The Doric order showed us that it is naught else but the continuation and the perfecting of the primitive system of wood construction. The sole fact of the visible imitation of wood assemblies clearly demonstrates the transposition that occurred from wood into stone. Now, it is a proven matter that before a series of trials led to the realization of the forms and dispositions of a fragile model within solid constructions, all the buildings of Greece were assemblies made of wood, which were coarse at first and later became more and more refined, until finally reaching a point where they were able to offer to art and taste the very combinations that established the system of Greek architecture.

The historical and undeniable evidence that we will produce elsewhere (*See* DORIC, WOOD, HUT, etc.) proves to us that many temples were initially constructed in wood and according to the same types as those that succeeded them in stone.

However, it does seem to us possible to determine the period of this transformation based on material evidence. It suffices for us to have established that this notion is to be placed first in the chronological order of Greek architecture. Besides, there is nothing to expect on this matter from the ruins of the most ancient buildings that one encounters in Greece. Irrespective of the authenticity of the periods in question, all these remains are extraneous to *architecture*; they are but ancient walls that time has not yet destroyed, and where there is no trace of art.

If we consult the most ancient writings, Homer presents us with descriptions of magnificent palaces; but we find nothing that could give birth to the idea of columnar orders, nor any regular system. For this poet, buildings attract attention because of the cost of their materials more than the value of their form. The choice and the polish of stone constitute their principal merit, just as the richness of metals seems to be the primary indicator of beauty in the works of sculpture. None of this material supports our research in the palace of Alcinous.

It is from the Doric order, whose history we only know in speculation, that we must obtain the evidence of the early trials of the art of building in stone. Be that as it may, this order's name does not prove that its invention was due to Dorus. Rather, this order received its name from having been used in the famous temple that this prince, according to Vitruvius, had built at Argos to the honour of Juno. Perhaps also, this name is due to the Dorians, among whom this style gained currency before becoming widely distributed throughout the rest of Greece. Nevertheless, it is certain that the most ancient edifices, at least those that exhibit the most evidence in favour of their antiquity, are of this order, which, as we shall see elsewhere, preceded the others.

But it is not doubtful that the interval of time which includes the period of Pericles and that of Alexander the Great, saw the three orders that constitute *architecture* acquire their perfection. The defeat of the Persians at Marathon had secured peace for all of Greece. Athens soon became the centre for the sciences and the arts. It is at this period, as Diodorus of Sicily remarks, that all talents experienced a sort of explosion. It is at this period that began the reconstruction of the temples destroyed or burned by the Persians. Then, these models of grandeur and beauty were constructed in the Parthenon, the Propylaea and other monuments whose remains still offer lessons for architects today.

Toward that period also, the Ionic order seems to have acquired the proportions and the ornaments that helped establish its rank between the order of strength and that of richness. The Ionic was the order of gracefulness. Did it see the light in Asia Minor, or did it receive from this country and its voluptuous climate, the taste for ornament, delicacy and gracefulness that characterize it?

Callimachus had already preceded the period of which we are speaking. If his invention (See CORINTHIAN) was limited to the substitution of the acanthus leaf for that of the olive in the capital of this order, then the Corinthian order, of which little remains in Greece, would have followed the fate of the other arts; and *architecture* – considered in the establishment of her system, in the orders, or in the execution of the most beautiful edifices – had, toward the century of Alexan-der, climbed all the steps from which it became perhaps necessary for her to progressively step down, especially in spreading her influence to the rest of nations.

The very ancient relations that seem to have existed between Greece and Etruria lead one to conclude, judging by the taste and the archaic style of sculptural objects that one discovers daily in the ancient country of the Etruscans, that either these communications took place at a time when art was not yet developed in Greece, or that certain causes had rendered Etruria stagnant, even in her *architecture*. The difficulty encountered by many people around this question is that they confuse the large constructions of city walls, which consist of nothing but the cutting and raising of large blocks of stone, with art properly speaking, which is the work of genius, taste, and the result of combinations inspired by the study of nature. However, with its Tuscan order, Etruria shows us such an affinity with the Doric order of the Greeks, that one cannot help but see the result of very close communications. We also find that the Etruscans probably used wood for a considerable time in their constructions and the ordonnance of their temples. The proof is found in the use of this material by the Romans during the time of Vitruvius, in its application to the temples they called Tuscan.

This stationary state of *architecture* considered as art is also confirmed by the other arts of design, which do not seem to have followed among the Etruscans the same progressive state that characterized them in Greece. However, it is to Etruria that Rome, in her early centuries, owed what she possessed in *architecture* and art. It is to her artists that Tarquinius entrusted the construction of this famous sewer, a work truly prodigious by its solidity, and in which some saw a presage of Rome's future greatness. The Tuscan taste for simple construction with few ornaments, suited for a considerable time the austere mores of a bellicose and poor republic. The opulence of materials and art did not take hold until the corruption of mores and the changing of institutions.

Augustus understood that the pleasures of the arts of luxury were to replace those of political liberty. He employed all the appropriate resources to realize this indemnification. He also used to boast of having transformed Rome into marble, whereas he found her in clay. Livy calls him the author and the restorer of temples. The greatest masters of Greece hastened to this new capital of the arts. During this period, *architecture* seems to have been taken to the highest degree that it could have attained in Rome, in practice as well as in theory, of which Vitruvius gathered the didactic notions in his treatise in ten books. The Pantheon was built then by Agrippa, Augustus's son-in-law.

The passion for great monuments increased even more under his successors. However, under Tiberius, Caligula, and Claudius, taste seems to have degenerated. Nero exhibited toward the arts less taste than mania and ostentation. He exhausted himself in colossal enterprises and wastefulness of all sorts. However, his reign was one of the most favourable ones to the great enterprises of *architecture*. Severus and Celer [the architect] constructed the palace known as the *Golden House*.

Under the fortunate reign of Trajan, *architecture* recaptured a taste for wisdom and grandeur,

light that a candle emits the moment it extinguishes itself.

The arch of Septimius Severus, signals one of the remarkable periods of the beginning of decadence. It is difficult to conceive how sculpture, since Marcus Aurelius, could have descended to the level exhibited by this monument. The arch, which is commonly known as that of the *Goldsmiths*, possesses almost nothing of the taste and character of good *architecture*. The profiles are faulty and the ornaments overburden and crush the members.

Sustained for some time by Alexander Severus's love for the arts, *architecture* seems to have finally succumbed during the fall of the Western empire. However, she still survived the

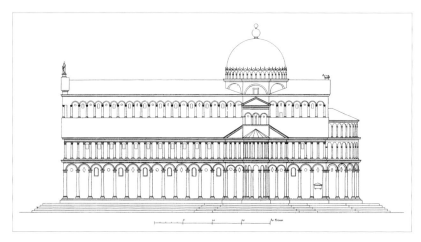

Fig. 24. Cathedral of Pisa, Buschetto.
From: A. C. Quatremère de Quincy, *Histoire de la vie et des ouvrages des plus célèbres architectes*,
J. Renouard, Paris, 1830

which seemed to reflect the character of this famous and wise emperor. The triumphal arches, the triumphal column, and the magnificent *forum* that time has more or less respected, all attest to the high degree to which this art was elevated under his auspices. The architect Appollodorus played a large role in all the enterprises of Trajan's reign. It was he who supposedly erected this famous column, a masterpiece among the marvels of the *forum* to which the emperor gave his name.

Hadrian, and the Antonines also, made *architecture* scintillate with the greatest lustre. The former practised this art himself. However, during the reign of the Antonines, as Winckelmann observes, art was beginning to decline. The lustre that it shed on this period resembles that bright

ruination of the other arts. In a century when there no longer existed a sculptor worthy of the name, Diocletian nevertheless displayed in his Thermae a grandeur whose preserved remains still compel our admiration. The immensity of that same emperor's palace at Spalato also shows the efforts of which *architecture* was still capable. It was around that same period – in the century of Aurelian – that the vast constructions of Palmyra and Baalbeck in Caleo-Syria, are said to have been built. Despite the licence in taste and the faulty details, one is astonished in the midst of these ruins by the grandeur of the plans, and the richness of the elevations and their ornaments.

One may inquire here as to why *architecture*, without the help of other arts, and after having arisen with them and through them, did not follow them in their fall. The reason for their different fates can be explained by many moral considerations that derive from the principle of their nature, that is to say, from the genre of their imitation. Suffice it to observe, that there is a part of *architecture* that is more subject than other arts to measures and technical procedures which allow copyists without genius to transpose, almost without evident variations, the elements and details of the works that preceded them. To this technical consideration, lets us add a historical one that demonstrates a different political influence on the arts of that time. During that period, statues were demolished and images were erased with much more ease than the destruction of

independent of the power of kings.

Abandoned to the furor of the Visigoths, Italy was emptied of all that Constantine had left. A general destruction turned into dust the greatest number of monuments of the ancient pride of Rome. What accelerated this ruination was a practice that was introduced by distress and ignorance to use materials from antique monuments in new constructions. A shameful forgetfulness of proportions, forms, and the purpose and propriety of these fragments, added still to the confusion of all the members of *architecture*, and by this mixture completed the loss of her idea and her memory. The method of building arcades on top of columns to make up for the lack of architraves, contributed to the gradual forgetting

Fig. 25. Campo Santo, Pisa, G. da Pisa.
From: A. C. Quatremère de Quincy, *Histoire de la vie et des ouvrages des plus célèbres architectes*,
J. Renouard, Paris, 1830

buildings. Additionally, cults could change in many temples without these temples changing their forms. Old columns were used in new buildings. Finally, almost no need remained for statues, but there was always a need to construct monuments. These were some of the causes of this inequality in the duration of the arts of design.

But a common fate was to soon bury them all under the same ruins. The transfer of the seat of the empire to Byzantium, by dividing the power of the state and the resources of art, dealt a mortal blow to the one and the other. In vain did Constantine will that his new metropolis attain the antique splendour of Rome; all his extensive efforts for its embellishment showed that the productions of genius are, more than one thinks,

of the original divisions in her imitative system. From misuse to abuse, things came to a confusion from which derived a manner of building and ornamenting buildings, improperly called, if you will, the *gothic taste*, whose works do not belong to the history of art, understood within the terms that we have defined.

Here begins a veritable interregnum in art and *architecture*. Like those rivers that disappear underground for a while and emerge only to recover a greater course, the art of which we speak, buried during the centuries of ignorance, finally came forth, having triumphed over the causes that had subjugated it; and its empire was to spread among the greatest number of nations on earth.

However, one must say that in the midst of the darkness that was widespread, a few rays of good taste were perceivable. The church of Saint Sophia, built by Justinian in Constantinople during the seventh century, transmitted to the architects of San Marco in Venice, towards the eleventh century, some of the rays we have mentioned.

During this period, the same glimmers of good taste were perceived in several Italian cities. In this same eleventh century (1063), was erected the great cathedral of Pisa, admired today for its beautiful conception and its materials borrowed from ancient constructions, which the architect Buschetto put to good use. Each of the following centuries, until the fifteenth, saw the rebirth and the progressive increase of the love of great enterprises and the traditions of ancient *architecture*, in the tower of Pisa, the church at Padua, that of the Trinity in Florence, in the basilica of the Sta. Croce and that of Sta. Maria dei Fiori in the same city, and in the Campo Santo of Pisa.

Thus, Italy was advancing with great steps towards the restoration of all the arts of Greece and of ancient Rome. Finally, Brunelleschi appeared.

Brunelleschi was the first who traversed the ruins of the monuments of antiquity with the scale and the compass in hand. The first of the moderns, he recognized and distinguished among the Greek orders, and he was the first who, after having discovered the laws and the principles of *architecture*, applied them with correctness and truth to new works. In building the vast cupola of Sta. Maria dei Fiori, he cleared the way for the great enterprises of modern *architecture*, and in the ordonnance of his church of San Lorenzo, reappeared for the first time, the Corinthian order with all the regularity of its proportions and the elegance of its capital with acanthus leaves. This architect deserves the title of the restorer of *architecture*.

Soon after came Leon Batista Alberti. He was the second of the modern artists to build according to the precepts of Vitruvius and the methods of ancient *architecture*. Being a successor of Brunelleschi, he sought in his own works, more elegance and variety of ornaments. His treatise *On Architecture*, the only one that the moderns can compare to that of Vitruvius, provided in its time, perhaps an even better taste for ancient art than the work of the Roman architect, whose many ambiguities had not yet been dissipated by the light of criticism.

Finally, aided by the enlightened protection of the genius of the Medicis or the sovereign pontiffs, by the rivalry that took place between all the cities of Italy, *architecture* succeeded in a short time in arriving at the highest degree that the moderns had attained. To mention, even in an abbreviated manner, the monuments produced in the space of two centuries by the most famous architects of Italy, would perhaps be an interesting way to end this abridged history. But no matter how abridged the presentation of these details can be, it would lengthen this article needlessly, as they have their place under the name of each artist.

ART It is not our task here, to embrace, even in the most general manner, all the conceptions under which the word *art* can be considered, for there will be so many necessary distinctions to establish in such a broad subject.

To mention but two, one must first distinguish between what is known as *mechanical arts* and *liberal* or *fine arts*. The latter necessitate a new division: that of the *arts of design*. The more the scope of the matter could be expanded, the more it is in the nature and the spirit of this Dictionary to restrict its theory to a single subject, that is to say, to the art of architecture. Such will be our task, following a very brief analysis of what constitutes the critical points common to the different arts, in other words, the points of view from which they can be considered.

Now, it seems to us that this kind of critique could consider each art in its *proper nature*, that is to say, in what constitutes its elements or its special attributes; in its *means*, that is to say, in what constitutes its particular effect on our senses and on our mind; and in its *ends*, that is to say, in what constitutes the kind of pleasure and impression that it can produce, or the needs that it must satisfy.

Although all the fine arts are children of a common mother, they differ no less among themselves in their proper nature, in their faculties and their goal.

They differ in their *proper nature*, because each in its respective attributes has a direct correspondence with only a certain given kind of need or pleasure. They differ in their *means*, because these means are limited by the diversity of their instruments, and by the barriers that nature has established between the different organs of the body and the different faculties of our mind. They differ in their *ends*, which are to please, inasmuch as the roads that they must traverse and the needs to which they must correspond, are different.

For example, although the pleasure of harmony is an attribute of music as well as architecture, the particular kind of means proper to these two arts, and the different organs that could enjoy them, are such that there is no resemblance between the evident effects of one or the other harmony. For, in what constitutes the proper nature of these two arts, there is the same difference that exists between the sense of hearing and that of sight.

What one can say about the essential nature and the proper means of each art, is more easily proven and conceived with respect to that which forms each art's ends or goal.

Thus, there are arts whose principal ends are to express, to paint, and to stir the passions within us. Their means are the images of either non material (as in poetry), or material things (as in painting). The goal of architecture, which imitates no living being and expresses only abstract relationships, is to produce in all of us the impressions that result from the ideas of order, proportion, grandeur, wealth, and other similar qualities.

Through intellectual means, that is to say, through the mediation of ideas, poetry portrays things to us. Through the use of the most material objects, architecture elucidates for us the most intellectual relationships.

We shall not expand here on the details and the applications of a theory, which even if abridged, would constitute the material for a voluminous book; but the words ARCHITECTURE, IMITATION, etc., offer some developments of this theory. It suffices

to demonstrate that since each art is different by its proper nature, its means and its ends, it is from the diverse applications of this fundamental distinction that must derive the theoretical definition of the *art* of architecture.

Therefore, we contend that with respect to her *essential nature*, architecture is an *art* based on necessity, and whose imitation, being purely ideal, is not material or factual; that she draws some imitative analogies from nature and from the arts which are her evident imitation; but that she imitates no reality; that her form is for the mind, only a combination of relations, proportions, and reasons, which please inasmuch as they are simply expressed.

We contend that architecture has two sorts of *means*: the *material means* or those of construction, which include all that relates to solidity, calculation, the science of mechanics, etc., that is to say, to physical need; and the *intellectual means*, which tend to produce what must at once please reason and taste: and this is what makes her one of the fine arts, or the arts of genius.

We contend, that considered in her *ends or goal*, architecture partakes in two principles: that of necessity, and that of pleasure. Consequently, architecture has a double aim: the first, independent from *art* intellectually considered, is to construct secure, commodious, and solid dwellings and shelters for the individual as well as the various needs of society; the second, is to make the plans, the elevations, the materials and their disposition, their forms and their combinations, their relations, their proportions, their ornaments, and the accord between the parts and the whole, serve either the pleasure of the eyes, or the one produced in the mind by every ensemble that becomes an imitation of the harmonies of nature, either in the intellectual or the material world.

Consequently, architecture could be defined as: *a composite art, a child of necessity and pleasure that must serve and please us by unifying the forms most befitting to the material needs of man and the harmony of relations best suited for the pleasures of the soul and the mind.*

If this definition comprises the universality of the uses of architecture and correctly indicates her double principle, it also clarifies that this art presents difficulties. Being obliged to serve us while pleasing us, and please us while serving us, it is clear that the material or technical side, and the moral or poetic side, are not separated by a great distance. Although the art of eloquence participates also in the requirements of these two conditions, one must recognize, however, that pleasure and necessity are much more contiguous, much more linked, and that the discourse which is their common means, is also their necessary point of agreement. But what is the relationship between the form required by necessity in architecture, and the form from which the idea of order and beauty derives? What analogy exists between the requirements of walls, pillars, and roofs, and the harmonies of proportion, composition, and ornament? We contend that the ideas of order, symmetry, and harmonious relations, have their principle within the nature of our mind. But the idea of their application to the art of building is so far from being a necessary property to the practice of this art, that no other people has taken this application to the same point and to the same perfection than the Greeks. Such indeed, was the intimacy of the relationship between the useful and the beautiful among them, that if one were to consider their architecture from the point of view of need, one would conclude that no other architecture bears its imprint more visibly; and if one were to examine it from the point of view of beauty and pleasure, one would be tempted to think that it never knew the law of necessity or need.

One must admit that such a happy alliance could have never taken place – and in fact, we do not see that it has occurred elsewhere – for so rare must be this correct combination of the elements of necessity and pleasure in the works of men, or in their senses and qualities. It is from this accord that *art* in Greece was born. Since then, the discordance of these two elements has resulted in the deterioration of its principles and taste, according to whether some causes, which cannot be accounted for in this article, gave a particular superiority to pleasure, that is to say decoration, over the system of order and the fundamental

reason for original types upon which are based the rules of architecture.

Indeed, every *art* must have rules that maintain the limits within which it can freely exercise its activities without repressing genius. But one can imagine that as long as these rules do not rest on a more solid foundation than that of arbitrary examples and authorities, either of the masters or of a blind routine, and as long as they are not based on a perfect accord between pleasure and necessity, their ineffectiveness will bring about their discredit.

AUTHORITY Taken in a figurative sense, this word, when applied either to the exercise of certain professions, to scholarly research, or to the works of the mind and the fine arts, designates generally the power exerted either by laws and customs, the examples of great writers, or the works whose merit is evidenced by the suffrage of all times and all nations.

In matters of taste especially, and with respect to those works which by their very nature escape the material judgment of measurements and calculation, it always seemed that in order to either prevent or appreciate disagreements, no other judge, no other regulator was found save the *authority* of the universal evidence of the past, or that of an uninterrupted succession of approvals transmitted to posterity by the most enlightened people in every nation.

In matters of art, and especially the arts of design, *authority*, as we just defined it, has always been regarded as inevitable, and even as useful as it is natural. If *authority* were to be banished, if it were that the student, sequestered from the past within the present, had no knowledge of the preceding works, one would understand how art, having to always be started anew, would remain in an eternal infancy. Doubtless, the use of *authority* has been, and can always be abused; but the spirit of routine, which could result from this abuse, warns us of one thing: that in this matter as in all others, there are some measures to be taken:

Sunt denique fines
Quos ultra citraque nequit consistere verum.

As soon as one speaks of *authority* in matters of art, that is to say the examples of the past, it is clear that the *authority* in question, above any other, is that of the antique.

Now it is precisely against this *authority* that the spirit of the moderns has revolted. It seems to the eyes of those who are informed by all that they observe in the progress and perfection of the knowledge of physical nature and natural sciences, that the same progression must take place in the arts that imitate nature. They think, and with good reason, that since ancient *authorities* in matters of science, are quite often found to be but errors, the same must consequently apply to the arts of genius and the works of imitation.

In the entry *antique*, we have treated at length the causes of this confusion between the arts and the sciences. Therefore, we shall not repeat here that there is an absolute opposition between their natures, and hence, a necessary opposition between their progress and their course. Thus, it so happened that as the *authority* of antiquity diminished for the sciences, it especially increased for the arts of design.

But, some may ask, if these arts find in material nature the visible models of the beautiful and the true, then why is the artist in need of *authorities* to guide him in his imitation? Why have a guide for one who has eyes?

Without a doubt, *authority* would have never entered the practice of these arts, if material beauty was not very closely linked to intellectual and moral beauty, and was for this very reason subject to the variation of opinions depending on time and place. But that which necessitated the intervention of *authority* in the study of the arts, more than any other reason, can be deduced from their nature and their history.

Experience, in fact, has proven that since no perfection is without finality – the very word perfection indicates a final point for each quality – and since art arrives at this point through universal consent, then, it finds in its very perfection the cause of its decline. When nature finds herself somewhat surpassed by art in a work of imitation, one observes how easy, and we even add, how necessary it is for the work of art to replace

that of nature among students. And herein lies, without a doubt, the danger of *authority*.

But if in a certain state of society and civilization, some particular causes were to interpose themselves between nature as an easily studied model, and the studying artist, would it not be inevitable, that in attaching himself to the works in which the laws of nature are written, he will adopt the easier study instead of the increasingly difficult one of an original which is out of his reach? From here derives the necessity and the strength of *authority* in the arts.

Reason and taste agree, however, that on this issue, there are some measures to be preserved. Indeed, one condemns, without a doubt, this excess of *authority* which implies an indiscriminate approval of everything; because by uncritically accepting or excluding anything, this excess will go as far as encroaching on the very rights of reason: our first guide. The important characteristic of *authority* is to assure us that this guide will not lead us astray.

What is known as taste in matters of art is naught else but the reason behind the feeling. It is for taste to establish the idea of the true and the beautiful, and to develop their principles and their effects in the masterpieces of art, in an often clearer and more intelligible manner than even the works of nature.

But, without a doubt, if there is an art that fears the mobility of opinions and the caprices of the spirit of change more than all the others, it is architecture. It is also in this art that a well understood *authority* can exert some fortunate effects. Having physically no visible model in nature, architecture bases her imitation only on an analogy with the works that agreeably affect our mind through the mediation of sight. Therefore, architecture cannot study enough the impressions produced by sight. Since essential beauty cannot be materially determined in architecture, the secret of this art must be to judge the beautiful first by that which pleases, but later, by that which must please.

Obviously, this method is somewhat dangerous. One could effectively run the risk of losing oneself in consulting the impressions of the few instead of those of the many, as well as the influence of a temporary and local taste instead of the perpetual and universal assent of enlightened people. Of course, the beautiful and the true in architecture would cease being subjects of controversy if one could consult all nations. The point about which all peoples at all times will agree, will indubitably be the one that will establish once and for all, the art, its principles and its effects. But how could one hope for such a formal and positive reunion of all peoples? Short of this, reason suggests that one ought to be content with either the plurality of tastes or opinions, or with the weight and the importance of suffrages. It is therefore agreed that what has been approved in the largest number of countries by the largest number of people, and especially the ones most enlightened and whose taste is the most cultivated, must prevail over the preferences of ignorant countries, centuries or people, and over the limited examples of local customs, or the ephemeral novelties of a futile and fleeting taste.

Such is the *authority* of the antique in architecture. Having been tried by the critique of many centuries and nations, the works of the Greeks have become a kind of equivalent to nature. All sorts of novelties and attempts at change have tried in vain to ravish Greece's sceptre in the realm of teaching and the *authority* of examples. No one has as yet avoided this *authority* without incurring the scorn of the following ages.

However, the *authority* of the antique itself requires a wise critique in the appreciation of such a great number of works that were produced with varying benefits, under many kinds of influences. The study and the imitation of antiquity in architecture will have to defend themselves against two kinds of excess, which are equally prejudicial to her *authority*. The first is the scorn of innovators, the other is the blind esteem of some fanatical zealots, who, without discrimination as to time and place, kind and number, admit everything as a model.

Naturally, the weight and the importance of *authorities* will depend on the subjects for or against which they will be invoked, that is to say, on their application, less in the details than in what constitutes the principles of art. Now among these principles, those that will be most exposed to attacks will be those that one calls principles of beauty, of imitative systems, of propriety and taste.

BIZARRE In architecture, this term designates the notion of a taste that is contrary to recognized principles, an affected search for extraordinary forms whose only merit consists in novelty itself, hence its flaw.

In ethics, one distinguishes between the capricious and the *bizarre*. The first seems to be the child of the imagination, the second, the result of character. Caprice manifests in tastes, the *bizarre* in moods. Caprice conveys ridicule, the *bizarre* conveys unbearability. Caprice implies lightness, and seems to be but an unfortunate habit that can be corrected; the *bizarre* betrays a flaw that cannot be changed. Finally, the capricious is not the *bizarre*, but it is difficult for the *bizarre* not to be capricious at the same time.

This moral distinction can apply to architecture, and to the different effects of the capricious and the *bizarre* that occur in this art. Capricious taste is one that makes an arbitrary choice in known forms, tending to imprudently distort the principles of art; *bizarre* taste is one that scoffs at them, intending to subvert any principle through the use of extraordinary forms. The first entails the idea of inconsequentiality, and implies the forgetfulness of rules; the second is a result of reflection, and declares an intent to despise rules or to make new ones. Caprice produces a childish game whose consequences can, however, be dangerous; the *bizarre* engenders a system that is destructive of order and of the forms dictated by nature. Caprice, in general, affects only the details; the *bizarre* attacks the constitutive forms of art. Misuses derive from caprice (*See* MISUSE); while vices are the children of the *bizarre*. Caprice laid down some of the laws that custom and the respect for antiquity have consecrated in ornament; indeed, the greatest artists, the most splendid centuries in art, and art itself, experienced its power. The *bizarre* is found neither in antiquity nor among the great modern masters. Thus, caprice could have occasionally manifested in the *bizarre*, but the latter assuredly never appears in the former. Vignola and Michelangelo have sometimes admitted some capricious details in their architecture; whilst Borromini and Guarini were the masters of the *bizarre* genre. If the *bizarre* in morals bears many of the characteristics that one observes in the arts, and if both emanate from the same principle, then one must note that the consequences of this principle differ as to the influence that they exert; in other words, as to the contagion of this influence. It should be noted that in morals, the *bizarre* is ordinarily a malady that afflicts few individuals; whereas in the arts, one may say that it is an epidemic.

This is explained to us by the two general principles that produce the *bizarre* in the realm of art, especially amongst the moderns.

The first of these principles seems to us to reside within the nature or constitution of modern nations; the other, seems to depend in particular, on the passions and interests which exert their influence on artists.

Regarding the first principle, one cannot help but recognize within the character of this modern malady, a particular tendency to be weary of better things, and a disgust that derives from the very excess of abundance. Indeed, it is from the midst of riches and indulgences that develops this malaise that poisons simple pleasures, rendering the simple beauties of nature insipid, and calling forth the affectedness of a corrupt taste.

Without citing the other arts as proof, one observes that modern Italy, through the revolutions undergone by her architecture, offers us the most striking example of what was just advanced. Masterworks of all sorts abounded in Rome, where, in the multiplicity of her monuments, the artist's eye revelled in lessons and models. There, the genius of the ancients that was resurrected by the Bramantes, the Sangallos, the Perruzzis, and the Vignolas, joined theory – which only addresses the mind – to the most visually eloquent practice. Who would have doubted that such a confluence of causes should have maintained taste in its purity, or at least preserve it from great deviations. Yet, the following

century was that of the *bizarre*. Some say, that the rapid perfection of art brings its downfall. Genius seemed exhausted by its own efforts; the eyes tired of simple forms, simplicity became known as monotony, wisdom became coldness, attachment to rule seemed sterile, and innovation replaced invention.

The works produced under the spell of this harmful principle are well known. Could it be true then, that the very perfection that genius brings to its works in certain periods, can become the principle of the harm that succeeds the good? This may be a paradox: we do not believe that the true, the good, and the just can be the causes of their contraries; and we hold that if a similar effect could result from the succession of good

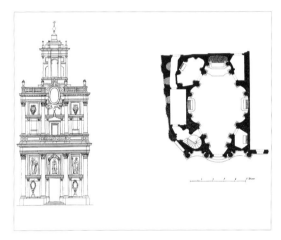

Fig. 26. San Carlo alle Quattre Fontane, F. Borromini. From: A.C. Quatremère de Quincy, *Histoire de la vie et des ouvrages des plus célèbres architectes*, J. Renouard, Paris, 1830

and evil, then it is neither direct nor immediate, and must derive from another less apparent and much more active cause.

We find this cause of the *bizarre* to reside in the immoderate taste for novelty which was introduced among modern nations by a dominant spirit of commerce. Its influence could only have been harmful to all the works of the mind and to the arts of design. Coming from mercantile interest, the habit of changing and renewing everything as promptly as possible in a multitude of objects of necessity or pleasure, need or luxury, could not but spread to the arts, whose models, however, can never change. It is true that these models are unchanging; but what can always change is the taste of those that produce them, and the fancy of those who judge imitation in these models. More than any other art, architecture is exposed to the influences of the spirit of fashion, because its true model does not strike the eye with a tangible form. In fact, being in a state of continuous mobility in the midst of society, could the art of embellishing houses and edifices have more permanent principles than the one that inhabits these buildings?

Thus, architecture summoned the help of the *bizarre*, which, in turn, always follows fashion, or hides behind it, because a reciprocal need unites them. Fashion would soon see its powers recede if the *bizarre* were to cease rejuvenating its lure. Their union assures their authority. The one is in charge of inventing, the other lends its charms to invention. The secret of the *bizarre* is known: it proceeds by exaggeration; it takes hold of the senses through excess. It is through the extraordinary that it gains votes. The *bizarre* offers the most incommodious forms and the most unusual contours and strange dispositions to fashion, for whom everything is good as long as there is constant change. Having entered architecture, the *bizarre* found ample material to develop its resources.

Doubtless, the arts of design, and especially architecture, would have protected themselves from the caprice of fashion and the eccentricities of the *bizarre*, had they found within the stability of morals, within the permanence of protective institutions, and the influence of a great number of necessities, among the moderns as well as the ancients, a veritable safeguard against the exigencies of the spirit of commerce, and particularly against this luxury of vain puerility which has nowadays become the principal nutriment for artists. Well, one can see that the meagre spirit of luxury cannot produce anything great. Everything then tends toward miniaturization according to the whim of an infinite number of small fantasies. Consequently, there was no greatness in artistic enterprises; and without grandeur in the cause, there can be none in the effects.

We have indicated one of the sources of the *bizarre* that affect the normal working conditions in the fine arts, within the general principle of the nature and constitution of modern nations. Let us indicate in a few words, the particular principle whose effects especially influence artists, driving them to the *bizarre*.

This principle is one that produces a false love of glory, and causes contempt for the beaten paths of predecessors. In every endeavour, the merit of originality is rare; and as originality always made the reputation of those who attained it, an ignorant vanity can easily convince that in order to have eyes fixed upon oneself, one must attract notice no matter the cost. Consequently, by confusing singularity with originality, the ambitious artist will wrongly neglect the study of the great models which is the true initiation to that of nature. Under the pretext that most followers remain behind their chosen master through servile imitation, we see him severing the link with all rules, holding all examples with disdain, casting himself in the most ridiculous innovations, and replacing the servitude of a faint-hearted routine by the excesses of a *bizarre* licence.

Let us agree: the more masterpieces multiply, the more difficult it is to produce seemingly new ones, and the more costly it is for vanity to recognize so many superior ones. Self-esteem prevails upon the envy that results from the prejudice toward the great credit that predecessors enjoy. We become accustomed to believing, and we strive to persuade others, that the respect that makes many disciples bow in front of predecessors, is naught but faint-heartedness. From here derives the mania for paradoxes and sophisms in literature. From here derives the reign of the *bizarre* in the arts, and especially in the art of architecture whose works do not have a visibly tangible and material model in nature.

Thus, it is sometimes a false love of glory and distinction, and other times a faulty system of study, and other times still, a principle of envy, that drive artists to carve strange paths for themselves that can only lead to the *bizarre*.

In fact, in order to distinguish themselves from great architects whose renown troubles them, these innovators entirely pervert the principles, the means and the ends of their art. For them, the genius of architecture no longer resides in observing a type consecrated by nature herself, in the varieties of character proper to each subject, in proportions and their relationship to our understanding, in the accord between forms and the impressions of our senses, and other knowledge of this sort. The resulting effects of all these accords would be too simple for the *bizarre* mind that holds them in disdain.

To the contrary, we will see, or better still, we have seen the *bizarre* place invention in strange and forced combinations, in the most difficult relationships to understand, in the most incoherent mixture of forms, in the configurations nearest the impossible, and in the most discordant of assemblages.

BOLDNESS This word is best defined by its opposite, which is timidity. There are few cases in the moral order of things where timidity is not a flaw, for it is often either an effect or a sign of weakness.

Contrariwise, *boldness* is almost always a praiseworthy quality, for it characterizes the strength from which it often derives; and as strength is the quality most pursued by man, it is needless to ask why he is inclined toward *boldness*.

If *boldness* is one of the characters or the effects of strength, then this quality, as with all other good qualities, is in itself significant as long as it occupies this happy medium between the proper and the useful. But, as with all virtues, it often happens that *boldness* is travestied by false pretences or distorted by exaggerations.

Accordingly, there is a feigned, simulated or fictitious *boldness*, one that presents that which in reality it is not, and mimics the appearance of true boldness; thus, it is known as *vaingloriousness*. There is also a false or flawed *boldness*, one that transgresses propriety and reason; thus, it is known as *recklessness*.

As with all the other arts, architecture has her natural and legitimate *boldness*, and she is exposed to the folly of vaingloriousness, and the vices of recklessness.

There is, in fact, a feigned *boldness* in the art of building; it consists in concealing the points of support, or searching within the stonework for

abutments that sometimes hide the means of solidity, while at other times giving the appearance of weakness to that which is strong. Many stone stairs have been constructed during the last century, according to the procedures of a feigned *boldness*. The secret of this kind of fiction is none else but the system of pendentives or squinches which befits the illusions of a *feigned boldness*, being a game that produces deceiving appearances. Such, for example, is the game that fakes the appearance of a wall by drawing all the joints. One may also classify within the means of *feigned boldness*, the use of iron and reinforcements that are foreign to true construction, and which hold finials and brackets in mid air, as in Gothic vaults, thus causing astonishment on the part of those

Fig. 27. Church of the Invalides, Paris, J.-H. Mansart. From: A.C. Quatremère de Quincy, *Histoire de la vie et des ouvrages des plus célèbres architectes*, J. Renouard, Paris, 1830

who are uninformed as to the ease with which these so-called difficulties are built. Thus, a feigned *boldness* is one that often mimics that which is flawed, without having the merit of building that which is difficult.

False boldness is known as *recklessness* in architecture, and one knows not where a vain pretension to skilfulness will lead the architect. Suffice it here to say that false *boldness* consists in building disproportionate masses over weak foundations, or in economizing on lateral supports in order to produce a delusive lightness, or in supporting vaults with thin members, or in imagining complicated compositions in order to have the so-called merit of producing new effects, etc. There is also a false *boldness* that harms judgment even when solidity is not compromised, as when several masses are stacked one on top of the other, or when height is taken for grandeur, or when oppositions are taken for contrasts, and variety for multiplicity, etc.

What has just been said about *feigned* and *false boldness*, suffices to give an idea of the true *boldness* in architecture; for to say that it must not be a game nor an excess, implies that it must rest on reality, which means a constantly evident reason in composition, and a tangible solidity in execution. No *boldness* exists if it does not rest on one or the other of these conditions, and in following them, architecture will imitate nature in the impressions made on our intelligence and our senses by the grandeur of her works. Now nature

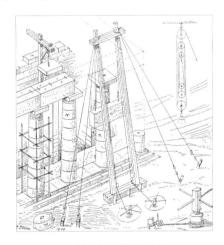

Fig. 28. Temple building.
From: Josef Durm, *Die Baukunst der Grieschen*,
A. Kröner Verlag, Leipzig, 1910

teaches the artist that the impression that most affects man is that of *grandeur* combined with *strength*.

Grandeur, that is to say *boldness* in dimension, is certainly that which most surely evokes in us the feeling of admiration. We delight in seeing pyramidal volumes rise up to the sky, we delight in vast interiors, immense vaults, and enormous columns supporting enormous entablatures. Any building that demands great efforts, great expense, and great perseverance, is sure to receive our consent.

Hence the necessity in architecture and for the architect to establish inventions and compositions, in plans and elevations, that produce this simplicity which is a necessary companion of

grandeur, and whose principle accrues in confidence in as much as the means that produce its effect are less apparent. This is why isolated columns reflect true *boldness* more than coupled ones. Generally speaking, any composition where unity prevails is also one that helps execution (or construction) to produce the impression of *boldness*.

If *boldness* in composition and in invention is necessary in the art of building in order for us to obtain the impressions that we seek, then the science of building is no less essential for the architect to regulate his imagination within the conceptions through which he seeks to astonish us. *Boldness* in construction will be the object of the observer's delight only when his mind is assured of the building's solidity and durability. For example, the economy of materials, in any construction, can only produce the delight that results from the lightness of structural supports, when one is certain that this economy is not prejudicial to their stability. There are some very skilful sections whose flaw resides precisely in concealing the secret of their artifice from the observer, thus painfully affecting the senses by the idea of danger that derives from the appearance of frailty.

Pleasing though *boldness* may be, when it is appropriately executed, it seems, however, that this is one of these qualities that should not be pursued too far. One may even advance that nothing should be built with the intention of appearing bold. *Boldness* may be the natural outcome of certain compositions, but it should not be their principle or their motive.

According to moralists, *boldness* in duty and in conduct does not consist in needlessly looking for danger, but rather in knowing how to confront it with reason. True *boldness*, according to them, is not one that makes a game out of scorning life, but rather, one who knows how to make a duty out of sacrificing it, when needs be. The same applies to architecture. Whether it is grand, simple, unified and strong, *boldness* will produce its effect without unduly searching for it. A *boldness* that is pursued runs the risk of becoming vaingloriousness or recklessness.

BUILDING (ART OF) This expression designates a different notion from the one understood by the word architecture, although *building* is encompassed by architecture, since all the ideas that it encloses, all the images and impressions that it produces, and all that it expresses intelligibly to the mind through the intermediary of sight, could not exist without the materials that embody its inventions. However, analysis shows that each of these expressions offers a different meaning. Thus, the *art of building* designates the material part of architecture.

What is said of the *art of building*, in relation to architecture, could be said of another synonymous term, namely, *construction*; but as with all synonyms, this term has its own nuance of meaning.

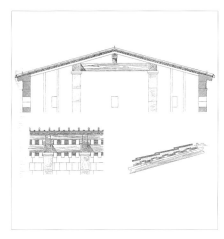

Fig. 29. Arsenal in Piraeus.
From: Josef Durm, *Die Baukunst der Grieschen*,
A. Kröner Verlag, Leipzig, 1910

This term comprises a higher significance than the one that applies to the material part of the work, and it should be used only to designate that part of architecture which depends on stereotomy, the calculation of forces, thrusts and resistances in large buildings, and all the processes of mechanics. (*See* CONSTRUCTION).

Following this analysis, the *art of building*, in each century, in each country, and regarding every work, depends on the diverse use of materials and processes necessitated by local requirements. In some countries where stone is rare and wood common, the *art of building* merges with that of carpentry, and consists of small materials that mortar combines with posts and crossbeams. Elsewhere, where both stone and large

forests were lacking, the *art of building* managed to form artificial stones, known as bricks. These bricks were first used in a crude state, after being well dried; subsequently the *art of building* found a way to render brick as solid as stone by firing it.

Demanding difficult extractions of materials, or expensive means of transport, or great effort in cutting and installing, the *art of building* in stone seems to have been adopted late even in nations where quarries abound. However, the relationships between the most ancient peoples, as well as the vestiges of their monuments, exhibit a particular taste for the use of enormous materials, and thus a great facility in their use. We do not know how long it took them to attain the knowledge that this *art of building* demands or presupposes.

Finally, it is evident that the *art of building* consists uniquely in that material part, which is for architecture what the more or less rough block is, no matter the material, for the art of sculpture.

CAPRICE To give an accurate and clear idea of *caprice* in the arts, and especially in architecture, we could do no better than consult the definitions given by philosophy in the realm of morals.

So we find that in morals, the word *caprice* is given to every desire that is devoid of reason, and is but a product of an imagination that cannot sustain it. Similarly, we maintain that in architecture *caprice* designates any invention, any unnecessary form that is not justified by the nature of things, and the reasons behind propriety.

We find that in morals *caprice* is the taste for something that befits neither our character nor our comportment, and cannot therefore occupy our attention for long. In architecture, *caprice* is a taste for all kinds of details and forms that are foreign to the constitutive elements of this art; and, since they are devoid of a rational basis, they cannot last.

In the word *bizarre*, we tried to establish the difference in idea between this word or that which it expresses, and the meaning of the word *caprice*. Here, we shall add that one reason for this confusion – even though the two words are far from being synonyms – is that very often and very naturally, we find on the one hand that the bizarre can derive from *caprice* and, on the other, that *caprice* can be covered by the *bizarre*, just as the small is included in the large.

If architecture was subject only to the laws of necessity, if she was limited only to the exigencies of solidity in construction and commodity in the disposition of buildings, then, without a doubt, *caprice* could never have found a way of creeping in. The measure of reason became for her a rule of necessity. However, if architecture were to stay enclosed within the circle of necessity, then she would have remained among the industrial arts. One can easily imagine what would have become of the art of building without knowledge of the virtue of imitation, the principle of proportion, or the charm of decoration.

Imitative virtue, in architecture, does not designate the property that other arts have of assimilating their work to the material reality of their models; but rather the intellectual and moral faculty of appropriating the laws and the combinations of nature, enabling architecture to act in her works as nature herself proceeded in all her creations. Well, one of the most important points of this imitation consists in what must be called the association of pleasure and necessity.

Almost all nations tried to realize this alliance. But the Greeks, being endowed with a moderate temperament that is equally distant from the extremes, have, better than any other people, imitated nature in this mysterious union whose principles and effects they applied to their archi-tecture. They understood that necessity and pleasure should be made so dependent on each other, establishing such a correlation, that the forms of necessity borrowed the appearance of pleasure, and those of pleasure appeared as if dictated by necessity; that the agreeable always appeared necessary, and the necessary always agreeable. This double disguise is the secret of Greek architecture. No other architecture suspected it. This union rests on a fortunate equilibrium that cannot be established in all societies, or in all climates, and is prone to an easy rupture.

It is in the nature of man, in fact, to misuse everything, but especially pleasure. Now, it is well known that the misuse of all sorts of pleasures is precisely responsible for these meretricious tastes called *caprices*. Similarly, in architecture, what is known as *caprice*, is naught but the misuse of the pleasing part of this art.

If we did not err in calling misuse in architecture *caprice*, if we knew what constitutes this pleasure, where it applies and the limits of its application, we would also come to know the nature of this *caprice*, its distinctive marks, and from whence it proceeds.

It is known that one distinguishes three kinds of pleasure in the art of architecture: the first resides more particularly in the domain of intelligence, and results from the harmony of proportions; the second comes from imitative instinct, and derives from the comparisons and correlations that the mind enjoys; the third can be more particularly called sensuous, since it addresses sight and comprises the domain of ornament.

§ I If the realm of pleasure were to have an authority that is proportionate to the source from which it emanates, and the effects that it must produce, then the pleasure resulting from proportions would be the highest pleasure, and the one whose principles should be more religiously respected; however, this is the principle that is most attacked and misappreciated. The reason for this is that there is nothing in all the rules of architecture that submits to mathematical evidence, nothing that the spirit of paradox[9] cannot negate. Yet this disadvantage is one that makes architecture an art; for she would cease being an art if everything were to submit to the test of the ruler and the compass. It is on this issue, however, that the false genius, that is to say the one of innovation, attacks architecture. Agreeing on principle, the true genius, or the genius of the true in architecture, admits the combined accordance between variety and the system of unity – as in nature – whence results the pleasure of proportions. It must have happened that *caprice*, or the misuse of pleasure, succeeded in many cases in prevailing over the very nature of the system of proportion, a system that is subject to many modifications, which, as with exceptions, serve to confirm the rule.

From this influence of *caprice* over the applications of variety to the forms of architecture, derived the changes whose least drawback is their uselessness, but whose principal danger is to entail more grievous changes that cause the upheavals of the bizarre. Thus, since the system of proportion in architecture does not have an infallible regulator, as the one found in sculpture for example; and since, in order to accommodate a great number of customs, architecture had to place the pleasure produced by variety in the first rank among these customs, *capriciousness* concluded that the more variety is produced, the more pleasure is increased. From here derived a great number of small licences in the general correlations of outline, in the proportions of the orders, in the useless multiplication of small parts, and many other variations that abuse the pleasure of variety, and serve to destroy the harmony of proportions and this accordance between unity and variety, upon which rests their system.

§ II The second kind of pleasure that we experience in architecture is that of comparison that the mind enjoys in every artistic genre, between that which is the model, and that which becomes its imitation. This pleasure belongs especially to these arts that have a tangible and visible example in nature. Architecture as we have seen (*See* ARCHITECTURE), by adopting the primitive construction in wood as a formal type, adopted also another, less material type, one that resides in the very spirit and system to which nature subordinated all her creations. It is by virtue of this application that architecture was assimilated to the other arts. The imitation of the primitive types of carpentry, soon became for architecture the theme or the manner of another kind of imitation of nature, which consists in making as she makes.

As a result of this spirit of imitation, the material model became, up to a certain point, the motif rather than the tangible object of a copy that had to answer to the propriety of a more elevated order. From here derives this imitation called metaphorical. Hence this more ingenious metamorphosis that disguises the imitated object of necessity under the veil of delight, which, by uniting the feeling of the useful or the necessary to that of pleasure, leaves he who does not know the secret of this alliance in doubt as to which of the two preceded or followed the other.

Thus, it is upon the association of necessity and pleasure that rests the principal imitative virtue of architecture; and herein resides also the source of pleasing comparisons that this double imitation procures to the eyes and the mind.

This is where the misuse of the pursuit of pleasure develops, thus constituting, as stated earlier, one of the principal characteristics of *caprice*.

Yes, the moderns have often misunderstood what constitutes the foundation of architectural imitation. First, they distorted it by separating one of its elements from the other, and then by abstracting its principal basis, and by making the pleasurable predominate over the useful. Having no longer necessity but only pleasure as a basis, they consequently added the unsubstantiality of a fantastical imitation as an aim to their inventions. Finally, when this misuse of pleasure no longer had necessity as a point of reference, it engendered what one calls *caprice* in architecture, that is to say, the application of ideas, forms, parts, and ornamental details about which one is at a loss to explain the principle and justify the use.

§ III We distinguished in architecture a third kind of pleasure: the one which actually addresses more especially and preferably the eyes; the one that embraces the domain of ornament.

Ornament in architecture, as we shall see (*See* ORNAMENT), can comprise two divisions: the first depends on the imitative system of the primitive types of the material model, whose presence – modified by art – one is forced to recognize in the building's profile, in the porticoes, the triglyphs, the metopes, the mutules, the torii, etc. The second applies to the essential members of accessory objects that have been borrowed from plants, leaves, from diverse productions of nature, or from more or less conventional signs.

The first part is subject only to the imitative propriety of type, and not to a scrupulous copy of forms which does not comprise the free imitation spoken of here. The second is linked to sculpture, and depends on an application in which art can, more or less, faithfully reproduce the objects of its imitation, where the feeling of pleasure seems to be the dominant one.

One must therefore acknowledge that this third kind of pleasure, in other words that of ornament in architecture, seems to have a less intimate relationship with *necessity*, consequently allowing *caprice* more influence.

However, it is fitting to observe that the Greeks, among whom the execution and the application of ornament in architecture were born, knew how to justify the use of ornament through a certain order of ideas and requirements that seemed to render them necessary. Indeed one could consider from many points of view that ornament was for them, if not a kind of hieroglyphic writing as in Egypt, then a kind of emblematic writing capable of evoking a certain order of ideas, of awakening all sorts of feelings through conventional images and, finally, of speaking through the intermediary of sight to a host of affections of the mind. Ornament must surely have had the virtue, which is sometimes found among the moderns, of indicating or rendering evident the purpose of many a building. (*See* ORNAMENT).

One must admit, in truth, that it did not take long for the interests of taste and pleasure to take hold of this arbitrary mode of writing. It was through the use of ornament, without a doubt, that *caprice*, which is only moved by the interest for pleasure, was able to erase from memory this part of utility that opposed the arbitrary and unreasoned use of the elements of ornament.

If the power of *caprice* explains this degeneration of ornament, as well as this separation that isolated it entirely from the demands of necessity, this separation and this isolation are best placed in order to elucidate the nature, the power and the effects of *caprice*.

CAPRICES The preceding article considered *caprice* in its abstract meaning, in the faulty and defective implications of the word, rather than the detailed applications to objects or forms through which these faults or defects are manifest.

If one were to enumerate here, all the kinds of *caprice* introduced into architecture by a foolish love for novelty, then one would certainly produce an article considerably lengthier than the preceding one. My aim here is not to present a useless and insipid review of these *caprices*. I shall confine myself to containing them within a general division, leaving it for everyone to include, as they wish, all those that will be omitted for lack of space.

Thus, it seems to me that the numerous *caprices* that one encounters in architecture can be classified into three categories, which I call: *caprices of construction, caprices of plan or disposition, and caprices of decoration or ornament*.

1° *Caprices of construction* are all those games of vain boldness which the builder, in order to show a useless and sometimes dangerous knowledge, imposes on the sight of an ignorant multitude. The pretended marvel of this sort of construction very often consists in disguising resting points through the use of irregular, and thus faulty, stonecutting; and sometimes, which is even worse, in using a hidden mechanism of armature that is foreign to any good construction.

One can affirm that the builders of antiquity never allowed themselves these kinds of *caprice*. It is true that the art of stonecutting, which the moderns call *stereotomy*, was sufficiently unknown for the ancient builders to even suspect its advantageous possibilities. This art has truly become very useful in regions whose materials are lacking in span and strength, and where certain means of industry, when used with some reserve, can compensate for the drawbacks of nature. It is here, however, that one discovers one of the principal causes of the *caprice* that multiplied in construction.

In fact, it did not take long for stereotomy to be misused. Soon, that which was but a resource of necessity, became the game of a vain skill. A childish ostentation of gratuitously vanquished difficulties came to consider the simple processes of an ordinary and easy construction as unworthy of a skilled man; thus, he wanted to build only that which is difficult, and the most beautiful construction was the one judged most audacious.

From here derived these numerous *caprices* of stereotomy, where the builder, moved by a principle that is contrary to that of the ancients, applied himself only to erasing the appearance of solidity; from here derived these bizarre vault sections, these elliptical and eccentric bends; from here derived these strange combinations in the stair sections and many other parts of edifices where *caprice* usurped the place of reason.

Thus, reason and taste concur in condemning these suspended ramps formed in such a menacing manner, and all these skilfully frightening constructions where one enters only on faith. Reason and taste will also be contemptuous of this charlatanism of means that leads one to believe in an apparent difficulty, which, in truth, does not exist. This refers to these deceits that lead one to believe, for example, that a vault is flatter than it actually is, that a projection is more dangerous, and that an overhang is bolder than it is supposed to be. All these *caprices* of construction, no matter how numerous, should be rejected and disavowed by the true art of architecture.

2° But the *caprices of plan* or disposition are no less numerous in modern architecture. In this regard, one can say that antiquity, without being entirely exempt from any reproach, still offers us the example of reserve and moderation. Concerning building plans, there are some differences to be noted between the art of the ancients and that of the moderns. The principal one relates to what one must call the regularity of execution and the wisdom of composition. One may find more of the former among the moderns, and more of the latter among the ancients. The reason is, it seems to us, that among the ancients architecture was a practice, whilst for quite a long time, architecture among the moderns, consisted more than one thinks in the art of drawing. If this is true, then one sees that in practice the architects of antiquity could easily commit irregularities in detail, but only with great difficulty could they fall into these *caprices* of plan and disposition, which are but a game for one who draws architecture.

This explains how these capricious combinations of forms, contours and mixtilinear plans, came to be considered as works of genius. It was then that the art of plans became like that of marquetry: an assemblage of lines in which the renderer's pencil aimed at nothing but producing plans that had never been seen before.

Now, what should have become and what in fact became of all the elevations that were obliged to correspond in their compositions to all the *caprices* of a plan that fragmented all forms and decomposed any kind of reasoned system, is well known. It is obvious from which school we just drew the notions and the examples of *caprices of plan* and disposition (for example, Borromini).

3° We still have to discuss the *caprices of ornament and decoration*.

Since ornament – as we said elsewhere, and as we shall repeat again – rests on two bases: the imitation of the types of primitive construction, and allegory, this division can establish some tangible rules in this regard, and determine the limits beyond which *caprice* begins.

The part of architectural ornament or decoration that derives from the imitation of types, cannot under any pretext lend itself to the *caprices* of variety. The forms of which we speak can receive ornaments that adapt to them, but they should not themselves be converted into ornaments properly speaking. For example, the parts that constitute the portico form its principal ornament; they can be enriched with diverse details that taste distributes to its liking on the members, but without altering their character. However, we have seen great architects, in the most imposing buildings in Florence, introduce *caprices* whose example was to later distort all of architecture. Baldinucci tells us in the life of the famous Buontalenti, that this Florentine architect was the first to introduce in the cornices and architraves, pediments whose rafters are turned upside down. Generally speaking, the representative parts of original types exclude any kind of variety that will convert them to arbitrary ornaments.

The same strictness, that is to say the exclusion of any kind of variety, cannot apply to this part of ornament which, as we have said, rests more or less on a system of allegory.

Doubtless it is desirable that the ornament of which we speak always retains, everywhere and in everything, the property of an intelligible writing whose signs more or less clearly express all the nuances of ideas, of character, demanded by the purpose of each building. In fact, as soon as the architect ceases to understand the meaning of the symbols or signs that he uses, everything here falls to chance, and it is here that all *caprices* triumph. When the artist is deficient in this intelligence, one always has the right to demand of him that he at least consults visual pleasure and general harmony. Thus, an economical, just and agreeable distribution belong to the sole judgment of taste.

Caprices of ornament that taste hastens to proscribe are also those that transport decorative sculpture into the deliriums or dreams of the arabesque, thus presenting impossible assemblages or kinds of combinations whose lack of verisimilitude can only be forgiven to the brush; but the reality of the matter used by architecture disenchants and ridicules these *caprices*. Only painting knows, through the magic of colours and the lightness of its processes, how to give life to these productions of the imagination without really giving them a body.

Taste will also proscribe the use of grotesque heads in architecture, which seem to be naught but studies of all kinds of grimaces. The Florentines have been prolific in this kind of *caprice* which never fails to contradict the gravity of their architecture by the opposition of a repulsive caricature.

But the *caprices* of ornament consist also in a kind of arrangement of forms that are outside the ordinary measures of a legitimate variety. It is in this genre that Borromini and the numerous followers of his capricious manner, distinguished themselves. We are referring to these cartouches cut along a curved outline, to these festoons and foliages without a model in nature, to these fantastical concretions of shells, rocailles, shields, palms, and other paltry figures, which are the productions and bastardized imitations of inventions, themselves degenerations of a taste tolerated by reason and justified by fortunate uses. We shall say nothing more about these objects to which the appellation *caprice* would give too

much credit and which, for some time, have been treated with general disgust.

CHANGE OF PROPORTIONS It is an important question in architecture to know whether the architect is free to change or modify the proportions of objects, in order to remedy the errors of sight, and correct the apparent alteration produced on the forms of objects by their distance and siting; or if all the illusions produced by nature ought to be left to the effects of optics, relying on the eye's judgment to rectify them; or if art should seek to anticipate them, correct, or exaggerate them.

This question has occupied most architects who have reflected on their art, and many find themselves divided about it.

To be clear, I must first warn the reader that the question is not these *changes of proportions* of which the architect is the undeniable master, and which consist in augmenting or reducing the height, the projection, the diameter of members, cornices, or columns, depending on the situation in which these parts find themselves, and the character that the architect wants to express, and the effect that he wants to produce. All these *changes* have taste as sovereign arbiter.

The question is to know if the apparent alteration that perspective causes in the aspects of buildings can in fact be corrected, either by narrowing, inclining, or elongating, or *vice versa*, all the parts whose siting and form seem to change; and whether one may dispose them in such a manner that the effect of these *changes* is imperceptible.

This is what Vitruvius teaches about this question, thus giving rise to great disputes:

"Now whether this appearance is due to the impact of the images, or to the effusion of the rays from the eye, as the physicists hold, in either case it is obvious that the vision may lead us to false impressions.
Since, therefore, the reality may have a false appearance, and since things are sometimes represented by the eyes as other than they are, I think it certain that diminutions or additions should be made to suit the nature

or needs of the site, but in such fashion that the buildings loose nothing thereby."[10]

Perrault, who united practice and theory, seems on this point, to differ from Vitruvius. We shall relate the principal reasons upon which his opinion is founded, and which we have extracted from the seventh chapter of his *Ordonnance des cinq ordres*.[11]

"From the celebrated story of the two statues of Minerva made to be set in a very high place, of which one is claimed to be unsuccessful because its sculptor did not change its proportions, one gathers that it is difficult to open the eyes of those who claim that art must correct the errors of the senses; especially since, regarding the different aspects of buildings, architects consider the excellence of their art to reside in the *change* of proportion. Thus, it is agreed that colossal columns diminish less than small ones; that the entablatures placed atop these columns have a greater height, for fear of their appearing too light. If the elements that compose your architraves, your friezes, and your cornices are too high, then incline them; for without this, they will appear too narrow. If they are at the level of the eye, or slightly above, then raise them, for without this they will appear to have little projection. This advice derives from all the reasons that optics can furnish; however, these changes, which are regarded as very necessary, have not been applied in the most acclaimed buildings, and chance alone seems to have presided over their use. I will explain.
The columns of the Temple of Peace, those of the Pantheon's portico, those of the Campo Vaccino, and the Basilica of Antoninus, have no more diminution than those of the Temple of Bacchus, whose shaft measures only ten feet. Furthermore, the columns of the Temple of Faustina, of the portico of Septimius, the Baths of Diocletian and the Temple of Concord, whose shafts measure thirty and forty feet, have more diminution than the arches of Titus, Septimius, and Constantine, whose shafts measure only fifteen and twenty feet.
Raised soffits. It is said that this practice should be made in order to render apparent the projection of the members. 1° *when it is viewed*[12] *from a distance*: In the portico of the Pantheon, where the view can be very distant, the soffits are not raised, whereas they are in the interior of the temple, since the view is necessarily close; 2° *when the particular elements do not occur at a great height*: In the Theatre of Marcellus, the soffits of the second order are raised, but not in the first. In the Coliseum, the soffits are raised in all four orders, and in the Temples of Vesta and Bacchus, whose orders are of the smallest proportions, the soffits are not raised; 3° *when one is unable to give the elements in question their proper projections*: In the architrave of the Temple of Fortuna Virilis, the soffits of the fascias are raised, even though the size of their projections is unusually pronounced. As to the inclination of fascias, it is said that they should incline forward when a very close viewing causes them to be seen obliquely, or when it is necessary to make them appear large, after having reduced them in reality. The examples of antiquity oppose this maxim, because in all the monuments cited, the fascias incline backward, whether they have their proper proportions or not, in their highest or lowest elevations. One must admit, however, that antiquity itself offers examples of the changes that we oppose; but these examples strengthen our principle by the ill effect that they present. We cite the most remarkable one.
In the Pantheon, the axes of the gradually recessed squares of the vault, in the form of hollow pyramids, meet at five feet above the pavement in the middle of the temple, instead of converging toward the centre; and these axes are consequently not perpendicular to the base of the pyramid, as would have been necessary to preserve the symmetry. Thus, these hollow pyramids appear

from below and from the middle to be the same as if they were directed toward the centre of the vault, and if the viewer were lifted up to that point. But as soon as the viewer leaves the middle of the temple, the obliqueness of these axes and the discord of the symmetry become apparent. This effect is much more considerable to the eye than if these recesses had had a straight orientation, as they ought, with respect to the vault. The only disadvantage of this straight orientation is that a part of the lower steps of each pyramid would have been hidden by the height of the steps as one moves towards the wall, and that more steps would be visible the farther one moved from the centre. But should one complain if the nose hides one of the cheeks in a face seen in profile? Having learned from this poor success, and even though he had praised the *change* of proportions, Labaco did not apply it in the hollow pyramids of the vault of Saint Peter's,[13] although this temple's great elevation above the Pantheon adds considerably to the disadvantage caused by the depth of the first steps in hiding the treads of those that follow. He doubtless recognized that nothing is more customary than to observe parts that hide each other, and that the eye is used to adjusting the proportions of entire objects by the judgment that it makes of the size of a whole of which it views only a part; and that this judgment, in general, authorizes no change in proportions, and that it never fails to prevent our being deceived by the alterations and adverse effects which, we imagine, must be the result of distance and varying positions. Thus, any change is useless.

We demonstrate that change is flawed. Whoever knows the proportion that an entablature ought to have, does not fail to see that the architect did not build it larger than it should be with respect to the column, no matter the height. There is also nothing easier than to judge if a man at a high window has a larger head than usual.

As a result, and according to the principle which states that what is carried has a calculated rapport with what carries it, this entablature, whose mass is larger than it ought to be when compared to its supporting column, will always present a shocking sight; the same occurs if, in order to avoid a statue in a niche appearing to lean backwards, you were to incline it forward, my eye will always perceive it in this ungraceful position.

But can the eye, one must ask, judge the size of distant objects with perfect precision? My answer is that the eye achieves this judgment by comparison. Indeed, it suffices to compare the size of the entablature to the other parts of the building, to judge if this entablature is in an exact proportion. Distance does not prevent it from making this comparison, for since everything diminishes in the same degree, this cannot remove the eye's faculty of perceiving the augmentation given by the architect to a particular part. Of what use then is a *change* that produces no good effect except at a certain distance, and assumes the eye to be in a constant position? None, since this supposed situation is improbable.

Thus, I believe that there is no reason to distort proportions so that they do not appear distorted, or to render an object defective with the intention of correcting it. Far from being defects, the views produced by distance and siting reflect the natural and true state of things; to change them is to deform them. All that has been said, and all that can be said on this subject, is that it is not certain if distance makes proportions appear to be other than they actually are, that it is certain that the *change* of proportions is the visible distortion of this same proportion; and finally, that it is more dangerous that a proportion appears distorted when it truly is, than when it is not.

However, what is to become of the unanimous opinion held by all architects and founded on the authority of Vitruvius, who teaches this *change* and prescribes its rules?

How is it that for the two thousand years that this change has been given as a precept, it has not been examined? It appears that any discussion was deemed to be useless since Vitruvius had thus decided, and, submitting to his law without practising it, it was assumed that all ancient architects observed it, for a profound reason, in all the buildings that they created, and whose remains we contemplate with an admiration that makes us believe that they ceaselessly consulted optics in order to determine even the smallest parts. The cited examples indubitably demonstrate the contrary, since it is frequent that, within the same views, proportions appear different, while they appear to be the same within different views.

In general, there is within us a sense that corrects all the errors of the senses, and it is the one that one may call the sense of experience and customs; its task is to reflect on the actions of our exterior senses. It is this very sense that retraces for us the true form of objects, when their distance or siting makes them appear other than they are. The judgment of experience adding to the image apparent to the eye, the knowledge of things that it possesses, such as distance and the siting of its object, and the size of things which it compares, prevent these images from being mistaken the one for the other. In fact, the images of a spark and a piece of paper, when these objects are near, differ little from those of a star or a white wall, when these objects are distant; similarly, an oval and an oblong square seen obliquely from afar, have the same effect on our eye as a perfect circle or square when seen directly."

It is with hearing as with sight. There is also a feeling that makes us distinguish between the words of those near us who speak low, from the words of those far from us who speak loud, even if in both cases the sound is of a similar faintness; for even if one were able to imitate this faintness caused by distance, there is nevertheless a multitude of indications that convey the difference between the faintness of one or the other case.

It is the same in painting; where the hues that are lightened in order to feign the distance of objects cannot equally render the same effect that results from distance. Therefore, without our thinking of the rules of perspective, without our imagination expressly examining the reasons and the different effects of distance that depend on the narrowing of angles formed by visual lines and the faintness of the hues of objects, common sense incessantly attends to all these things, and observes all these occurrences; and if sometimes it is found to be lacking, then, it is a sure sign of its usual adequacy.

Therefore, to make indispensable the *change of proportions* suggested by Vitruvius as a precaution against the illusions that can be caused by distance and obliqueness, one must assume that whatever belongs to sight, depends only on the eye; which is not true, because at the same time sight also uses the judgment of common sense for correction, and it so happens that this judgment never fails, otherwise perspective and painting would always deceive. There is no more reason to assume that a circle is an oval when it is seen obliquely, than to assume that an oval is a circle when the oval is painted so as to appear circular.

These reasons, while insufficient to completely destroy those of Vitruvius in favour of the *change of proportions*, are nevertheless adequate enough to give this precept the limits that it needs. Vitruvius himself recognizes that a great deal of taste and knowledge are required to use this precept and, in my opinion, one encounters few cases where this maxim of the *change of proportions* can apply.

CHARACTER This word is the same in French as the Greek word *characteer*, which derives from the verb *charassein* (to engrave, to imprint) and signifies, in the proper meaning of the word, a mark, the distinctive sign of a particular object.

One could cite few words that are applicable to more objects in a metaphorical sense, but which are more often used in a figurative one. Indeed, it suffices to think of the infinite variety of distinctive signs which approximately marks all that is embodied in the material realm and all that is comprised within the variety of ideas in the intellectual world, to realize that no other word contains a larger number of applications than the word *character*, if it is indeed true that no object exists that is not endowed with a distinctive variety to a certain degree.

Ordinary parlance however, and more particularly that of all theories, teach us that the word and the idea of *character* are only applied to a certain kind or a certain number of distinctive signs, that is to say, to those that eminently hold the property of designating and distinguishing an object among many others that resemble it. For example, there is no physiognomy that does not have its more or less distinctive variety. However,

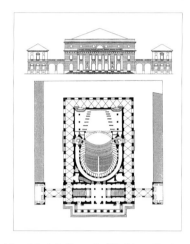

Fig. 30. Théâtre de l'Odéon, Paris.
From: Julien Guadet, *Éléments de la théorie de l'architecture*,
Librairie de la construction moderne, Paris, 1909

the word *character* is only applied to a small number of physiognomies, that is to say, those that are distinguished by some salient traits that remain engraved in one's memory.

The same can be said of all the physical properties whose innumerable levels could distinguish an infinite variety of material objects, as well as all moral qualities whose nuances differentiate in a more or less evident manner the labours of intelligence, the works of the mind, and the productions of the arts of imitation.

****

Having to confine ourselves here to these arts of imitation, and even more particularly to one of

them (architecture), we maintain that the use of the word *character*, as authorized by the usage of theory, does not indicate any distinction in a work of art irrespective of its measure or quality, or according to a vague and general sense, but rather a supereminent distinction that endows it with primary importance.

It seems to us that this superlative distinction is manifest in the works of which we speak here more especially under three principal and different expressions, which need to be preeminently explained. These expressions in the use of the word *character*, each presenting a particular meaning, will perhaps assist us in distinguishing the three different acceptations of this word and, consequently, the three kinds of qualities that it expresses.

1° One uses the word *character* in praising a work of art; for example, when one says that this work *has character*. One understands by this expression that this work, in its principle and its effects, in other words in its conception and execution, is endowed with qualities whose nature is expressed in the words *strength*, *might*, *size* and moral *loftiness*.

2° Another use of the word *character* is an expression similar to the first, although comprising quite a different idea as when a certain work is said to have *a character*. Now, far from the generic sense of the word, implying that the work has a distinctive mark, one must note here that, on the contrary, this work is distinguished by a special quality known particularly in the works of imitation as *originality*.

3° A third expression in the use of the word *character*, seems to us to indicate another distinctive quality, as when a work is said to have *its character*. It is evident that the possessive pronoun *its* indicates here an idea of property, understood in a different meaning from the banal and ordinary sense. Now this property is that of the ability that a work has, to convey to us its particular nature, and its purpose.

In resuming the three points of view according to which each work can be submitted to the theoretical analysis of the word *character*, we believe that the attempt to apply them to works of architecture could provide a sufficient summary of the vast notions that this matter comprises.

****

The first expression, consisting in a work *having character*, applies therefore to every art of building, to every monument of architecture endowed with the faculty of impressing the mind and the senses by the qualities of *strength* and *size*, whose expression can result only from the double principle of *unity* and *simplicity*. But history teaches that the same thing happened to these two principles as to other primary causes whose activity, development and duration are independent of people's wills and wishes. There were times propitious to the qualities of which we speak; such were those periods of civilization where feelings were unspoiled, where minds could conceive of only a small number of principal ideas and powerful means, and where for a lack of a more or less superfluous array of ancillaries, the necessary in architecture was centred in a reality of excessive solidity and an ambition for eternal durability.

This explains why the monuments of this first age of civilized societies are distinguished either by the use of enormous materials, or by the composition of colossal masses. It was under the sole influence of instinct, and in the absence of the methods and calculations of a refined science, that the primitive art of building impressed its works with this *character* of strength and energy. Only, following the development of knowledge with its economic methods and its abridging means, this character was no longer achieved.

But to this somewhat material cause, which compelled the art of early ages to seek the principal merit of monuments in strength and size, one must also add a moral cause which derives from the very principle of the mores and institutions of the time, that is to say, from the state of *simplicity* in the needs of the mind, and from the *unity* of the means that satisfy them.

It must be recognized that the more needs and desires multiply in a state of society, the more there is an increase on the part of private interests to seek small combinations which are no longer suitable to satisfy real needs, but to incessantly create new ones either in the physical or in the moral realm. Thus, the same cause begets them and multiplies them, while they all tend toward the same end, which is to satisfy the desire for novelty. Now at the time when the art of building excelled by the *character* of strength and size, we observe that this *character* was favoured by a general spirit in rapport with public mores. It seems that the expenses and the pleasures of architecture, instead of being subdivided on a small scale between a multitude of subordinate works, found themselves concentrated on a large scale within a small number of monuments that made the principal qualities of the art shine with much strength.

It is also clear, that such monuments must be the product of some great affections that embrace the entirety of a country's inhabitants, and that concentrate on some vast subject of common admiration, the totality of impressions which everyone will later apply to the requirements of private luxury and innovation. It is from the need to put oneself at the level of a great and universal feeling that derived all the grandeurs of religious or political edifices which also survived their ruination; and this generating cause was the reason, from the earliest ages until our present time, for the survival of their remains, their narratives or traditions. The more this principle is reduced, or is disseminated through shabby private enterprises, the more its influence is enfeebled, and the weaker becomes the virtue of that which produces in art this strength and this size that one expresses by saying that it *has character*.

****

The second meaning in which the idea of *character* applies to the art of building in general, or to the work of architecture in particular, is the one we express by saying, of either the one or the other, that it has *a character*. This expression, we contended, has the purpose of expressing the quality generally known as *originality*.

Now one understands by *original character*, whether in art in general or in a particular work, that which designates the one or the other as not being copies. The word *copy*, grammatically understood, means nothing in a moral sense. This word, being a synonym of *double*, always indicates a procedure that is more or less mechanical, which, by reproducing or multiplying an original, finds itself (with certain exceptions which we will not discuss here) excluded from the veritable domain of imitation – the imitation of nature – and is consequently outside the domain of invention.

In considering *character* then under the aspect of *originality*, in a sphere other than an art in itself – that is to say, in its conceptions, its ideas, its points of view, its correlations, and its propriety, where the artist draws the means and the effects – one easily understands how natural it is, over the course of the years, for the ever increasing succession of works to make it increasingly difficult for the following ages not to fall in the ways opposite to those of originality.

In truth, the easier it was for those who were the first to tread these paths to follow the inspirations of a free feeling and to model themselves on methods developed by simple needs or after the indications of nature, and the farther one moved from these paths, and the more artificial needs begat different requirements, the easier it was to lose sight of the directions of an original feeling; it was then that the vain ambition of originality often led to what is but its caricature.

Indeed, it must have happened that, feeling left behind by a very large number of models one despaired of being original, and one believed in being condemned to trail behind the footsteps of predecessors. From this difficulty of acquiring what we called *character*, that is to say, a special and individual imprint, must have derived the two misuses that have always marked the fortunes of works of art. Soon, two paths unfolded, the one for the minds and talents who no longer thought and saw for themselves and who, by limiting themselves to repeating what had been thought and produced before them, precipitated the disgust and the indifference that derive from monotony. The other path is the one upon which –

whether by foolish pride or by base interest – innovating minds that despise the past throw themselves, and who, not for being but for appearing original, go so far as to repudiate the fundamental principles of the real and the true, and rush into the excesses of the ridiculous and the bizarre.

It is evident, not because of what we have just said, but by virtue of the nature of things, whose eternal lessons we simply recalled that, in certain ages, it is given for a few works to be noted for their originality, that is to say, to have a *character* – a special quality that is not borrowed. Now this result must occur every time that a long succession of efforts and successes gives birth, whatever the artistic genre may be, to works inspired by the boldness of genius which knows how to proceed independently from any conventions other than those whose observance is prescribed and ordered by the original study of nature.

****

The third meaning, which more often designates the word and the notion of *character* in architectural theory – whether one treats its productions or whether one judges the talents of their authors – is the one indicated by the third expression mentioned above, when a monument is said to have been given or not, *its character* by the architect; that is to say, a *character* proper to it.

Before entering into the analysis of some aspects of the theory of the word *character* in its third application, we should state why we reserved much more space for this application than the first two, as well as for a series of didactic developments which we have not treated until now. The reason is as follows.

Character, as the first two divisions of this notion explained, is a quality which in two of its aspects in works of architecture depends on certain causes upon which neither the power of man nor that of instruction can exert an influence. Nothing indeed – especially with respect to the first acceptation of the word *character*, that of strength and physical size – nothing, I say, could cause societies in the process of modifying and aging, to retrogress towards the simplicity of the early ages and towards the feelings that harmonized the art of building with the state of physical and moral needs of that remote age.

This, the theory of *character*, understood as the most emphatic expression of the needs and taste of a nation in its youth, can only be considered today as a purely historical theory. With the help of historical traditions or some ruined remains one can recall or compare the notions that exempted monuments from exhibiting taste, invention or delight, being qualities whose absence was compensated for by a powerful instinct for solidity or gigantic size; but these kinds of notions can lead only to a negative result regarding the causes that could reproduce them. Hence, it is obvious, with respect to this issue, that the didactic theory of art could extract from it no practical document, no profitable lesson for the present time. This *character* of strength and power belongs to a principle that cannot reappear because of someone's liking or will.

The same can almost be said of the *character of originality*, considered either in the natural course of causes which, at certain periods, as if spontaneously, produced men who are said to have been the students of no one but themselves, or envisaged more particularly in these accidental encounters of privileged geniuses which seem to be the exceptions to the circumstances in which they found themselves. In the one case or the other, theory could well account for these facts or their causes, but no didactic teaching can be assigned to resuscitate or propagate their effects.

On the contrary, it seems to us that the third kind of *character* is an entirely different matter, which consists in the art of impressing each building with a state so appropriate to its nature or its use, that one can read in its salient traits what it is and what it cannot be. This distinctive property, which one expresses by saying of a monument where it is evident that it has *its character*, while constituting at the same time one of the principal merits of art, has the additional feature that its secret can be taught not only by examples, but also by practical documents.

It is therefore to this didactic theory that we shall limit ourselves by abbreviating the precepts of taste comprised in a matter which can be infinitely extended, if one were to survey all its details.

****

The art of characterizing each building, that is to say, of rendering evident through material forms, and explaining the qualities and properties inherent to its purpose, is perhaps of all the secrets of architecture the most valuable to possess and at the same time the least easy to predict.

Character, understood as a synonym of *indicative property* of what the building is or what it must appear to be, cannot be developed by the artist without the concurrence of two corresponding impressions. Through the effect of the first the artist must render a faithful and true account of the qualities or special ideas with which custom endows a monument; the effect of the second, is to make known to the artist the exterior means that art could employ in order to correspond to the expression that must be manifested to the eyes.

The first, and without doubt most important condition to realize this manifestation, is the knowledge of the special purpose of the monument, followed by the kind of ideas that correspond to it and which are capable of finding within the language of this art the proper signs to clearly express the monument's idea. To produce this effect there is, first of all, a gradation to be observed in the extremely variable use of lines and forms, masses and materials, ornaments and wealth, which art could apply to the whole as well as to the details of buildings, with a variety of modifications. This kind of scale provides the architect with a very powerful means to establish differences of physiognomy that are so evident, that even the least learned eye is not mistaken.

Thus, we believe that an essay on the theory of *character*, considered from this point of view, could rest on the development of three of the principal means to manifest the purpose of buildings, 1° *by the forms of the plan and of the elevation;* 2° *by the choice, the measure or the manner of ornament and decoration;* 3° *through the massing and the kind of construction and materials.*

We shall briefly survey these three divisions.

****

We shall unite under the same point of view and under the same critique some insights into the means exhibited by the forms of the plan and the elevation to characterize buildings, that is to say, to render their purpose evident.

The two aspects of which we speak are so closely related that nothing could be prescribed to the one that is not applicable to the other. The plan, in truth, is something hidden to the eyes and especially to the minds of many; however, it is upon the plan that the form of the elevation depends. It is therefore very important for the expression of the proper *character* of architecture that a plan conceived at random, without the intelligence or anticipation of the elevation's relation with the forms required by a building's purpose, does not bring about the daily misapprehensions into which the observer will surely fall.

One could generally say that there are few buildings that cannot by their very purpose direct the architect toward the more or less simple or more or less complicated path of ideas that the plan requires. The uniformity of customs will therefore produce a certain uniformity of distribution in a school or in a hospice, for example, and this effect must be correlated with the elevation, whose simplicity of line will become the obligatory *character*. One could generally say, as the plan goes, so does the elevation. A great diversity of uses, functions, residents of varied social standing, all necessitating numerous varieties in plan, as in a large public establishment, will therefore allow the architect to reflect this state of affairs in the exterior combinations of forms and lines that will influence the aspects of the elevation.

Admittingly, there are often only slight differences of character between one building and the next. Many purposes, of a more or less similar nature, will endow the plan and the elevation with more or less indicative nuances.

But there are other buildings whose original idea and actual purpose do not permit the architect to confuse them under the appearance of a plan, or especially a common and banal elevation.

For example, in spite of the modifications introduced to scenographic displays by modern usage and by the customs of our theatres, their interiors still offer within the circular part of the hall, an enclosure that always corresponds to the tiers of ancient circular theatres. It seems to us here, that there is enough material to suggest to the intelligent architect a characteristic motif of plan or elevation that distinguishes and reveals the monument for what it is. Is it not astonishing that among all the theatres erected in our modern times, the idea did not occur to any of their authors to grasp this simple trait of exterior *character*?

If the circular form of a plan and elevation is the exterior distinctive sign, and consequently the proper *character* of a theatre, then we believe that one would just as obviously sin against the guidance of nature, by unnecessarily applying the circular form to other buildings, as was done, for example, in the building that serves as a market for grain and flour.[14]

Very often still, the architect's pencil, toying on paper with all the forms of plans and elevations, takes pleasure in introducing circular shapes and lines to plans and especially to the exterior elevations of houses; only the slightest notion of propriety tells us that to adopt a convex form of elevation for the access to a house presents an obvious contradiction to the natural idea of entry. In vain would one invoke the physical possibility of such a building; it is a weak reason, for the purpose is not that which is materially achievable but what must morally be, that is to say, according to the laws of sensibility and intelligence.

Intelligence and taste require especially from the architect, in the means that he employs to characterize buildings in their plans and elevations, a wise discernment and a proportionate use of resources that tend to establish among them a kind of hierarchy or gradation that easily reveals their purpose. Now, it is a misconception of this order of proportion to indiscriminately apply to houses as well as palaces, and civic institutions as well as religious monuments, the same wealth of plans and splendour of elevations.

If, for example, one characterizes (in the manner of the ancients) the plan and the elevations of a temple by sumptuous peristyles crowned with pediments, by wings of columns, and by the most lavish architectural articulation, then, would it not be, comparatively speaking, a reduction in distinctive merit or in characteristic value, to apply the same luxury of plan and elevation to a building intended for the affairs of money and commerce? Since examples, in such a matter, are the best lessons, we shall invoke here the authority of the ancients, in the evident difference of *character* that they knew how to establish, between their temples and their basilicas.

If we are to believe more than one piece of evidence, it seems that even the pediment was not indiscriminately applied to the elevations of temples and those of civic or political constructions, and even less so to private constructions. In fact, architecture does not have at her disposal a large number of signs that correspond to all the impressions that she intends to produce, to risk weakening their value by the prodigality of their use. It is only by applying them with much discernment and economy, and in a just proportion, in the moral sense of each building, that she can preserve their property as a language intelligible to all.

Thus, the use or the absence of columns, their varied number in elevations, and the appropriate choice of orders, must become for each building the reliable means to indicate their purpose as well as the idea that the observer should form. This leads us to the second means of characterizing buildings.

****

What is known as *decoration* and ornament is perhaps the means to characterize buildings that is easiest to define and explain.

Decoration, independently of the resources of architecture, comprises those of painting for the interior of monuments, and those of sculptural ornament, which are applicable, according to the architect's wishes, to his exterior as well as interior works. These means are obviously innumerable. However, far from serving to characterize monuments, that is to say, to imprint them with their essentially distinctive sign, these means will only be elements of confusion as long as the mind that regulates their use is not founded upon a rule of art. Now, here are two of the most important rules.

Firstly, it is certain that decoration, understood in a sense without convention or without any particular restraint, is the art of employing all of architecture's riches. But, as we shall prove elsewhere (*See* DECORATION), the expression of richness is not proper to all buildings, and especially to the same degree, for such is the nature of their diverse purposes. The art of the architect must not be more free to indiscriminately use the means of decoration than is the art of the writer or the orator to apply the flowers and pomp of rhetoric to the style of all the subjects that it treats. It is therefore to the characteristic genre of every building that is given the task of determining what it prescribes or that which it accepts to employ in its expression through decorative resources.

Secondly, decoration – philosophically considered according to the moral use that it comprises, and according to the goal towards which it must tend – is in actuality a kind of language whose signs and formulas must also have a necessary rapport with a certain number of ideas. If decoration ceases to be so, then one can see in it only a dead language, a hieroglyphic writing whose meaning has been lost, and which, having consequently become mute for the mind, is naught but a fruitless entertainment for the eyes. It would therefore be in vain for this language to present the most varied means to render the purpose of every building clear and intelligible, if the artist lacks the knowledge of the signs at his disposal.

Having to only summarily indicate here some of the means of characterizing monuments by their decoration, we still have to say that the most important condition to observe consists in an economy of decorative means, and in an enlightened discernment between objects of ornament, which are only too habitually used in every place and in every subject.

For example, if one places festoons everywhere, what would be the significance of this commonplace? What characteristic value does this banal use of common festoons, scrolls, and foliage without reason have? What could these pateras, these genii, these quivers, these lyres, these grotesque heads, indiscriminately placed on the surfaces of all buildings tell us or teach us? What meaning is the observer supposed to assign to them, if the decorator himself has no idea of their value? Painting and sculpture, used on a large scale, could without doubt furnish the architect with the most noble subjects for decoration, as long as these subjects – as well as the motives behind their inventions and their judicious combination with the architectural elements – are in harmony with the indicative *character* of the building's special purpose. But who has not noticed the uselessness, to say the least, of these vast compositions abandoned to the caprice of a brush, that invade all the spaces of an interior and even the architectural elements, leaving the observer uncertain as to the forms of the place where he stands? This excessive abuse of decorative means, in which each of the two arts loses the value of its *character*, accustoms the eyes of the public to no longer evaluate decorative objects with respect to the *character* that they must convey and strengthen, but solely with the indifference with which one treats the objects of a banal and insignificant luxury.

We must say the same thing about the numerous classes of attributes that should be used with much reserve, by applying their varied signs and symbols to the characteristic qualities or properties of each monument, that is to say, its purpose. We explained earlier, however, that the Greeks and the Romans – although by then, the sole action of time had already produced many misuses of some of the allegorical signs of ornament – knew how to arrange and appropriate symbols and characteristic attributes for their principal edifices.

The use of attributes always offers the architect a vast field of application, and numerous means to reveal to the observer the purpose of monuments. Invention in this matter has no fewer limits than the genius of allegory, but it is exposed to the same drawbacks, that is to say, that its emblems are rendered obscure by dint of new combinations and a lack of thoughtfulness in their use. There are qualities that must be preserved in this area of ornament; one must avoid presenting the mind with enigmas instead of inscriptions. There are accepted ideas and there are certain agreed upon attributions that must be respected or managed with care.

However, the true spirit of ornament in the use of attributes warns especially against falling into this routine of banalities which, by being everywhere, adds nothing of value anywhere, and which, instead of characterizing buildings, can only serve to erase any idea of *character*. One cannot count the many different kinds of industries that multiplied ornaments in a variety of materials, and threw them into circulation, thereby rendering them insignificant by their very multiplicity. How many sphinxes, lions, eagles, vases, trophies, candelabras, tripods, altars, caducei, quivers, crowns, laurel branches, etc. become a tedious filling, and occupy in buildings solely the same role as embroidery in fabric!

****

We said that there was as third way of indicating the purpose of buildings by a *character* appropriate to each, and that this way could more or less consist in a relative genre of *construction*, and in *the very nature of materials* which the architect had the art to employ.

Let us first state, that by the word *construction* we designate here not only simple building or the science of cutting stones, but this area of art which, with the aid of taste, relies on science to produce fortunate effects on our senses and our imagination. The art of theatre decorations offers a daily demonstration of the diversity of impressions that could be produced by compositions inspired by the dramatic situations that architecture must suit. This is where one is convinced, more than words can say, of the variety of resources that art can also find in the combinations of masses and materials, of solids and voids, of contrasts produced by bold and multiple apertures, in tall vaults, or in heavy and low roofs, depending on the characters of variety or uniformity, liveliness or gravity, terror or voluptuousness, that each building can render more or less evident.

The diversity of materials that art could employ must also count among the means of construction that converge within the expression of *character*. One of these varieties will consist in the very dimension and volume of stones, not only because of the building's size, but also because of its kind of purpose, whether it will comprise ideas of strength, gravity, richness or delicacy, delight and elegance. The very quality of these materials and their mode of work could be included within the sphere of propriety and the effects capable of strengthening the impression of *character*.

We shall go even farther, and suggest that the variety of colour in the materials of construction is still one of these practices that an intelligent taste can make good use of, in favour of the *character* it intends to make evident. We mean to speak of the sensuous impression that we experience in beauty; the very rarity of certain materials, their combinations, as well as the manner of diversifying their effects. Although some reject this sort of pursuit, on the basis that real beauty needs no adornment, one still observes that beauty in nature does not decline all outside ornament.

Generally speaking, there is a over-reliance on examples of ancient monuments, which even in their dilapidated condition shine with a beauty that strikes the eye. However, we are far from realizing the extent to which the ancients developed material opulence and all the pursuits of luxury, even in the smallest details of their architecture. New discoveries forced the conclusion that not only did marble, metal and all precious materials enter their constructions, but that different colours of painting were generally applied to the stones of their most beautiful edifices. (We shall develop this subject in greater detail and authority elsewhere. *See* COLOUR).

Here, we shall consider only the use of colours, be they natural, artificial, or material, as a physically active way to put a building's character en rapport with its purpose. Indeed, the stone or marble colour could have a particular effect on the largest number of observers. By delighting the eye, marbles of a clear and lightly streaked tone produce a similar impression on the mind. If veneered marbles of a dark tone that is austere and uniform were to be successively displayed in front of our eyes, then our mind would receive an impression that leads to sadness or seriousness. Those who know the sepulchral chapel in Turin, complete in black marble, and even that of San-Andrea della Valle in Rome, attributed to Michelangelo, could confirm the impression of which I speak, with the physical means that I mentioned.

COLOUR In speaking of *colour* in relation to its use in architecture, the reader needs no forewarning that this word is not used here in the sense given to it in painting.

Since nothing in architecture represents physical nature, and since the forms of architecture owe their value to an order of things that is independent of matter, then she has no need of *colour* in order to fulfil her true purpose. It must be said that architecture can produce her greatest beauty with the most common of materials; and that all her singularities, all the richness of the most precious and remarkable substances, will never alone be able to captivate the admiration of an intelligent eye or the feeling of a connoisseur.

This is not to say that architecture scorns or must scorn any adornment. Ornament, which forms part of her constitution, is a sufficient indication that it is in her interest not to neglect the agreeable, and to grant to the senses what they rightly demand. In this, nature offers both lessons and examples.

Additionally, architecture has always drawn on the resources of painting, especially in interior decoration, whether in providing areas that only painting can fill, or in borrowing certain effects of contrast in the hues and the variety of tones, which render apparent the reliefs of ornaments, thus producing a vivacity that is agreeable to the eye.

Therefore, there is no reason, regarding the use of *colour* in the interiors of public or private buildings, to reject a practice that suffers no contradiction. The same can be said regarding the more or less frequent usage in all countries – but more general in some nations – to cover the exterior of houses with *colour*. Many a reason of utility, not to mention that of pleasure, have made a practice out of this usage, especially if wood enters into the construction, or in order to protect weak sheathing against climatic influences. One cannot deny also that in countries where this fashion prevails, as in the South of France, in the Lyonnais, or in the Genoese states, etc., such diversity of *colour* gives a great air of gaiety to buildings. However, the luxury of stone construction in houses finds itself impaired when covered with *colour*, for that puts the most expensive materials on the same level as the ordinary ones.

In general, one could say that in every art, but especially in architecture, there is a certain beauty of instinct so to speak, and that there is a corresponding sentiment among most people that leads them to admire the grand, the rich, and the rare. This explains why it is difficult in certain countries to use taste as a gauge to approve of painting the exterior of great stone buildings, because the value of a work in stone finds itself hidden and concealed behind a cover of *colour*; but also because this practice can be seen as a kind of charlatanism which aims at capturing the approbation of the eye at the expense of that of the mind.

For a long time, the idea of endowing the exterior of monumental architecture with *colour* did not occur to anyone. The works of antiquity, whose investigation was limited to examples found in Rome, could not have inspired this practice. It is after the sphere of research was enlarged through travels to include countries that were inhabited by the Greeks, that much new information offered hitherto unknown facts, resulting in the conclusion that there was frequent use of *colour* in antiquity in temples which were constructed in the most solemn order, that is to say the Doric.

We must say, for we have ascertained it ourselves, that most of the temples, either at Paestum or in many an ancient city in Sicily, are constructed of a stone that is not suited to polish, and thus it was deemed necessary to cover it

with a coat of stucco. However, this material was not painted in a uniform manner. Numerous vestiges of *colour* prove that this stucco received the most varied tones; that the divisions of the entablature had different hues; that the triglyphs and the metopes, the capitals and their annulets; and even the architrave's soffit, were coloured in different ways.

The research that was conducted even in Athens, in the Parthenon, the Propylea, the Temple of Theseus – all of them made of marble – corroborates this taste for the use of varied hues endowing backgrounds with nuances that appreciably enhance the bas-reliefs and other accessories. This is akin to the ways – of which we are certain – in which marble sculpture enhanced with *colour* many details of drapery, armour and accessory objects.

From this matter it seems to us that we can infer two things: first, that since the principal beauty of architecture does not depend on the quality of materials, nor on *colour* or cost, this art in reality needs only the resources of order, proportion, the harmony of forms, and the observance of the proper pleasing character. Second, since architecture accepts the use of *colour* in the interior of monuments, she has just as much right to use it on the exterior, depending on the diversity of materials; and in the same manner that she employs marble of all *colours*, in columns, capitals, friezes, cornices and other parts, as long as one use or the other is motivated as a means to express character, and not produce a bad mixture.

COMPOSITE (Order) The nomenclature that was consecrated by preceding *lexicons* and *treatises on architecture* notwithstanding, our object is to prove that the *composite* order exists neither in theory nor in practice, and to reveal the source of the misunderstandings that bestowed an imaginary existence on this so-called order.

In fact, it is not among the Romans, where some pretend to locate the origin of this new order, that one finds the proper authorities to justify this pretension. I hope to demonstrate decisively, that a thorough examination of the use and modifications of the orders in Rome, far from establishing the birth of a new order, proves on the contrary that no one ever suspected its existence.

The order known as *composite* owes its existence to the moderns; but one must specify the kind of misunderstanding to which it must be attributed. I see two principal misunderstandings: the first, I would call an *error of reasoning*, which results from the ignorance of the principles upon which the character and genius of the orders are founded; the other, I would call an *error of fact*, whose source resides in the very ignorance of monuments and the ambiguity of examples.

§ I *On the error of reasoning*. I said that the existence of the *composite* order is based first on an error of reasoning. Vanity as much as ignorance contributed perhaps to the production and justification of this error. Since the renaissance of the arts, the moderns spared no effort in order to realize what they called conquests in the domain of architectural invention. On the one hand, they expressed regrets that there was almost nothing left to invent; on the other, there was presumptuous boastfulness about the pliancy of new discoveries. Nothing is more ridiculous, it seems to me, than the despair of some and the ambition of others. But it appears to me that they differ in such a way only because they agree on placing invention where it does not belong. (*See* INVENTION).

Those who believe that there is nothing left to say in architecture err when they confound the orders, or that which forms the elements of this art, with the results and infinite combinations to which these elements can inexhaustibly lend themselves. As to those who believe that one can always find something new regarding the orders, they persuade themselves that change suffices for invention, and that they make new compositions by decomposing the antique.

We demonstrated elsewhere that the orders or modes of architecture are to this art what the tones are to music, or the principal colours to painting; that to look for new orders in architecture is equivalent to expecting new types of proportion in the human structure. Suffice it here to demonstrate that the so-called *composite* order has no other origin but the false idea of invention

which has for a long time tormented those who look for, and consequently fail to know genius.

The principal illusion of those who believe in the possible discovery of some new order rests on an obvious misunderstanding. In fact, they think that a new adornment in the capital suffices to give birth to a new order. They believe that it suffices to change the profiles of a base, to substitute a quarter-round for a scotia, or adapt some symbols or national allegorical emblems in order to give the column the honour of an important discovery in architecture, and so that they acquire fame for the new-born order, believing themselves to be its creators.

One reflection could have spared much expense in this kind of invention; and it is that each of the orders is based on the expression of one of the principal qualities that architecture manifests; and that these qualities, which are to the moral sense what the primary colours are to painting, can be reduced to a small number beyond which there could be many nuances but which are far from being complete colours.

"The orders," says Galiani correctly, "are but architecture's means of execution; and there could fundamentally be only three that express this art's diverse degrees of richness. Now, as nothing could be richer than the superlative, or of a lower materiality than the concrete, no order deserves this name if it surpasses one or the other of these terms; because to do more would be an excess, and to do less would not suffice. As to the terms of the comparison that one can place between the high and low degrees of richness that befit architecture, they only render the idea of a thing that is less rich than the richest, and more rich than the poorest."

If one were to apply this very judicious reflection of Galiani's to the other qualities or properties of which each of the three Greek orders is an expression, one would reach the same conclusion, to wit that one cannot take the orders beyond or short of the means that manifest their character without altering them by one of these two excesses. Thus, instead of adding to the character of simplicity and energy of the Greek Doric, the so-called order that the moderns named *Tuscan* succeeded only in contriving a poor product. The same applies to the so-called *Composite*, which, being a mixture of the Corinthian and the Ionic, lost the character of both and failed to have the richness of the one and the elegance of the other.

It should not be inferred from this that architecture is limited to the monotony of three orders that should always and everywhere be employed without variation. Since we used the colour comparison, let us continue the analogy and its deductions. Not only does architecture use and

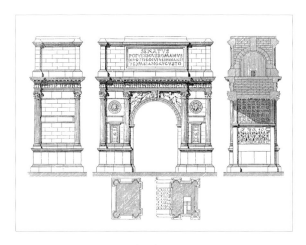

Fig. 31. Arch of Titus, Rome.
From: Julien Guadet, *Éléments et théorie de l'architecture*,
Librairie de la construction moderne, Paris, 1909

should use the three orders in their integrity, depending on an aptness to the kind of building, but she should also accept adjustments that are proper to the numerous modifications required by taste. These are the adjustments that correspond to what we termed nuances in colour. Who has ever contested that the architect has the right, for example, to introduce some variety of measures in the proportions proper to each order, in the profiles, the modifications of detail, the ornaments, and the influence borrowed from other orders? But all these things belong more to minor accessories than the essence of every order.

What was said about the ensemble and the system of ordonnance that constitutes the proper genre for every kind of column, and the borrowed

details that can be made without producing a new order, can rightly be said of the capital, which, far from constituting the proper nature of an order by itself, is but its physiognomy. Whoever is knowledgeable about these matters does not attribute to a quarter-round, a volute, or foliage, the property of determining that which establishes the veritable differences between the orders.

For example, the decorative adjustment of the Corinthian capital, or such and such an adjustment of detail, such and such a change or mixing of details, cannot constitute a new order. The ancients, as we shall soon see, had infinitely diversified the capital without changing its essential type.

The error of reasoning that we oppose regarding the existence of the so-called composite capital, resides in the false opinion that accessory ornament is the principal important element of the capital, and that each modification or mixing of ornament produces a new type. Now if this is obviously erroneous, as the facts will prove, it is so even more to make the existence of a new order depend and derive not from a new composition of general proportions, nor from a special distribution of outlines, or a new type of capital, but solely from a new combination of the accessories of this capital.

Now, the so-called *composite* order, with very few exceptions of details, has the same proportions, the same outlines, the same type of capital as the Corinthian; it only differs by the introduction of Ionic volutes and their mixing with Corinthian foliage. There is therefore nothing here that constitutes a new order.

Let us now demonstrate that this error of reasoning is based on an error of fact, and on the very ignorance of monuments.

§ II *On the error of fact*. The period, when the kind of order whose existence I contest began to gain ascendance among the moderns, was far from being that of analysis and experience. The monuments of antiquity were beginning to emerge from the dust of time and oblivion; the learned research of artists and antiquarians had not yet allied an enlightened critique to all these precious remnants of ancient art upon which a better coordinated system of precepts and authorities was to one day be based.

A famous monument, on account of historical subject matters represented by the art of the chisel, was preserved in such a way that it drew particular attention to itself. I speak of the arch of Titus. This monument, which is remarkable on many levels, is ornamented with four columns whose capitals are composed of Corinthian foliage and Ionic volutes. From this, some inferred the existence of an order that they called *composite*.

This kind of supplement to the architectural orders soon entered all teaching methods, and even the monuments. Architects became absorbed in the means to specify more precisely this

Fig. 32. Composite order. Baths of Diocletian.
From: Josef Durm, *Die Baukunst der Etrusker und Römer*,
A. Kröner Verlag, Stuttgart, 1905

amplification of the Corinthian order. But all these efforts served to prove the vacuity of this invention. A simple look at the authoritative monument demonstrates this. Indeed, upon examining the architecture of the arch of Titus, one does not find in the profiles of the entablature, the column base, its proportions or the details of its ornaments, any differences other than those ordinarily found between one Corinthian ordonnance and another of the same name. One even finds more tangible differences, for example, between the Corinthian portico of Nero and that of the Pantheon; or between the latter and the Corinthian thermae of Diocletian. The only variance in the arch of Titus is that of its capital.

But if the combinatory variety of ornaments in the capital sufficed to constitute a separate order, and if there were as many orders in antiquity as there were variations on the Corinthian capital, then there must be hundreds of orders as we shall see.

The ancients, and especially the Romans, seemed to have considered this order's capital as a resource that could lend itself, through the grandeur of its development, to the allocation of all sorts of symbols and allegorical attributes. It will be evident, through the enumeration of all the accessories, that only the taste for decoration enters in the composition of the crowning of this order, and that the joining of the volutes to the acanthus leaves was but one among the many combinations imagined by the excessive taste for variety. This mixture of adjustments that belongs to two capitals was not the only one.

If this kind of mixing of two capital ornaments could create a new order, there would be no reason to refuse the same distinction to the mixing, which was just as common, of the Doric as well as the Corinthian capital. Perhaps, too, there will be no hesitation in preferring this amalgam, since it is simpler and more natural than that of the so-called *composite* order.

To complete the demonstration that the association of the Ionic volutes to the leaves of the Corinthian never had the privilege of designating a separate order among the ancients, it suffices to examine the compilation of composite capitals transmitted to us by antiquity. One can find some capitals where the volutes were formed by a ram's horns. Other capitals exhibit a volute formed by fishes whose bodies bend upwards toward the abacus, bringing their tails, in the shape of a flowerwork, to the middle of the abacus. Above the astragal, a bough is surmounted by two sphinxes uniting in a single head, and whose wings stretch until they reach the volutes. Elsewhere, the capital's drum is in the shape of a basket where four large split leaves ascend from the astragal to the volutes, which emerge from the basket in the form of a ram's horns.

It is generally known that a Corinthian abacus has four horns; but there is a capital that has eight that are equally spaced, with a rose between each pair, and underneath each rose, there is a head. There are also heads of ram whose horns form volutes.

Another Corinthian capital is without an abacus, or volutes, and with nothing that takes their place. It is a simple capital ornamented with a single row of foliage upon which birds are perched.

One could say that there is almost no subject or allegorical figure that the taste for ornament did not use in the fashioning of the Corinthian capital. Their enumeration would be too lengthy. Suffice it to say that one finds figures of men at arms, figures of genii, victories, griffons, and pegasoi.

We have considerably shortened the enumeration of the antique *composite* capitals, the drawings of which can be consulted in *Della Magnificenza ed architettura de' Romani* by Piranesi. Let us end by the mention of various capitals from this compilation: truly Doric capitals with their echinus and their abacus crowning two rows of Corinthian foliage.

The reasoning and the authority of facts or examples concur then to prove in the most decisive manner, that the so-called composite capital – of which modern architecture intended to make a new order – is but a variation among a great number of other mixtures imagined by the ancients within the ornament of the Corinthian capital.

I shall end this discussion with a very judicious reflection by de Chambray:

"The architect does not employ his industry and learning to find new orders so that his work acquires value, or to become a skilled man any more than an orator invents new words that have never been said in order to acquire the reputation of being eloquent, or a poet makes verses of different rhythms and measure than is customary. This affectation is puerile and impertinent, and if one were to occasionally take such a liberty, then it must be so befitting that its reason is plainly obvious. Thus did the ancients act, and with such restraint that they limited all their licence to the form of the capital, of which they made a hundred brilliantly successful compositions that befit particular subjects; and one could only impertinently step outside these compositions."

The entire theory of the so-called *composite* order, seems to us enclosed within this quote from de Chambray. It is evident that he accepts variety in decoration within the Corinthian capital, depending on the nature of monuments, and the allusions that they comprise. But he does not believe that a new combination of ornaments should constitute a new order.

COMPOSITION This word designates either the act of composing (one speaks of *being in the heat of the composition*), or the object itself that has been composed. (One speaks of *a good or a bad composition*)

It is under the first acceptation that we shall consider this word, that is to say, in the purely didactic meaning of the idea of *composition* in architecture.

Let us first note that the words *composition* and *conception*, which are sometimes used indiscriminately, are not in fact synonymous. One could use the word *conception* to express that operation of the mind which embraces only the principal motif of an idea, its general correlations, and a vague idea of its disposition. *Composition*, on the contrary, consists in embracing not only the general idea, but all its developments, as much in the choice of its details, their propriety, their rapport with the whole, as in the means that must assure the execution of the whole and its parts.

In this regard, the painter and the sculptor enjoy an advantage which is denied to the architect. They are at once both the composers and the executors of their works. The ideas and the means to realize them emanate from the same author. The means available to the architect to realize his compositions depend on many processes, and necessitate the convergence of agencies that are foreign to him. Nothing, therefore, is more important for the architect, as he composes, than to constantly have his mind directed towards the means that must realize his inventions.

Also, it is never too early to form the mind of the student toward submitting his *composition* to the control of the means of execution.

The study of *composition* must not consist in imagining on paper some divisions of plans which are agreeable by their variety and their symmetry, or elevations that seem to offer either picturesque massing arrangements, or new outlines and aspects. Often, all these efforts lavished by the imagination in drawing form, will present parts that are either unexecutable, or that demand incalculable expenses for their realization. It is never too early to train young architects to compose projects of an easy and useful application, that economically unite the useful and the agreeable, solidity and propriety.

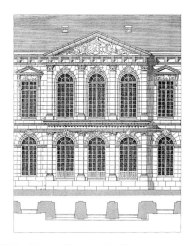

Fig. 33. Bibliothèque Nationale, Paris, court elevation.
From: Julien Guadet, *Éléments et théorie de l'architecture*,
Librairie de la construction moderne, Paris, 1909

It must be said that in modern times, especially in schools, architectural *composition* has been too emphasized in student exercises. Without a doubt, it is good to exercise the imagination, but it must be done with caution. One could remark that this abuse derived from the same cause that once multiplied the lectures and the compositions of rhetors in Rome. It is well known that this was the effect and the sign of decadence and abandonment into which true eloquence fell, when the freedom of the tribune disappeared. Similarly, since the causes that once supplied the great enterprises of the art of building ceased to exist, one observes projects and vast *compositions* on paper assume a peculiar increase, wasting talents that are no longer required by the needs of society.

CONCEPTION As already mentioned under the word *composition*, this word designates what in the mind or in the imagination of the architect is the primary thought, the general and abstract idea, or the incomplete esquisse of a composition of the ensemble, but not of the parts or the details of a monument.

Thus, in the moral realm, similar to the formation of beings in the physical realm, *conception* is a kind of abbreviated formation of a plan or a drawing, which is given definitive development by the composition.

However, nothing is more important than this beginning of creation. The artist is well advised to give ample attention in his thoughts to this first seed. "That which is well conceived, can be clearly stated," said Boileau. Before deciding in an often banal drawing on the massing and the ordinarily routine relations which are the fruits of a practice without art, the mind should be well acquainted with propriety, constraints, and the formal conditions of any enterprise.

Instead of submitting his composition to a *conception* previously elaborated in his mind, it often happens that the artist demands from the routine of composition the idea that he has not yet found. From this habitual exercise of the hand and the pencil, to which many students exclusively apply themselves, results the inertia of this interior faculty of the mind, which consists in assembling for the purpose of a well considered *conception*, the elements that will compose it.

The word *conception* is often mentioned in descriptions, accounting particularly for what constitutes the ensemble of a monument, and praising especially the fortunate *parti* of its plans, or the general effect of the volumes that compose it. Thus, one speaks of the church of Saint Peter and its connection with the magnificent piazza that precedes it as a great conception; also, one speaks of the junction of the palace of the Tuileries with that of the Louvre as a fortunate and beautiful conception.

CONSTRUCTION This word serves to indicate the manner in which a building is made. Thus, in speaking of an edifice, one says that the *construction* is fine, solid, skilful, bold, light, economical, or that it has all the contrary vices. It also serves to indicate the materials used or that can be used to execute the work; for example, a building's construction can be of quarry-stone, of ashlar, of brick, of wood, etc.

As a part of architecture, *construction* is the art of executing all that is included in the composition of an edifice. The essential aim of this art must be to unite perfection, solidity and economy. One obtains perfection by entrusting the execution to good workers; solidity, by endowing every part with the proper dimensions relative to the weight to be carried, the resistance to forces, its position, and the consistence of materials; economy, by using the most befitting materials, of

This misuse, one at least suspects, comes from the fact that those who renewed ancient architecture first were painters, sculptors or renderers, who were especially interested in decoration because it fell more within their province than construction, which demands special knowledge. However, in the splendid antique buildings of which these artists sought only to imitate the ornaments, one observes that the columns, the pediments and the other principal parts of decoration were essential to the edifice; this is what gave to their works the character of grandeur and propriety that still arouses admiration, even though the remains are devoid of the greatest part of their ornament.

The special protection that has been accorded until now to those who occupied themselves only

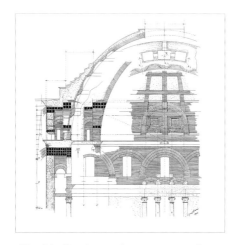

Fig. 34. Pantheon, dome construction.
From: Josef Durm, *Die Baukunst der Grieschen*,
A. Kröner Verlag, Stuttgart, 1905

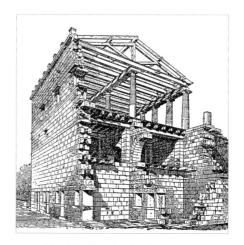

Fig. 35. Stoa in the Aegean.
From: Josef Durm, *Die Baukunst der Grieschen*,
A. Kröner Verlag, Stuttgart, 1905

good quality, careful implementation, without waste or superfluous work.

WHAT ARE THE CAUSES THAT RENDERED CONSTRUCTION EXTREMELY COSTLY, AND OFTEN LACKING IN SOLIDITY?

Since the renewal of ancient architecture, the majority of those who have devoted themselves to the study of this art have neglected the study of *construction* in favour of composition and decoration, which they considered to be the principal aims of their art; whereas it is certain that a building could fulfil the object of its purpose even though it is not decorated, another, whose decoration is beautiful, would fail to fulfil this purpose.

with composition and decoration is because most architects today disdain *construction* in order to give themselves to the most ostentatious part of architecture. Hence all these projects where one observes that the principal aim is sacrificed in favour of shallow accessories, where almost no attention is paid to the use to which an edifice is destined, nor to the expense needed to execute it.

There has not been enough reflection on the nature and the aim of architecture. Unlike poetry, painting, sculpture, and music, this art is not an art of pure pleasure that could endure all the deviations of the imagination; to the contrary, it is an essentially useful art, demanding much knowledge, prudence and skill in order to unify beauty, commodity, solidity and economy within the same edifice. Truly, this is what the science of the architect consists of – a science which is difficult to acquire. Even though our nation boasts of being among the most educated, one could perhaps say of her, with Plato, that she would have difficulty in naming one accomplished architect.

Being generally more decorators than builders, architects today barely know the methods of the arts that they must employ in order to execute their projects. Thus, when they are charged with the execution of an important edifice, and being unsure of the means, they change and vary the work incessantly; they repeatedly start over parts of the work without being satisfied, and after many attempts which are as costly as they are useless, they put themselves in the hands of

reasoned description of the project, in order to justify the disposition, the forms and the dimensions of all the composing parts, and so that those for whom the project was built can judge for themselves if the architect has fulfilled their goal.

It is not enough that the project contains all the necessary parts for which the building is destined, that the ensemble of details exhibits beautiful forms, that the ornaments are well chosen, with good taste, and relate to the building's genre; the project must in addition be built with solidity and economy. This is why it is very important, once a project's distribution and decoration have been fixed, to examine all its parts anew, to account for the means of construction, in order to understand if they are the best,

Fig. 36. Columbarium at Varengeville.
From: Julien Guadet, *Éléments et théorie de l'architecture*, Librairie de la construction moderne, Paris, 1909

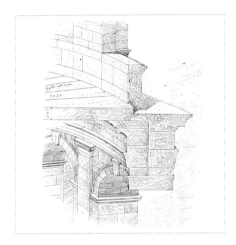

Fig. 37. Amphitheatre at Arles.
From: Josef Durm, *Die Baukunst der Grieschen*, A. Kröner Verlag, Stuttgart, 1905

contractors who are usually greedy, cunning people, who do not cease to lay traps for them by uselessly squandering materials and by superfluous work. Such is the source of this infinity of abuses that ruins the richest individuals, and drains the state without producing anything.

ON THE MEANS TO RENDER CONSTRUCTION LESS COSTLY

For a public edifice or a building of some consequence, the architect should be given a detailed account prepared by someone with good knowledge of all the particularities of use to which it is destined. This account will serve to guide the architect in the composition of the project.

The architect should be bound to provide a

the most simple, the least costly; if they are the most befitting to the building's genre and to the materials available in the country where the project is situated. Without this wise precaution, one risks to uselessly waste much time on materials, costs, and superfluous work, which are badly combined, and could only be executed through extraordinary and ever so costly means that one could avoid by predicting them.

ON THE CONSTRUCTION IN CUT STONE

This manner of building is the most beautiful, the most solid and the most durable, demanding much art and knowledge; but it is also the most costly. However, it is the only one that should be used in buildings or parts of buildings that demand high solidity. The solidity of stone work must be independent of the cement or mortar used in it. It has been observed that all ancient constructions of the sort were made without mortar, that the stone was cut with such precision and accuracy that the joints were barely perceivable, and that in those which were visible, it was not possible to fit a knife blade, no matter how thin.

All the art of construction in cut stone consists in coursing and setting. Many ancient constructions reveal that the Romans used clamps of bronze or iron, which were sealed with lead in order to more solidly unite the stones. They sometimes used keystones made of solid wood and cut in a dovetail fashion.

CONTRACTURA The Latin word used by Vitruvius to designate what we call diminution in the art of tapering a column. In translating this word as *diminution*, Perrault observes that – in order to conform to the usage of the word – this expression applies to the narrowing that a body can experience in its different dimensions. The most correct word in French, to express the idea of *contractura.*, is that of *narrowing*. (See DIMINUTION).

CONTRAST This word derives from *contra stare*. *Contrast* is synonymous with *opposition*; but as with all synonyms, these two words, whether in their etymology or their ordinary use, offer a variety of tangible ideas.

It seems to us that between these two words and what they express there is a distance that separates the idea of what is *contrary* from the idea of what is *different*.

Doubtless, whatever forms a *contrast*, forms also an *opposition*, just as the more contains the less, and the *contrary* contains a *difference*. The idea of *opposition*, in nature and in the arts that imitate her, indicates a position that enhances and distinguishes the reciprocal qualities between creatures and between works of art. The idea of *contrast* seems to us to express such a shock, such a hostility between the objects at hand that one of the qualities of these objects must give way to the other.

The art of painting best explains the precise value of *contrast* and of *opposition*.

Now it is very obvious that painting, considered from the point of view of the technique of colours, exists only by virtue of *oppositions*. Indeed, what are its hues, its half-tints and varied nuances, its gradations of chiaro-scuro, if not *oppositions* whose infinite differences enhance – in the most measured manner, and through means that belong only to painting – the effects that nature produces in all her creations in their smallest parts?

This is the way painting operates by virtue of the infinite *oppositions* that it exploits through the use of a small number of colours. But these oppositions are naught but imperceptible differences of light and shadow, chiaro-scuro, the strong and the weak.

Painting also knows, through a different use of means, how to imitate nature when, in certain accidental effects, she presents not only a graded succession of differences that please the eye but, on the contrary, some abrupt and rapid movements from one order of things to another, which surprise the senses by shaking the imagination. Such are certain sudden transitions from tranquil views to ones in a wilderness full of menacing rocks, or vice versa; and such is the lightning that furrows the horizon, or the flame of the volcano and the fires that light a dark night. Such are the *contrasts* in nature which the painter produces by not subtly passing from light to dark, but rather with bold and sharp means that manifest all the different effects of colours; this is what properly distinguishes an *opposition* from a *contrast*.

The same applies to many other arts, but with the varieties that relate to their proper nature. Since theory in this matter best explains the value of *contrast* and its difference from *opposition* in the arts that exert a more direct action on our senses, we believe that the art that renders this action more tangible and easy to appreciate is music.

Indeed, no other art operates more than music in these necessary successions of differences known as *oppositions*, which are contrary to monotony; and no other art utilizes more easily the resources of *contrast*, in other words, these sudden and unexpected passages from sounds that approach silence to explosions that resemble those of thunder, which are energetic means that music uses to pass from the most gentle expression of feeling to the noisy *contrast* of the most stormy passion.

Poetry, which has the widest reach of all the arts, is not subject to an exterior sense or a particular organ, and possesses innumerable means of operating through infinite *oppositions* within the diversity of ideas, sentiments, affections and characters, that it sometimes treats as simple variations, while at others it *contrasts* in order to better affect the mind. Of all the applications of this theory in the art of the poet, the most tangible is the one that concerns theatrical or dramatic action. This is where the poet instills *contrasts* in certain characters, or certain roles that may appear exaggerated were their *contrasts* not necessary for the general effect, in a manner akin to what painters call a strong foreground.

Thus, the effect of *contrast* is to suddenly transport the mind, through an unexpected impulse to enjoy a surprising impression, which by virtue of its power cannot be of long duration, nor can it be repeated. Here, the reason or the feeling for propriety must establish the limits of the likely for each subject, but especially for each art. In fact, each art could develop its own theory regarding this matter. And as each art influences the mind through particular means, and as each art addresses different organs, it is possible that the general principles that apply to all the arts in what they share in common comprise some exceptions and different applications regarding the proper nature of each.

It may even be that some arts may reject the uses of *contrast*, while admitting the uses of opposition in their language.

One may first posit that *contrast* resides in the arts that express images, and move the mind in manifold ways, capturing its bents, and transporting our imagination with the greatest speed from one place to another, from one feeling to another.

Now, if there is an art that is unskilled in exerting this influence, it is architecture, for it particularly addresses the understanding by acting on the intelligent rather then the sensory part of our mind. It is through the correct relations of harmony, the reasoned combinations of forms, lines, contours, masses, measures, and the reciprocal accord between the parts and the whole, that architecture delights us. But this delight is above all else that of judgment, for architecture first addresses reason. The admiration that it calls forth is of the kind produced by the general harmony of nature. This impression is that of order. Now the feeling of order does not produce these strong and abrupt emotions which are the effects of surprise, and these *contrasts* that one may call skilful disorder.

On the contrary, architecture seems to employ more of what we termed *oppositions*; and we shall even add that it is in the nature of her means to use these differences in measures, projections, simplicity, richness, proportions, heaviness, lightness, and others that form the melody as well as the rhythm of its language. It is by the effect of *opposition* and its *differences* in their innumerable degrees that architecture establishes, in each edifice, this harmony of effect and character that transports the mind towards the feeling of admiration, which is a feeling quite different from that of astonishment, whose virtue belongs to *contrast*.

However, we do not claim that the resources of architecture do not have the means to make us experience the effects of *contrast* by the diversity of constructions, forms, or fanciful elevations. We contend only that these abrupt comparisons, like the sudden passage from an elegant and tastefully decorated Ionic interior to a rustic underground tomb, cannot be in the domain of architecture properly speaking, for these *contrasts* are not allocated to a particular place or a given time.

This sort of *contrast* can only belong to the decoration of some interiors, or to scenographic representations that offer us, not only the idea, but one may say, the reality of the most *contrasting* locations from one moment to the next. In the palazzo del Te, the effect of the sudden and unexpected passage from the preceding elegant gallery into Giulio Romano's *Hall of Giants*, where the painting accumulated enormous masses of rocks on top of the figures of giants, must have produced the impression of a true *contrast* when the colours were still bright. One could also mention the decorative marvels in many holy places that make us swiftly experience the passage from the obscurity of a tomb to the brightness of daylight, which is a *contrast* that operates within architecture, only not by her own means.

The same applies to the theatre. Nothing better expresses the idea of diverse and also *contrasting* characters, than when the architect represents a prison, a tomb, a catafalque, a temple, a ball-room, or a gallery. But all these elements are built on the stage, and they are made salient by their *contrasts*.

Furthermore, there is an art that is naturally devoid of any kind of *contrast*, although it comprises oppositions. We speak of sculpture, which by its very nature is the most isolated art. Indeed, if *contrast* results from the unexpected and sudden encounter of contraries, it can only occur in those arts that operate in succeeding images, where a natural progression can be interrupted in order to produce the unexpected shock of *contrast*.

Now the ranking of the arts in this modest theory would be: *poetry*, *music*, *painting*, *scenography*, *architecture* and *sculpture*.

CONVENTION In customary usage, this word designates any act that results from the coming together of many people. The very formation of the word indicates the idea of alliance so clearly, that I shall not insist on its elementary meaning.

I shall not enumerate the sorts of uses to which the word *convention* applies. I shall quickly move on to the use of the word in fine arts theory in general, and promptly bring the discussion to architectural matters.

In examining the principles of imitation in every art, it is apparent that there are certain pacts or adjustments known as *conventions*, between the imitator and nature, and then between the art and the observer. Through these *conventions*, art produces in us the delight that we demand of it.

Indeed, nature does not address the mode of imitation proper to each art save under a certain rapport or special aspect. Each of these rapports or aspects forms the imitative domain whose property is expressed by every art's name. Whether each art represents material forms through ideas or metaphoric images, or whether

through material forms it manifests moral affections or sensations, each art in reality, can grasp nature only from one side or from one particular point of view.

One could quite realistically liken the fine arts, in their individual relations with nature, to the image of these students placed around their model; where every different position permits each to behold one side, one aspect. The same applies to the imitative representation that every art produces of the same subject.

Thus, when painting and sculpture imitate an object – the one through colour and without the reality of relief, the other through relief and the roundness of forms, but devoid of their colour – they offer the spectator one of those necessary

Fig. 38. Belvedere Farm, main barn and tower, D. Porphyrios.
From *Demetri Porphyrios, Selected Buildings and Writings*,
Academy Editions, London, 1993

conventions to which he must subscribe as the condition for the existence of these arts. Through a peculiarity, which we shall not explain here, the delight that pertains to these two kinds of imitation derives precisely from this lack of complete imitation. (*See* ILLUSION).

But these two arts are subject to other *conventions* still with nature or with their model. For example, they can never seize but a moment of a certain action. Even if the figures that they display in the attitudes of the most energetic movement, can be seen as such only in the briefest moment that passes away after a first look, there is, however, between the arts and the spectator a tacit *convention* through which the latter will want nothing more.

The kinds of adjustments or *conventions* made between the arts in their imitation of nature, and the senses to which their imitations are addressed, would form an inexhaustible subject of a long book. One can even add that almost all the rules of painting and sculpture (that is to say the rules of their abstract theory) are naught but a compendium of *conventions* from which derives all the virtue of their effects.

What has just been touched upon about the *conventions* of painting and sculpture in relation to their model and the observer, will be more palpable still when applied to the other arts, and especially the scenographic arts. Thus, pantomime, which speaks through movement and expresses itself through gestures; and music, whose movements are in the combinations of stress in the voice or the effects of instrumental sounds; and the representations of scenography, despite its accomplished means of illusion, all reinforce the system of *conventions* of which we speak, if one were to compare all that these arts lack with all that is possessed by their model.

I think that I have said enough in order to indicate the meaning of *convention* in the fine arts. However, so that the entire meaning of this word and its associated notions are clearer, I would add that it is sometimes used in a good sense and at other times in a bad sense. Every artistic constitution has necessary *conventions* which are the conditions of its existence. There are also some less basic *conventions* which are the consequences of earlier ones. Still, there is a point where theory compels us to stop, beyond which the arbitrary and the bizarre are found.

This is what effectively we would call – reprehensibly – a style of *convention*, or a form of *convention*, designating all that derives from the abuse, the excess, or the misunderstanding of the *conventions* of which we spoke. Such are, for example, all these compositions whose object is to flatter the eyes through a choice of strange forms, and whose assemblage nature disavows. Nothing explains this difference in *convention* better than what is known as ornament, whose ideas and forms derive from a certain order of *conventions* admitted by nature and sanctioned by

taste. But soon, as if that which is an exception can in turn become a rule and produce other exceptions, the most irrational and least agreeable inventions of ornaments began to proliferate, like those parasitic plants that are always ready to replace the good grain. But this will be better explained in the following application to architecture, which is our object.

The art of architecture – leaving aside the intellectual correlations of its imitative system, which is adopted from the general economy of nature, her laws and combinations, thus making architecture an art of genius – belongs still to the imitation proper to the fine arts by virtue of particular *conventions*.

This second kind of imitation, which we have developed elsewhere (*See* ARCHITECTURE, WOOD, etc.) and which seems to rest on a material order of things, exists solely through the effect of various *conventions*. Thus, this artistic metaphor, or the transposition of the system and procedures of carpentry into the system and procedures of stone construction, cannot exist without a considerable number of *conventions*; in other words compositions that judgment ties to reality. Also, one should not be astonished that this art has been exposed, especially among the moderns, to two sorts of misconceptions. The basis of this imitation being to a certain point changeable, caused sometimes too great a severity of reasoning, and at other times too great a complacency of imagination, which served to constrain or expand *conventions* beyond the point that judgment indicates as being the happy mean.

In the absence of any real model found in nature, judgment has determined – and the experience of centuries confirmed it – that the simplest building, that of the Greek type of primitive wood construction, which was formed by the instinct of nature so to speak, became for architecture what the works of nature were for painting and sculpture.

However, it became necessary for the rustic type of wood construction, which answered in its coarseness to the most simple needs, to undergo numerous modifications through the change in materials, and the necessity to have the most varied combinations in order to satisfy the exigencies of taste, symmetry, and the eye's delight.

From here derived a second order of *conventions*.

But the issue here was unlike the imitation of natural objects in painting for example, where a faithful image of a given model is produced. This would have been but a purely mechanical repetition of a purely material object; and where there is only repetition, there is no imitation in an artistic sense. Thus, the need to compromise with all the forms of the model developed a more material kind of imitation than the one mentioned above. Hence, without leaving the intended fiction, each part of carpentry found itself transformed into a simple commemorative representation, which, being subject to a new harmony of relations, forms and symmetries, produced pediments instead of roofs, modillions instead of rafters, and triglyphs in place of beams. Architraves and entablatures replaced summers, columns replaced vertical supports, diverse capitals replaced plates, profiles of all sorts reminded the intellect and the eyes of projections, intervals, and the divisions of the original building, with a pleasing variety.

The more the exigencies of the most opulent societies, and the increasingly pressing needs of luxury applied to more public proprieties and private uses, the more the architecture of exteriors and interiors, of the most complicated plans and elevations, found it impossible to remain within the rigorous constraints of her primitive formation.

A third order of *conventions* also took place but the list is too long to enumerate here. We shall therefore mention but a few. For example, the use of superimposed orders with all the details of the entablature that represent the top of the edifice through the details of the timber-roof (such as the purlines and the rafters). One of the most accepted *conventions*, is the use of pediments in the interior of monuments where there is no need for protection from rain; the use of cornices and entablatures in the interiors of houses and apartments, etc. Engaged columns and pilasters, which in reality are naught but the representations of columns, since they cannot be true supports, must count among authorized *conventions*. One *convention* that gives rise to controversy is that of twin and coupled columns, especially in isolated colonnades, where their merging shafts produce unequal masses. This abuse is less severe if they are held back to back.

Ornament also gives rise to a considerable number of *conventions* whose enumeration would be too long, and which derive from subtle nuances where taste is the only judge.

Enough has been said in this article and in the entry PROPRIETY, in order to explain to a clear mind the importance of knowing and appreciating the different sorts of *conventions* accepted in architecture, and the necessity to respect propriety. Two dangers assail this theory, which is naturally exposed to two excesses. There is that of the rigid minds who wish to enclose architecture within the narrow circle of that which can be demonstrated as necessary, and who repel even the most usual *conventions* of antiquity, disregarding the exceptions brought about by new needs among modern people. It would be proper to say here, *Summum jus, summa injuria*. But most dreaded is the contrary excess of those who abuse received *conventions* in order to deny any rule, who admit no other law than that of *caprice*, and who, instead of seeing exceptions as confirmations of a principle rather than its destruction, conclude that since there are curved lines, then there must be no straight ones, consequently recognizing no authority but the arbitrary.

CONVENTIONAL Such is the appellation given to all that exists or that is made by virtue of conventions.

In the arts of design that have the nature and form of the human body as a fixed and real model, there is often a misapprehension between a *conventional* manner, and what is known as a *style of convention*. The meaning here, is understood in the sense of a manner or style that an artist adopts, and which, instead of having a natural truth for a principle, is generally the result of either a false and exaggerated imitation of the style of some master, or of a system where some artificial rules are substituted for those that guided the greatest artists.

The fact that the two arts of which we spoke have in nature a material model that impresses the senses, does not necessarily entail that it suffices to have eyes and an experienced hand in order to reproduce truths and beauties; for these truths and beauties still need to submit to a reasoning that disengages them from all that could harm the effect of imitation, if art were to limit itself to no other function than that of a mirror. Here is where genius, followed by theory, in order to attain what is known as the *beautiful ideal*, has established certain *conventions* with nature or, better still, with that which is improperly known as the *individual model*. It is evident from these *conventions* that if the model is in nature, nature is not always in the model; that is to say, the true model does not reside in partial productions which are several generations removed and subject to a multitude of accidents, but rather within the general laws of nature where the individual is most often but a more or less defective exception.

Now this system is one of those high *conventions* in which the theory of painting and sculpture approach the first rate *conventions* by virtue of which architecture draws her imitation from the high source of the general system of order, harmony, and proportion that nature communicates to the genius of the artist who knows how to obtain his principles and rules.

Thus, it is in this sense that the adjective *conventional* can and must become a word of praise.

COPY The etymology of this word, which is the Italian word *copia*, seems to us to indicate with enough precision, the veritable meaning attached to the idea and the act of *copying*. *Copie* and *couple* in French signify the *double* of a certain object. Hence, *copiare* [Italian: to copy] signifies to make the double of this object.

This is, as one observes in the realm of imitation, the precise use of the word *copy*, and the definition of the idea that it expresses.

To *imitate*, as mentioned in the article *imitation*, offers a wholly different idea, with a much wider, and at the same time more elevated meaning. Its general definition is found in the idea which expresses the repetition of an object by and with another object, which becomes its image. It is clear that the analysis of this theory could present as many kinds of imitation as there are different manners with which to reproduce an object within another object.

But there is also a triple division of imitation, considered in the simple idea of the action of repeating an object.

There is the manner of producing a repetition through an image which demands of its author the resources of genius, of feeling, of the imagination; this is, properly speaking, imitation in the moral sense of the word.

There is a material imitation. It is that which produces the repetition of an object by mechanical procedures and unfailing means, and where consequently moral action has no effect.

There is between these two sorts of imitation yet another means of repetition, which is equally distant from that which characterizes genius in an artist and that which constitutes the routine procedure of the worker; it is the art of the copyist.

In fact, the *copy* in the truly imitative arts, is more the result of the talent of the artist than a technical operation independent of its user. The *copy* supposes an accuracy of sight, a facility in execution, and a feeling for the beauty of the original; consequently, it requires talent and intelligence.

Copying is therefore not an entirely foreign matter to the art of genius, but only to the genius of art or to invention.

We should also add that the idea of imitation applies to the repetition of the works of nature, while the idea of *copy* applies to the repetition of works of art.

Since it is generally from works of art that one learns, as in a mirror which best assembles traits, to know and imitate those of nature, it is ordinarily through *copies* that beginners proceed. This is why students' studies begin with *copies*, and it is by *copying* that those who intend to take up imitation begin.

We have said that the idea of *copy* excluded that of imitation, and that invention eminently constituted the true imitation. Hence, if one must begin by *copying* in order to learn how to imitate, then one must not indulge for a long time in work that holds the inventive faculty within an inertia which sometimes prohibits it from developing.

Yet there is in the study of works of art a way in which to emerge as an imitator rather than a copyist. Herein resides the very secret of sentiment and of genius. But this secret, which the teachers can reveal to the students through the lessons of an active teaching and through examples, is difficult to communicate through the documents of an abstract theory, which are frequently without value.

One has seen great men imitate the works of their predecessors, and appropriate even their taste and manners, without being less reputed as original or inventive. Indeed, it is always possible to exercise on the ideas and the conceptions of others the very action of invention. It is possible to follow their progress without tracing their very footsteps, and to pattern oneself on the spirit rather than the letter of their inventions, in such a way that, while profiting by their examples, one also acquires the right to serve as a model for those who follow. Still, such a study of imitation is less the study of the works that properly belong to their author, than that of nature whose maxims and lessons these works rendered practical. This is how great men succeeded each other, without following each other in the same career.

Therefore, what differentiates he who imitates preceding works from he who is but their copyist, is that the first knows how to read in the inventions of others the maxims or the inspirations which produced them, and having studied the paths through which their genius passed, he learned to tread similar paths; while the other, repeating borrowed ideas in servile works, crawls behind, instead of walking by himself.

Therefore, since it is with the purpose of forming imitators that one compels students to begin by being *copyists*, one must be guarded from letting them ignore the goal to which they must strive. It is advisable to explain to them the middle ground that must be kept between a precocious ambition which rejects any constraint, and a servile docility which dares not shake the yoke of the first studies.

There is perhaps no other art whose teaching requires more the practical application of this distinction, than the art of architecture. There is effectively no other art where the confusion between the idea of copying, and the idea of imitating, is more easy to enter. If, as we have often said, the idea of copying (in the arts of design) applies to works of art, whilst the idea of imitating applies to the work of nature, it is easy to understand why the art which has no positive model in nature, finds and produces more easily copyists rather than imitators.

Moreover, this is what experience has proved.

In fact, since teachers have but works of art to present to students, their minds and eyes become accustomed to search for the principles and the rules only in the monuments made by human hands. One needs either a deep sensibility for the beautiful and the true, or a considerable power of understanding, to attain that which in abstraction is the ideal model of architecture, and to deduce from it the combinations applicable to the material work. It is simpler and shorter to repeat what has been done by the banal means of measurements and the compass. And indeed one must admit that since there is no other art where ideal imitation is further removed from ordinary capacities, there is also no other art where the copy, in the true sense of the word, is more within the reach of the greatest number. Measurement and the compass do not suffice to repeat the painted or sculpted figure, while a building, on the contrary, can be faithfully and mechanically copied.

In vitium ducit culpae fuga, said Horace. *The fear of committing an error causes you to fall into a vice.* This is what happened in many an artistic genre, but especially in architecture. The monuments of antique art, since the renewal of the arts, did not for two centuries cease to be the type upon which the greatest masters ordered their conceptions, and formed their taste and their manner. One could really cite them as examples of that which distinguishes the imitator from the copyist. The simplicity of the plans, their accordance with the elevations, the purity of the style, the respect for the types, the observance of proportions in the whole as well as in the details of the orders, in addition to a judicious appropriation to modern usage, of forms, measures, ornaments, combinations to which other countries and customs gave birth; this is what distinguishes the imitation that those two centuries made of ancient architecture.

But soon the pride and ambition of a vain originality raised the pretensions of all novelties against the effects of judicious imitation. To design after the principles of antiquity was considered the domain of copyists. For fear of *copying* what has developed for centuries, nothing better was imagined than to simply do the contrary. One knows well, and it has been said elsewhere, what results from the fear of being a copyist. Novelty was mistaken for invention, and it was not realized that while there is novelty in all inventions, there is reciprocally no invention in all novelties.

Such is the vice that one may fall into when one wants to avoid the mistake of the copyist. If there was a choice between a mistake and a vice, I do not think that the choice could have been in doubt.

CORINTHIAN (Order) This name is given to one of the three orders of Greek architecture which especially expresses the character of richness and magnificence in edifices, through the ensemble of its composition and its forms, its measures and its proportions, and the order of ideas to which it relates.

What is known as *order* in architecture (*see* this entry) can be considered under three headings: that of its measures and proportions, which belongs to the didactic part of this art; that of its character and its significance, which belongs to the theoretical part; and that of its origin, formation, and composition, which belongs to the historical part. In this article, we shall deal only with the last heading. (*For the other two, see the entries* ORDER, ARCHITECTURE).

The word *Corinthian* is misleading when it comes to the origin of the form and composition of the order in question. Doubtless, the Greeks were the inventors of architecture as an art of imitation, and the discovery of the orders, understood as the means to manifest their correspond-

ing qualities through the combination of expressions, forms and diverse ornaments, was quite certainly the work of their genius. However, long before the age of Greek architecture, another nation had raised vast edifices. Egypt had fashioned the columns and ceilings of its temples from quarry stones, and its column capitals were characterized by a great variety of configurations.

Today, as the diverse Egyptian capital forms and their irregular use are known in great detail, one is led to believe that these diverse measures, forms and ornaments were used without any rational system that aims at a determined expression of quality, genre, or character. Of these, one notes the capital in the form of a vase or an inverted bell, which is sometimes devoid of

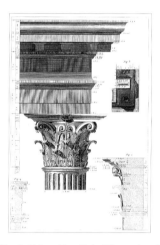

Fig. 39. Corinthian Capital, Olympian Zeus. From Stuart & Revett's *Antiquities of Athens*, Reprint, B. Bloom, New York 1968

ornament, and other times ornamented with leaves of lotus or other plants.

The type of order which was undeniably born in Greece, where one may say it was *endemic*, is the Doric (*See* DORIC). Judging by the considerable number of Doric edifices still extant, and the very small number of *Corinthian* ones that could be cited, one may conclude that the *Corinthian* order was but little employed, or that it was used during the period when Greece no longer built great enterprises, having lost her power and her riches.

There is even reason to believe that the communications between Egypt and Greece occurred at quite a late date, and that the Doric order had been in use in most temples for a long time.

Be that as it may, it is undeniable that the type of Greek *Corinthian* capital is found in the Egyptian bell capital, and that its ornamental motif made of olive or acanthus leaves exists also in that of the lotus or palm leaves. There is also no reason not to believe that Callimachus's story was imagined in order to nationalize the idea or invention of the *Corinthian* capital.

This suffices to explain that the name *Corinthian*, given to this capital does not imply that it was invented in Corinth, unless, as we said earlier, the substitution – attributed to Callimachus, who came from Corinth – of the acanthus leaf for the other plants served to justify the name.

We said that the extant ruins of Greece offer little indication of the use of this order. Enough remains, however, to show us that its capital was fashioned according to a taste different from the one that followed. In fact if one were to examine the capitals of the monument known as the *Tower of the Winds*, one notices almost no resemblance with those of later times except the general form of the vase. Its decoration consists of two rows of leaves: a lower row of acanthus leaves, and an upper row of pointed and elongated olive leaves. There are no caulicoles, no volutes, no channels cut in the abacus, which is entirely circular.

The capital of the choragic monument of Lysicrates, ordinarily known as the *Lantern of Demosthenes*, whose shaping is richer and more varied, is still far removed from the later use to which it was subjected. A single row of acanthus leaves occupies its lower part, from which other foliage emanates and unites, conforming to the flexion of the volutes.

If the length of this article were to permit the gathering of many more details regarding the origin and the formation of the capital that became one of the principal traits of the *Corinthian* order, then one would most probably conclude that its initial use was in the form of a smooth vase. This is observed in the exquisite bas-relief of an archaic style (like that of Aegina), found at the villa Albani, where it adorns the columns of a temple front.

Similarly, some caryatids show a capital in the form of a vase or inverted bell, without any orna-

ment. Other caryatids exhibit the same form of capital with ornaments of little relief, that is to say without projection, of which one finds many examples in Egypt.

Is this one more reason to give an Egyptian origin to the *Corinthian* capital? Beyond the lack of historical proof, one could still oppose this opinion by saying that the very nature of things in one or both countries, considering the facts and examples, may have produced a capital form that we are compelled to regard as independent of its accessory ornaments. In fact we observe that in Egypt this form was generally the result of the need to raise the structural supports in many a monument where certain kinds of capitals, formed by superposed parts, could have naturally justified the bell

Fig. 40. Egyptian and Corinthian capitals.
From: Josef Durm, *Die Baukunst der Grieschen*,
A. Kröner Verlag, Leipzig, 1910

shape. Who could deny then that after custom had consecrated the type of Doric capital in harmony with its proportions and all the correlations that derived from the imitation of the primitive wooden model, that the need would arise in Greece for columns befitting higher proportions, leading naturally to the development of a more elevated type of capital with a more elegant configuration? Since we find no corroborating evidence to this effect in historical documents or in a chronology of monuments, it seems to me that we should limit ourselves to the induction that the genius of the Greeks transposed the analogies that it found in the study of the human body and its principal varieties and proportions, to an order of things that did not receive a material model from nature.

Thus were born the forms, the measures and the ornaments of capitals, with the differences in proportion and variety in the three orders. But these kinds of modifications emerge imperceptibly and grow unbeknownst to their contemporaries. Once custom and taste have naturalized and sanctioned them, they enter the language of art, and one uses them without thinking of going back to their originating causes. Finally, when in the course of the following centuries one inquires as to their origin, one is left with nothing but hazardous conjectures. This is perhaps the most reasonable opinion that a wise critique can give regarding the origin of the Ionic and *Corinthian* capitals.

If the analysis of the *Corinthian* capital – as evidenced by certain extant Greek monuments and other more ancient indications – informed us as to what the *Corinthian* capital was before the modification of its ornament attributed to the sculptor Callimachus, then we must look outside Greece for the models in which the art of architecture searches today for its rules. It is in Rome, in this capital of the ancient world, and in monuments that were undeniably the product of the manner and the chisel of the Greeks, that one must look for the most beautiful compositions of the *Corinthian* order.

To begin with, the capital – which is its most characteristic attribute, and which adorns the most beautiful edifices of Rome, and in buildings that were undeniably the products of Greek work – is composed of a drum in the shape of an elongated vase without swelling, and an abacus or top plate whose sides are channelled. The capital's body is ornamented with three rows of leaves, forming what is known as a *panache*, that is to say, their extremities curve and incline forward. The four angles of the abacus are supported by volutes that emerge from the second row of leaves, and seem to be themselves supported by stems known as caulicoles, in the manner of certain plants. Smaller volutes merge also on the four sides, towards the middle of the abacus, and seem to support what is known as the eye or the rosette of the capital.

Such is the general description that has for a long time been adopted regarding the *Corinthian*

capital. I said general, for it cannot be that such a composition, which has no fixed and necessary basis, would fail to produce some small and numerous varieties. There are a very few capitals perhaps that exhibit no difference.

The most important one, if not for composition then at least for the very nature of objects imitated by sculpture, relates to the kind of foliage. The olive and acanthus leaves seem to rival each other for prominence. The acanthus has an aspect that is richer but also appears heavier and less lively. The partitions produced by the olive leaf are firmer and endow the sculpture with a livelier effect.

The height of the rows of leaves, the number of their denticulations, their spacing, correlations and curvature, are details that defy description. One can even add that there is no rule that determines them. All of this is necessarily subject to proportions and taste, which is the only judge of the good effect of these details that depend on the dimensions of edifices and the distances from which they are viewed.

Doubtless, the capital is the accessory of an order, and its ornament is also but a detail of this accessory. Here however, as in other cases, the accessories occupy a larger place in the description than the principal matter itself, consisting in proportions of which we shall give the most customary rules based on the best models.

The most general proportions of the *Corinthian* capital, are those that give seven to eight diameters to the height of its shaft, without counting the base and capital. To obtain the height of the capital, add three and a half small modules to the measure of the lower diameter, which makes one sixth of a diameter.

Dividing this height into seven parts, give four to the rows of leaves, that is to say two to the first row, and two to the second row. Divide each leaf into three parts, with the top part given to the descending curve of the leaf. The remaining three parts – of the seven – are for the small stems, the volutes and the abacus.

As to the base, the most customary and best proportion given it, is that of the attic base, whose height often measures half a module.

The shaft of the *Corinthian* column receives entasis and fluting, although it is just as common to have it smooth.

The entablature is one of the most important parts of the *Corinthian* order. It is usually divided into twenty parts: six for the architrave, the same for the frieze, and eight for the cornice; but the monuments reveal that these measures are variable.

In the temple of Jupiter Tonans, as in that of the Sibyl, the frieze is larger than the architrave. This height is found to be smaller in the Pantheon's portico, in the temple of Peace, and in the Antonine basilica; but in the Pantheon's interior, the architrave and the frieze have the same height.

The architrave comprises three divisions or bands, although there are some with only two. The common rule is to distinguish eighteen parts to the architrave: the top cima reversa measures three, the fillet measures one and a quarter, whereas the large astragal below the cima reversa measures one part. The top division measures five parts; the small cima reversa, one and a half; the middle division four, and one half for its astragal; and the lower division three.

What is special about the frieze of the *Corinthian* order, is that it can receive the greatest opulence, or remain completely devoid of ornament, without indecorousness. One must also say more generally, that this order admits the greatest magnificence of ornament, and is also capable of dispensing with any richness of detail save that of its proportions and its forms. Its shaft can remain without fluting, and its base can have profiles without ornaments. Its cornice and frieze admit all the luxury of decoration; however, it can exclude any decorative detail (as shown by some splendid examples) without becoming disordered and altered. Also, there is much diversity in the measures and the ornaments of this part of the entablature.

Thus, the character of richness and magnificence that is associated with the *Corinthian* order derives from its proportions, the numerous and varied elements of its composition, as well as the ornaments and details with which sculpture embellishes its forms. By considering this order as one of the hues that architecture can employ, one must also appraise its ability to be modified in order to accommodate various nuances, depending on the character that the architect intends to render more evident.

We have said elsewhere that this order does not suit all kinds of edifices; we shall not repeat here the rules of taste that proscribe, prescribe or modify its use.

CORRECTION The words *correction* and *purity* are often used as synonyms. It seems to us that they should only be compared in order for one to explain the other. In fact, there is something in common between them when considering certain mechanical works. A work that is *correct* is one that is devoid of mistakes, and in this view, the word *purity* obtains, since the word *pure* implies that something is without blemish or admixture.

If one were to transpose the meaning of these words to the appreciation of the spirit of the arts, one would find a tangible difference. It would seem that the idea of *purity* is more applicable to the abstract quality of the genre, the taste, or the invention of a work of art, whereas the idea of *correction* pertains more particularly to execution.

For example, the word *pure* in architecture designates any building, any composition or conception that appears to be the product of a high intelligence, of a clear aim, of a right feeling for the harmony of forms and the proportions of a proper character. It seems to us, on the other hand, that the word *correct* refers to any building or composition that is the result of an exact observation of rules, that causes no objection to be raised, that would satisfy even the eyes and the mind, only without arousing any particular impression, especially that of admiration, or capturing the imagination.

However, the *correction* that derives from the observation of rules is a quality that one cannot too highly recommend in this art where intellectual independence and the mania for innovation can destroy everything without supplying any suitable substitute. Architecture, more than any other art, is in need of a shield that protects her from the easy aberrations and the deviations of the spirit of caprice that rejects any constraint as a destruction of genius; whereas the triumph of genius in this art, as well as all the others, is to be or to appear free precisely when under shackles.

Such is the virtue of rules; it is to give more impetus and energy to the artist. We also observe that the most beautiful masterpieces have always been those that have become rules themselves by identifying with the rules, and owing their quality to the merit of *correction*.

DECORATION In artistic parlance this word expresses two different ideas. By *decoration* in general, one designates the art of decorating an object; and when one says more specifically *a decoration*, one designates the work or the product of the art of *decoration*.

Both meanings are applied to architecture, designating either the art that includes all parts and all kinds of exterior and interior ornaments, or designating, more particularly, the array of objects, subjects and compositions that the architect's taste or genius impressed with pleasure and delight on what was otherwise a work based on need and necessity.

If one were to consider *decoration*, or the art of decorating, abstractly and within the general idea of the word, one cannot help but recognize that taste partakes in the very nature of the human mind, exemplified in the need for variety, which in itself is naught but the need to alternately move from action to rest. Changing impressions, for the mind, is like the change of positions for the body. The more delightful objects increase, the more pleasure will the mind experience.

Indeed, when an advanced state of society multiplies the physical needs of man, his mind cannot but desire more numerous intellectual sensations. This is when imitation comes to his aid.

The advantage of imitation is its power to choose, coordinate and assemble within the same subject, the diversity of scattered impressions arising from the objects at its disposal. Then, through the illusions that it produces, it makes us experience in a few moments, and in a small number of points, a multitude of sensations that in reality would have required the course of

many years, and the confluence of many circumstances. Such is, for example, the true cause of the pleasure produced by imitation in drama. This virtue belongs no less, although in different degrees, to the other arts of imitation, which can be considered, in an advanced state of civilization, as the true decorators of society.

Thus, to decorate or to embellish an object, is to adorn it with accessories that reinforce the impressions proper to this object; it is to multiply the ways in which it can be considered; it is to make available for the mind certain comparisons or combinations which, through their variety, enable it to behold different views; it is to present the mind with new safeguards against monotony and boredom; it is, in one word, to give pleasure to the mind.

If the taste for *decoration*, as we just defined it, derives from the very nature of the mind, then we shall find that the origin and the model for this taste is within nature herself. In fact, could it not be that nature herself had in mind the delights and the pleasures of man by placing him in the middle of this spectacle of infinite variety that composes the whole of her creations; and would it not seem that in the numerous varieties of agreeable forms, colours, divisions, and embroideries of all kinds that she took pleasure in making and in diversifying within the exterior forms of her spectacle, that she invites man to spread the same luxury in works of arts.

However, there is a question here that raises a doubt. Did nature, no matter the class of her creations, ever produce useless details; that is to say, ornaments whose sole purpose is to please the eye of man. Although many natural productions contain accessories of form or colour whose purpose we cannot explain, there is nothing that authorizes us to judge them useless, for the secrets of the underlying structure of a great number of beings are unknown to us. On the contrary, in judging that which we cannot fathom by that which we can explain, we must admit that that which appears to us to be a parasitic ornament is either a cause whose effect we cannot see, or an effect whose cause is unknown to us; but that everything has a reason and a purpose.

Accordingly, that which we call ornament or *decoration* in nature is either the effect or the principle of a necessary order.

Moreover, we are compelled to recognize that the general system of nature is such that she constantly places pleasure side by side with necessity, making the former always derive from the latter.

Without expanding on the principle of a theory whose evidence is found within each individual, it suffices for us to deduce, through a necessary analogy, that decorative art is compelled to conform to the conditions willed by its own principle.

This principle, in fact, leads us to the following two consequences:

The first is that since the taste for *decoration* has its model in the works of nature, architecture must then operate in her works as does nature, that is to say that the inventions of architecture must rest on a more or less tangible need.

The second is that before being and appearing necessary, *decoration* in edifices must employ ideas, subjects, and images, which by their combinations and choice, are most congruent with the principal object, that is to say, the purpose of each monument.

By the word necessary, we do not suggest that *decoration* is indispensable for every edifice in all its parts. Taste, or the feeling for customs, consists in knowing how to appraise the proper measure of ornament needed by different buildings. And sometimes even the absence of ornament can be seen as a means of *decoration*. Since the ceremony of language, the richness of diction, and the luxury of images do not fit all the forms of speech, and as there are some forms of speech whose simplicity or absence of adornment make for all the adornment, the same applies to architecture, where there are edifices whose character would be destroyed or weakened by *decoration*, and whose beauty derives from the absence of all ornament.

Therefore, a necessary *decoration* is one whose absence would produce a deficiency of meaning, or a misconception; one whose presence explains to the spectator the object for which it is used; one that reinforces the impressions that this object must produce, and develops their character.

A necessary *decoration* is also one that draws the incentives for its inventions either from the core of the principal idea of the monument or from the relations between its accessory elements.

Now, in order to leave the circle of abstract ideas and the realm of the systematic theory where we have been examining the principle of architectural *decoration*, we shall consider the three kinds of tangible means that architecture possesses to embellish the forms that answer to necessity: 1° *the instinct or the natural need for variety*, 2° *analogical imitation*, 3° *the use of allegorical signs or historical figures*.

FIRST PARAGRAPH
On the instinct or the natural need for variety.

The means that architectural *decoration* obtains from the instinct for variety are common to all peoples and are found in all their works. From this instinct derives this large number of details, embroideries and denticulations that have no precise significance. These details are found in every country and resemble these fantasies and trivial games that all children repeat everywhere, having learned them in no particular place and from no particular person.

In considering Greek architecture from the standpoint of one of the elements of *decoration* (that of ornament properly speaking), one is compelled to recognize that with respect to the execution of the edifice, this element is no different in a piece of furniture, around a vase, or other similar objects that receive most of their ornaments for the pleasure of the eye, thus incurring no other meaning.

To be excessive in one's proofs is to expose oneself to doubt regarding the proofs comprised in the other elements of *decoration*. Such was the abuse that compelled some to pretend to explain the differences in capitals by means of the differences in head-dress, the column flutings by the falling dress-folds of women, or by the tree bark and other arbitrary forms, and even more arbitrary similitudes.

There is a place to be made in architectural *decoration* for the genius or the instinct for variety. It is in this place for example, that should be classified the rosettes in coffered ceilings, the various kinds of foliage in the Corinthian capital, the Ionic volutes, the ovolos, beads and the tracery, and in general all the sculptures in an entablature. It is not that many of these details are entirely capricious, as if they did not belong to a natural order of things; on the contrary, it is well known that art could not help but borrow these details from nature. However, the subject at hand is their transposition into architecture, and it is precisely this application that can be criticized for having no plausible and incontestable reason within a natural analogy.

We should mention, however, that certain critics have attempted to explain this transposition of plants into ornaments with fortuitous reasons such as those that make these plants grow over the ruins of abandoned edifices. Such hypothetical explanations do not account for all the other details and profiles in buildings. In observing that this taste, which is common to all peoples, is also subject to all the products of human industry, it stands more to reason to recognize that there is a certain category of objects within *decoration* which is the pure result of the universal instinct that searches within variety for the simple visual pleasure.

If one is compelled to admit that many decorative objects, considered as to their origins and the reasons for their use, derive from the caprices of chance and depend on the instinct for variety, then one ought not conclude that the architect must abandon disposition to the chance of caprice and the variations of instinct. This is the point that explains the difference between architecture as an art, in that it is subject to rules founded on the causes of our delights; and architecture without art, that is to say, one that follows only the mechanical impulse of instinct in its compositions.

Although a good number of ornaments could not appease a rigorous critique regarding their origin and their necessity, nor justify the reasons for their introduction into *decoration*, the decora-tor is no less required to know how to use them for another sort of purpose: that of the effect that one expects from the number, the mode and the nature of these objects.

Now there is an effect that is produced by ornamental objects, even the least significant ones by themselves; it is one that modifies the character of an edifice in one direction or another, whether by multiplying the impressions of distraction and delight, or by affecting the observer's mind through the feeling of gravity and simplicity, or by inspiring the idea of richness, abundance and luxury through the choice of objects and the manner in which they are developed.

Depending then on whether the architect *decorator* intends to emphasize one or the other of these general ideas that the language of his art can only express through more or less ambiguous signs, he will strengthen the massing with lines, forms and proportions, and with the more or less lively or more or less restrained effect of this category of objects known as *ornaments*.

Moreover, architecture has the means to pleasantly affect us, and these means consist in the order and harmony that are produced by any tasteful arrangement. Considered in such a manner, ornament comes to be identified with the principal merit of architecture. Indeed, a beautiful edifice can be abstractly defined as a spectacle of harmonious relations and agreeable details. Now these relations and details of ornament are of such importance for the success of the whole, that a building that uses ornament poorly could fail to achieve its purpose as a congruence between reason and taste. And, conversely, it may be said of many a derided building, and for good reason, that it would accrue a higher opinion among people of taste, if its *decoration* were to be removed or replaced by another.

One could compare that part of architectural *decoration* that consists in the use of ornaments, which are more or less arbitrary signs that catch the eye, to the purely instrumental part in music which pretends to be an indeterminate language that is understood by the ear without the words and the inflections of the voice.

SECOND PARAGRAPH
On imitation by analogy

The second source from which architecture derives its means of *decoration*, is the *imitation* that we call *analogical*.

It is in the nature of human faculties to create only by combining created things, and to invent only by imitating. The invention of architecture gives us the proof and the example. We have shown elsewhere how this art was able to derive the types of its constitution from the primitive constructions dictated by necessity, and how it was able to convert the more or less fortuitous elements of a coarse industry into reasoned combinations.

Now it is through this same imitation by analogy that an important part of architectural *decoration* evolved from the forms of primitive construction. In fact, there is no architecture whose imitative and decorative system is more visibly inscribed within the primitive nature of things than Greek architecture.

The Greeks accomplished two things that made their architecture excel over all other architectures. First, they adopted a model which was derived if not from nature, and she does not make buildings, then it was at least formed by her inspiration and under her dictation. Then, in order to satisfy the needs of delight, they made it such that every necessary part, justified by the laws of solidity, was transformed into an embellishment where the necessary appeared to be disguised rather than hidden.

Consequently, this architecture developed a kind of imitation of nature by virtue of which delight was not only situated near necessity, but was rather its product. Thus, since the principal ornaments derived from the very forms of construction, there were few objects of *decoration* that did not answer to reason.

These objects need only be indicated, since they derived from an analogy with the necessary objects of construction. Everyone knows that the principal elements, forms, details and relations from which the true richness and magnificence of edifices is composed, derived from the constitutive parts of the primitive model. The authority of this imitation was such that it came to be identified with the delight that results from *decoration*, to the point that it evokes the same pleasure that one experiences while observing nature herself – as if by instinct. Cicero expressed this effect with much sense and good taste when, admiring the decorative beauty of a pediment, and recognizing its origin in the roof that protects from the rain, he exclaimed that edifices should still be crowned with a pediment even if one were to build in Olympus where it does not rain.

Therefore, the decorator must display a scrupulous attention in his compositions, to all the imitative analogies of architecture. He must realize that the members to which he wants to add ornaments are themselves already ornaments; that the profiles, bases, capitals, the parts of the entablature, the pediments, and many other objects that became the essential *decoration* of architecture, should not be diverted from their original meaning by foreign accessories, nor distorted by an excess of parasitic details, nor by a search for certain contours and configurations with which decorative fantasy tried, for some time, to replace the genius of architecture.

One can see how the spirit of ornament and *decoration*, which is auxiliary to architecture, can even pretend to decompose and recompose architectural forms. As mentioned earlier, one must admit that, properly speaking, many an ornamental detail, many an accessory to principal forms, found their way into architecture by the sole instinct for variety, without any other reason for their use. As a consequence, the paradoxical and innovative mind concluded that everything in *decoration* must be arbitrary, because not everything in *decoration* was founded on the necessity of reason, or the reason for necessity.

Decorators formed a false idea of invention, and this seems to have further influenced their works. They mistook the exact observance of the same forms in the architecture of antiquity as a sign of a lack of genius, and they called monotonous that which was regular. They mistook the moderation in effect for a poverty of means; the purity of form for timidity; they replaced the wise and intelligent economy with the excesses of luxury; and the simple caution in achieving a harmonious and wise variety, with lavishness in contrasts and diversity. However, the examples of the two opposing styles have proven that the more scrupulous observance of types or the constitutive forms of architecture can be associated with all the variety required by the taste for *decoration*, when this taste knows how to obtain its motifs from the works of nature through imitation by analogy.

The general system of Greek architecture and its division into three modes demonstrate how the tempered expression of the primitive forms dictated by necessity compels the use of *decoration* in edifices, depending on their purpose, their character, and the multiple degrees of richness or economy, embellishment or simplicity. These degrees and the diversity of their use constitute a kind of highly intelligible language in *decoration*, when, on the one hand, the artist has the skill to speak it, and, on the other, when the spectator knows how to understand it.

THIRD PARAGRAPH
*On the use of allegorical signs
or historical figures*

The principal source from which architectural *decoration* derives the most befitting means to make an edifice a kind of historical book, or a poem which assembles the greatest ideas or the most varied impressions, is the use of allegorical or historical figures or signs.

Through the use of allegorical means alone the work of an architect becomes an ensemble of relations and ideas that address not only the intellect but also the feelings and the imagination. The architect no longer evokes in us the impressions that correspond to his aim through simple and indirect references, or through more or less abstract combinations, or a choice of intellectual correlations; rather, the art of architecture here, having become a historian, explains in clear terms the material object and the moral goal of the edifice. Thus, *decoration* supplants inscriptions by conveying more and better

instruction than all the legends painted on walls and frontispieces.

When it is directed by such a spirit, *decoration* serves also to determine the purpose of an edifice even after it has fallen into ruins. How many monuments would have remained nameless were it not for some small fragment of their *decoration* that indicated what they were, and the purpose of their construction?

All the details that *decoration* borrows from painting and sculpture, in order to produce this effect, are too numerous to occupy a place in this simple analysis. However, one could divide the principal means that these two arts offer to architecture into three classes:

The first class comprises allegorical attributes;

The second is composed of complete or partial figures;

The third embraces the subjects of composition.

1° Under the name attribute, we group all the symbols or emblematic figures which, having received a tangible existence through the medium of sculpture, accrued the value of these monograms that can be read by everyone. Within this group, one could classify the festoons, scrolled foliage, plants or fruits which have always and everywhere been used in religious ceremonies, and which art imitated in durable materials, shaping them into clear and intelligible attributes for sacred edifices or for monuments dedicated to pious solemnities.

Thus, the sacrificial instruments, the sacrificers' ornaments, sacred vases, heads of immolated animals, bandlets, pateras and all that was included by ancients cults are received as attributes that enrich the *decoration* of modern architecture, which in turn uses them as conventional signs that explain the purpose of a certain kind of building.

It is well known that each divinity had its particular attributes among the ancients, but it is also known that each divinity was naught but a kind of symbol standing for the diverse properties of nature, or for the ideas behind the physical or the moral order of things. Doubtless, no one believes in Jupiter, Venus, Apollo, or the Muses, etc., any more, but as no one ceases to believe in the qualities, feelings, and intellectual powers that these fabulous beings represented, their names and their attributes have remained as emblematic figures consecrated through the poetry of language and that of architectural *decoration*.

Therefore, there is nothing to prevent the eagle, lightning, and the club, from representing eternity, omnipotence, or strength; the lyre and the laurel from signifying harmony and glory; the helmet and the lance of Mars from designating war; the palm and the crown from announcing victory; the olive branch from expressing peace, etc. Thus, the ear of Ceres, the serpent of Esculapius, the tripod of Apollo, the bird of Minerva, the cock of Mercury, can be the expressive signs of abundance, science, divination, vigilance, etc.

Accordingly, the instruments of the arts, the sciences, and all the objects that serve the purposes or uses to which an edifice is destined, become its natural signs. Thus, through the use and combination of attributes, the open field of *decoration* is as varied as it is wide. But it is vital for the significant value of these attributes that they not be employed without purpose, and for their respective uses not to be confounded. Yet, how many are the examples of imprudent and improper mixtures of all these attributes used without discernment as to their value, in the manner of an ignoramus who assembles the characters of writing to amuse himself, or to utter the sounds of syllables without relation to nor a knowledge of the ideas that connect them?

Thus, the decorator ought to know and respect all the attributes and their relationship to the purpose of the edifice. All the more reason to express the same spirit in the practice of the second class of objects; that which includes partial or complete figures.

2° By partial figures, we designate those that represent but a portion of the human body and others beings, with busts, animal heads, and in general all mutilated configurations such as herms, and combinations of different natures from which the genius of the arabesque composed

all its repertory, and of which painting and sculpture could indefinitely modify the variations.

By subjects of complete figures, we designate all those that painting and sculpture can personify by producing in different corporeal forms that which belongs to the realm of poetry. Few are the conceptions of this art that the decorator cannot endow with intelligible forms with the help of allegory.

If the figures and their subjects are chosen with the necessary intelligence, they will add to the effect of the character of an edifice, irrespective of the edifice's purpose or the kind or mode of its architecture. A triumphal arch, a gate for a city or an arsenal, a theatre, a hospice, a market, a water tower, a palace, a temple, etc., and all sorts of monuments could offer to painting and sculpture subjects of complete figures that speak at once to the eye and the mind of the observer. However, one must be guarded from abusing these resources, for indiscretion contributed substantially to diminishing their value; and soon, redundancy and ambiguity accustomed the observer to regard them as insignificant signs.

With respect to sculpture in particular, and the objects of its realm, there is a kind of misuse that comes from certain routine habits in architectural projects, in which the artist multiplies the bas-reliefs and statues on all surfaces and on all the tops of monuments, solely as a filling-in. And in how many executed buildings does one not see these mundane *decorations* where the observer cares little to know their motives or their reasons?

The banal use of niches is also a customary source for this sort of *nonsense* in sculpture. If the artist becomes accustomed to consider statues as signs of an arbitrary ornament, or as an indifferent filling-in, then soon the public will no longer concern itself with the meaning of these figures which are either nestled in walls or isolated on roofs, and where the eye and the mind will search in vain for a form and a motive.

There is also a custom that recommends that this kind of luxury of *decoration* be reserved for public monuments and edifices of a certain importance. Perhaps the severity of these principles in architecture is offset by the resulting economy of work and expense. It is important for that which is accessory to not appear to be as expensive as the edifice, either in fact or in opinion, for it is often the case where one of the two remains incomplete. If one had to place statues in all the niches, for example, who is to say if such a measure would not cost more than the walls that house these niches.

3° It is especially in the third class, the one that embraces the subjects of great compositions in painting or sculpture, that *decoration* amongst the moderns seems to have considerably surpassed the magnificence of antiquity in the scope of its conceptions.

and the progress as well as the extension of the scientific procedures of perspective, have particularly contributed among the moderns, to an increase in these grand paintings that one may appropriately call spectacles of *decoration*.

This is not to challenge the ability of painting to decorate the largest spaces, for many are the examples that testify to the appropriate use of this art in grand decorative compositions; but many of these examples, in the ceilings or the vaults, show us that these compositions must always be governed by a relationship of lines and compartments that remind the eye that it is architecture that provides the basis, and determines the field and the spaces that are allocated to the decorator.

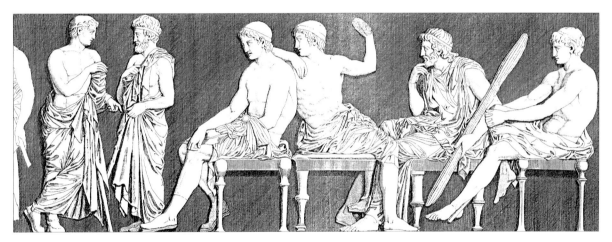

Fig. 41. Section of the Panathenaic Frieze.
From Stuart and Revett's *Antiquities of Athens*,
Reprint, B. Bloom, New York, 1968

Neither the historical narratives, nor what can be deduced from the architectural remains, lead us to believe that the ancients ever used painting to cover the whole extent of their cupolas or their largest vaults. We know that decorative painting was used in their temples; but – as the painted subjects in the temple of Minerva at Syracuse or in the enclosure around the throne of Jupiter at Olympia demonstrate – it seems that these were a series of separate paintings, easily accessible to the observer. The grand compositions of the [Cnidian] Lesche at Delphi, or the Pœcile at Athens, which represented the most numerous subjects, were painted on the wall, like Raphael's compositions in the Vatican. Certain causes, which include the heightening of modern cupolas

Now such has not always been the system of decorative compositions followed by painting. Far from being confined within architectural forms, the decorator invaded the domain of the architect, and destroyed and remade the forms, dimensions, combinations, profiles and orders to his whim, thus replacing the general architectural effect with a painted one.

A vast space allows the painter to address only the eye. But how can an observer grasp the totality of a subject, the connection between its various parts, or appreciate the characters of its figures, or judge the truth of its forms, the beauty of the faces, and the correctness of proportions, all at a distance of one hundred or two hundred feet?

What else can one also add regarding the use of painted columns, or the views of buildings that form a background for this sort of composition, since these views can appear true from only one particular perspective, while from another they offer a frightening image of ruin and collapse.

The great compositions of sculpted figures have specific applications in architecture, outside of which their effect will be nullified. One may say that sculpture is the natural *decorator* of architecture. Ancient monuments, and some modern ones, demonstrate the degree of magnificence attained by edifices that are enriched with the inventions of sculpture, whether the figures are modelled in the round or in bas-relief.

The Greeks and the Romans were particularly adept at sculpture, whether in the pediments of their temples, or in the development of the art of writing their mythological traits or the high deeds of their history through the use of figures in bas-relief. Although most of their monuments stand denuded today, one can still judge by what remains from the *decoration* of the Parthenon in Athens, by the Trajanic and Antonine columns, and ancient triumphal arches, the rich and wise abundance of their sculptural compositions in poetic and historic subjects, that stand, so to speak, for religious history and political annals.

As we have remarked earlier, there is one genre of sculpture that is particularly appropriate to architecture. This genre is that of the ancient bas-relief, which apparently had never been practised in a way that rivalled painting; and one can be permitted to doubt if there ever were isolated bas-reliefs, like the tableaux that the moderns have made. Their exclusive purpose as the accessories of architecture explains and proves that a certain simplicity of composition, the absence of distances and perspective in the background, and even the rigidity of their style or execution, were the proper characters of their use.

Therefore, in composing historical and allegorical subjects, the decorator must be careful to use sculpture only with the means that are of the nature of this art. Any encroachment on the domain of painting, whether in the degradation

of the plans, or in the distance or foreshortening implied in perspective, or in the contrasts between the massing and the effects, must be excluded from the bas-reliefs that belong to architectural *decoration*.

As I intended to treat *decoration* from the standpoint of a general theory, I shall not prolong this article by expanding on the details of practices in *decoration* that are appropriate to every kind of building, or to every detail in various architectural parts. In order to consider *decoration* – which constitutes nearly half of architecture – in all its elements, one would have to leave the prescribed limits of an article in this dictionary. Everything that relates to details is found first in the entry ORNAMENT, and then in the entries CAPITAL, BASE, COLUMN, FRIEZE, ENTABLATURE, etc.

DECORATION *considered as*
SIMULATED ARCHITECTURE
either on the walls of edifices, or in theatres.

§ I With respect to the first of these issues, *decoration* imitates on the smooth surfaces of buildings the grand compositions of real architecture. It emphasizes the projections or recesses, and simulates the materials, forms and ornaments by means of linear perspective and colour.

This kind of *decoration* was known and practised in antiquity. In the reign of Augustus, according to Pliny (Bk. XXXV, Ch. X), appeared a kind of *decoration* of walls that consisted in the representation of porticoes, country houses and landscapes; while the exterior walls exhibited views of maritime cities and ports.

This same taste, known today as the arabesque, flourished among the Romans, and consisted in small-scale reproductions in the interior compositions of houses.

We do not know – through lack of evidence and also because the ravages of time have erased traces of this kind of *decoration* in extant ruined edifices – the extent to which this *decoration* was cultivated in succeeding centuries, except that it reappears in the fourteenth and fifteenth centuries along with the other elements of painting. The

Campo-Santo in Pisa is still full of historical paintings, though in a degraded state, but where one can still admire a considerable number of views and compositions of buildings that serve as a background for the figures, and represent to us the state of architecture at the time.

Two conditions that united in Italy must have facilitated and expanded *decoration* with simulated architecture. The first consisted in good plaster work, the second in the good practice of fresco painting or equivalent procedures such as those of distemper, and also oil painting. We should also add that deterioration through cracking in this kind of work can be repaired at modest cost.

Some cities in Italy are especially known for the practice and the propagation of this kind of *decoration*. The city of Genoa, for example, gave this *decoration* great renown, for there is no palace where it is not found, either standing apart, or in concurrence with real architecture. The exterior walls of houses are painted with columns, niches, statues, balustrades, bas-reliefs, etc. Through these *decorations* of modest cost, simple individual houses gain the appearance of the richest palaces. And in these palaces, the luxury of this kind of simulation is greatly developed, especially in exteriors where gilding mixes with marble imitations.

The Venetian and Lombardian schools have produced illustrious artists in this genre of decoration. We shall borrow from the famous Algarotti, a distinguished man of letters as well as an enlightened art lover, some details on a subject that has rarely occupied art historians.

According to Algarotti, the three great masters in this school were *Dentone (Girolamo Curti)*, *Mitelli* and *Colonna*.

Although his style was severe, and his work apt to be a model for architects themselves, *Dentone* (says Algarotti) can incur the reproaches of certain licences. His intercolumniations were often so wide as to be unrealizable. There are columns of his, in the palazzo Vizzani in Bologna, that rest on consoles in lieu of stylobates. He is also blamed for having given very heavy proportions to the Ionic order of the famous *decoration* of *dei servi*, where the illusion was taken so far that

it was said that a dog collided with the wall, thinking that it was climbing the painted stairs.

Colonna, whose grandiose compositions are full of relief, and who could be called the Annibale Carracci of *decoration*, has often displayed the fault of over-abundance in invention. The great hall in the palazzo Locatelli, which was painted by him, is a proof of this excess, for it has enough *decoration* to suffice for three large halls. Moreover, he is blamed for licences that overstep the bounds of the freedom that can be granted to a decorator. This abuse has been faithfully imitated and followed by his student Pizzoli in the otherwise substantial ceiling of the church of the *Madonna del Soccorso*.

Mitelli, *Colonna*'s rival, had an agreeable manner of painting; his colours are pure and subtle, and his character is noble. He could be seen as the *Guide* to *decoration*. But still, he could be reproached for his very thin columns, his heavy bases and his disproportionate capitals.

Algarotti also mentions *Chiarini* as an excellent imitator of these masters. In equalling their qualities, he even knew how to avoid their failings. His designs were severe, and the forms and proportions of his edifices were elegant. He may well have surpassed the others, and his chapel of the *Annunziata* is perhaps the masterwork of the Bolognese decorators.

It is clear from Algarotti's critical remarks of the best works of the great decorators, that the art of architectural *decoration* in painting must be the best imitation of what constitutes beautiful architecture in reality; and that nothing that is proscribed in the model can be tolerated or excused in the imitation.

§ II The second area of simulated architecture is the theatre. Generally speaking, although scenic representations include many a motif with respect to the location of the play, most of these representations demand paintings – be they exterior or interior – of temples, public squares, palaces, halls, galleries, etc., that can belong only to the domain of simulated architecture.

Decoration in the theatre can claim some indulgence for its compositions. It is well known that because of the limited space on stage, as well as the multitude of scenery flats and the demands of artificial lighting, that the decorator occasionally needs to use certain broken forms in various groupings; however, the experience provided by some decorators proves that the most successful effects of theatrical illusion can generally be allied with the regularity of the plans and the appropriate proportions.

Unfortunately, works of this kind are the most temporary. It is quite useless to say that all we have left of the works of the ancients are narratives, for these narratives teach us that the joint resources of painting and machinery must have produced all sorts of illusions. Agatarchus, Democritus and Anaxagoras wrote treatises on this subject. They taught, said Vitruvius, that "...given a centre in a definite place, the lines should naturally correspond with due regard to the point of sight and the divergence of visual rays, so that by this deception a faithful representation of the appearance of buildings might be given in painted scenery, and so that, though all is drawn on a vertical flat façade, some parts may seem to be withdrawing into the background, and others to be standing out in front."[15]

These words of Vitruvius prove that *decoration* in the theatre was executed in painting, and differed from architectural *decoration* which was in solid construction.

Baldassare Peruzzi seems to have been the first in the sixteenth century to have renewed, with prodigious success, the prestige of theatrical illusion, and united it to the greatest beauty in invention and composition.

After him, the most famous practitioners of this genre are Bibiena and Servandoni. The latter elevated the charm and the value of scenic compositions to a point where they became a spectacle that captured the charm and the interest of the play at hand.

In the *decoration* of theatres, there are two parts that must be united by the artist who intends to succeed: invention and execution. The particular aspect of this art is that these two parts are so mutually necessary that the presence of the one cannot excuse the absence of the other.

DIMINUTION The ancients used the word *contractura* for what we call *diminution* in columns, which consists in a gradual narrowing of the column shaft, either from the bottom to the top, or from the lower third to the top.

Some looked for the origin of the *diminutions* in columns in trees, which may have served as types; others, like Vignola, believed the cause of the form of swelling [enlargement, entasis] resided in the analogy with the human body. All these etymologies are as problematic as their research is trifling. Nor is it necessary to go back to Egypt in order to find the reason for the pyramidal form that taste, in accordance with common sense, gave to columns.

To satisfy the two most important things in architecture, that is solidity and the appearance of solidity,[16] which constitute one of the principal parts of beauty in architecture, said Perrault judiciously, architects made the columns larger at the bottom than at the top.

Vitruvius suggests that *diminution* varies depending on the size of the column, and not the number of modules. According to him, a fifteen foot column should be diminished by a sixth part of the lower diameter, and a fifty foot one by an eighth; and he regulates the *diminution* of the column sizes in between in the same proportion. Yet the remaining monuments of antiquity do not prove the application of this rule. One does not observe a different *diminution* in the columns of the Temple of Peace, the portico of the Pantheon, those of the Campo Vaccino or the Basilica of Antoninus, for example, from that of the Temple of Bacchus, whose columns are one quarter of the height of those just mentioned.

There are some very tall columns, like those of the Temple of Faustina, the Portico of Septimius, the Temple of Concord and the Baths of Diocletian, whose *diminution* is greater than the one observed in columns half their size, such as the columns of the arches of Septimius Severus, and Constantine. Finally, the *diminution* of those columns less than fifteen feet is not one sixth of the diameter as Vitruvius suggests, but rather one seventh and a half; and this is also the *diminution* of the fifty foot columns mentioned above. This proves that these kinds of rules should never be taken rigorously.

The same applies to the different *diminutions* that some try to establish among the different orders. The rules and the examples are also contradictory on this point. Perrault, however, makes an exception of the column he calls Tuscan; he believes that in order to find a middle point among the diverse opinions on the subject, it should be given six parts of a diameter, whereas the others receive seven and a half.

It will be apparent, from the table that compares the differing diminutions and the differing dimensions of columns, that the ancients never regulated their buildings according to the system of Vitruvius, since there are different *diminutions* in the same order, and in the same size of column, as there are similar *diminutions* in similar orders of equal dimensions. One observes in this table that the Doric columns of the Theatre of Marcellus, and those of the Coliseum, which are nearly of the same size, vary in their *diminution* in a ratio of twelve to four. And, on the contrary, one finds the same *diminution* in the column of the Temple of Fortuna Virilis, and that of the portico of Septimius, where the former is Ionic and measures twenty-two feet, while the latter is Corinthian and measures thirty seven feet.

From all the different *diminutions* given to all the columns, seen in the examples presented in the following table, Perrault (*Ordonnance des cinq espèces de colonnes*, Chap. VIII)[17] extracts an average by adding the number of the smallest *diminution* to that of the highest, and then takes half this number, which ranges to eight minutes. He states:

" ...if we add the size of the smallest *diminution*, which is that of the Doric column of the Coliseum at only four and one-half minutes, to the size of the largest, which is that of the Theatre of Marcellus at as much as twelve, half of these sizes, which together make sixteen and one half, is eight and one quarter. Similarly, if we add the size of the smallest *diminution* of the columns that remain, which is six and one eighth in the column of the Basilica of Antoninus, to the largest of ten and one half in the column of the Temple of Concord, half of these two sizes, which together make sixteen and five eighths, is eight and five sixteenth. Now this dimension of eight minutes, which makes almost exactly a seventh part and one half of the diameter, is one fifth of my small module, or four minutes, taken from either side of the column. I have not listed the *diminutions* of the Moderns because they are the same as those of antiquity, which vary from author to author and from order to order."[18]

The *diminution* of columns, still according to Perrault,[19] is carried out in three ways. The first and most usual way is to begin *diminution* at the bottom of the column and to carry it up from there to the top. The second, which was also practised in antiquity, is to begin the diminution about one third of the way up the column from the column base. The third way – for which there is no precedent in antiquity – is to make the column thicker near the middle and to diminish it towards the two ends, that is to say, towards the base and towrads the capital. This practice, which gives the column something like a belly, is called enlargement.

Perrault had no knowledge of the ruins of the city of Paestum, where there is a Doric edifice with columns that have a swelling [enlargement] that the Greeks called *entasis* (*See* ENLARGEMENT).

There are many geometrical procedures used or proposed by architects to draw the *diminution* and the swelling of columns. Vignola invented an ingenious one, where the two lines that form the profile of the column curve towards the extremities in the same proportion, by curving twice as much towards the top as towards the bottom because the superior part of the *diminution* is twice as long as the inferior one.

TABLE OF COLUMN DIMINUTIONS AFTER PERRAULT.

	Shaft Height Feet, inches			Diameter Feet, inches			Diminution Minutes	
DORIC								
Theatre of Marcellus	21	0	0	3	0	0	12	0
Coliseum	22	10	1/2	2	8	3/4	4	1/2
IONIC								
Temple of Concord	36	0	0	4	2	1/2	10	1/2
Temple of Fortuna Virilis	22	10	0	2	11	0	10	1/2
Coliseum	23	0	0	2	8	3/4	10	0
CORINTHIAN								
Temple of Peace	49	3	0	5	8	0	6	1/2
Portico of Pantheon	36	7	0	4	6	0	6	1/8
Altars in Pantheon	10	10	0	1	4	1/2	8	0
Temple of Vesta	27	5	0	2	11	0	6	1/2
Temple of Sibyll	19	0	0	2	4	0	8	0
Temple of Faustina	36	0	0	4	6	0	8	0
Campo Vaccino	37	6	0	4	6	1/2	6	1/2
Basilica of Antoninus	37	0	0	4	5	1/2	6	1/8
Arch of Constantine	21	8	0	2	8	2/3	7	0
Interior of Pantheon	27	6	0	3	5	0	8	0
Portico of Septimius	37	0	0	3	4	0	7	1/3
COMPOSITE								
Baths of Diocletian	35	0	0	4	4	0	11	1/3
Temple of Bacchus	10	8	0	1	4	1/4	6	1/2
Arch of Titus	16	0	0	1	11	2/3	7	0
Arch of Septimius	21	8	0	2	8	1/2	7	0

DISPOSITION This word, in architecture, designates the order and the arrangement with which the intelligence of the architect imprints the details as well as the ensemble of a building.

The same words change significance sometimes within the diverse languages that use them. Vitruvius lists *disposition* among the five divisions of architecture.[20] But it seems that among the Romans this word corresponded to what we would call today *distribution*, or even to the art of designing architecture; because, he says, there are three parts to disposition: *ichnography*, *orthography*, and *scenography*, that is to say, the plan, the elevation and the perspective view.

Nowadays, we use the word *disposition* in a more general and more theoretical sense. One speaks of a *skilful disposition*, a *faulty* or a *shabby disposition*; and this nearly always applies to the idea of a general ordonnance.

Nothing can repair a faulty *disposition* in a building, neither the luxury of ornament, nor the wealth of materials. *Disposition* is to a building what configuration is to a body.

Disposition differs from distribution in that the first embraces all the elements of architecture and all the relations within a building, while the second designates especially the arrangement and order of the parts that compose the exterior.

Disposition in an edifice is to consider in the exterior as well as the interior, all the requirements of site, orientation, need, customs, character, aptness, the principles of art, and the rules of taste.

Distribution in an edifice, is to combine in the best possible order, and in a manner that brings the useful and the agreeable into accord, all the rooms, halls, galleries, and apartments that form the ensemble of an interior. (*See* DISTRIBUTION).

On account of the scope that custom gave to it, the word *disposition* in fact includes all the components of architecture. Both construction and execution depend on a good combination of parts; and the aim of *disposition* is to assign to every object its proper place and use, and to choose ornaments and find their correct allocation and their harmonious dispensation.

Disposition, then, exhibits such a general acceptation that one could reduce all of architectural theory to this article. As it is in the nature of this dictionary to allocate the notions of each article according to the divisions of knowledge, this one has occupied much less space than its definition implies.

DISTRIBUTION It is the division, the order, and the arrangement of the rooms that form the interior of a building.

Distribution is one of the most important parts of civil architecture; an art that aims towards making healthy, commodious and agreeable dwellings. A good *distribution* subdivides the premises occupied by a building, increases the enjoyment of the inhabitants, and renders its tenancy more profitable.

The issue of *distribution* among the ancients, is one of which we have the least precise notions. Private dwellings are never apt to survive the upheavals and the revolutions that destroy cities. Without the discovery of those buried by Vesuvius, we would be limited to the ever obscure and problematic descriptions of some writers from antiquity. However, the small number of well preserved houses at Pompeii could shed only a limited light on the *distribution* of

interiors. Nothing is more subject to customs and domestic habits.

One observes a simple and almost uniform *distribution* in the plans of these houses. However, an exception should be made of the Pompeian country house, where the refinement of ornament, of passages and interior conveniences lead one to assume that these amenities, which belonged to rich proprietors in urban or country houses, must have evolved very far.

Modern artists agree on the likelihood of this conjecture, following the research made on the villa Adriana in Tivoli. Indeed, one observes there some apartments where the *distribution* was of the highest art: baths, where all conveniences were arranged in the most industrious and

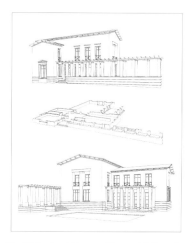

Fig. 42. Villa in Athens, Demetri Porphyrios.
From *Demetri Porphyrios, Selected Buildings and Writings,*
Academy Editions, London, 1993

refined manner; rooms of ample size, lit in a manner very appropriate to the climate and their use during certain hours of the day; rooms whose doors are arranged in an enfilade. Finally, one is compelled to recognize in these shapeless ruins, that the Romans had taken the art of *distribution* and the luxury of convenience, farther perhaps than the moderns.

However, such was not the opinion of a modern architect (Le Camus de Mézières, *Génie de l'architecture*), who speaks of the *distribution* of the ancients, after the descriptions left to us by Pliny, of his two country houses.

"...let us briefly survey the buildings of the ancient Romans, those masters of the world.

They put everything into the exterior decoration, as did the Greeks, and their interiors were not at all convenient; there was no proportion between successive rooms; the exterior decoration governed their size. Vast galleries were the principal feature of these ancient buildings. Take the descriptions that Pliny gives of his country houses. We find in that of the Laurentine an immense area of land, much sumptuousness, great magnificence; but no private comforts. Their skill extended only so far as to take advantage of the site, of the exposures most favorable to health, and of the delight that wise men feel when enjoying a pure and temperate air in every season, despite the changes in weather. Another lesson to be learned, is the art of taking advantage, in architecture, of all that a climate offers that is pleasing to the eye and to the mind, relative to the site. Among the large and the numerous rooms, there were some where one could enjoy the sight and even the sound of the sea; in others, secluded among gardens, that sound was heard only as a distant murmur. In those parts that enjoyed neither sight nor sound of the sea, the profoundest peace and quiet prevailed. In these various situations, there were apartments and chambers for the day and for the night, grand rooms for assemblies and banquets, and others, less large, for gatherings of the family and of a select circle of friends. There were private rooms, where the master could isolate himself form his household at the end of a long gallery, to work and to rest.

The whole bespeaks great ceremony, much profusion, and a faulty conception of luxury. This is apparent in the size and extent of each room and in its use. If we consider the exterior of the buildings that composed the Laurentine, the length of the principal front appears to have been some hundred and seventy toises; (to give a comparative idea of this extent, we note that the garden front of the Château des Tuileries is one hundred and seventy toises in length, and that the full length of the Château de Versailles, on the garden side, is two hundred and seventy toises.) but it may have been as much as two hundred and forty toises, if the lodgings of the slaves and freedmen stretched as far as the corresponding part on the other side in order to give the whole a perfect symmetry. This was no more than would be needed if we consider that the ordinary banqueting chamber was ten or eleven toises long by a little more than six wide. The great court was thirty toises by twenty-four, and the small, circular court was twelve toises in diameter. The gallery, which Pliny himself likened in size to those of public buildings, was forty-five toises long by five toise wide; a second banqueting chamber was twelve toises by eight; and the adjoining room was twelve toises by about six wide, as was the tennis court.

Estimate the size of the whole from these measurements; add the gardens and remember that this was the house of a Consul, who had several others equally large and equally splendid.

We might cite the houses of Cicero, as described by Sallust, those of Pompey, or the magnificence of buildings erected by Lucius Lucullus, Sulla, and many other Romans; but these descriptions, however interesting, would be of little use for the present purpose. They would show us only the way in which the ancients lived, which was very different in internal arrangement from ours in France. Our manners are not the same, nor are our customs, etc."[21]

This last reflection of the author that I have just quoted should, I believe, have rendered his judgment as to the taste in *distribution* among the ancients a bit more guarded. If taste is intimately tied to climate, to ways of life, social customs, and the prejudice of ostentation and vanity, and since all these things can only be very different depending on the country and the century, then it is difficult to conceive how to propose rules or practical examples in this matter.

There is agreement on only one point, which is commodity; for without doubt, it must form the basis of *distribution*. But commodity itself is a local matter that depends on customs, which being different in all places, must produce different results in all places.

The art of *distribution* is very perfected in France, and especially in Paris; but this does not mean that one might propose the modern *distributions* of Paris as models for imitation in all places. This simply means that in Paris the art of multiplying the enjoyments of luxury within small spaces has been perfected; it also means that since the land available for building in Paris is very expensive, and since an apartment house included as many houses as storeys, it became necessary to take from a small piece of land the best advantage possible; and this is what perfected the art of *distribution*.

After reading d'Aviler, Laugier, Blondel, Mézières and others who wrote on this subject, one is compelled to acknowledge that there are no rules to propose in this matter. The customs in England do not admit the enfilades of rooms which are sought after in Italy; and the small apertures, the passages, the concealed rooms that qualify the French *distributions* are neither practicable nor suitable in London or in Rome.

There is a part of *distribution*, which one may call etiquette, which consists in regulating the number, the measure and the disposition of ceremonial rooms such as the salon of exhibition, of reception, etc. This part is even more subordinated to the customs of nations, and cannot be the subject of a general theory. Besides, all that could be said on the subject in this article can be found in each partial article composing the art of *distribution*, such as *apartment, chamber, cabinet*, etc.

It is all the more difficult not just to prescribe rules, but even to state somewhat general precepts on the art of distribution; for, despite the regional customs of each country, the architect must, in his plans, submit to the private opinions of his patron.

In addition to these condescensions for the ideas or the whimsy in private buildings, there are, within all the buildings consecrated for public use, some local and indispensable facts, to which *distribution* must also conform.

Here are some general maxims for private houses, given by d'Aviler, to which one does not pretend to add more authority than they should have.

1° A building must present itself well and have a propitious entrance.

2° The best location for the main body of a house is between the court and the garden.

3° The storehouse and the stables must be placed in such a manner that the living quarters are not inconvenienced, which can be avoided by placing them as wings, on each side of the court.

4° One of the wings, that of the storehouse, should connect to a vestibule that leads to the dining room, so that serving is done conveniently.

5° Irregular forms for rooms should be avoided. They should be used only when such irregularity in some forms of details provides more importance, grandeur, or a more advantageous situation for the room.

6° When one intends to arrange a long enfilade in a large building, one should avoid the occurrence of rooms for domestics within this enfilade.

7° Although symmetry should be observed in general, there are cases, however, where it can be disregarded in interior *distribution*, as long as one arranges for a correlation on the opposite sides.

8° It is an indispensable rule for interior *distributions* to be in accord with outside decorations.

DORIC This name designates one of the three Greek orders, which, through its form, proportions and the character of its details, expresses especially the idea of strength and solidity in architecture, and recalls most evidently the origin of this art among the Greeks.

Before broaching the subject of the origin, system and the history of the *Doric* order, a preliminary observation will be made to establish precisely the principal points of this theory.

As a consequence of all the architectural treatises, and even more as a result of all the edifices built in Europe before the second half of the eighteenth century, many minds may still hold an inveterate opinion regarding the form and the proportions of the *Doric* order. It could be said, particularly from an artist's perspective, that there are not only two shades of meaning, but two rival modes, vying for the official title and the name *Doric*. They differ from each other in style, character, proportions, the presence or absence of a base, the form of the capital, and the details of the profile.

This difference is such that when the renewed Greek *Doric* reappeared, whether in the drawings of travellers, or in some attempts in modern edifices, some saw it as a local style forming an exception to a general style; while others saw a coarse adumbration of the order which the Romans perfected; and others still, saw a new order.

The countless discoveries of this kind of monument of antiquity reproduced over time, have shed enough light on this question allowing us to affirm that after all there is but one *Doric*; and that the *Doric* of the moderns is but an improper modification that entered their architecture as a consequence of their forgetting of antiquity, and through a prolonged ignorance of the authentic monuments where this order received its original and truly distinctive character.

If we were to cite here the most famous architectural monuments of the most splendid centuries of Greece, and if we were to produce the authorities that are still extant of this long misunderstood order, we would be needlessly lengthening this article with an extensive list of evidence that a multitude of descriptions from travellers has spread throughout Europe since the middle of the last century. These descriptions would prove that this order – which has been considered since its reappearance as an adumbration that received its perfection with the Romans – was used in the most exalted periods of art by the most famous of architects, and applied in edifices of the most noble character.

Thus, the *Doric* order – as we shall consider it, along with the two others – is the order that was perfected by the Greeks. The *Doric* is not an attempt at making architecture, but rather its very complement. It is not the adumbration of an expression which has since been ameliorated by taste and experience; it is rather the result of the experience and taste of many centuries. It is not a local style as was initially assumed; it is a general style. It is not a groping in the dark, it is rather the very perfection of art – its originating type.

I. *On the origin of the Doric order.* To speak of the origin of the *Doric* order is to speak of Greek architecture. Thus, to deal with the origin of this order is to go back to the very birth of art.

The imitative and proportional system that forms the distinctive character of Greek architecture has so marked the *Doric*, that it cannot be regarded as an effect, but rather the very principle of art. For this reason, we attribute to the *Doric* not only the pre-eminence, but also the antecedence over the other orders.

Vitruvius, the most ancient writer on architecture known to us, but the most modern writer with respect to the objects that he treats, assigns to the *Doric* order, or perhaps only to its name, a kind of etymology whose only worth is the trouble to change the ending of words. Such a tradition was apparently propagated in Rome, about the *Doric* order. This order owes its origins, according to Vitruvius, to Dorus, king of Achea and the whole Peloponnesus. "*For Dorus, the son of Helen and the nymph Phthia... built a fane, which chanced to be of this order, in the precinct of Juno and Argolis...*"[22]

One is at pains to reconcile in the work of this writer, what has just been related with what he says below about the true origin of the *Doric* order, and that which established its system. In fact, he places the origins of this order in the imitation of timber work and the first trials of the art of building in wood. Then, he elaborates on the details of this transposition; explains its consequences; and concludes with this maxim, which contains the principle of Greek architecture in general, and of the *Doric* order in particular. "*Hence the ancients held that what could not happen in the original would have no valid reason for existence in the copy.* " *Ita quod non potest in veritate fieri, id non putaverunt in imaginibus factum, posse certam habere rationem.*[23]

If the *Doric* order was the result of the bringing together of such connections and relations, how then could one assume that the temple at Argos owed its *Doric* ordonnance to chance? But it matters not, especially nowadays, to conjecture as to the cause which gave this order the name of one country rather than another. Such research may have some historical importance for those who would like to go back into the mists of time and recapture the first threads of Hellenistic traditions, but any such discussion is completely foreign to the true origin of the *Doric* order.

The imitation of primitive construction in wood: this is what the origin of this order in Greece undoubtedly presents to us. No single man, no single architect could claim the honour of this invention. Some have claimed, with little discernment and reasoning, that what is known

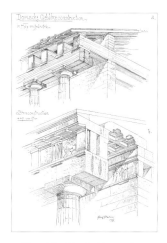

Fig. 43. Doric Tectonics.
From: Josef Durm, *Die Baukunst der Grieschen*,
A. Kröner Verlag, Leipzig, 1910

as the *rustic hut*, was one day copied by an architect, and that the success of such a copy was the cause of its multiplication. The flaw in such an hypothesis is that it particularizes and individualizes that which is but an abstraction. As we related elsewhere (*See* ARCHITECTURE) it is not the rustic hut – as this appellation indicates, a coarse work answering a common need – that served as an example to art; it was the already highly developed wood construction that with time became the very type of stone construction. Before the *Doric* order, fashioned by architecture, emerged from this imitation, the model was long in being perfected through a highly developed combination of relations and proportions. An imperceptible progression of toil and taste

modified the supports, the roofs, the porches, the ceilings and all the elements of wood construction. Thus it was that such a model acquired in the mind the power and authority of nature.

It was therefore slowly and belatedly that the stone shed [bâtisse] came to replace the already regularized wooden construction. It is a hard and difficult matter to be in need of so fixed a model. One does not ordinarily make trials and improvise in stone. Everything indicates therefore that such a transformation could not have been carried out and become definitive, save after a succession of slow operations, some of which were readily understood, while others, having escaped even the attention of contemporaries, eluded more easily the research of the ages that followed.

If the origin of the *Doric* order resides undeniably in the imitation of the forms of wooden construction, one must consider this order as the perfection and complement of a system of relations and proportions which art was successful in rendering as necessary and as positive as those of nature. The genius of the Greeks, as we shall see, was able through a new correlation to join this system to that of an imitation of another kind.

II. *On the imitative system of the Doric order*. To establish the most characteristic difference between Greek architecture and other architectures, one cannot overemphasize that the model of the former was already an assemblage of various parts and relations linked together. Accordingly, only time and customs must have imperceptibly constituted a general system of proportions, with determinate forms and invariable rules. In fact, the effect of this imitative system must have naturally disposed the mind to associate it, through analogy, to the imitation of the system that governs organisms.

By closely emulating the primitive forms of wood construction, the system of the *Doric* order, consisted therefore in the introduction into architecture of the same spirit, and the same course which nature follows in all her works. Having no positive model in nature, this art would have fallen prey to all the flights of fancy, had it not been for the simplicity and unity of a form, which being founded on reason and determined by necessity, served to contain the attempts of the imagination within the realm of imitation.

However, we must agree on the nature of the imitation with which we are concerned. The sphere of imitation is very wide, but yet the imitation proper to architecture has nothing in common with what is understood by this same appellation in the other arts. In fact, the column does not imitate the tree or the beam in the same sense that a painting does; the architrave, the frieze or the cornice, the triglyphs, the mutules, cannot affect this resemblance that draws together the imitating object to the one being imitated. The idea of imitation in the *Doric* order comprises only that of

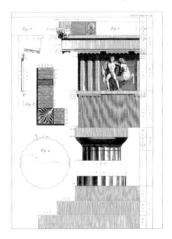

Fig. 44. The Parthenon Doric.
From: Stuart & Revett's *Antiquities of Athens*,
Reprint, B. Bloom, New York, 1968

representation or fictitious indication. Whoever excessively besets this idea will cause it to vanish.

This imitation is simply a convention to lend oneself to. In adopting a model, art could only imitate it in the sense and with the means at its disposal. It is by conserving the traces of combinations inspired by need, and by appropriating their elementary facts, that art succeeded in avoiding the drawbacks of arbitrariness, and in appropriating the general laws of nature, which makes nothing without reason and useful purpose.

The entire system of this imitation consists of a congruence with its chosen model; a congruence that reveals a middle ground between freedom and constraint. Thus the column did not receive a base, because the beam did not need

such a supplement to achieve solidity. The column borrowed from its model the diminution of its shaft, but art gave it its fluting and other accessories, which no longer have a relation to the model. The triglyphs imitate the ends of beams, but yet this imitation is limited to exterior surfaces. The pediment is modelled on the ridge-pieces of a timber roof, but still it is used in interiors where a roof is not admissible, and yet if one were to build an edifice on Olympus, where it never rains, said Cicero, the edifice will be no less crowned with a pediment. Such is therefore the spirit of imitation in architecture: it depends on allegory; and the *Doric* order – having conserved to a great extent the traces of its original types – is the one that best consecrated the fortunate link of which nature abounds with examples, by which I mean the agreement between pleasure and need.

Greek architecture possesses still another kind of imitative system, one whose effect produces a more active impression on our mind. It consists in that architecture proceeds in her works as nature proceeds in hers. Architecture succeeds in attaining this system, by applying the general rules that nature has fixed in the shaping of organisms. Now, nature has so willed it that organisms exhibit such a correlation between the whole and the parts, that it is possible to know the whole from each part, and each part from the whole. Such is also the law that the genius of the Greeks thrusted upon their architecture, by uniting together all its members in a symmetry whose effect is such that each member gives the measure of the entire *ordonnance*, and conversely, that the whole determines the dimension of each member.

Vitruvius, in what he related about the proportions of the male body, taken as a model for the proportions of the *Doric* order, and those of the female body, which is imitated in the Ionic order, only meant to give us as a metaphor. It is quite evident that nothing positive nor material, could have formed or will form part of such a mode of imitation. Such was the case, as with many other truths, that time transformed into fables. This is what must have happened to the tradition of the metaphoric system of the Greeks, who combined the properties and qualities of their architecture, with those that the arts which imitate the human body were able to recognize and study in sculpture.

It was, in truth, an ingenious and prolific system; which, having ordered the art of building on the principle that governs organisms, endowed the whole in an edifice with necessary and reciprocal relations to each part, so that an art which could have turned – as has happened everywhere else – into a game of caprice, became instead –as in the human body – a combination of relations given by nature.

The *Doric* order is the one that possesses more manifestly this imitative and proportional character.

III. *On the proportions of the Doric order*. By imitating the system of proportions presented by nature, Greek architecture imitated her further by conforming to the spirit in which such an application is to be considered and understood; that is, one must be guarded from believing that the idea of proportion in architecture, more than in nature, implies that of invariable measures.

Nature herself never imposed such measures in the works of her creation, where nothing is subjected to a mathematical uniformity. Such is also the case in *Doric* edifices, where, if one discovers a set of relations that are generally the same, one also observes a certain measure of variety, which is the result of the freedom given to art to more or less express the qualities and effects needed to tangibly suit the character it wishes to convey. One must not be astonished by such freedom, nor complain against it, because, without it, the artist falls captive to tedious practice, and becomes nothing more than a servile copyist. Furthermore, every work that is condemned to mechanical repetition ceases to have a rapport with the taste and intelligence of the observer, who will see in it nothing but the uniform product of a mould or a template.

The comparison of a certain number of Greek *Doric* monuments will render this theory sensible through facts as well as through reasoning.

The following shows the variety of proportions which one observes in the principal *Doric* edifices measured in Greece, Sicily and Magna Grecia by the architects who visited these countries.

Column and capital measurements, taken together

Temple of Minerva in Athens [Parthenon]

	Feet	Inches	Fractions
Shaft height	30	7	5
Capital	1	6	10
	32	2	3
Top diameter	4	7	0
Lower diameter	6	2	8

The column is 5 2/6 diameters high.

Propylea in Athens

	Feet	Inches	Fractions
Shaft height	24	10	5
Capital	2	2	8
	27	1	1
Top diameter	3	8	6
Lower diameter	4	9	0

The column is 5 3/4 diameters high.

Theseum in Athens [The Hephaesteion]

	Feet	Inches	Fractions
Shaft height	16	0	10
Capital	1	6	8
	17	7	6
Top diameter	2	5	4
Lower diameter	3	1	3

The column is 5 2/3 diameters high.

Temple of Segesta in Sicily

Shaft height	28	8	1
Lower diameter	6	0	1

The column is 4 3/4 diameters high.

(Quatremère gives no total measurement here. *Trans.*)

Temple of Corinth. (See Leroy, t. II, p. 44)

Shaft height	23	0	0
Capital	2	6	0
	25	6	0
Lower diameter	6	0	0

The column is 4 1/6 diameters high.

Temples of Selinunte in Sicily.

The first.

Height of column	15	9	0
Lower diameter	4	1	2

The column is 3 7/8 diameters high.

The second.

Height of column	26	9	2
Lower diameter	5	4	8

The column is 4 25/26 diameters high.

The third.

Height of column	25	6	4
Lower diameter	4	11	4

The column is 5 4/6 diameters high.

The fourth.

Height of column	25	11	8
Lower diameter	6	8	7

The column is 3 7/8 diameters high.

The fifth.

Height of column	28	11	7 1/4
Lower diameter	5	5	3

The column is 5 1/3 diameters high.

	Feet	Inches	Fractions
The sixth.			
Height of column	47	7	6
Lower diameter	10	1	8

The column is 4 5/7 diameters high.

This temple has not been entirely finished, the columns remain smooth, with the exception of three which have been fluted, the first with salient edges, the other two with filets.

The Temples of Agrigento

That of Concord.	20	7	8
Height of column	4	4	0
Lower diameter			

The column is 4 4/5 diameters high.

That of Juno.			
Height of column	19	7	2
Lower diameter	4	2	6

The column is 4 2/3 diameters high.

That of Hercules.	31	4	1
Height of column			
Lower diameter	6	5	6

The column is 4 5/6 diameters high.

The other temples of this city are either totally ruined or less important; that of the giants, of which one can still find some remnants that allow conjecture as to proportions, had not been completed when Agrigento was destroyed.

The Temple of Minerva at Syracuse

Height of column	28	0	0
Lower diameter	5	10	9

The column is 4 4/5 diameters high.

The Temples at Paestum

The large temple.			
Height of column	26	10	7
Lower diameter	6	2	5

The column is 4 1/3 diameters high.

The small temple.			
Height of column	16	0	0
Lower diameter	4	0	0

The column is 4 diameters high.

I have only used as examples, the best preserved antique monuments, whose measurements have been faithfully recorded, thereby guaranteeing their precision. A larger number of authoritative examples will add nothing to the conclusions which one can draw from this parallel. We observe in edifices of the same type and the same century that the height of the *Doric* column exhibits variations, which, at times, reach more than one diameter. If one were to apply this comparative examination to all the parts of the ordonnance, one would encounter the same variety in detail and the same uniformity of style.

The proportion of the entablature, that is its most general rapport with the column, has in the Greek *Doric* a character that is in perfect agreement with that of the whole ordonnance. In the temple of Minerva in Athens [Parthenon], and that of Theseus, the ratio between the entablature and the column is of one to three; in the temples of Paestum, it is of one to two and a half; in the temples of Syracuse, it is of one to two and a quarter; in the temples of Agrigento, it is of one to two and a quarter. Thus the proportional mean of the Greek *Doric* entablature was nearly a third of the column height. The Romans, and after them the moderns, took it to a quarter, and since then there is a weakening of the character of strength and solidity.

Generally, among the Greeks, the architrave's height measures three quarters of the column diameter, the frieze one diameter, and the cornice one quarter of the diameter. The opposite occurs among the Romans and the moderns who allow the architrave to have half a diameter at most, and make the cornice nearly one diameter.

The average height of a capital, including the echinus, the abacus and the fillet, is of half a diameter among the Greeks, whereas the moderns allow it a third of a diameter at most.

We shall not multiply these details which need to be seen in order to appreciate their rapport with the character of Greek *Doric*. These proportions must also be compared with those of the other two orders, in order to understand how architecture, by modelling her works on the organization of the human body, seems to have established, through the variation of forms and proportional adjustment, precisely the same kind of difference between the statue of a Hercules and that of a Venus or an Apollo. Like the sculptor who wanted to express the highest degree of strength in the imitation of the human body, by exaggerating the swelling of muscles, the protuberance of the bones and the projection of forms, architecture proceeded to impart to the *Doric* order the energetic character of strength, and to boldly articulate everything that tends to produce the idea of solidity, strength and durability. Who knows, if it was not for the very reality of solidity – whose quality is so energetically expressed by the *Doric* – that this order owes the distinction of having survived nearly everywhere among the remains of Greek cities, while other edifices lie in ruins?

IV. On the modifications of the Doric order among the Romans. No art owes its origin or its perfection to ancient Rome. When this country began to make its mark on history, the arts of design, and especially architecture, had already reached in Greece a high degree of progress. The lack of positive historical information on the relations between ancient Etruria and Greece prevents a clear understanding regarding what the first country owes to the second. We shall refer the reader to another article for a few critical developments on the subject.

What is plainly evident, and can be demonstrated by undeniable facts, is that around the time of the birth of Rome, Etruria had attained a very remarkable degree of artistic culture, especially in architecture. It was to Etruria that Rome owed her first great works of construction – as is evidenced in the *cloaca maxima*, built under *Tarquinius* [Priscus] the elder – its taste for the architecture of temples and the religious rites that regulated their disposition. *Ab Etruscis haruspicibus disciplinarum scriptis... dedicatum.* (Vitruvius, I. I, chap. VII).

We shall see (in the article on Etruscan Architecture) that Rome during the time of Vitruvius – that is under Augustus – still counted temples which were constructed following the Tuscan mode, whose description – according to this writer – does indeed demonstrate that their architecture, like that of the Greeks, had been based not only on the trials of wood construction or carpentry, but that they had preserved, even when constructing with more solid materials, the vestiges of the use of wood, no longer as an imitation, but even in reality.

The Tuscan ordonnance in Etruria, was therefore a composition that originated either in Greece, or was born of the same principle; and consequently – as Vitruvius demonstrates – it was completely consistent, save a few exceptions, with the ordonnance of the Greeks.

There is no doubt that what has been called the Tuscan order was adopted in Rome, and reigned there until more frequent communications with Greece – especially after the conquest of that country – served to spread the knowledge and the use of the Greek *Doric* order. This order, at the time of Vitruvius – paying close attention to the description which he gives, and to the proportions as well as certain details which he assigns to it – this order, was a kind of combination and blending of the Tuscan and the *Doric*. Also, with respect to proportions, Vitruvius, who did not see the original monuments of Greece, modified their character in a totally arbitrary fashion, as if, one might say, under the inspiration of his Tuscan order.

It is indeed remarkable that, having given to the Tuscan order a height of seven diameters, *sint ima crasitudine altitudinis parte septima* (Book IV, chap. VII), and having related that the Ionians had adopted the measure of a male foot for the *Doric* proportion – which is the sixth part of his height – Vitruvius adds: "*It is true that posterity, having made progress in refinement and delicacy of feeling, and finding pleasure in more slender proportions, has established seven diameters of the thickness as the height of the Doric column...*" (Vitruvius. Book IV, chap. I).[24] *Posteri vero elegantia subtilitateque judiciorum progressi, et gracioribus modulis delectati, septem crassitudinis diametros, in altitudinem columnae doricae constituerunt.*

From this, one can infer the important modification that the *Doric* order suffered in Rome at the time of Vitruvius.

The second modification concerns particularly the capital. Its echinus was reduced by removing its chamfered form, and the fullness that the Greeks gave to its graceful outline. This was replaced by a torus of little saliency, accompanied by an astragal. The abacus, whose ample spread used to present a large support for the architrave and an imposing crown to the column, was reduced to a weak plate of modest thickness, which was changed from being simple and smooth to admit profiles and even ornaments.

The entablature was the object of a third modification. Its parts were subjected to the same system of elegance and variety, while losing the height with which the Greeks had endowed them. The architrave received two faces, thus depriving it of the idea of solidity required by its character. The triglyphs, by virtue of their proliferation, often became objects of whim, and thus people lost sight of their original and representative principle.

The addition of the base that came to modify the primitive character of the *Doric* did not occur at the outset; this fourth modification happened only gradually. Vitruvius, in the article that concerns this order, makes no mention of a base, and yet in the *Doric* of the Theatre of Marcellus, one notices that the shaft at the bottom begins to terminate with a slight *cyma recta* – similar to the one in the other two orders – which serves to connect the shaft with the torii at the base. Lastly, regarding the base of that which is known as the *Doric* order of the Colosseum – even though it cannot be affirmed that it is a true *Doric* – it is quite likely that the custom of giving a base to the Tuscan served to justify this modification which became associated with the *Doric*.

We have already seen that one of the principal characters of this order in Greece was the use of triglyphs in the frieze in an unvarying order. This is where the Romans made a fifth modification. In fact, Vitruvius, in agreement with the example that is still extant at Cori, teaches the manner with which to distribute several triglyphs within the interval of the intercolumniation of a diastyle temple, and he opposes this disposition to that of the pycnostyle or monotriglyph. "*Some of the ancient architects said that the doric order ought not to be used for temples, because faults and incongruities were caused by the laws of its symmetry."* (Book IV, Chap. III.)[25] And here he relates the disadvantages of the metopes and the triglyphs that occur at the corner, as always having something defective. (*est mendosum*) "*For this reason*, he states, *the ancients appear to have avoided the scheme of the Doric order in their temples.*" (Book IV, Chap. III.)[26] "*Quapropter antiqui evitare visi sunt in aedibus sacris doricae symetriae rationem..*"

It is evident from this passage that Vitruvius had little knowledge of what had existed in Greece, if by *antiqui* he meant the Greeks. If, on the contrary, he wanted to speak of the Roman architects, his predecessors, then this will serve to prove that the Doric was little practised in Rome.

It is therefore not unlikely that the Tuscan and the Doric, having had a common origin, and having relations of kinship with each other, were united in the so-called Doric of the Colosseum, where the suppression of the triglyphs in the frieze, the addition of a base, and the lengthening of the column, reaching a proportion of eight and a half diameters, do not allow one to recognize the true Greek Doric. Nevertheless, leaving aside this bastardized ordonnance of the amphitheatre of Vespasian, it is evident that the Roman Doric, though with lengthened proportions and with modifications to the principal points which formed its character, still retained, especially in relation to the two other orders, a few of the qualities which had determined its rank and its fame in Greece.

V. *On the state of the Doric order since the renewal of the arts.* When architecture reappeared in the fifteenth century, the first efforts of artists and scholars aimed at recovering the characters and proportions of the ancient orders. The ruins of Rome offered then the only possible field for exploration. But, of course, as is the case with all preliminary research, no critique occurred. Various monuments separated by an interval of many centuries acquired equal authority under the rubric of the antique. Experience, new discoveries, and new points of view were needed to establish the beginnings of comparison and discernment.

There soon arose another kind of misuse, which was a result of the limited availability of facts: it was the systematic mind set. To every order was assigned an unvarying fixity; every architect developed a method based no longer on three but on five orders, whose elements were deemed to have existed either in the ruins of Rome or in the writings of Vitruvius.

On the one hand, the remains of ornate Corinthian capitals of varied compositions led to a belief in the existence of what was termed a composite order, as if a few sculpted details in a capital sufficed to form a particular order. On the other, Vitruvius spoke of a Tuscan order, of which no authentic monument had yet appeared; now this so-called Tuscan appeared more simple than the Doric and was therefore arbitrarily placed at the bottom of the architectonic ladder. And since Vitruvius gave to the column of his Tuscan temple seven diameters, the newly created Tuscan order was also conceived as having seven diameters, a base and a smooth frieze; and was deprived of all richness and variety.

In this new ranking, the Doric occupied second place, for it had a frieze ornamented with the triglyphs. To be of consequence in this new arrangement, from the so-called Tuscan to the so-called composite, the Doric was thought to be taller than the Tuscan, and was assigned eight diameters. It was subsequently given a base, whose absence would have contradicted the new system of progressive opulence. The so-called Doric of the Colosseum provided the authority for this base, and a slight embellishment of its profiles was deemed satisfactory. Thus was established the gradation of the five orders, according to the modern system .

It has already been mentioned that in architecture there are but three degrees, which, regardless of various appellations, always form a higher, a lower and a middle term. Whether these degrees are characterized by the qualities of strength, simplicity, lightness, elegance or richness, the orders are but the means of expression of the highest, the lowest and the middle terms of these qualities.

Thus, to aim at that which is more simple than simplicity is to produce poverty, and that is the so-called Tuscan; and to aim at exceeding the richness of the Corinthian is to produce luxury and excess. That was the error into which the modern architectonic system fell, having pretended to surpass that of antiquity.

Consequently, this character of simplicity disappeared from the *Doric* order, and with it that of strength or solidity - which resulted from its short proportion - the size of the abacus and of the echinus, and the height of the entablature. Thus, the very indicative signs that originated the types and forms of the *Doric* composition were diminished. This significant ensemble of forms, of details and proportions, was modified in such a manner as to produce only variety instead of a contrast with the other two orders.

It is useless to relate here the minor differences among the moderns who sought to establish the progressive system of what they called the "five orders." All that differentiates them, consists in that half a diameter with which some like Palladio and Scamozzi augmented their *Doric*, taking it to a height of eight and a half diameters.

Vignola, who was considered the legislator of modern architecture – and in many ways he still passes for one – composed his *Doric* by uniting the variations of the new systems in a temperate middle course; this, however, without suspecting the existence of the truly ancient system. He gives to his column sixteen modules, or eight diameters in height, and to his entablature, four modules or two diameters. He places dentils in his cornice; gives two faces to the architrave; gives a profile to the abacus, which he ornaments with rosettes and an astragal; and he rests the column on a base composed of a *cyma recta*, a filet, a quarter-round [ovolo], and a plinth. The metopes of his frieze are ornamented with *pateras* , and he places the last triglyph centred on the axis of the corner column.

This order, was obviously composed in total ignorance of the Greek *Doric*. But modern architects departed from the Greek *Doric* even farther than Vignola. Many took the liberty of eliminating the triglyphs and the metopes from the frieze, and there were those who even gave the column

a proportion of nine diameters. Some assigned to it an Attic base, others fluted it to a level measuring two thirds of its height and carved the flutes in a semi-circular fashion; others still cut out ovolos and heart-shaped leaves in the echinus, giving a *cyma* to the *abacus* and ornamenting the soffit with rosettes.

From all these modifications, one can conclude that if that which is *smooth* is synonymous with that which is simple in architecture, and if that which is simple is indispensable for the idea of strength, then the *Doric* order as a whole and in each of its details has been reduced to a light hue rather than a sharp-contrasted colour and, consequently, architecture has been robbed of one of the most energetic forms of its language.

Architecture, as has often been said, must have the right to modify its tones by varying the character of each order. These variations, like musical semi-tones, are but light shades in the expression of that special quality which is proper to each of them. Thus, a Corinthian order, without overstepping its bounds, could admit some simplicity, and a *Doric* order, without renouncing its character could afford some elegance. But if the differences between the orders are reduced to slight intervals, and if they are separated more or less by a single diameter, by faint projections of profiles, or by imperceptible additions and diminutions, it would be a vain effort to make such weak articulations intelligible to the eye. Clearly, this kind of adapting of effect or impression, will offer nothing salient to most people, and it will even cease to have a well determined value for the architects themselves. This is what happened to the *Doric order*.

VI. *On the use of the Greek Doric in the eighteenth century.* Modern Rome, the unique and privileged heiress to the arts and monuments of ancient Rome, was for a long time the only school where modern architecture drew her lessons and its models. We have seen that the proximity of Etruria and the first communications between this country and Rome, must have grafted, so to speak, at an early period, the style and the proportions of the Tuscan ordonnance, which was an emanation from, or rather a very ancient modification of the Greek *Doric*. We have also seen that during the reign of Augustus, the rules and prescribed proportions given by Vitruvius to his *Doric* were at odds with and, on nearly all points, in opposition to or dissimilar to that of the Greeks; the *Doric* temple at Cori offers a striking example of these differences.

This explains how it came to pass that in ancient Rome and in the midst of the varied uses of other orders in her monuments, no *Doric* bearing the character and style of the Greeks was found. But perhaps there is a kind of exception to what was just stated in the columns of the church of San Pietro in Vincoli. These columns recall the qualities of a *Doric* which is different from that of common usage. There is reason to believe that these very columns – each of which was made from a single block of marble – were imported into Rome along with others of a Corinthian and Ionic order, and loaded onto ships which the Romans filled with statues, *colossi*, and other works in marble.

Be that as it may, no truly Greek *Doric* monument was found in ancient Rome, and despite the quests of antiquarians and artists, the original *Doric* remained unknown. No exception will be made of old travellers who, like Spons and Wheeler, traversed Greece in the seventeenth century, without having communicated in their accounts or superficial drawings, the slightest impression of the true *Doric* order. The same could be said of Cluvier and d'Orville's work on the monuments of Sicily.

Research and discoveries of this sort were awakened and encouraged by the revelation of the *Doric* temples of Paestum, about which in 1745, the baron Joseph Antonini published some rather circumstantial accounts and details to excite the zeal of others. According to Grosley, it was in 1755 that a young Neapolitan painter who had lost his way in this deserted region happened to discover these monuments and related the account of his impressions, which, when accompanied by his sketches, served to bestow on the ancient city of Paestum a renown which she had lost for many centuries. In short, the proximity of

Naples encouraged many artists to determine to undertake this journey; and today, no other antique site is as well known as this one.

However, the very precise knowledge of the Greek temples of Paestum, which preceded by a considerable time that of other monuments, made it such that the *Doric* style of these temples became the subject of bizarre conjectures, until the time came when more numerous and similar discoveries enabled the greatest number of critics to draw the parallels that were to shed light on the matter and impel general opinion.

In a country which is beholden to the exclusive empire of fashion, a new intention, running contrary to the opinion which initially treated the *Doric* as an exceptional style, soon came to treat the Greek *Doric* as a unique and exclusive order; a kind of common-place which was indiscriminately applied, and preferably to the most ordinary constructions. Nothing could have done more to discredit the taste for the *Doric* than this banal application. As soon as this most noble and wise order – which requires at once the simplest and the most regular combinations – was subjected to the flights of caprice, it lost its proper signification; and it is doubtful, in the present state of affairs, whether it is possible to encounter in some grand and noble project, the opportunity to reinstate the *Doric*'s true character and preeminence.

However, if the course of events allowed architecture to procure two orders, or rather two modes of the same order – where one is but a softened version of the other – would this constitute grounds to use them both? The first, or the baseless Greek *Doric*, with its shorter proportions and all the regularity of its intercolumniation and its frieze, will find proper use in edifices where a simple plan and symmetrical elements accord with the expression of a serious character, uniting the ideas of strength and solidity. The second, being the Roman or modern *Doric*, may find use in various compositions where, instead of prescribing the simplicity of the plan, it will be compelled to adapt to the exigencies of many situations, such as discontinuous elevations, changing lines and other variations which are incompatible with the severity of an imposing character.

The *Doric* that I call modern, is therefore a nuance, or rather an intermediate tone in the architectonic scale, between the Greek *Doric* and the Ionic.

The lack of an element complementary to harmony in modern architecture, served more than one thinks to weaken her means of expression. It seems, therefore, that modern architecture needs a reinstatement of this grave tone that it lacks; however, not in the spirit of fashion, but rather through the fundamental system of art and from the perspective of a theory of taste. But this fundamental and regulative tone must be restored to its rightful place. The use of the *Doric* order must be regarded not only as a simple effect, but rather the very principle, and the generative type of architecture. It should be considered as a rule, which, far from bending to the whim of caprice, serves on the contrary to rectify the freaks of fancy, or the flights of the paradoxical mind, which thrive on contesting everything in order to confound everything.

The Doric Frieze. It has been said and demonstrated, in many articles, that the triglyphs and metopes of the *Doric* order represented naught else but the tradition of the beams of a floor and their intervals which were later filled with masonry, when the beam ends were left uncovered.

This practice of construction, which consists in revealing in masonry buildings the pieces of wood that form their structure, is quite natural and belongs to the custom of wood construction witnessed in a variety of countries.

The Greeks have for a long time unified both timber and masonry work in their constructions. The custom of leaving some pieces exposed on the exterior must have inspired the idea of covering them with some embellishments, and hence was born the ornament of the triglyph, which has since been sanctioned by an ancient custom, and was later regularized by the perfected art of stone or marble construction.

In the edifices that were henceforth amenable to just symmetry, the regular adjustment of the triglyphs and the metopes, became the subject of a few difficulties which, according to Vitruvius, compelled some architects to avoid them. Among these architects he mentions Arcesius, Pytheus and Hermogenes, who, before erecting a *Doric* temple to the honour of Bacchus, changed instead the design and made it Ionic. "*This is not because it is unlovely in appearance or origin or dignity of form, but because the arrangement of the triglyphs and metopes (lacunaria) is an embarrassment and inconvenience to the work.*" (Book IV, Chap. III)[27]

One cannot deny that in the adjustment of the *Doric frieze* there are two difficulties, which consist in either placing the last triglyph at the corner as did the Greeks – thereby requiring a small and progressive enlargement of the metopes in the direction of the corner – or, if the triglyph is to be centred on the axis of the corner column, dividing

Fig. 45. Parthenon, corner.
From: Josef Durm, *Die Baukunst der Grieschen*,
A. Kröner Verlag, Leipzig, 1910

the metope into two parts at the corner of the frieze; this becomes quite irksome to the placement of sculpture or ornament in the metopes, as in the Parthenon.

The imitation, which one is bound to recognize in the triglyphs as representing the visible extremities of beams, compelled some critics to search for ways to justify its origin and regularize its use, through some mathematical demonstration. But, to be absolutely rigorous, the beams of every floor, in general, are to be placed only in the same direction as the area to be covered; thus there is no need – especially when comparing those beams to the manner in which the triglyphs of the *Doric frieze* are grouped – to establish another row of beams on the other side of the building, thereby making a chequered ceiling.

It must therefore be concluded that the adjustment of the triglyphs and the metopes at the four corners of the parallelogram in a *Doric* Temple is a convention whose rigour should not be too closely tested.

By establishing the triglyph at the angle, the Greek architects were not hampered by the difficulty that the matter could have presented, if in a fictitious imitation, one were to proceed according to reality. However, Piranesi pretended to justify the possibility of having a triglyph, or a beam's end, presenting two faces, on each side of the corner, as shown in his *Della Magnificenza dell'Architettura dei Romani*. This is a veritable game of fancy that could never have existed in reality; it is an imaginary solution to a useless problem.

What good does it serve to go to such pains to materially and geometrically explain that which – as we have demonstrated many times – should be understood as a fictitious imitation, not a servile copy? No doubt, the triglyph representing the beam in a floor should not appear in a place where that which it represents could not occur. What must be recognized is that the corner triglyph, completes and ends the frieze, and gives to this part an appearance of solidity which one delights at finding in every corner. As to the small inequalities in the widths of the metopes near the corner, and the variation in intercolumniation necessitated by this adjustment, experience proves to us that the effect of these matters is hardly perceptible to the eye.

Irrespective of the side that an architect might take regarding this matter, there will always be these small irregularities which are of consequence only for the compass. Perhaps it might still be observed that of the two sorts of adjustments, that of the corner triglyph will present the least disadvantage. There is yet another observation to be made in its favour. Since every mutule of the cornice has to correspond to every triglyph, then the last triglyph, when placed at the precise centre of the corner column, causes in the soffit of the entablature the occurrence of a space whose adjustment is difficult. Instead of the palmette which the Greeks quite naturally used, one observes in this location the formation of three kinds of compartment: that of the corner, and that of each of the two semi-metopes on each side, thus producing small divisions which are quite disagreeable, and whose adjustment is no less awkward.

EFFECT In works of art, an *effect* is a quality whose characteristic is to stimulate other qualities, to make them stand out, to attract and fix the eye and the attention with something exciting.

This quality is such in art only because it is felt and studied in the works of nature; and, here as elsewhere, it is best defined by its opposite. Thus, there are physiognomies without *effect*, where despite the regularity of features and the beauty of the complexion, they exhibit either in the eyes, or in the colour or the countenance, a certain lack of liveliness that endows the face with expression and intelligence, and the gaze with feeling.

Effect in painting is an indispensable quality, where its opposite would be monotony. Nature contains beautiful sites, which, for the painter, may lack this contrast of lines, masses and accidents that the eye searches for especially in imitation. These are sites without *effect*. The same may be said of objects that are deprived of light or that receive a vertical sun; because there is a lack of contrast between shade and light which alone produces, more or less, the *effect*.

All of the above aims at naught else by defining the nature and the conditions of this quality known as *effect*, through tangible comparisons.

Architecture also has her own kind of *effect* and her manner of producing *effect*. Considered simply from a certain abstract but purely material view – either as an assemblage of solids and voids, or a composite arrangement of smooth and projecting parts – it is evident that there is a basis for much contrast in architecture, and consequently many combinations capable of producing many an *effect*. From these combinations derive also the contrasts between light and shadow. The fact remains that a uniform mass of solids without voids or projections cannot produce any impression other than that of monotony, which is the lack of *effect*. Such is the case of an Egyptian pyramid, where everyone is condemned to repeatedly behold the same grandeur and always experience the same impression. On the contrary and irrespective of any different intellectual predilection, anyone who lives opposite the Louvre's frontispiece, St. Peter's colonnade, or the Pantheon's peristyle, can always obtain new impressions from these monuments, and would find it difficult to exhaust the observations deriving from their *effect*.

We believe that the two principal *effects* produced by architecture, can be attributed to two different means; that is to say, this art has one *effect* that derives from composition, and another that depends on execution.

architecture than the use of columns or pilasters. It is not the size of an edifice (says Le Roy) that determines its *effect*. Who has not observed that the view of the frontispiece of the Pantheon affects us more strongly than that of the basilica of St. Peter's in Rome, although the basilica's portico has wider and taller columns? This is so because St. Peter's columns, being engaged to the wall, cannot produce the variety of *effects* conveyed by the depths of peristyles.

The *effects* of architecture result from its capacity to offer two kinds of sensation through its compositions: the first has the quality of a still life, where its immobile objects do not change with respect to us, even if we change our vantage point; the second is qualified by an active and

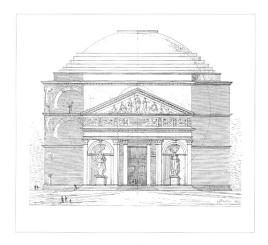

Fig. 46. Pantheon, Rome.
From: Josef Durm, *Die Baukunst der Etrusker und Römer*,
A. Kröner Verlag, Stuttgart, 1905

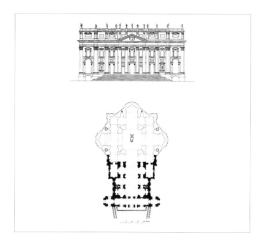

Fig. 47. St. Peter's, front elevation and plan, C. Maderno.
From: A.C. Quatremère de Quincy, *Histoire de la vie et des ouvrages des plus célèbres architectes*, J. Renouard, Paris 1830

The *effect* that is due to composition derives, above all, from the varied use of solids and voids. Thus, the variety and the harmonious combination of the lines of a plan, determine the variety of aspects that multiply these impressions that the eye transmits to the mind. But the *effects* that convey a great idea of the building by multiplying its perspectival views are produced by the volumes which compose the elevation. Through this variety of aspect, an edifice becomes a kind of spectacle whose scenes seem to change, either because of the points from which they are viewed, or because of the changing play of light over the solids and voids throughout the day.

As some writers have observed, nothing better demonstrates the *effect* of the impressions of

animated nature, where the appearance and aspect of the same edifice seem to change when we change our location.

Effect in architecture depends also on a moderate use of variety. If, as we have seen, a volume entirely smooth and devoid of any detail leaves the eye and the mind completely inactive, then, for a contrary reason, the extreme multiplicity of parts and details compiled one on top of the other, will cause us great pain in seeing and judging; and because of the great pretension to produce *effect*, we end up producing none at all.

With respect to decoration, *effect* depends then on a moderate use of the means of variety. Gothic architects excessively multiplied the details in the frontispieces of their churches, and by going beyond the point, they failed to produce *effect*. Too many or too few divisions in a building are equally harmful to *effect*. Divisions in buildings facilitate the act of seeing; but too many of them avert the sight from weariness, and too few avert it through indifference. Therefore, if *effect* is a quality whose use in architectural composition is to allure the observer and to give pleasure to sight, then the efficacy of this quality can be annulled either by the excess or the want of details.

There is a second kind of *effect* and a way to produce it in architecture. It is one that depends on *execution*, understood here not in the sense of the science of construction, but rather designating the purely material means that endow each part with form and value. The measure or the method of this kind of *effect* cannot be established by projects and drawings.

Some imagine that in order for a building to have an increased sense of *effect*, the architectural members, the massing, the details and the profiles must be left in a neglected, incorrect or unfinished state like the esquisse or the adumbration of certain decorative figures.

The best works of the Greeks categorically contradict this opinion. No other architecture is more dedicated to *effect* and for *effect* than that of the Greek Doric temples. There is no other architecture whose profiles and details are pronounced with more energy and projection. All the parts of these grandiose masses with a bold *effect* are sculpted and terminated with precision; and all are ordered for *effect*, without there being the least pretension of making an *effect*. Fine and slender fillets are followed by a capital of massive appearance; a deeply carved part is followed by a delicate and light projection. There is *effect* precisely because it is not applied everywhere.

In the *effect* of its most colossal masses, Greek architecture followed the same system as Greek sculpture in the execution of the most enormous statues. Contrariwise, and in every art, the moderns want everything for *effect*. This is the surest way of having no *effect* at all.

In such a manner, the successive decorators of the church of St. Peter's have exaggerated the *effect* of some of the sculptures placed on the nave's archivolt. Doubtless, the execution of ornaments meant to be seen from afar demands a certain boldness for its *effect*; but one that does not exclude the finesse or the purity of the work. The remains of antiquity furnish us with models for the *effect* that befits the placement of such an ornament. Here again, one observes that the *effect* of execution, like all the other qualities in architecture, consists in a happy mean between extremes, or what in music is called a *forte* and a *piano*.

EFFECT This word can be understood in a more general sense, signifying simply the result experienced by observing the works of nature and art.

When one judges the *effect* of an architectural project, one designates nothing else but fore-

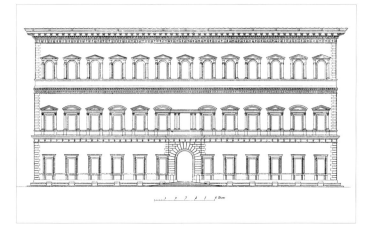

Fig. 48. Palazzo Farnese, Rome. A. Sangallo, M. Buonarotti. From: A.C. Quatremère de Quincy, *Histoire de la vie et des ouvrages des plus célèbres architectes*, J. Renouard, Paris, 1830

seeing what will be its appearance once it has been completed.

Nothing is more hazardous than such forecasts when one's conjectures are based only on delineation. That is why it was customary in the past, in the case of important monuments, to build a small model in relief, the only effective way to predict the building's true impressions, whether those depending on the play of light or those resulting from the relationships between projections, the distribution of members or profiles, and their relation to the whole.

When Paul III wanted to complete the Palazzo Farnese, where Sangallo had executed the exterior up to the level of the entablature, Michelangelo was summoned to collaborate on this enterprise, and his project was selected. When charged with the execution of such a large cornice, he did not feel that his drawings or their general approval were sufficient authority to carry out the task. He knew that calculation can often be flawed when passing from the small to the large scale, and how insufficient were even the rules of optics in judging the *effect* of volumes and their details. Therefore, he was not content to build a small model of the entablature in relief, but built a life size model of it at one of the corners of the palace.

Generally, it must be said that *effect* – understood as the result of any architectural combination, especially regarding the impressions produced by the character of each monument – cannot be determined from the simple observation of drawings, even by architects. This is even less so in the case of the public or the builders themselves. Are they really equipped to make a judgment based on reduced images which are for the projected building what an adumbration is to a statue?

ELEGANCE In looking for the qualities that this word expresses within etymology, one finds the verb *legere*, or *eligere*, from which derives the Latin word *elegantia* which indicates the idea of *choice* or *choosing* that comprises the qualities of *gracefulness*, *lightness*, and *delight*, that often explain this word.

Elegance in architecture concerns particularly what is known as gracefulness, but especially lightness. Thus, in opposition to the Doric order, the character of gracefulness is evident in the Ionic, in its ornaments, and also in the lightness of its profiles and proportions. But *elegance* as lightness distinguishes the Corinthian order above the others. This applies to the essential and proper type of each order, but does not prevent the heaviest from acquiring a relative *elegance*. Thus, a Doric order may appear *elegant* by comparison to another, while an Ionic or a Corinthian order – in their variations of character, proportion or ornament – may not seem *elegant*.

Elegance is applicable to everything in architecture for it contains the ideas of delight and lightness. There could be *elegance* in construction,

in form and in disposition, as well as in the details and ornaments.

Elegance in construction is manifest through a choice of valuable materials and their skilful facing built upon good foundations, and where the joinery forms pleasing divisions. Such must have been the *elegance* in the stone facing of the temple of Cyzicus mentioned by Pliny (Bk. XXXVI), where all the joints were marked by a fillet of gold.

Elegance in form and disposition requires a harmonious combination of projecting and recessed parts in plan and in elevation, as well as an ingenious rapport between solids and voids, graceful contours, pyramidal volumes, and a temperate use of bossage that enhance the smooth parts and break the monotony of materials. No

Fig. 49. St. Sulpice, Paris, Servandoni.
From: A. C. Quatremère de Quincy, *Histoire de la vie et des ouvrages des plus célèbres architectes*, J. Renouard, Paris, 1830

other architect exhibited this kind of *elegance* to the same degree as Palladio.

Elegance in ornament or in decoration consists, first of all, in the moderate use of the objects that form the infinite repertory of the decorator. The dress and the head-dress of women, the luxury of fabrics, the lavishness of embroideries, diamonds, pearls, gilding, all are the opposite of *elegance*, which consists in a tastefully made choice of all that makes beauty shine without pretending to replace it. The same applies to decoration in architecture. Nothing destroys more surely the feeling and the effect of *elegance* than the pretentious belabouring of everything with decorative details; for not only *elegance*, but also richness itself are destroyed by this excess. But there is also a choice of light ornaments, there is a discreet manner of distributing them, and there is a charm in execution that makes them shine, all of which are merits linked to the effect of *elegance*. But the architect also needs the feeling for this *gracefulness which is more beautiful than beauty itself*, that cannot be defined but is explained through examples. I can elucidate this matter only by a comparison with Greek statues that have become like mirrors where all the effects of *elegance* are reflected, and which language cannot explain.

The opposite of *elegance* in architecture is either heaviness or thinness.

ENLARGEMENT OF COLUMN Vitruvius informs us that the *enlargement* [renflement] in the shaft of a column was known as *entasis* among the Greeks.

Enlargement is a slight augmentation of the diameter in the lower third of the column. It derives form a more or less tangible and progressive diminution found at the bottom as well as at the top of the shaft, thus producing an effect which is akin to that of a belly.

Vitruvius, as we mentioned, spoke of this swelling. *With respect to the enlargement made at the middle of columns, which among the Greeks is called entasis, at the end of the book a figure and calculation will be subjoined showing how an agreeable and appropriate effect may be produced by it.*[28] Unfortunately, this figure as well as all the others that accompanied his treatise have disappeared; the moderns have sought to repair this loss but their opinions have differed.

Initially, one may theoretically ask upon what principle or what motif, whether it is necessity or pleasure, does the practice of the *enlargement* of columns rest.

If one were to look for the cause in some necessity, it will be difficult to point to a single reason based on a real or an apparent solidity that justifies this practice. The same does not apply to what is known as diminution in the shaft of a column. This practice derives, at least indirectly, from the common sense that states that the strong supports the weak. Hence the universal use of the pyramidal form in many buildings, for it pleases because of its accord with our instincts even when it is not materially necessary. And this is so true, that an opposite form, even with the most manifest solidity, will displease us for it runs counter to our senses and our reason. This is why the need to satisfy reason and feelings must count among the requirements upon which the rules of architecture are based.

Thus, having found no reason that materially justifies the *enlargement* of columns based on construction or necessity, we shall look for a cause within some imitative analogy.

Could one not suspect that the metaphorical rapport between the human body and that of a column, of which Vitruvius spoke, became the object of a flawed and literal imitation? We have already demonstrated many a time that the imitation of the human body in architecture can be only an abstract transposition of the principles of order, symmetry, and proportion that nature offers as an abstract or speculative model. Vitruvius is perhaps not the inventor of this system of formal imitation where the type for *Doric* columns evolves from the male body, and that of the Ionic from the female body, and where the volutes derive from women's head-dress. Could anyone have prevented the belief in such similitudes that were adopted by certain systematic minds that have even assigned a belly to a column as a new trait of resemblance with their imaginary model?

Others, having abused the primitive transformation of trees into beams, and then beams into columns, tried to explain the cause of *enlargement* by the accidental protuberances of tree trunks, which is as futile a hypothesis as the first one, hence needing no refutation.

As soon as one realizes that the *enlargement* of a column does not rest on a principle of necessity, and as soon as one finds no origin based on the slightest probability, then one is compelled to ask whether the cause does not reside in the simple delight in shape and variety. We are inclined to believe that there is no better explanation.

In fact, one must recognize that in many objects and accessory details in architecture, a certain part must be reserved for this instinct for variety that ceaselessly tends to embellish the forms based on necessity to the point of losing sight of their originating principle. Thus, it is admissible to assume that the very outline of a column may have imperceptibly become the object of research, and that a certain pleasure was taken in breaking the continuity of the shaft by a gentle curve.

In fact, as we mentioned above, there is a generally accepted practice that adds interest to the shaft by a diminution that is found in many a natural object. Is it not possible that this practice led to a refinement in outline? This seems to us to be the most likely conjecture regarding the origin of *enlargement* in columns.

Since the drawing that accompanied Vitruvius's article on *enlargement* has not come down to us, many modern architects have proposed various methods.

Vignola has imagined an ingenious manner of regulating this *enlargement*. He draws the profile in such a way that the two lines that make the column's profile curve towards the ends by the same proportion; and they curve twice as much towards the top as towards the bottom of the column, since the upper part is twice as long as the lower.

In his *Traité des quatre principaux problèmes d'architecture*, Blondel showed how this line can be drawn at one stretch with the instrument, found by Nicomedes, that drew the line known as the first conchoid of the ancients.

Perrault thinks that this practice serves only to trace the line of diminution that starts at the bottom of the column without curving, but which, on the contrary, arrives at the top perpendicularly, unless the curvature begins above the lower third, which in this case must display two parallel lines. Furthermore, he does not think that the column must diminish at the bottom, since (he says) this was never practiced by the ancients nor by most of the moderns.

However, Perrault seems to hold another opinion in his translation of Vitruvius, where there is a note regarding a new method of drawing *enlargement*. Perhaps, in his treatise on the *Ordonnance des colonnes*, he meant to say that no

remains of ancient monuments display columns with *enlargements*.

This opinion was quite prevalent until one of the three edifices of ancient Paestum, the one that was thought to be an *atrium*, served to dissuade commentators. Paoli, in his dissertation on this monument, tells us that the first artists who saw and drew it, did not notice this characteristic in the columns, or had neglected to make it tangible in their drawings. In fact, the artists employed by Count Gazzola did not differentiate in their plates regarding this issue between the columns of the atrium and those of the two temples of Paestum.

It is, however, certain that the columns of the *atrium* display a tangible *enlargement*; and Paoli remedied the omission of the early renderers with a plate where the column is drawn to a large scale, thus not only showing this *enlargement* clearly, but also demonstrating the nature of the system according to which it was executed.

Here is the rule that he proposes, following the example of the monument at Paestum, for the purpose of harmonizing the *entasis* or the *enlargement* of the column with its diminution. For the *enlargement* not to have the appearance of a belly, he proposes that, after the line of diminution has been drawn and starting from a point slightly lower than the bottom of the column, a perpendicular line is drawn, starting from the same point, which should not be exceeded by the *enlargement*.

EURYTHMY *See* SYMMETRY

EXAGGERATION Such is the name given in ordinary language to any expression that tends to give a larger idea of the reality or the appearance of things by increasing their qualities or their quantities; and sometimes by diminishing them, in which case it is known as an extenuation.

Morally speaking, any *exaggeration* is a defect, since it is distant from what one may call real truth; but such is not the case with the *exaggeration* found in the imitation that qualifies the art of rhetoric or the arts of design. There is always a fictive part in these arts that requires certain resources without which they would fall short of their model.

Therefore, the art of rhetoric has one *exaggeration* that is faulty, and one that is not only permissible, but also necessary.

A faulty *exaggeration* is one that needlessly carries our mind beyond the idea within which the subject or the object ought to be conceived. It uses grand means in order to produce small effects. This is what is generally known as an *inflation*.

A justifiable *exaggeration* carries ideas to the level of extraordinary things, where the forms of ordinary language could not elevate our imagination. This is what is known as a *hyperbole* in the art of oratory and in poetry.

Similarly, in the arts of design, there is one *exaggeration* that is not only permissible but also necessary, and there is another that is faulty.

The first kind of *exaggeration* occurs in three areas which we shall succinctly analyze.

1° Abstractly speaking, there is in art a necessary *exaggeration* which is an indispensable condition of imitation; for any imitation of what is alive and natural would be inferior to its model if art, which has no life nor reality, were to slavishly reproduce the model's appearance. The artist, therefore, uses a kind of *exaggeration* in which the qualities of many individuals are assembled within one; for example, he represents his subjects more as they ought to be rather than as they are; he represents his subjects in the best light that befits the effect he seeks; he articulates their form, their contours and characters with propriety.

2° With respect to ideas and images, the artist, like the poet, has the right to use the kind of hyperbole that befits his field, and to apply it to the representation of things and individuals. Through the use of allegory, he could appropriate many fictions that will magnify the aspect of his subject. Painting and sculpture are filled with these poetic *exaggerations* that portray an action or an individual within an order of ideas that is superior to that of ordinary things.

3° Regarding execution in particular, there is another kind of *exaggeration* that consists in enforcing the tone of colours and the contours of forms, depending on the nature of the subject or the location of the work. We shall not discuss the augmentation of dimensions in objects seen from a great distance. But sculpture, being subject to the same requirements, seems to have acquired the right to use the hyperbole of dimension, not relatively but materially, that is to say in its production of colossal figures, not because of distances, but with the intention of making them colossal.

Thus, it is easy to understand that if there is a legitimate *exaggeration*, there is yet another that should be condemned for the abuse, the excess or the misplaced use of the means discussed above.

Many of these considerations are also applicable to architecture. This art, in truth, does not have a material model in nature to which it can compare itself, and from which it can receive fixed rules. If architecture's true model resides in the spirit of the rules that nature follows, it is easy to misappreciate, misunderstand and misinterpret the principles that will permit or prohibit the use of *exaggeration*, in other words, the means that will attenuate rather than augment its effect.

Thus, wherever there is an unjustified affectation or pretension towards the strong or the grand, then the very idea of strength and grandeur will disappear. Wherever the pretension to solidity, to lightness, to simplicity or richness is very obvious, then there is a failure of effect. There is no proper quality of architecture that does not have an *exaggeration* that is legitimate, and one that is faulty. Solidity may turn into heaviness, lightness into weakness, simplicity into poverty, and richness into luxury or confusion.

For example, the height of an edifice is one of those aspects that impress the most; but if it is solely the result of a vain difficulty that has been overcome, then *exaggeration* becomes a defect. Solidity in construction is desirable, but on condition that it appears to be based on a certain need; otherwise the senses will be repulsed. It is desirable to have more voids than solids, especially in interiors; and the eye delights in observing all the points of support on the exterior; but if one detects an affectation in this kind of *exaggeration*, then one suspects naught but some feats of strength that depend on a faulty use of a mechanism that is hidden to the eye but not to the mind nor to instinct.

Generally speaking, since architecture rests more than any other art on the harmony between taste and reason, it must be particularly guarded from the abuses of *exaggeration.*

EXECUTION The arts of imitation have such an immediate relationship with man that one is not surprised to find the two principles of human nature contained within them. These principles refer to two properties, the one corresponding to the body, the other to the mind.

Accordingly, one can say that each art is composed of an intellectual part, and a more or less material part. The former consists in the workings of the mind, the feelings, and the power of the imagination. What constitutes the latter depends on the more or less tangible signs used in each genre of imitation, or the more or less material and mechanical means through which the artist manifests his thoughts.

The latter part, is usually known by the name *execution.*

One can distinguish and consider separately the part that *execution* plays in the arts, depending on their degree of material imitation. The more material and mechanical are the means of an art, the easier is its *execution* distinguished and analyzed. Accordingly, the distinction between the two parts of art is somewhat more tangible in sculpture than it is in painting, and it is clearer still in architecture.

In the other arts, the one who thinks is also the one who executes, whereas the inventor or the author of a work of architecture is not its executor. He must use instruments other than his own, and not only must he employ the manual work of others, but his own manual cooperation is impossible.

However, this does not imply that the material *execution* of an edifice is independent of the architect's authority; for *execution* is composed of a large number of practical procedures with which the architect must be familiar in order to supervise and direct all the operations. Thus, although he does not personally build, he must be the one who directs the building. In this view, *execution* in

architecture differs from that of other arts, it is remote rather than immediate.

But architecture is divided into two parts, and if the part known as *construction* is still subordinated in its execution to the mind of the architect, then it must be considered, in the whole and in the details, as dependent on him alone and on his genius. *Execution*, in this case, is so particular to the architect that buildings are recognized by the manner of their *execution*, just as paintings and statues are recognized based on the manner of the painter and the sculptor.

GENIUS This word derives from the Latin *ingenium*, from the verb *gignere*, which signifies in its simple meaning to *engender, produce. Genius* in French is the name given to this moral faculty of man, whose characteristic is to *produce* and *invent.*

Following another definition, derived from *ingenium*, in so far as it signifies *in nos genitum*, this word must fundamentally signify an aptitude, a natural or innate disposition in us that makes us inclined for such and such a study, or for such and such an area of knowledge, or work.

We must also say in advance that the word *genius* – understood, not in the theoretical meaning of moral faculty in the domain of art, but allegorically, as a personification consecrated by the religion of the ancients – applies also to a large number of figures which we shall treat in the following article.

In the present article, the meaning of the word *genius* is considered under the two theoretical concerns allowed by its double etymology.

In the first of these concerns, *genius*, being a creative faculty and a principle of invention for each kind of human activity, does not lend itself to an analysis that develops all its virtues and clearly explains its actions, any more than it can teach the secret of acquiring it. There is no teaching in this endeavour, which by general agreement is considered to be a gift of nature. It is only through its effects, and through some of the means that produce it, that one could give some satisfactory notion.

Thus, though products that are reputed to be works of *genius* by common acceptance, and through the means that these works reveal, it is possible to subject this creative faculty to a kind of analysis that could explain it up to a certain point.

For example, it has always been commonly held, that men of *genius*, or who have always been known as such, are those who produced the largest body of work. From century to century, and by common consent, it was hardly ever mentioned that a recognized work of *genius* may have been the sole product of its author. Consequently, facility and fecundity came to be considered as two characteristic attributes of *genius*. But, obviously, this fact, considered as the result of the productive faculty, can neither explain its principle, nor teach how to reproduce its effects.

What some call *inspiration* is also but a metaphorical figure, which is only suitable to explain the effects of *genius* without accounting for its nature. One uses this figure in order to explain that certain works appear to be the result of some fortunate moments where an exalted feeling quickly grasped these ideas, these fleeting insights that research cannot reveal, and which particularly elude the effort of labour.

Following such observations, *genius* came to be considered as a lively, easy and rapid action that is often separate from the collaboration between work and study, which were regarded as foreign to *genius*. But it is impossible to verify that these rapid movements called *inspirations*, are not themselves the result of the unseen and unknown work of those who experience them. In how many endeavours does the imagination – which one might term the memory of feeling – compile, unbeknownst to us, a supply of ideas which appear to germinate spontaneously, only because the seeds had been planted in us without our knowledge. Thus, *genius* has its proper manner of operating, which only it can reveal and define.

It would be erroneous to conclude from the definition of *genius* as a natural gift that its recipient needs no assistance from study. Work is no less necessary than culture, even in the soil most favoured by nature. It is true that work without *genius* produces only bad results; but *genius* without work can also yield only miscarried results.

We said that the word *genius*, in ordinary usage, had another acceptation according to which it designated a certain aptitude or natural disposition that carries us towards such and such an endeavour, work, or knowledge. It is in this sense that one is said to have a *genius* for a particular art or a particular profession. However, this expression is ambiguous, because it is possible that the word *genius*, in these cases, applies to the art itself. Thus, while concurring that this often implies having or not having the necessary aptitude or innate disposition (*in nos genita*) to succeed in such and such an artistic genre, it could also be understood that since each art has its own *genius* or its proper nature, it is this very property that may be foreign or ill-suited to the artist in question.

Following this distinction, a correlation or reciprocity obtains. Each art, each kind of knowledge, study, and endeavour, has its particular *genius*; that is to say, an ensemble of objects, knowledge, and means that determine its being. But this being will not possess the *genius* of this art if it lacks the faculties that correspond to each of the elements that compose this art.

GRAND, GRANDEUR Why do people admire all that is *grand*? The answer to this question is of little concern to us. Artistic theory is linked to moral sensations in as far as one wills it to be. To account for the causes and principles of these sensations falls in the domain of metaphysics; to ascertain their existence and to deduce consequences ordinarily suffices for artistic theory.

Now, it is a universally agreed upon fact, that what is *grand* excites admiration in the works of nature, and produces the same effect in works of art. Therefore, *grandeur* is a quality – a foremost one perhaps. In every field, the people who expressed it were placed and remained in the first rank. Such is the very nature and effect of this quality that nothing can replace it, whereas it can replace many others. The absolute lack of *grandeur* cannot be excused, either by the elegance of details, the carefulness of execution, or the luxury of ornaments. On the contrary, *grandeur* in thought, in invention, in composition, in design, or in effect, permits itself to have a multitude of defects and negligences.

Such is the power of the impression that all that is *grand* produces in us, in the moral and physical realms, that even crimes are able to extract from us a kind of admiration, when a certain perseverance, an obstinacy in evil, and the boldness in the manner of its execution, give it a character of *grandeur*. This is because the idea of *grandeur* never proceeds without that of strength, and because something in our instinct admires and searches for a quality that is the principle for our preservation.

Thus, *grandeur* is one of the foremost merits of architecture; and I mean *grandeur* in all its kinds, that is to say moral or material, as well as the

Fig. 50. Spanish Steps and the Trinità dei Monti, Rome. From: Julien Guadet, *Élements et théorie de l'architecture*, Librairie de la construction moderne, Paris, 1909

linear or proportional *grandeur* in building. The first consists in the expanse of surfaces and volumes; but if accompanied by a smallness in detail, then it loses a large part of its effect. Thus, the exterior of Gothic edifices and churches presents the most considerable mass of building that can be imagined; but the idea of *grandeur* is particularly weakened by the idea of minuteness in detail. On the contrary, the interior of these edifices – although made in the same architectural manner – impresses the senses by its *grandeur*. It is because in these interiors the small details are few, whereas on the exterior they proliferate.

In no other construction was linear *grandeur* taken to such a high level as in Egyptian pyramids. This *grandeur*, one must admit, is the only

merit of these edifices, without which no one would have ever spoken of them; for this kind of monument is a stranger to the resources and delights of art. But whoever beholds them feels so small and is forced to admire these masses that seem to rival mountains. Since nothing in these uniform masses diverts from the sentiment of unity and simplicity offered by the whole, then, their impression and their *grandeur* influence the senses with as much strength as possible. Yet, since nothing compels the eye to exercise the faculty of comparing, and since these masses do not in themselves offer a means that could awaken the idea of rapport or combination, considering that they are devoid of divisions and somewhat of parts, then the impression of this kind of linear *grandeur* promptly tires the mind; and once the feeling of admiration has dissipated, nothing serves to awaken it, while uniformity almost immediately causes boredom.

The two examples we have just cited demonstrate that linear (or dimensional) *grandeur* alone does not suffice to produce in us the complete sentiment that our mind awaits and expects from monuments. There is another *grandeur* whose impression is more certain, and which produces its effect at much less cost: it is the moral *grandeur* which, in architecture, I would call proportional, because it results especially from a rapport of the whole with its parts, and each part with the whole.

In order for the *grand* to be manifest, the object that realizes it must be so simple as to strike us at first glance – that is to say in its entirety – and at the same time strike us by the relations between its parts. The numerous repetition of small impressions will never produce *grandeur*. In order to embrace the idea of the scope of a building, our mind has to make an effort; but the proliferation of small parts, far from enlarging, actually diminishes this power within us. One could traverse the entire globe, says Sulzer, without finding it *grand*; because if one were to conceive of only the part of the earth that one occupies, then the imagination is not compelled to make an effort to form an idea of this part; but if one were to conceive at once a distance of one hundred leagues[29] or more, then one needs a mental effort; hence the idea and the sentiment of *grandeur*.

We attribute the character of *grandeur* to visible objects composed of diverse parts having a tangible and necessary rapport with the whole; that is to say, when they consist of large parts which in addition to their variety still remain in such an accord with the whole that they always bring the observer's eye back to that very whole.

In order for a city seen from afar to appear *grand*, it is not enough for it to present a large quantity of houses; these houses must also be distributed in *grand* parts, in clusters or quarters. The city in its various parts must also present *grand* towers or domes, around which less elevated buildings are assembled.

Fig. 51. St. Paul's, London, Christopher Wren.
From: A.C. Quatremère de Quincy, *Histoire de la vie et des ouvrages des plus célèbres architectes*. J. Renouard, Paris, 1830

A palace will never invoke the idea of moral *grandeur* spoken of here solely through a multiplicity of doors, windows, columns, ornaments, and details. This idea will be realized when various parts are disposed and linked with each other in such a manner that the small parts are not perceived in their relationship with the whole, but rather in their correlation with the principal parts to which they belong. On the other hand, these principal parts must be so linked together that they result in an inseparable and harmonious whole. Thus, the eye of the connoisseur is obliged, as it were, to behold the edifice only as a whole, and to be impressed all at once by the totality.

One of the surest means to impress the character of *grandeur* in all works of art, and especially those of architecture, is to endow the whole with simplicity, which results from the small number of principal parts. Then, the eye and the imagination are diverted from details, or at least their effect impresses the mind only in the correct order, that is to say, last.

One cannot give the architect lessons or advice save on that which relates to moral or proportional *grandeur*; whereas linear or dimensional *grandeur* derive from causes that are almost never subordinated to the architect. In the expanse of their plans and the solidity of their construction, edifices are subject to all sorts of circumstances and considerations in which the principle of beauty very often plays no role. There are periods and countries where the economy is the primary regulator of architectonic conceptions. Nothing *grand* is produced in these periods and countries; for even though it has been said that moral or ideal *grandeur* can be manifest in a small building, it remains natural for the small to seek the small, and for the taste for minutiae to be allied to small enterprises as if by a certain affinity.

Contrariwise, it is difficult for an architect in charge of building on a large scale and with large dimensions, not to receive inspiration from the dimensions themselves in order to achieve *grand* forms and *grand* proportions. Naturally, he finds himself compelled to display all the strength of construction in such masses; hence the appearance of solidity. Now this appearance constitutes one of the beauties of the edifice, and one of the ways in which the idea of the *grand* is communicated to the observer. The *grandeur* of masses pleases us in the works of nature because it humbles us, and because our smallness aggrandizes the soul by elevating it towards the idea of the principle of every form of *grandeur*. In works of architecture, the *grandeur* of masses pleases us because it makes us proud. Man is proud to feel himself small next to his own manual work. He enjoys the idea of his own strength and power.

HARMONY This word applies more particularly to works of music and painting than to those of architecture. However, when the true sense of this word is ascertained, one is led to believe that the idea that it expresses applies not only to this art as well as to others, but that it may have originally been borrowed from the art of building.

Indeed, in its original acceptation, the word *harmony*, which is the Greek word *harmonia*, meant *link*, *joint*. Thus, it properly signifies the union between objects that hold together, adjust, ally, meet, etc.

In speaking of the walls of Tyrins, where the largest stones were held together and linked by the smallest, Pausanias uses this word. Each of the smaller stones, he stated, served as a harmony to the larger ones. "...as certainly the purpose of each of these small stones is to serve as an adjustment for the larger stones." Ὡς μαλιστα αυτων εκαστον αρμονιαν τοις μεγαλοις λιθοις ειναι.(Pausanias, Book II, Chapter XXV).

However, music seems to have used the word *harmony* in a more particular way. The word is given a special meaning that designates the scientific part of this art, which consists in simultaneous action, and in the combination of sounds. From this customary use of the word in music derived a kind of ambiguity that led some to assume an entire technical similitude applicable to the other arts. They imagined: 1° that every art borrowed this word from music; 2° that in borrowing this word, every art owed to music not only the moral idea of *harmony*, but that each of these arts was supposed to imitate musical modes, and to proceed by means that completely corresponded to the nature of musical elements.

Such were the systems advanced by certain speculative minds that aimed to transfer the *harmonic* procedures of music, to the *harmony* that suits the other arts; as if it were possible to have a parity of practical *harmony* between the art that addresses the ear and the one that addresses the eye. Thus, in painting, the nuances of colour came to be ranked in hues and half-hues, in order to correspond to the tones and the half tones of music; and some applied themselves to establishing between the accordance of sounds and that of colours certain correlations that the difference between our perceiving organs has proved to be impossible, imaginary, and purely nominal.

Such a similitude has been imagined in architecture. A passage of Vitruvius, in which he recommends to the architect that he possess a tincture of music, led to the belief that music must share a common system of *harmony* with architecture. However, if Vitruvius finds it commendable for an architect to know music, he explains his reasons, and he indicates where the application of this knowledge is useful. It is, he states, in order for the architect to know how to dispose the vases that reverberate sound within the structure of a theatre; and in order to recognize by sound, the degree of tension in the strings of ballistae and other war machines.

Thus, the theories based on these passages are as ineffectual in their principles as they are in their applications.

However, one could cite many erudite men, among whom figures the great Blondel, who took enormous pains to give consistency to purely nominal analogies, regarding what they called the *harmonic* in their architectural treatises. For example, according to some fanciful parallels, the Attic base (who could have ever suspected it!) represents a *si mi sol si*, which is augmented by a *la* when a pedestal is added, resulting in the chord *la si mi sol si*. But there remains the two filets that terminate the upper and lower part of the scotia; and these two mouldings confound the logic of this bizarre system, here as well as elsewhere. But Blondel and Ouvrard assign to them the roles of *spira* [Ephesian spira?] *whose modulation*, so they say, *makes one appreciate with greater pleasure the essential notes in chords*.

Enough said, perhaps more than enough, about a bizarre idea that the least reflection will cast away. When one considers that there is no work of art or industry that is not, to some degree, an assemblage of parts; and that the mode of combination proper to each art depends on the diversity of elements that compose it in such a manner that, since each art has its proper mode that may not apply to another, their only commonality is that general and abstract law of the necessary correspondence needed by the parts in order to produce the whole and the pleasure that results from observing it, that is to say, that of *harmony*.

Thus, the idea of *harmony* should first and foremost, apply to what one may call the general system of architecture. *Harmony* exists, not only when the parts are of the same style or taste, but when all the parts are found in such a reciprocal and necessary rapport that no part could be displaced or transposed without rupturing the general bond, which is the fundamental reason that established their place.

In order for the pleasure of *harmony* to become evident within the system of an architecture, there is a certain condition that the very definition of the word indicates as being indispensable. Indeed, if *harmony* is a link between sundry or discordant parts, then our sight and mind should be able to understand the parts and the knot that

Fig. 52. The Philippeion at Olympia.
From: Josef Durm, *Die Baukunst der Grieschen*,
A. Kröner Verlag, Stuttgart, 1905

ties them together, in order for this link to be grasped. Now, in order for this to occur, the parts must be neither too similar nor too dissimilar. Too much unity in the forms that constitute the elements of an architecture, will cause the principle of *harmony* or concordance between forms to weakly impress the senses. Such is the flaw of Egyptian architecture; its elemental type is too simple, its imitative system approaches identical similarity too closely. When everything is simple, everything becomes monotonous; and the principle of *harmony* has no tangible application.

On the other hand, when the elements of an architecture are too dissimilar or too incoherent; and when the reason that assembled these parts is too confused; or when these combinations – as

in Gothic architecture – seem to be made only by chance; and when the eye and the mind cannot perceive a necessary link between all these objects and their details, neither because of the reason for the need nor the need for the reason, there can be no *harmony* that results from the system of such architecture.

Now, in examining outside the realm of abstractions what is designated by the word system in every architecture, and what is regarded as *harmony* in the customary practice of this art, we conclude that *harmony* must preside over the *combination of a building's plan*, the *disposition of its elevations*, and *the distribution of its decoration or its ornaments*.

There is *harmony in the plan* of an edifice when that which constitutes its whole is the result of a single thought; when all the distributions – each designed for its proper use – are coordinated within a general motif; when each part, in relation to the need that justifies it, seems to be naught but the product of a propriety dictated by the pleasure of symmetry; and finally when, with simple lines and a clear and easy to comprehend parti, architecture unites – in an altogether uniform and varied manner – the diverse constraints of the project in such a way that nothing seems to have cost either pain or difficulty in combination. The *harmony* of the plan must become the principle and the basis for the general elevation, from which one could sometimes except certain palace fronts that do not form a noteworthy ensemble.

Harmony in elevation consists first in the correctness of the principal relations of length, width, and depth that a building's mass must present and that the eye should easily understand. This kind of *harmony* between the principal dimensions forms part of the system of proportion to which the works of nature and the human body – to a certain extent – offer analogies and examples. One cannot prescribe a precise rule in this regard. All sorts of circumstances that depend on the place, the point of view and the position must be taken into consideration by the architect, and serve to guide him. But the most important principle of *harmony* to observe in the elevation is one that lays the disposition of the ensemble of volumes, as well, as the style that regulates the ordonnance, the judgment that clearly designates the purpose, and the unity that gives it its proper character. This is what is most rarely encountered in a complete manner in the elevations of a great many buildings.

The *harmony* of decoration, in its theory and its applications, offers precepts that are perhaps easier to deduce and observe. Indeed, every order already shows us – whether in its proportions or the relations established between the form of each of its ornaments – the rule and the example of the true use of decorative *harmony*. It is obvious that the multiplication of ornaments, be they light or delicate, would be ill fitting to the order whose object is to express strength or solidity, and vice versa. An enlightened sentiment once compelled the founders of the orders to regulate the degree of strength, lightness, or opulence of each, as well as the kind and the measure of ornament that befit its use and its character. Thus, in the decoration of each building, one must follow the principle of *harmony* whose consequence is prescribed by the utilized order. *Harmony* in decoration consists not only in the measure, but also in the choice of ornament; but the laws of this *harmony* are contradicted when buildings whose use demands an exterior character of simplicity, are endowed with opulence and decorative luxury; and, conversely, when the building that demands opulence is devoid of ornament. One infringes upon the laws of this *harmony*, when one is mistaken as to the kind of ornament that applies to the kind or the purpose of each edifice, or its different constitutive parts; as, for example, when light subjects or the caprices of the arabesque are used in a church, or in any other building destined to a solemn use. *Harmony* also prescribes the sparing use of the means or the resources of decoration, and the calibration of effects in the diverse parts of an edifice depending on the different uses in its interiors. If, for example – as it has happened many a time – one were to display all the pomp of *decoration* in the stair of a palace, then what remains for the interiors?

Without doubt, this theory could occupy a long and important treatise, because it comprises varied notions and applications to each of the different arts; and wherein architecture will especially find ample substance for development. However, because of the analytical nature of a dictionary, and because these notions are distributed over a great number of articles, it was deemed proper to only present a summary here.

HUT This name is given to every poor dwelling made of common and light materials, more often of wood – or of earth intermixed with wood and covered either with thatch in the countryside or with planks in cities – or of any other economical material.

Regardless of the manner in which it is considered, the purpose that it serves, or the country and the time where it is used, and no matter its form, the *hut* is always the first adumbration or the common repetition of more accomplished or more important constructions.

We shall not deal here with this second kind of *hut*, which, in an advanced state of civilization, is produced either by the numerous uses of an infinity of needs, or the slender means of the poor inhabitants of the countryside. The article *hut* can find a place in a dictionary of architecture only in an abstract and theoretical respect; that is to say, in as much as the expressed meaning of this word presents a trial or an adumbration of construction in the origin of every society; hence it is possible to discern the seed whose succession of ideas and efforts fostered later development.

We do not pretend to apply this theory to all kinds of buildings in all nations on earth; nor can we offer a knowledge of all the varieties of *huts* or early dwellings that every society experiences, depending on a multitude of local causes. This retroactive knowledge is perhaps even impossible, for lack of sufficient traditions among a large number of nations. Many kinds of reasons could have combined to form these poor dwellings in different countries, and Vitruvius gives us sufficient indications to prove that this first seed may have remained sterile with respect to art in many places, as the facts demonstrate.

This, did not occur in Greece; and we can affirm, on the basis of historical material, diverse traditions, and the evidence of her own architecture, that the primitive dwellings of this country were made of wood. Thus, Thucydides tells us that Attic *huts* were formed from a wood assembly. These wooden constructions could be disassembled at will and re-erected elsewhere. As soon as the Peloponnesian war was declared, Pericles ordered that the wooden houses of the entire Attic region be demolished, and their materials brought to Athens, in order to protect them from the enemy's fire. (Thucydides, Book II).

One is compelled to believe that the system that constituted the most perfected Greek architecture in all her parts is clearly a representative image of all the elements of a natural composition in wood. It is therefore much less a question of proving the representation of the Greek *hut* in Greek architecture, than to show how and why no other kind of *hut* could have produced that which distinguishes this architecture; that is to say, on the one hand, her imitative property, and on the other, her proportional virtue. If one were to enumerate, based on the authority of facts and theories, all the known or supposed ways of making primitive dwellings known as *huts*, then neither the *huts* made of branches and foliage, nor the plastering with earth, or artificial or natural caverns are capable of becoming perfectible models, let alone inspiring any imitation whatsoever.

What could the art of earlier times have found to imitate in works whose very nature deprived them of all that could secure calculations, combinations, and the reciprocal relations of various parts? There was only one material (wood), one combination (that of assemblies), one ensemble (that of projecting and recessing parts), one necessary rapport (that of load-bearing and load-borne objects), that could perpetuate and reproduce itself in another material such as stone, and secure a set of already combined relations, already determined spaces, and already formed elevations.

Perhaps this is one of the better reasons that one could give for the enduringness and the perpetuity of Greek architecture: she alone had what must be termed a system that was not the work of chance; she alone was born of a seed fertile in combinations. She alone found in the *hut*, which

was her primitive type, a whole that was already united by necessary relations; an ensemble composed of parts subordinated to the principle of necessity; a model capable of lending itself in the art of building, to that which is largest, that which is lightest, and that which is more refined; and finally, a model capable of adapting itself to the necessities of all countries and climates.

Therefore, in Greek architecture, when one puts forward the *hut* as having been her model; it is obvious that one must be guarded from believing that the *hut* in question is the rustic habitation known ordinarily by this name, especially in the case of an agricultural state.

Doubtless, our *model hut* is but a system of theory founded on primitive facts, but having become a kind of *canon* at once fictitious and real, whose necessary or probable cause can be always verified by introducing all the intended modifications to inherited forms or new proposed uses. Yes, this type, which one should never lose sight of, is the rule to redress all the misuses introduced to this art, sometimes by an ambitious innovation, and other times by a blind routine. Through its powerful virtue, a clever critique will banish these depraved customs, these faulty deviations, to which architecture is exposed more than any other art. This valuable type will always be like an enchanted mirror, whose effect cannot be endured by a corrupt art, and which, by reminding it of its true origin, is always able to bring it back to its first virtue.

IDEA, IDEAL adj. According to its Greek derivation and the accepted theoretical definition, the word *idea* signifies the kind of image left in our mind by the impressions of objects. Thus, metaphysically[30] speaking, *idea* and *image* are two synonyms.

However, some metaphysicians would like the word *idea* to signify the representation of all that pertains to the moral domain, and the word *image* to designate the representation of all material objects, or those that fall in the realm of the senses. Indeed, one speaks of the *idea* of the just and the unjust, the *idea* of duty, of soul, of Divinity; and one never uses the word *image* to express those kinds of representations. This latter word is therefore exclusively suited to the representation that operates in our mind, of all that impresses the exterior senses; and, very appropriately, one speaks of *grasping and retaining the images of corporeal beings*.

Yet common usage in this kind of subject, authorizes the use of the word *idea*, and indeed one speaks indistinctly of the *idea* or the image of the sun, of having the *idea* of, or of representing the image of a man, a statue, or a building. This is why the word *idea* belongs in the vocabulary of the arts of design.

Therefore, this word is used in architecture to designate the impressions left in the mind by the objects that belong to the art of building; thus one speaks of having the *idea* of a monument, of conserving the *idea* of its plan, its elevation, its ornaments, etc. The same word is used concerning the invention or the composition of an edifice. In this case, as in all others, the artist invents and imagines only by making a new whole out of various parts he holds in his mind; thus, the product of this invention is but a composite effect, that is, a new image formed by the combination of many other partial ones, of which the imagination makes a new ensemble. But the artist must have this new ensemble present in his mind before realizing it; this is what is known as forming the *idea* of a composition.

The more lively and powerful the impression of an observed object, the more distinct is its *idea*. This liveliness and this force of impression depend either on the nature of the mind or on memory, or on the extent of study. Reflection, and the practice of combining, offer the artist the greatest facility to clearly represent all that he proposes to realize; the clearer the *idea* held in his mind, the more truth his representation of this *idea* acquires, and the more accessible it is to the comprehension of the observer.

One uses the word *idea*, in the arts of design and in the art of designing architecture, synonymously with the word *esquisse*. Thus, one speaks of rendering the *idea* of a composition, or of fixing the *idea* of a project for a monument. This bears the same meaning as the word *croquis* or rough sketch, that is, an object's abbreviated or reduced image, which nevertheless suffices to fix the general notions or to recall the whole.

The word *idea* is used in yet another sense, as when one speaks of making from an *idea*, painting or drawing from an *idea*, or reproducing from an *idea*, the appearance of a monument. This signifies, in general, the act of making from memory or from the imagination. But fundamentally it is as if one spoke of painting or drawing, not after a given model – or what is known as *after nature* – but according to the type or image that one has formed of it; it is as if one were to reproduce the appearance of a monument, not after reality, but rather from the image of it preserved in memory.

As a consequence of this capacity, of which our mind is endowed, we are able to compensate, in the imitation of many an object, for the actual and immediate observation from nature; by fashioning after careful study, a kind of type which stands as its exemplary *ideal*; and this is at once the principle and the explanation of what theory calls the *ideal* in every genre of imitation.

We should add, however, that the word *ideal* has two distinct meanings.

The first, which is ordinarily understood in a negative sense, is synonymous with imaginary, with fantastic, with fictitious. According to these meanings, the word *ideal* could be applied to any work which, instead of being conceived and executed in accordance with the laws of nature, and following the principles of truth and the rules of taste, appears as the product of a disordered imagination, which mistakes its own dreams for the inspirations of genius and falls into the false in order to produce the new.

The second way to understand the word *ideal* is more particularly applicable to the arts of imitation that have in nature an evident model. In this sense, one opposes, in the theory of imitation, the word *ideal* to the word *natural*. Thus, the imitative manner which one may qualify as *natural*, is one that is restricted to the exact copy of the model taken individually; while the *ideal* imitative manner, is one which represents objects or beings, considered from a general point of view, in other words, as they can be, or as they could be.

In the latter sense, the *ideal* is the result of an operation of the intelligence, whose object is to assemble within one individual, all the perfections which are ordinarily found scattered in the many. For such an operation consists in various parallels and generalizations that can be wrought only in *idea*, and through the effect of an abstract system. The result of this system, for example, is known as the *ideal* of such a subject, of such a nature, or such a composition, etc., that is to say, the characteristic type, the generic principle of such and such a subject of imitation, which is deduced from a nature considered in her intentions and in the general laws of her works, rather than her individual productions.

This imitative theory seems of little application in architecture, which does not operate on the basis of a real and material model. However, when one thinks that the system upon which this art is founded, and the principles upon which it is based, are necessarily the result of intelligence; and when one recognizes that every system that derives from the general laws of nature belongs to the *ideal* order of things, then perhaps one is permitted to propose that no art more than architecture rests on the principle known as the *ideal*.

ILLUSION The idea associated with this word, etymologically speaking (*illudere*), is that of trickery. When applied to imitation in the fine arts, this word expresses the property or the faculty that they possess to delude us with the images that they present. But to what extent, in what measure, and with which means? This is the subject of a theory that will not be developed in this dictionary, that is, that architecture, by its proper nature, is truly unable to achieve the artifice of *illusion*.

Every *illusion* that art produces is an effect of imitation, in that it makes us mistake for a reality that which is but a fiction. Now this effect necessarily supposes that art pursues the identical resemblance of a model in its practice.

But we have sufficiently demonstrated, in many articles, that the kind of imitation proper to architecture is simply abstract; and that this art imitates the principles, the laws and the rules that nature follows in her works, as well as her many intellectual consequences. Thus, there is no *image* here, in the ordinary sense of the word. Now, when there is no *image* or resemblance, either of real objects or of physical effects, there can be no way of producing what is known as *illusion*.

In vain can one cite the artifice of *simulated architecture*. On the contrary, nothing could better prove that this does not concern architecture, since in this matter it is not this art that fools us, but rather painting. Architecture is the material of this trickery, but not its agent.

IMAGINATION It is the moral faculty which has the property of retaining, reproducing, and retracing either the images of external objects, or the impressions of internal feelings.

Since we can only understand the effects produced by our moral faculties by borrowing signs from corporeal beings, language – as mentioned in the entry *idea* – has borrowed from the painting of material objects or the delineation of figures the terms that we use to designate these incorporeal traces left in our understanding or our minds, and the feelings that we experience, by the reciprocal relations of things. Hence, as we have already seen, *idea* and *image* have the same significance.

As a consequence of this system of borrowing from physical objects, *imagination* has been considered from two points of view. It is assumed to be either a sort of repository where the impressions produced by external objects or internal feelings are classified and, in this case, *imagination* participates in the property of memory; or, it is considered to be a kind of laboratory where the received impressions, that is to say their images, unite in diverse combinations, thus producing new ensembles, new associations of objects, feelings, and impressions; and in this last point of view, *imagination* participates in the quality known as genius.

In fact, *imagination* is often understood as *genius*, and these two notions are easily confused. However, *imagination* differs in that it is one of the instruments of the creative faculty. This faculty is one of the necessary conditions of the activity of imagining because genius is perhaps less a single faculty than a union of faculties, among which one also counts *judgment*.

Genius is assisted by the *imagination*, especially in architecture, and *imagination* needs to be tempered by judgment. Without the faculty of *imagination*, that is to say the elaboration of images stored in memory within new combinations, the architect will be a copyist who repeats within the same appearances, and the same givens, the works of those who preceded him. But if judgment were to fail to preside over the kinds of combinations made by the *imagination*, then this absence of judgment will beget the two defects which served, in certain periods, to vitiate the very constitutive elements of architecture.

Under the pretext of *invention*, but in fact in the name of *innovation*, even the most renowned architects laid claim to genius, not only by arbitrarily combining, without any principle, the elements of the system upon which this art is based, but also by compiling the most incompatible elements. They denied that there was or that there could be a reason that regulates architecture; they reversed all the principles and all the forms, and pretended that since nature does not produce buildings, then architecture has no regulating principle – as if nature had no general laws that apply to all kinds of works.

The other defect is produced by the lack of judgment – understood as the regulator of *imagination*; and without overturning the foundations of architecture, it is manifest in the disposition of edifices, when in order to flaunt his *imagination*, the architect subjects the necessities of construction, the propriety of composition and the pleasure of decoration to arbitrary and strange uses, and a false picturesque effect. (*See* CAPRICE).

IMITATION Each art has in nature a general model common to all the arts, and a model that is particular to it. To consider nature in the universality of her laws suggests that her *imitation* belongs to all the arts. Consequently, there are rules for *imitation* to which each art is subject, if not in the same manner, then at least to the same degree. Similarly, there is a universal grammar

common to all languages, and a grammar which is particular to every dialect.

For an art to be reputed an *art of imitation*, it is not necessary that its model be based on physical and material nature in a manner evident and conspicuous to sight. This kind of model belongs only to those arts that address the eye through the mediation of corporeal forms and colours.

Likewise, it is not necessary for all the arts that fall in the domain of poetry, to base themselves on a model as easy to understand and conceive as dramatic art, which finds in human characters, passions and ridicule, the original models after which the artist moulds his portraits. The other genres of poetry, without the benefit of such clearly defined models, do not possess any less

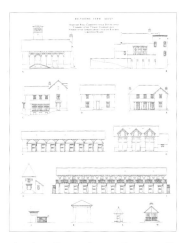

Fig. 53. Belvedere Farm, Ascot, Demetri Porphyrios.
From: *Demetri Porphyrios, Selected Buildings and Writings,*
Academy Editions, London, 1993

the privilege of *imitation*. Only, it must be said that the way in which these arts imitate nature is qualified by something more abstract, more general, and which also requires a wider outlook; because to restrict the poet to what is known as *imitative poetry*, amounts to reducing his available field of *imitation* to these onomatopoeiae whose choice of expressions and sounds – that resemble what that they signify – seem to counterfeit their very appearance.

Therefore, when nature is said to be the model for all the fine arts, one must be guarded from restricting the idea of nature to that which is evident and material. Nature exists as much in what is invisible in her as in what is apparent to the eye. Thus, to take nature as a model in certain works of art, is to imitate her by adopting the very rules that she follows in her works; by operating in accordance with the same principles that guide her actions in the formation of her creations; and, finally, by proceeding in works of art, in a manner which follows the direction that she prescribes to her means, by adopting the same ends as those towards which she tends.

To imitate, then, does not necessarily signify to make the image of, or to produce the resemblance of a thing, a creature, a body or a given work, because one could imitate the artificer without imitating the work. Therefore, one imitates nature by making as she makes, that is, not by repeating her work properly speaking, but by appropriating the principles that served as a rule for this work, in other words, her spirit, her intentions and her laws.

In order to elucidate the way in which architecture has the right to be included among the arts of *imitation*, we deemed it necessary to incorporate this preliminary development of ideas comprised in the word *imitation*; that is, the two different manners in which art imitates nature.

Elsewhere, we gave an account (*See* ARCHITECTURE) of the sort of *imitation* that every art of building makes from the elements of primitive construction, which early societies gave as models to the ages that followed. But once this sort of *imitation* is introduced and perfected, it is no longer the artist's own making, for he no longer imagines it and is instead bound to conform to it. Thus, in Greek architecture for example, the artist who composes a monument according to the system borrowed from what is called the primitive type of building in wood, is not known to be its original imitator; he only adopts a consecrated mode of *imitation* that resembles the system or the mechanism of a language which is adopted through use and common consent. The same can be said of many commonly used details and ornaments, which, like the tropes, figures and metaphors of a language, allow the author the sole merit of successfully applying their *imitations*.

But the *imitation* that is truly proper to architecture – which like the other arts rests on nature – being less direct, is no less real, only its principle

is more abstract. Because it is through the *imitation* of causes that art imitates the effects of nature, and reproduces her impressions. The architect imitates nature when, in the creations that are dependent on his art, he follows and renders sensible to our eyes and our minds, the system of harmony, of the whole, of reason and truth, which nature reveals as a model in all her works.

But, let us say it, the secret of this system could only have been revealed and applied to the art of building among a people where the *imitation* of organisms and of live nature familiarized the eye with the very models in which the laws of proportion and the variety of types of every character were impressed in the most evident manner; and where the examples of all the harmonies that man can apply to his works were manifest. In a word, it is the true *imitation* of the human body that revealed the theory and the practice of proportion.

Now, if one were to except Greece, no other nation in antiquity was able to learn from this school of thought. Everywhere else we see that the spirit of *imitation* of the human body has been chained and debased by the routine sway of political and religious customs. All sorts of reasons tended – as they still do in many countries – to steal away, to obscure or distort the true knowledge of models of art, and to perpetuate the trials or imperfect adumbrations of the forms of the human body. Now, these coarse productions of a failed *imitation*, having stood between nature and the artist's vision, came to eliminate even the artist's awareness of the imperfection of his work. This is what happened in ancient and modern Asia, in Egypt, and in the Middle Ages.

The Greeks suffered at first under the yoke of this instinct, but they knew how to overcome it. Among the causes of this liberation, there was a most powerful one, whose effect has not been sufficiently noted in the writings that claimed to give us the moral history of *imitation* in Greece.

It was inevitably through idolatry or the cult of divine images that the *imitation* of the human body spread everywhere. Having universally consecrated this practice, religion perpetuated and sanctified the forms of idols. Consequently, the most ancient idols were the most revered. As a result, it was impossible to ameliorate the forms of idols among many a people; for this amelioration would have discredited their value, by removing the prestige of their antiquity. This instinct, which is common to all religions and all countries, took place also among the Greeks; and one learns from history and extant writings that their primitive idols were also made with the coarse instinct of *imitation* without art.

In all respects this state of affairs persisted among the Greeks until a new practice was introduced into the institutions of their country, one that allowed for the emancipation of *imitation*, by providing a multiplicity of occasions on which statues were raised to personages who were not gods, and for causes which had naught to do with religion.

Indeed, the practice of raising statues to victorious athletes at stadia was developed at an early period in Greece. History has preserved a few notions which prove that this genre of sculpture was made initially according to the erring ways of the rigid style without art or life which characterized all Egyptian sculptural figures. Thus, according to Pausanias, who gave an eye-witness description, the statue of the athlete Arrachion had the legs close together, the arms stiff, hanging, and stuck to the body.

But soon, something that could not have happened elsewhere – that is, in countries where statues were naught but religious idols – occurred in Greece. It so happened that this same constraint lost its hold on the very genre of purely human representation, and the need to express movement and the appearance of life became apparent. Let us add that these statues, which were destined to be honorific and commemorative images of known and living people, must have awakened the feeling of comparison, and motivated the need to judge the relationship between the model and its *imitation*. Thus, the games of the stadium and the exercises of the gymnasium naturally became the schools where the representation of the human body found its most effective lessons. As imitative truth was no longer hindered in the execution of its works by the obstacles of religiously consecrated forms,

art accrued the increasing obligation of rivalling nature.

Without a doubt, that liberty to ameliorate the forms of design through the study of the human body, begat in Greece this true *imitation* whose secrets were unknown to the rest of the world, and which, before the experience that we have just related, were unknown among the Greeks themselves. Since then, it became impossible for the artist not to manifest the same expression of truth within the statues of divinities. Their simulacra gradually left the coarse envelope of forms devoid of art. Finally, the gods were cast in the likeness of man, until the time came when genius opened to the artist a new path: that of ideal truth, which bestowed a kind of super-human beauty upon the statues of divinities.

Thus was the *imitation* of nature in the arts of design among the Greeks formed, expanded and perfected.

But such a principle could not remain limited to a small number of applications. As soon as man found the truth somewhere, he wanted it everywhere. As soon as the charm of *imitation*, founded on the causes of nature was felt in some parts, the need for this pleasure was communicated to other parts. And architecture, being so closely linked to the arts of design, could not remain a stranger to such an influence.

This brief history of *imitation* among the Greeks, demonstrates how the imitation that constituted their architecture was born and developed, and how the principle of reason, of truth and harmony was introduced to the art of *imitation* through the influence of a powerful analogy which adopted a system of proportions that was no longer based on arbitrary and variable elements, but rather on the assimilation of the system that nature applies in the organization of living beings.

Now this system of proportions, which was borrowed from nature, could only have appeared among a people who had realized its applications in the *imitation* of the human body; and it is by applying this system to her endeavours, that architecture deserved to be ranked among the fine arts.

The study of the human body had instructed the eyes and accustomed the mind to distinguish the variety of characters and differences in form; from here derived the tangible expression of the principal qualities of strength, lightness, power, etc. Hence, architecture found the kind of model, according to which she could appropriate an analogical correspondence between the same properties and the same qualities that are rendered evident and perceptible in the three orders and the nuances that they comprise.

This was how the spirit of an indirect *imitation* of nature realized this successful assimilation of the human body that some critics have rendered absurd by ridiculously straining its application. Indeed, many writers, and Vitruvius is numbered among them, have imagined that there must be some rigorous relationships between the male body and the Doric column, or between female hair arrangements and the Ionic capital, or between the falling folds of a robe and the flutings of a column. (*See* IONIC).

To call these kinds of parallels, which one may characterize as encounters rather than resemblances, an *imitation*, falls, without a doubt, in the realm of ridiculous fables. But the misuse to which some have subjected this system of *imitation*, by treating it in an excessively materialistic way, cannot destroy its existence nor weaken its truth. The sound theory of art, consists in freeing the true – a matter that can be easily travestied – from a double bias that emanates from a single source, and which consists in the denial of that which cannot be demonstrated physically, or its depreciation to the most material level possible.

The aim of this article has been to demonstrate the many different levels existing within the realm of *imitation* in the fine arts, and to prove that it is erroneous to give the name of art of *imitation* to that which only has a positive and material model in physical nature.

IMITATION This word is often understood in the sense given to the word *copy*; when, in a work of art, one intends to designate the absence of that quality known as originality. Also, the word *imitate* may sometimes be used as a synonym for the word *copy*, in order to designate the artist who not only formally reproduces an object without adding anything to it, but also when he servilely reproduces another's manner of doing and composing.

In this sense, the word *imitation*, often designates a work that repeats the style, the manner, and the taste in execution of the work of another master.

Imitation in this case is understood as the opposite of *invention*.

INGENIOUS This word seems to apply in general to any work or artist that displays genius; yet it also expresses another nuance. Thus, in speaking of a work that demanded the greatest compositions and all the depth of genius, one does not call it *ingenious*. Rather, this appellation is given to the work that demanded an intelligence that distinguished itself by the use of fine and delicate inventions, by an economy of means, and by effects that provoke more surprise than admiration. He who discovered the laws of gravity was a man of genius; he who imagined the barometer was *ingenious*.

When applied to all the arts of design and to architecture, the word *ingenious* designates less the idea of invention in general, than the invention of details that is synonymous with skill and intelligence.

The name *ingenious* will not be applied to great thoughts, to the new and bold conceptions of great painters, or to sublime and renowned sculptures; but it will designate – as Pliny himself stated, in speaking of the painter Nealces – these dexterous episodes that explain a subject, and the richness of indirect motifs that assist the mind in discovering that which would have remained an enigma for the eye.

Thus, in speaking of the above-named painter, Pliny said that he was *ingeniosus et solers in arte*, or *ingenious* and adroit in his art; and in so doing, Pliny defines the word using the same association of ideas that we used in our definition. Nealces was to paint a naval battle between the Egyptians and the Persians. This battle was to take place in the immensity of space where the Nile reaches the sea; and in order to impress on the observer that the waters were those of the Nile, the painter drew the scene of a crocodile ambushing a donkey who was quenching his thirst.

The same writer uses the words *argumento ingenioso*, or *ingenious* motif, to designate the allegorical invention by which the painter Parrhasios represented, in one and the same object, the seven or eight different characters expressing the variations and contradictions of the people of Athens.

Of all modern painters, Poussin is one who more aptly befits the appellation *ingenious*, in the sense given to it by Pliny. Several of his paintings like the *Dance of the Four Conditions of Life* and *Et in Arcadia Ego*, shine with these ingenious motifs, which are the result of an imagination crowned by the sort of research that earned him the appellation: *the intellectual's painter*.

assume that it was invented for pure pleasure. What pleases in this building is precisely what would have been very displeasing in the work of a less *ingenious* architect. Everything is dictated by the site, and one could even believe that the architect himself dictated the building's placement. The space is small and narrow, whereas everything that fills it is large, and appears to fit comfortably.

The architect also exhibits an *ingenious* talent in the choice and the use of ornaments, their application to different spaces, and the meanings that they accrue in new combinations.

INVENTION In ordinary parlance, this word accepts two meanings. The word *invention*, in

Fig. 54. Palazzo Massimo, plan, B. Peruzzi.
From: Julien Guadet, *Élements et théorie de l'architecture*, Librairie de la construction moderne, Paris, 1909.

Fig. 55. Palazzo Massimo, elevation, B. Peruzzi.
From: A. C. Quatremère de Quincy, *Histoire de la vie et des ouvrages des plus célèbres architectes*, J. Renouard, Paris, 1830

Similarly, in architecture, the *inventive* artist will be distinguished from the *ingenious* one. This art, perhaps more than any other, comprises the quality that this word designates. This quality is not the one that produces great effects, but rather, it is one that enables the architect to profit from all sorts of situations preventing even the suspicion that a certain difficulty was overcome, whether it be the defects of irregularity, the lack of space, or the most irksome constraints. If one were to ask for an example of this sort of quality, then, I think that no architect would hesitate to name the palazzo Massimo, the *ingenious* work of Baldassare Peruzzi, who knew how to advantageously utilize an awkward and irregular site. Such is the merit of this quality that one may

fact, is given to the thing invented, as in speaking of a machine as a *useful invention*. But the same name is also given to the quality of the mind which invents; and one says of a man that he is *inventive*, or that he lacks *invention*.

We shall consider this word here under the second meaning.

Consequently, in the language of the fine arts, *invention* is synonymous with *creation*; and these two words are drawn together by a common notion, which also serves to define them. One must stipulate, in fact, that man creates nothing in the elementary sense of the word, and that he only finds new combinations of pre-existing elements; the same applies also to the inventor who finds these combinations.

Man's need for *invention*, or for the pleasure that he experiences and demands from all the arts, comes from the constitution of his very being; from the nature of his mind. This mind, so closely united to the body, experiences – either by itself or as an effect of this union – a ceaselessly renewed need to move from rest to action, and from action to rest. This alternating succession is a condition of being. Continuous action or continuous rest would lead to its end.

The need of which we speak, which is the need for change, blends with the ordinary course of life, in work and in pleasure, in the joys of the body as well as those of the mind. Man demands certain pleasures of all the arts, and these pleasures derive from images of all kinds that either stir his passions or delight his imagination. But, additionally, man wants every art, within its proper sphere, to always find new means to please and move him.

In this respect, it can be said that, within the domain of their imitation, each of these arts possesses inexhaustible resources to satisfy this appetite. Nature exhibits an infinite variety of resources in all her aspects; she is no less prolific in the diversity of qualities and talents dispensed among individuals. Indeed, as each individual differs from the other by his physiognomy, so has each individual, within his moral faculties, a more or less distinct manner of conveying and communicating the impressions of the objects of nature.

Hence the innumerable varieties of the subjects of imitation, and also the ways in which these subjects are treated.

However, nature bestows upon some individuals, the privilege of distinguishing themselves from most others by a superior faculty of conception; to bring objects together, to combine them, and to present their effects or images in a more lively and true way, and with more brilliant colours; hence what is known in the arts of imitation as the styles or manners of the great masters.

Here, too, it came to pass that the greatest number of imitators who were deprived of that privileged vision that characterizes the inventive genius, instead of studying nature herself, were content to study her within the imitations of others; and instead of the original images of the great model, they were reduced to a reproduction of its pale second proofs. Such is the lot of those known as *copyists*; a numerous tribe, whose insipid repetitions end up discrediting the very value of the originals that served as their models. And this is one of the causes of the feeling of indifference, and sometimes disgust, held in certain ages towards the works that bear the mark of genius, where *invention* shines the most.

Now, those who seek to please through originality endeavour to find new ways; but this sought-after originality always has something artificial that soon becomes an oddity [*bizarrerie*]. The public's taste bites the bait of novelty and proclaims as inventor he who leaves the beaten track; and calls *invention*, that which is but an innovation. Soon, any respect for consecrated principles and rules is considered servile or timid, and the field of imitation falls prey to the dissoluteness of caprice. This is more or less the story of all the arts in modern times and among modern peoples.

Such is the fate that *invention* suffers, wherever the mind fails to find the degree of constraint that it needs, justly combined with the measure of independence which is no less necessary.

Thus, we observe that in Egypt and among all the peoples of Asia, where the mind was enslaved either by a religious power or by the yoke of routine – a necessary effect of the caste system – art was never able to find the liberty required for the development of the imitative faculty. In matters of art, there is no *invention* where there is no imitation of nature. But this imitation cannot occur where it is forbidden to leave certain forms and prescribed givens.

The fortunate circumstances that converged among the Greeks served to emancipate the imitative faculty which was also initially enslaved by the shackles of routine. (*See* IMITATION). As soon as it was permitted to modify religious signs; as soon as the expression of their idea was able to free itself from the conventions of sacred writing, then, the effect of this freedom was the need to compare the work of art with that of nature, and to slowly approach her models. With free imitation, *invention* was born; but it had to exchange the slavery of routine for the knowledge of rules that the very study of nature imposes in order to curb the licence of *invention*.

These rules that nature prescribed, by identifying themselves with imitation, fortunately found a guaranty of freedom within the realm and the spirit of religious institutions. If the artist was indeed free to impart to his work the impressions of natural truth, the scope of his imagination still adhered to the respect of a certain number of types, characters, combinations and consecrated modes. These conventions drew for art the circle where genius could exercise its action, for it was regulated without being restricted. In politics, there is no liberty without abiding by the law; likewise, in matters of art, there was no *invention* without subjecting oneself to rules.

Yet the moderns, while inheriting the art of the Greeks and their rules, found no obligation to follow other than that which derives from taste – an often very variable arbiter. Different customs, another religion, and the varieties of time and climate, in many ways rendered the rigorous principles and the ancient ways of seeing inapplicable to the new needs of the art of building. The sixteenth century in Italy reproduced many such examples, especially in architecture. But nothing in the opinions, the practice, or the institutions of the time could have acted as a safeguard against the continuity of a borrowed style, which was applied without the necessary link to the needs of another order of society.

At the time of their renewal, architecture and the other arts were no longer the native productions of the countries where they were reappearing. Architecture was succeeding a manner of building that had rooted itself along with many customs that were foreign to her domain, and to which she had to make many concessions. Thus, there was necessarily a confusion of ideas about the nature of this art. Since the ancients themselves never pretended that architecture could be confined within geometric measures, and since, on the contrary, nature had taught them what the ideal principle of architectural imitation could

have and should have been, it was believed that what was known as the *ideal* in the arts was synonymous with the imaginary and the arbitrary; and that since there were no models for buildings in nature, then there must be no kind of imitation for architecture. Subsequently, it was believed that rules could not exist because the rules of this art were not subservient to geometric rigour.

Consequently, the imagination believed that it had the right to transgress everything, to dare anything, to destroy everything, and to produce anything. Thus, the name *invention* was given precisely to anything that was disorderly, as if no *invention* could occur within rules; whereas what precisely characterizes the *invention* proper to the fine arts is not independence from any restraint, but liberty within rules.

We have already said that every *invention* consists in a new combination of pre-existing elements. What, then, are the elements that the true inventor could and should combine? This undoubtedly applies to those elements that fall under the rubric of an order of ideas, of relations, of objects which already have among themselves a connection of kinship (in other words, they are *homogeneous*). Indeed, to assemble within one individual, beings of different natures, is to create monsters; it is to spin chimera. Thus, in all the arts, this question can relate only to the elements or the objects that form the natural domain of each. Any other manner of understanding the combinations which are within the scope of *invention*, would be an absurdity of the sort that Horace expressed in the following verse:

Humano capiti cervicem pictor equinam
Jungere si veli, etc.

This condition of imitation, which belongs to the means of *invention*, needs only to be stated in order to be demonstrated. Therefore, its consequences are such that every kind of art is limited to a certain order of imitable objects, beyond which there are but heterogeneous combinations, as, for example, when the elements of different genres of poetry, or of certain arts of design, which are separated by moral or material boundaries, are mixed together.

But the theory of imitation and the delight that it provides have also taught us that the boundaries prescribed to every kind of art and the links that relate the artist to his chosen field are the most active cause for the impressions that the one and the other produce. Theory, in agreement with experience, teaches us that by rupturing these links, art itself is dissolved and loses its virtue, or the power that it exerts on our mind. The reason is that our mind, being a unity, rejoices only through unity, and finds no pleasure in divergent or incoherent sensations. This is the source for the elementary rules of the different arts.

Now, these rules have in truth been invented by no one. If they appear to have been the result of the masterpieces of some great men, one must be guarded from believing that they did not exist before. Only, these great men and their works have more lucidly manifested the rules that guided them. By their examples, they rendered these rules tangible, and compelled their successors to teach them more clearly.

Rules are naught else but observations made from nature. They exist before one discovers them. Man does not make these rules, he proclaims them. The most beautiful works are those where they are demonstrated most brilliantly.

It must be said that far from rules being injurious to *invention*, *invention* does not exist outside rules; we should add that *invention* would be worthless if it were possible not to have rules; for there would be no way to judge *invention*.

If one were to compare these principles to the attempts made by many innovators in architecture – and to the great efforts to deny or destroy rules by substituting for them the chance of caprice or the caprice of chance – then one will be convinced that no art is in more need of rules, and in no other art is *invention*, or the art of new combinations, in more need of being contained within a determined circle of pre-existing elements.

Well, it must be said, and it is not repeated often enough, that in their application to the plans, elevations and ornaments of edifices, the elements of architecture are not composed of all

the forms imaginable. If such were the case, then these fortuitous elements, without relation to each other, devoid of a reason which unites and explains them, would turn the works of the art of building into the very prototype of disorder. Considering these forms from the most abstract view, it is clear that the eye can only delight in their combination as long as an evident reason provides the unifying link. Outside the virtue of this reason, there is nothing within any assemblage of forms that provides attraction for the eye or meaning for the mind.

This is what has been demonstrated more or less clearly by the various architectures that could not find in their original principle, and in the imitation of the laws of nature, a principle of

Fig. 56. Atlantis Perspective, Léon Krier.
From: Léon Krier, *Architecture, Choice or Fate*,
A. Papadakis Publisher, London, 1998

order and reason, a system of necessary forms and combinations, derived by analogy from those that govern the works of the Creator.

Therefore, the rules founded on such principles are not arbitrary. When one proposes that there could be more than one imitative system, one does not destroy rules by virtue of this proposition; in fact, one would only be claiming that there could be rules that have been individually deduced from the same principle. One would no less recognize that there is a responsibility to observe the general law of order, and that *invention* cannot free itself from constraint.

This is what those so-called *innovators* in the architecture of the seventeenth century failed to understand. In the disorder of their imaginations, they employed all the types of the imitative system of Greek architecture, and made a game out of confounding and distorting them by sometimes denying their origin, sometimes their meaning, and other times their relation to the corresponding parts of the same system.

Nothing, indeed, could present more inconsequence and aberration of judgment than the so-called *inventions* of these innovators.

If the column, one might have said to them, is to your eyes only a perpendicular support made of materials whose only requirement is the assemblage needed by solidity; if what the column supports in the composition of the edifice is neither the image nor the representation of anything; if this composition as well as its elevation must not present the imitation of any model or pre-existing type; if all that falls under its embellishments, is the result of caprice or chance, and must signify nothing either by itself or by its location; then one would ask you why you use objects, to which the suffrage of many centuries has assigned a precise significance, in order to mean nothing. Why have columns, capitals, abaci, architraves, entablatures, pediments? And if by *invention* you mean the decomposition of these elements that you preserve without being able to distort, is it not obvious that your *invention* invents nothing; that it is but a negation instead of a creation?

There are numerous other critical considerations to develop on this subject; but this should suffice to demonstrate the futility, or better still, the nullity of *invention* of the innovators of the seventeenth century, who failed, in their own manner of innovation, to produce even the new, since they only reproduced in a state of disorder and confusion those elements ordered by reason throughout the centuries.

The goal of this discussion has been to demonstrate that in no artistic genre does *invention* exist without rules; and that far from opposing genius, rules favour it and assist it, by protecting it from the deviations of caprice; and that since *invention* consists in finding successful combinations of pre-existing elements, its field of application is wide open; and that within this boundless circle,

combinations will always remain innumerable; and that, finally, it is genius which is very often lacking in combination, for combinations will never be wanting for the true genius of *invention*.

IONIC (Order) Such is the name given to one of the three orders of Greek architecture, which, in its intermediate form, its proportions and the character of its decoration, is situated between the Doric and the Corinthian; that is to say, the two principal qualities expressed by the art of building.

These two qualities are strength or solidity, on the one hand, opulence or luxury, on the other. Between these two characters is found that of elegance or grace, namely, the *Ionic order*. The imitative spirit developed by the Greeks through the study of the human body within the other two arts of design (*see* IMITATION), must have suggested to their architects some ingenious analogies that transferred to the art of building the same varieties of mode, character and proportion, which distinguish between the sexes, the ages, the properties of each constitution, and their pertaining faculties.

Man can proceed in his works only through assimilation. Such was the manner in which Greek architects proceeded in establishing the modes that constituted their architecture. Nothing was more natural than the transfer of the principle of type that differentiates corporeal structures into architecture. Having endowed the Doric order with the character of strength and its corresponding qualities, the same system of assimilation must have inspired the borrowing of the ways in which nature imprints the formation and the proportioning of bodies, and their consequent application to the characteristic forms that properly express the qualities and properties of architecture.

This was the source the *orders*, in as much as they are considered as modes that tangibly determine – like the tones of music for the ear, and the colours of painting for the eye – all that the varieties and combinations of form can produce, in a manner analogical to the impressions willed by the architect.

This is how the order called *Ionic* was established, and came to occupy a middle place within the harmonic system of architecture, between the simplest and heaviest order, and the more opulent and tallest one.

The system in question – as proven by the monuments, the rules of antiquity, and the most irrefutable notions – belongs exclusively to the Greeks. No other architecture exhibits this system's idea or example. Only the Greeks knew the orders.

Some however, searching in a very material and narrow way for the origin of the orders, attack either the meaning of the orders's names, or the composition of their capitals. Nothing has been more unavailing than the conclusions based on names, for everyone knows that chance is

given to the *Ionic order* does not prove that Ionia was its cradle. The imitative spirit that produced the three orders of Greek architecture derived from abstract causes that history never understood. As soon as the effects developed, people wanted to return to their source and learn their secrets through the study of words and names which are, quite often, the deceptive interpreters of a lost tradition.

There is a misapprehension that should be noted regarding the origin of the *Corinthian order* as well as the *Ionic*: it consists in understanding an order only through its capital. Thus, regarding the Corinthian, it is held that the capital with a bell ornamented with foliage occurs frequently in Egypt, and that the idea for this form and its

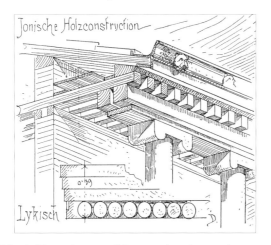

Fig. 57. Ionic Tectonics, possible precedent in wood construction.
From: Josef Durm, *Die Baukunst der Grieschen*,
A. Kröner Verlag, Leipzig, 1910

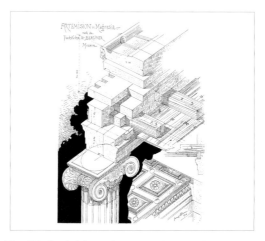

Fig. 58. Ionic Tectonics, artemision in Magnesia.
From: Josef Durm, *Die Baukunst der Grieschen*,
A. Kröner Verlag, Leipzig, 1910

almost always present behind the naming of objects, inventions and practices. Thus, the pretence according to which the *Ionic order* was invented in Ionia is a futile affair based on naming; and the same applies to the name carried by the Corinthian order. Contrariwise, we believe that since an order is part of a system of forms, proportions and ornaments, which are correlated by a reason and an association of diverse relations, then it cannot be the invention of one man or one country. For this reason, we have demonstrated (*see* CORINTHIAN) that Callimachus did not invent the order that bears the name of Corinth, and that his invention – if indeed it was one – was relegated to the substitution of one leaf for another within the capital. Additionally, the name

decoration could have been transplanted in Greece. But as to the column and its character, its forms, its proportions, and all the correlations that constitute the Corinthian ordonnance, nothing of this sort exists in Egypt. The same with the *Ionic*. Even if the manner and the ornament of the capital could have derived from the Asiatic style, and even if it were probable, according to the remains of Greek antiquities in Ionia, that the order that bears this name may have acquired this country's predilection; still, nothing justifies this country's claim to the honour of an invention – understood in the sense of the word *order* – which could not have been a local discovery, nor a partial one, nor connected to a precise period; but rather the product of successive trials.

Enough said about a subject that no discourse could completely clarify, save that it is important that profitless opinions do not succeed in replacing historical certitude. We shall now move to a shortened analysis of the *Ionic order*.

In considering the *Ionic order* only in its column, we find that it exhibits three division: the shaft, the base, and the capital.

The shaft gives rise to few observations and varieties. The ancients as well as the moderns readily endowed it with flutings carved in a semi-circle. Sometimes they number twenty-two, as in the temple named Fortuna Virilis in Rome; but more often they number twenty-four, and rarely thirty-two. As to its proportion, the shaft, including the base and capital, comprise nine

of the edifice. One observes that the higher torus alone receives ornaments, which are sometimes filets, and sometimes knots as in the Erectheion.

The *Ionic* capital is the part of the column whose articulation occupied modern architects the most, in order to adapt it to building compositions. We have seen that this capital is composed of volutes whose contours occupy two of the four sides. The other two, that is to say, the lateral sides, are formed by what is known as the *baluster-side* whose heavy end rests on the reverse side of the volute. Thus, this capital has two of its sides ornamented in one manner, and two in another. When the *Ionic* order is used in a disposition of isolated columns, as for example in a temple front with columns at right angles, it

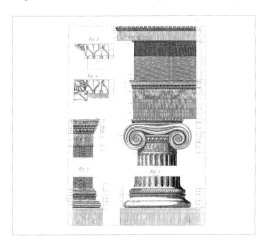

Fig. 59. Erectheion Ionic.
From: Stuart & Revett's *Antiquities of Athens*,
Reprint, B. Bloom, New York, 1968

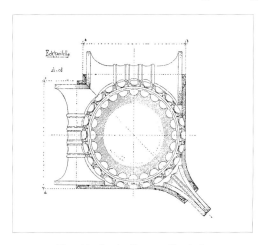

Fig. 60. Ionic Corner Capital.
From: Josef Durm, *Die Baukunst der Grieschen*,
A. Kröner Verlag, Leipzig, 1910

diameters in height – *quae novem ionicae*, said Pliny (Bk. XXXVI, Ch. XXIII) – which is a middle measure that admits some variety.

If we briefly discuss here the *Ionic* base, of which we gave some details in the entry BASE, following Vitruvius and modern architects, it is to show that some of the rules pertaining to details that were prescribed before there was knowledge of Greek architecture must allow certain modifications. While ordinary precepts recommend that the base height be divided into three parts: the higher torus, the middle scotia, and the plinth, all the *Ionic* monuments of Athens display a base without a plinth; and it is divided into three nearly equal parts: a torus on top, a scotia in the middle, and a torus at the bottom which rests on the steps

is necessary that the corner capital presents the two sides with volutes in the front façade, and on the other, the one with baluster. If other columns are found on the same line as the return angle, then the corner capital will be in baluster, whereas the other columns of the same alignment, presenting their front sides, will be in volutes. Hence the difficulty in the use of the *Ionic order*.

In the Ionic monuments of Athens, such as the Erectheion, where the architects wanted the corner capital to offer two similar sides, the one in the front of the building, the other on the side, the angle volute is elongated and curved similarly on both sides of the corner. However, this curve presents an irregularity – especially in plan – which is less evident in the elevation, one that modern architects endeavoured to avoid. Did they have any better success?

The need to give two volutes to each of the four faces of the capital, compelled them to imitate within the *Ionic* capital the double volutes that figure as accessories in the Corinthian. To realize this, they had to eliminate the baluster of the lateral sides, and widen and carve each side in order to facilitate the doubling of the volutes or their union.

The *Ionic* capital has also been modified by varying its height. Nothing in this regard, was determined by the Greeks. The monuments of Athens exhibit within the collar, which is below the echinus, a small frieze of ornaments that augments the height of the capital.

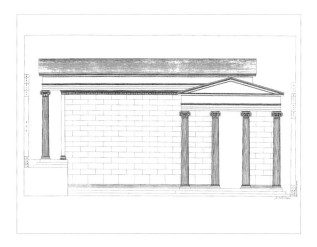

Fig. 61. Erectheion.
From: Stuart & Revett's *Antiquities of Athens*,
Reprint, B. Bloom, New York, 1968

The moderns went further. They attached garlands to each eye of the volute, that occupy the height of the collar on each side.

At the beginning of this article, we have defined the *Ionic order*, in all that characterizes it, as that which occupies the middle term between the qualities of the other two. This results from the ensemble of its proportions and outlines. Now this ensemble, especially in the profile of the entablature, is in accordance with the qualities of which each order is the expression.

The somewhat material imitation of the primitive types of carpentry is what particularly endows the Doric order with the character of strength, gravity of bearing, and solidity that distinguish it. This must have influenced the spirit

that established the character of the *Ionic*, thereby expressing less tangibly in its entablature the traces of the constitutive parts of wood construction. Accordingly, its architrave had less height and was less simple than that of the Doric; it was ornamented with three dividing bands. Thus the *Ionic* frieze no longer exhibited the ends of beams that the triglyphs represent in the Doric, and it became either completely smooth, or ornamented with figures. Similarly, the cornice no longer had mutules, which signify by their sloping position the ends of rafters in a timber roof.

Modern architects had a different opinion as to the application of dentils in the *Ionic* cornice. Since Vitruvius claimed that the dentils were equivalent to the triglyphs, and that they indicated the ends of purlines, some wanted to exclude them from the *Ionic*, while others made them a property of this order. Such a debate is useless, if it is true that notable examples demonstrate that they can be included, or omitted and replaced by another ornament. In the *Ionic* ordonnances in Athens, the cornices bear no dentils, and the members are always carved in an ovolo.

Thus, the character of the *Ionic* entablature and the column is a middle term between that of the Doric and that of the Corinthian. It comprises neither the austere solidity of the one, nor the luxury of mouldings and opulence of the other.

IRREGULAR Generally speaking, this appellation designates any work of art made without rules, or contrary to them.

In architecture, this word designates the kind of work and the manner in which it has been produced. Now this manner can be evident through the absence of rules, or through false rules. The *irregular manner,* then, is one which is professed by certain countries, certain centuries, or certain artists, who recognize only the regulation of chance and fancy. It is also this manner that only recognizes as a rule the erring ways of a routine that is foreign to any calculation, and to any law of reason.

In opposition to the meaning that we have just given to the word *irregular*, it must be acknowledged that there can be a *regular manner*; that is to say, one that recognizes rules, but only those rules founded on the science and observation of nature.

If one were to consider the state of the fine arts, past and present, among all the peoples of antiquity and the existing and known nations today, one is obliged to admit that the majority knew only what we call the *irregular manner*; either because of ignorance of all rules, or because of the irrational practice of the traditions that administer them.

Therefore, since the *irregular manner* has always reigned – and still reigns in many countries – then it would certainly gather the largest number of ballots, were this matter to be submitted to a vote. And so it is not surprising that many minds adopted an indifferent scepticism regarding this matter, while others opted in favour of the *irregular manner* and the freedom to dispense with rules.

The basis for the judgment of primacy, founded on the large number of votes, is strengthened still more by the idea that the *irregular manner* is generally instinctive. One is therefore compelled to conclude that, since everything that concerns the animal part of man is an impulse of nature, and since this impulse influences many a judgment that depends in the final analysis on moral faculties, intelligence and taste, then the manner that is based on instinct can be regarded as natural.

This is how the support of nature is invoked in favour of the *irregular manner*, because this manner, so it is believed, is also the effect of natural causes, and the somewhat necessary result of human constitution in a great number of nations.

Suffice it here to make a comparison in order to destroy the sought after support behind the ideas of *nature* and the *natural*. Do *vice* and *virtue* not share human proclivities in an unequal manner? Would one say that vice is not condemnable because it results from nature? And would one conclude that since most people have vices, then the majority of suffrages would prefer vice to virtue? A similar comparison could certainly occur between ignorance and knowledge. As with vice, ignorance is also based on a natural instinct. Who would dare invoke the authority of this instinct in favour of ignorance?

Accordingly, the same applies to that moral faculty known as *taste*. There is an uncultivated and depraved taste, as well as a cultivated and perfected one. What effect does the argument of number and the multiplicity of suffrages, in favour of the *irregular manner*, have on this discussion? Do we not see in every country, and in every century, how the number of ignorant or false savants greatly outweighs that of the learned? Who, then, has ever pretended that the majority of opinions makes the law in this case? The same applies to every art that demands special study and a distinct culture.

But as in every country where the majority – for all sorts of general or particular reasons – is excluded from expressing opinions as to the merits of works of science or art, and where the suffrage of common sense cannot be admitted, so it is with many nations that remained in a sort of infantile state regarding the arts and sciences. Thus, number has no effect here. Ten ignorant nations have no more right to oppose one learned nation, than the nine-tenths of a population have to oppose the one tenth that is accomplished through learning.

This being the case, the first question must be to know if the nations where the *irregular manner* – or the one foreign to the rules of nature – reigns and has always reigned in all the other branches of knowledge and culture, display the same expanded knowledge, the same accomplishment as the other nations who profess the opposing manner; that is, the one founded on the principles of nature. The second question is to know if the practice of the *irregular manner* among these nations derives from a true choice, an enlightened discernment, or simply an instinctive impulse and the result of a blind routine.

But it seems to us that these questions carry with them the most decisive answer. Who does not realize from the first look that, despite the ancient state of their civilizations, the peoples of Asia, as well as their spirit and their knowledge, are still far from the level attained in the physical and moral sciences by most of the younger nations of Europe? Well, what is the state of their arts? It is the stagnant state of routine and instinct. But this state is precisely the contrary of the one demanded by the spirit of observation, which is the principle behind all the perfection of human faculties. Where the empire of routine reigns, artists will not and cannot act by virtue of a free and reasoned choice. Where there is no freedom to reason and choose, everything remains subordinate to instinct. And such is the true definition of the *irregular manner*.

LICENCE, LICENTIOUS We stated elsewhere (See CONVENTION, ART, etc.) that each imitative art is limited by its particular nature to represent but a single aspect or side, so to speak, of the universal model, or of nature; that, consequently, this art is confined to an often narrow enclosure, in order to produce its proper genre of illusion; that certain reciprocal concessions accordingly established themselves between art and nature, or rather between the artist and those to whom his work is addressed; and that their conditions are on the one hand, that nothing will be demanded of an art beyond what is comprised in its nature and in its means, and on the other, that each art obtains certain extensions that somewhat facilitate the broadening of the imitative realm within which it is practised.

Therefore, conventions are kinds of pacts or accords, by virtue of which we lend ourselves – without too much improbability – to everything that can facilitate the combinatory effects that the artist employs in order to please us by captivating our senses and our minds. There are conventions that one may call necessary for they relate to the essence of art and form the indispensable conditions of its practice. There are others that relate more specifically to the execution of details, rather than the whole system, and are naught but consequences of the necessity that admitted the first conventions; such conventions are known as *licences*. The first conventions enter less in the circle of rules than in that of principles; the others, that is to say *licences*, are, on the contrary, *the exceptions to the rules*.

Without being an art of direct imitation, architecture, as we have seen elsewhere, partakes in the properties of other imitative arts, primarily by

imitating the laws that nature follows in the order and harmony of her works. But architecture adopted a more tangible and material model by joining to her imitative combinations, the type of primitive constructions that a long custom had naturalized in Greece. It is upon this model that rest the practical system of its imitation and the rules that derive from it.

But it is evident that architecture could not rigorously conform to the conditions of a purely mechanical imitation. When it came to satisfying all sorts of social exigencies, the primitive type was constrained to give way to many a concession; from here derived exceptions which, in turn, authorized new ones, and which are sometimes called *conventions*, and other times *licences*. For

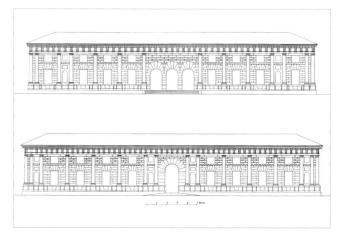

Fig. 62. Palazzo del Te, G. Romano.
From: A. C. Quatremère de Quincy, *Histoire de la vie et des ouvrages des plus célèbres architectes*, J. Renouard, Paris, 1830

example, in a rigorous argument, the interior of a Doric temple should not have an entablature, since the exterior parts of the entablature represent the ends of beams, which cannot exist when compared to a material reality, nor can they consequently be seen at once from the inside and the outside. The same can be said about the method of placing mutules under the pediment, which, as everyone knows, being the parts that indicate or represent the roof's rafters, can only be likely placed on the longitudinal sides of the building. But the custom of symmetry transformed the method in question into one of those conventions that no one thinks of contesting.

These examples are mentioned in order to explain the line that separates *conventions* from *licences*. Tracing this line is not a difficult matter, if one reasons that conventions relate to the system of architecture, which they first established and then completed by giving it rules; whereas *licences*, instead of being deviations from the system, are naught else but authorized infractions to the rules of this system.

Licence, as the meaning of the word indicates, signifies *permission*. Any permission that is given supposes that there is something disallowed; in fact, in every art, rules prescribe, forbid, or permit. Therefore, *licence* is the permission to do what is generally forbidden; thus *licence* does not violate the rule, since it is but an exception, and every exception is in fact an acknowledgment of the rule.

The needs to which architecture answers are so numerous and varied that a multitude of cases exist where the architect is forced to sacrifice the rigorous observation of rules for the sake of pressing social proprieties.

For example, we observe that the rule of equality that must regulate the distances between columns, was generally observed by the ancients; yet they also admitted many exceptions to it. The inequality in the middle intercolumniation in the front peristyle of Roman temples was a *licence* – but an authorized one – that was justified by Vitruvius on the basis of the requirements of the cult in some religious ceremonies. Nothing bears better the character of *licence*, that is to say a necessary exception; and at the same time, nothing better explains its difference with *abuse*, that is to say the unnecessary derogation of a rule, than the practice of this exception by the moderns in many a monument, where nothing warranted such an irregularity.

Furthermore, nothing rests on more fixed rules than the tripartite division of the entablature; however, there are examples from antiquity that show the suppression of one of these divisions. And one observes the motive for this suppression in the interior order of the large temple at Paestum, which supported another; because it is evident that in such a place a complete entablature would have greatly shortened the higher order. Such *licences*, therefore, need to be authorized by an evident reason and necessity; it

would be a grave error, in this case as well as in many others, to convert into a rule that which is but an exception to the rule.

Just as there are *licences* or exceptions to rules justified by need, there are also *licences* of lesser importance whose only judge is taste, and whose aim is to give a better effect to the whole or to a particular part of a monument. Thus, in all the details that constitute the proper character of each order, of each member, of each profile, the artist is permitted many modifications. Regarding many details of proportion, the rules fixed only a certain middle ground which taste freely constricted or broadened to a certain degree, depending on the building's location, the perspectival distance, and many other considerations deriving from the very nature of the character of the monument.

We did not intend that this entry be an enumeration of the *licences* that need and taste authorize in architecture (the list would have been too long); rather, we have given an idea that is at once general and precise regarding what should be understood by *licence* – a word whose meaning is often confused with that of *convention* and *misuse*. (See these entries).

We have established the essential difference that exists between *convention* and *licence*. As to the difference that separates *licence* from misuse, it clearly derives from the meaning of the first of these words; for, if a *licence* is a *permitted thing*, then it cannot be a misuse. A permission is founded only upon plausible motives, which are the necessity to tolerate a small drawback in order to avoid a greater one. But every infraction to a rule that does not have such a motive is misuse.

Certain confused minds in modern times have concluded that, since it is sometimes permitted to depart from rules for plausible reasons, then one may depart from rules for no reason at all. Instead of regarding the exception as proof of the existence of rules, they regard the exception itself as a rule. Henceforth, they recognize no rule, and we have seen what became of architecture under this anarchic regime.

Usage is often inconsistent in the meaning it gives to words. That of *licence* has a different meaning in ethics, thus producing the word *licentious*. In architecture, the adjective *licentious* expresses a different idea from its substantive form. As we have seen, *licence* signifies that which is permitted. On the contrary, in architecture, *licentious* expresses the idea of all that is or must be forbidden.

Doubtless, the predilection that was responsible for transposing this word into architecture was above all else that of Borromini and his school.

MISUSE People misuse all things. There is *misuse* of the good and even of truth itself, when their application and its consequences are taken to excess. They are also misused through erroneous applications. Nothing is easier, and consequently, nothing is more common than the *misuse* of the principles of art and imitation. After writing a long article about these *misuses*, one could write an even longer article regarding the causes that produce them. In this entry, we shall merely indicate one of the most fertile sources of this *misuse* that has always proliferated in architecture.

Since there is no rule, irrespective of the artistic genre, that does not admit some exception, it is quite natural to think that the principles upon which architecture is based exhibit less of an absolute inflexibility than other arts. It suffices to examine the nature and the number of conventions that constitute the system of this art, to understand that many a convention is based either on the instinct of taste, or on a more or less ideal imitation of the works of nature, or on the properties of our visual faculty, or those of our intellect. This art, considered in the materials that give it life, would seem to participate little in moral and intellectual properties. Yet, this art is perhaps the one whose works and effects bear the most reasoned relationships with our mind, necessitating those refined conventions to which we lend ourselves, depending on the kind of imitation.

Accordingly, the principles of imitation and the rules of execution in architecture demand certain concessions from us without which architecture would cease being an art and would enter the sphere of mechanical works. Now we must recognize these concessions as exceptions to the rules of architecture.

Well, it is precisely these exceptions that become the most ordinary and natural cause for *misuse*. Now, what is said here about *misuse* in architecture applies in the same manner to all sorts of *misuse*.

Exception is a more or less slight deviation from the rigour of rules. There is no class of rules, no matter the subject, that does not experience these deviations. The principles of morals themselves have applications that are more or less rigorous according to the many circumstances that modify human action; and similarly one observes that from exceptional modifications emanate paradoxes and sophisms.

One cannot recount how many *misuses* derive from certain exceptions to principles characterized by a mathematical regularity, or from the rules of the analogical system of imitation that architecture adopted. In the entries *architecture*, *wood*, *tree*, etc., we prove that irrespective of the beliefs of the whole of antiquity, no person in good faith could refuse to see, in the Doric order especially, the imitation of a primitive wooden construction which has since been modified by the very necessities of this transposition. Here, two kinds of *misuse* running in opposite directions are committed by those who acknowledge this imitation. Some profess a strictness in the observance of this imitation that would destroy its charm; others, arguing against the restrictions which only the nature of this imitation should bring to bear, prefer to reject its use altogether. Consequently, they recognized no other regulator but caprice and the genius of arbitrariness.

Hence it is evident that the results deduced from the principles upon which taste in architecture rests need to be treated with much reservation. In this essay, we have spoken only of the principles of taste. As to the principles relative to construction, that is to say, those of solidity and durability which are based on the material and incontestable basis of experience and the demonstrations of science, we shall consider the infringement of these principles to be an error or a flaw rather than a *misuse*. We have nothing further to add about this issue in this article.

To return to what is generally known as *misuse* relative to art, we maintain that architecture is somewhat like language where there are numerous manners of speaking that are contrary to the rules of grammar but which gained authority through extended use to the point that there is no way to correct them; whereas other manners that lack the authority of time are rejected – as they must be – by writers who are in a position to establish the rules of language.

Similarly, we observe two sorts of *misuse* in architecture, according to the authorities that have more or less approved them. The first acquired legitimacy not only by force of habit, but it became so necessary that it has almost been accepted as a rule. Such is, for example, the enlargement [entasis] of columns; such are the modillions built perpendicular to the horizon and not following the incline in the sloping parts of pediments; such is the method of putting modillions on the four sides of an edifice, and on the cornice that serves as a base for the pediment. In fact, as representations of the ends of bridging-joists, modillions should strictly be found only on the sides where rafters and queenposts are supposed to rest. It is therefore contrary to the reality of the model imitated by these objects to locate them in parts of roofs where there cannot be rafters, queenposts or purlines. Such kinds of *misuse* are called licences.

This is not the case with the second sort of *misuse*. A *licence* is an exception to a rule; *misuse* is an extension given to an exception. (*See* LICENCE).

If certain worthy examples admitted these *misuses* in some instances, one must emphasize that they acquired only a precarious authority. Palladio wrote a chapter on this sort of *misuse*, of which he distinguished four kinds, consisting, according to him: 1° in using a cartouche to support any object; 2° in affecting a large projection to cornices; 3° in applying bossage [rustication] to columns; 4° in breaking pediments, leaving them open in the middle.

If Palladio were writing his chapter on *misuse* today, it would probably have been much longer.

Perrault, in his time, had already increased the list of *misuses*; and even though it is easy for us to add to his list, we shall not further enlarge this article. Reference to these *misuses* is found in a more useful manner in the different entries that contain the precepts of antiquity and the examples of the great masters. Here, with the help of a general theory, we only meant to point to the most fertile source of what is known as *misuse* in architecture.

OPTICS *Optics* is a physico-mathematical science that teaches the workings of vision. The principles of this science form the basis of delineation in painting, and these principles are no less useful to the architect.

The rules of *optics* in architecture (according to Perrault's *Ordonnance*) remedy the errors of the senses. As the images of objects appear smaller and less clear when they are distant than when they are near, and as objects appear different in straight views in comparison to oblique views, some imagined that this was a defect for which architecture must compensate. Hence the systems that proposed to change the proportions as well as the location of architectural members and their accessory elements. Some even based their system on the authority of Vitruvius. Perrault has shown that all this theory was false, because the mind has the property to rectify the ways of seeing things, and knows how to place things back in their natural state. We have discussed this matter in the entry CHANGE OF PROPORTION.

ORDER This word, in architecture, enjoys a general acceptation that needs no definition, since all the synonyms, such as *arrangement*, *disposition*, etc., could not provide a clearer idea.

Order is one of those primary ideas that carry within them their own explanation; it serves to explain other ideas, rather than the reverse; in addition, fewer words enjoy a wider use.

In its application to architecture, this word signifies in general – as in the works of nature and in all human productions – a certain system of disposition in the elements of a whole, and their reciprocal rapport with that whole; which shows that an intelligent purpose presided over this system. Chance produces no *order*, that is to say, no state of affairs that denotes the necessary existence of anticipated and permanent correlations. Nothing could occur or advance in a similar manner by chance; rather it is the contrary effect; that is to say, the continuity, the perpetuity and the return of the same causes, the same results and the same phenomena that have always proven to human reason the existence of providence – a source, and an immutable principle of *order* that governs, *par excellence*, the universe.

The works of man, then, approach those of the author of nature as more applications are discovered of the intelligent principle which man alone among all created beings received from Divinity.

Fig. 63. Atlantis, Léon Krier.
From: Léon Krier, *Architecture, Choice or Fate*,
A. Papadakis Publisher, London, 1998

It is through *order* that this intelligent principle is evident; this is also what we admire in the organization of societies, in the laws of nations, in the productions of genius, and in the works of industry. It is towards the perfection of *order* that the meditations of philosophers, the research of scientists, and the works of artists are aimed.

Among all the arts, there is none where the existence and the application of *order* are more evident than in architecture, considered not only in her physical relationships with human needs, but, more particularly still, in the intellectual combinations which art, as a production of the mind, takes pleasure in manifesting and rendering evident to the eye, in order to satisfy both reason and taste.

That which is known as *order,* then, is a matter about which there is general agreement. One might say that it is in the nature of man to be so disposed; but in this realm as in others, all do not reach this agreement; and those who approach it the most, are those who studied the laws of the book of nature, which, although open to all, are understood by only the few. This study attains its highest degree only among peoples and individuals where the greatest and the most perfect civilization has cultivated the proper faculties to understand the correlative properties that unite physical objects and intellectual matters, in their causes and in their effects.

In ascertaining the identity of the peoples who devoted themselves the most to this study, one also remarks that, among them, the arts of imitation attained an eminent degree of correctness, harmony, truth, and proportion; all of which are qualities that emanate from the general principle of *order*.

As already mentioned, among these arts, architecture – which consists only of a series of relations – is the art whose perfection can most easily be measured by a governing *order*, and by the evidence through which it is reflected.

There is no doubt that some element of order prevails, even in the most different architectures. An absolute negation of *order* cannot exist in any human product; and one will always find some idea of *order*, even in the most formless hut among primitives; but it is evident that the notion of *order* in matters of theory, can apply only to the work that exhibits its character to the highest degree.

Now, *order par excellence* in architecture, rests on the most complete system; that is to say, the one that exhibits most openly the principle of intelligence; the one that coordinates the rapport of each part with the whole, and the whole with each part, in the most correct and permanent manner, and through the harmony of proportions.

But the greatest confusion reigns around the idea of proportion, which we shall treat elsewhere (*See* PROPORTION). This word is very improperly used to designate the main relations between the individual parts of an ordinary object. Without a doubt, every object exhibits relations of height and width, etc., but these simple relations of measure do not make proportion. Clearly, only *organisms* truly have proportions. Accordingly, neither the height nor the thickness of a tree can be deduced from the thickness of a branch, because one knows the many ways in which chance will render this rule faulty and misleading in generalizing its application. Contrariwise, every animal is organized in a manner so constant for its species, and where the rapport between one of its members and its whole body are so uniform, that one part makes the whole known (*es ungue leonem*); and the same can be said reciprocally of the whole.

This is what one calls proportion; this is the image of *order*. If it is impossible to deny that this is *order*, *par excellence*, applied to the works of architecture, it will not be difficult to discern from the various known architectures, the one that merits preference above all others. It is clear that this offers us a measure that depends neither on caprice nor on prejudice.

We do not pretend, here, to traverse all the countries on earth, in order to examine all the ways of building according to this parallel; but a short exposé will suffice to illustrate this theory.

Only two architectures can be submitted to this research: the architecture of Egypt, and the one called Gothic.

Was there in Egypt, a principle of *order* that was so regular, so generalized and permanent, that one could deduce from it a true system of proportion? Regardless of the favourable bias towards the monuments of this architecture, we believe it to be an error to apply to them the same properties as those of Greek architecture. First, the extraordinary simplicity of the volumes of Egyptian buildings, their constant monotony, and the utterly routine spirit of this nation in all her products, compel us to conclude that a study of relations intended to please the mind more than the eye, is as unlikely as it is useless. One knows that a temple, in its ensemble as well as in its parts, was necessarily subjected in Egypt to the types that were once consecrated by a religion that was the enemy of any novelty; one is

therefore easily persuaded that such an edifice required neither the particular genius of an architect, nor these multiple trials that he requires in order to discover the causes of the art's impressions on our minds. In Egypt, *grandeur* and *solidity* were the qualities that religion had permitted the architect to express; but grandeur and solidity can exist without any system of proportion. Massive columns, massive lintels, and massive walls; herein lies all Egyptian architecture.

It is true that one finds in Egyptian architecture some diversely tapered columns, as well as some varied and even some very diversified forms of capitals; but there is no evidence of a necessary, established rapport between the forms and the ornaments of a certain capital, or the structure and decoration of a certain column; it has never been established that there was an invariable rapport between the height of a certain capital and that of a column; one also encounters a capital with foliage, for example, and composed of many levels within the same column, which is sometimes lower, sometimes higher or more slender, and other times thicker or thinner. It is true that a certain uniformity of measure reigns between the height and the width of some columns; but this is found everywhere, and this relationship is established by the most simple procedures of construction. Fixed measures certainly existed everywhere in Egypt, and a temple, or a column was made in the same manner as a statue, that is, with the compass; that is all. But the compass, or the simple and mechanical use of this instrument, do not provide the harmonic relations of taste and beauty upon which *order* rests *par excellence*.

The excess of uniformity and servility in Egypt opposed the establishment of a system of proportion that results from *order* – a result whose property is to manifest the intelligence that produced it. There were general measures, that is to say, those that necessity and habit establish in the routine products of industry and among its principal elements; but a regulating module that could become the measure of all buildings, and which is evident in each of their smallest parts, was unknown.

The excess of simplicity and routine uniformity in Egyptian architecture opposed the discovery of a system of correlations, which are at once fixed in their principles and variable in their applications, depending on the differences of character and ideas that art expresses. Contrariwise, the kind of building known as Gothic was born out of the changing fortunes of many heterogeneous elements, and took place in a time characterized by such confusion and ignorance that the extreme diversity of form, solely inspired by caprice, prevented the introduction of any true system of proportion in an architecture whose mixture of constitutive elements, in truth, presents to the mind naught but the idea of disorder.

Let us be clear about the true notions that this matter comprises, because many have formed a mistaken idea regarding *order* and proportion in architecture. When one enters the interior of a Gothic church, one is struck by the regular disposition of the pillars and the arcades that compose it; one admires the intertwining of its vaults; the lightness, and what is known as the boldness of its masses; but all these merits, regardless of their value, hold no relationship with the principle of order which we qualified as a system of architecture. Many things prescribed solely by instinct are capable of producing beauty in this art, while being devoid of proportion in the proper sense of the word. Examine Gothic architecture, then, and inquire if her pillars have any fixed correlations with their constitutive parts; she will answer that the same pillar could have the same width for a height that varies by three times, six times or even more; that nothing here is designed to be constant, neither in buildings in general, nor in one building in particular, irrespective of its size. Ask if the capital has a rapport of size, form and ornament with its pillar; it will answer that caprice or chance are the only determinants. Ask if she has members, projections and details that correspond to such and such a disposition; she will tell you that she never worried about other relations save those of building and execution; she will show you the heaviest supports side by side with the most slender spindles; she will show you groupings of small columns that support nothing; and sometimes, a multitude of useless supports, while at other times volumes that overhang with no support. If you were to inquire about the reasons for the exteriors of churches, she will answer you with an ill-understood confusion of parts and incoherent details, carved with the most ignorant capriciousness. Her elevations are never proportioned to their supports, and she derives vanity from a process whose only purpose is to give the appearance of a tour de force.

Therefore, there is no proportional system in the Gothic; there is no governing principle of *order* that endows each part, each detail, each ornament, with a reason capable of coordinating them with a whole, as well as other parts, other details, other ornaments.

It is quite useless to demonstrate that such a spirit never animated Indian architecture, which is the product of an even more limited instinct, and where the luxury of the most disordered ornaments replaces the very forms that could constitute a mode of building. Also, one should unquestionably be spared the search for the slightest indication of the principle of *order*, in the sense given to it in the present context, within the light structures of China, and among a people where everything has been reduced to routine. Let us now demonstrate that the principle of *order* which we failed to find in any known architecture, is not only legibly written in Greek architecture, but it could not have been otherwise, since this principle owes its birth, so to speak, to this architecture.

Indeed, one must remember (all the proofs will not be listed here; see the entries ARCHITECTURE, WOOD, DORIC, etc.) that Greek architecture – on the evidence of her monuments and the determining developments and modifications that rendered her applicable to all nations – was not created solely by this universal instinct for stone cutting and assembly. She alone possessed, during the centuries that formed her, a kind of model; and this model was itself a combination of assorted elements brought together in a constant rapport by necessity and reason. Therefore, she was born out of a pre-existing combination, whose principal facts she adopted; hence her principle of *order*. Wood, which formed the early buildings of Greece, produced a composite assemblage of pieces that were subordinated to naturally uniform relations. This is what induced stone construction, in its assimilation of the principles of wood construction, to adopt this regularity of disposition and yet avert the immutable fixity of routine, because of the influence of the spirit of imitation. Only the spirit of *order* and proportion was acquired from the model; and variety introduced a sufficient dose of freedom, so that architecture became pliant to the expression of many qualities.

But by adopting a system of proportions in the first combinations of wood construction, art also needed to study the spirit of proportions in yet a greater model: that of nature. Then, as the imitation of nature was being perfected by the art of design in the images of the human body, this same spirit of imitation must have necessarily exerted an influence on architecture; such a confluence occurred in Greece but nowhere else.

Now, reflecting on the common link that unites all the arts, it becomes at once apparent, how and why the ignorance of the proportions of nature in the human body must have reacted on the art of building of the Egyptians, the Goths, the Indians and other peoples; and also how and why the architecture that possesses the most *order* or fixed proportions, belonged to a people who raised the study and the science of proportion in painting, and the delineation and the sculpting of the body, to the highest level.

This is where the architect, comparing his work to that of nature, appropriated a new model by analogy; and this model (as we have stated in the above-mentioned articles) consisted not in the positive form of a particular being, but in the system of laws that govern the organization of all living beings. Since each of these beings is a compound of members and organs, where all the dimensions in every species are such that a single part indicates the measure of other parts and that of the whole, likewise, the architect appropriated the condition of regulating the constitutive parts of a building in such a mutual correspondence

that the measure of the whole could determine that of the column, for example, and *vice versa*. The same applied to the secondary parts; thus every part of the entablature was endowed with the property of communicating the measure of the whole entablature; a simple triglyph could determine the width of every intercolumniation; the intercolumniation could indicate the column's diameter; the column's diameter could become the regulator of all the spacings in the edifice; and all these proportions happen to be, as they are in nature, not just geometric facts that could have reduced this art to servile monotony, but only a general principle of *order* admitting many modifications; in one word, comprising the same varieties of which nature offers us both the precept and the example.

But when this imitation of the proportional system of the body was transposed into architecture, it was not reduced to a simple principle of abstract *order*, suitable to solely satisfy reason.

The arts that imitate the human body, do not limit the study of natural proportions to the simple regularity that it brings to the imitative method. The result of this study was to fix the attention of the imitator on the deriving effects; and these effects are the diverse impressions of delight brought by the very variety of proportions that nature modifies within her creations, depending on their gender, the different qualities that suit them, as well as the properties that she distributes in varying degrees among creatures.

The imitation of the human body could not have remained for a long time without discerning these varieties within its models; without perceiving that every kind of physical or moral quality was distinguishable, in the exterior structure of bodies, through varieties of proportions that become the faithful indicator of a characteristic property. Thus, strength, lightness, agility, dexterity, grace, nobility, and beauty, were represented to the mind through a certain accordance between forms and proportions, in such a way that the eye could not be mistaken. Proportions were a kind of language that first expressed the most evident and salient qualities, and later their nuances. No one is unaware of this graded scale of physical and moral characteristics, that all the natural genres of Attic statues offer us as a compendium.

The same occurred in architecture, as soon as she acquired an organization which assimilated it to the works imitative of nature.

Architecture needed to express to the eyes and the mind, the character of physical or moral qualities that could be rendered evident through the accord of her constitutive forms; their mutual rapport; the diversity of volumes; the variation of measures; and the meaning of details and ornaments, through everything that manifests such and such a quality, or produces within the observer, such and such a determinable impression.

This was one of the results of the principle of *order*, no longer understood in a universal or physical sense, but in the moral significance given to it by the mind and by taste.

It is indeed in the nature of *order*, that every work of art – like every work of nature – bears the exterior character of the qualities that constitute it. Clearly, we are speaking here only of moral or intellectual *order*. Doubtless, any building could suffice for the material needs of its use, without art having to fashion exterior forms for the purpose of pleasure; but pleasure is also a need for a man cultivated by society, and it is this need which is the father of the fine arts. As soon as this need was felt, it required of architecture that her appertaining principal characters be rendered evident by the building's forms, proportions and details, and through permanent signs.

The principal characters are those to which the ideas of power or force, grace or elegance, lightness or richness, adhere. Now, as these ideas – that necessarily result from lines, forms and measures – manifest themselves in the clearest manner by heaviness or lightness, a certain progression must have been established between these two qualities, in the relative proportions of each edifice, as well as the supports or columns.

Hence this gradation of heaviness or lightness which, in Greek architecture, distinguishes and characterizes each of the modes applicable to buildings. What the Greeks called *ergasia*, and the Romans *ratio columnarum*, is what we call an *order of columns*.

Indeed, *order*, and the character of the quality that it expresses, do not exist solely in the different kinds of columns; but they are distributed throughout all the parts of a building; only the column is their indicator or regulator. This is why the name *order* was given to the supports of different proportions, of diverse styles, forms and ornaments, known as *Doric, Ionic,* or *Corinthian*.

In the respective entries, we treated each genre of *order*, its formation, its character, its properties, and its differences with the other *orders*; and we shall not enter into additional details on this subject here.

In analyzing the general notions of *order* as applied to architecture, the goal of this article has been to show how and for what reason *order* was understood – not as an ordinary disposition, but as a systematic use of proportions – to be the privilege of Greek architecture; and how each genre of column, called *order*, stood as a type of proportion that art implements in varying degrees, whether in a material sense for the eye, or in a moral sense for the mind.

It is indeed true that each *order* of columns – by the nature of the proportions that constitute it, and by the effect of the character of these proportions – expresses a principal quality to which its measure, its form, and its ornaments correspond. But it should not be understood that each of these three modes is limited to that which is absolute in each of these qualities.

Thus, the Doric *order*, which signifies strength, can express many degrees and diverse nuances of this quality, through many degrees of heaviness and massiveness. The slightest knowledge of the Doric monuments of antiquity teaches us that they had a considerable number of nuances. In fact, in the kind of imitation of abstract qualities – such as the properties of the human body as in the expression of corporeal strength – one can discern a considerable number of gradations from heaviness to a beginning of lightness. Such was the case among the Greeks, where the gradation ranged from the Doric, which was less than four diameters in height, to the one that approached six.

If the Doric *order* is the one that presides over the imitation or the expression of force, of simplicity and of all the varieties which are like the semi-tones of this mode, the Ionic *order* that follows expresses, through the rise of its shaft, the more slender form of its mass, the elegance of its capital, and the suppression of the details that recall its primitive construction, that it is the representative of this character which, in the form of the human body, belongs to such a gender or age and which, in the moral scale of sensations and ideas, is the attribute of certain forms of discourse, of certain modes of eloquence or poetry.

As one cannot strengthen that which is already strong in an absolute sense, without producing heaviness, nor lighten that which is elegant without producing thinness, one cannot also go beyond that which is rich without falling into the excess of luxury; and the Corinthian *order*, being at once the type and the image of elegance and richness, finds in the varied use of its proportions, its forms and its ornaments, the fulfilment of all the gradations comprised in the expression of its assigned quality. Experience has proven that it was a mistake to attempt to surpass this *order* in the formation of the so-called composite.

Each of these *orders*, then, is the indicator of the forms, taste and character upon which is based the system of moral *order* found in Greek architecture; and she alone succeeded in uniting physical *order* with proportions, or the positive correlations of the whole and the part, in such a way that all that constitutes delight, ornament and richness was also distributed to every part.

What we have just said about the characteristic property of the three Greek *orders*, and about the kind of quality of which each offers an expression, should demonstrate what was and will always be the error of those who have attempted or will attempt still, to invent new *orders*. This error stems from the false understanding of the kind of columns known as *orders*, and the resulting kinds of ordonnances.

It has already been remarked that there are three very distinct aspects within the three Greek *orders*: their form, their ornament and their proportion. Each of the three *orders* is distinguished from the others by each of these three aspects; now, there is already a great misapprehension in pretending to invent a new order by changing one of these three aspects; because if one were to change only the form without changing the ornament, or the ornament without the form, or one or the other without proportion, one would have produced nothing new; one would have produced merely the inconsequential and the disparate, because these three aspects are necessary to each other, and depend on a common reason that unites them, not arbitrarily, but by virtue of the general principle of harmony.

For the invention of the Greek *orders* comes less than one thinks from types and their apparent forms. In fact, the Greeks did not invent *order*; they only recognized that in architecture, as in everything else, there was the *higher*, the *lower*, and the middle point between the two; since, whether one knows it or not, whether one wills it or not, buildings will always express in their appearance, a higher or a lower aspect of solidity, gravity, simplicity or lightness, pleasure or variety.

Since between this higher and this lower, there cannot but be a middle point that unites these opposing qualities to a certain degree, the Greeks did nothing else but establish these three terms: in the Doric, by the characters that best express the idea of solid supports, heavy ornaments, and short proportions; in the Corinthian, by the most elegant forms, the richest decoration, and the most slender proportions; in the middle or Ionic order, by the medial use of forms, ornaments and proportions that are equally distant from the simplicity of the one and the richness of the other.

Consequently, the transposition of the qualities of each *order* does not depend on caprice, for that would disassociate what common sense had united: because each of these three things, *form*, *ornament*, and *proportion*, according to the sole judgment of the eye and the most common instinct, have a necessary correlation with the other two. It would be in opposition to the very nature of things to place that which is richest over that which is poorest and vice versa.

Such is the elementary principle of the *orders*; but this does not mean that it is against nature to give to the solid *order* a capital other than the Doric, or to the elegant *order* a capital other than the Corinthian. Nothing, without a doubt, would oppose this in general theory, as long as in each of these orders the new capital corresponds to the most simple character of the one and the richest character of the other. In fact, many a variety occurred in this genre, especially with respect to the Corinthian; and if they rarely met with success, it is because these novelties were only distinguished by an excess that added nothing to the expression of the given character, either because they fell short of it, or because they went beyond it.

Such has usually been the fate of the so-called inventions whose authors invented nothing, and could have invented nothing; because nothing is to be found outside the law of nature; and once this law has been discovered by the genius of art, in the three combinations that we developed, nothing remained for the spirit of innovation to conquer, save the bizarre, that is to say, disorder.

But the most ignorant of pretensions has been the belief that one was inventing a new order with a change in the leaves or the symbols in a capital. Nothing prevents the oak leaf, the fleur de lys, this or that symbol, from being substituted for the acanthus of the laurel leaf, and a multitude of these variants are found in antiquity. But then, one would not have made a new capital, but a new ornament for the capital; even less a new *order*, for an *order* does not derive from this, any more than the proportion of the human figure derives from clothing or hair style.

We have already articulated many of these considerations, in the entries where the descriptions of the Greek *orders* is found, and we shall not lengthen this article with new notions on this subject. To conform to the usage of dictionaries, which according to the received nomenclature, multiplied without reason the names of the *orders*, we shall merely list here, their simple designations.

Attic *order*.
Caryatid *order*.
Composite *order*.
Corinthian *order*.
Doric *order*.
Ionic *order*.
Tuscan *order*.
Rustic *order*.

ORDONNANCE This word is a synonym of *disposition* and *distribution* (See these words); but in its application to architecture in general or a building in particular, it is assigned meanings that differ from each other, as the species differs from the genus.

In general theory, *ordonnance* designates an elementary part of the art of building. Thus did Vitruvius try to distinguish among all the things that constitute architecture, *ex quibus architectura constat* (Bk. I, Ch. II) between *ordinatio, dispositio* and *distributio*. But these distinctions are very arbitrary, and if the use of these words ever endowed them with some evident variety of meaning, it would be quite difficult nowadays to perceive it, and to transmit its nuances into their corresponding French words.

We shall state here only that the use of the word *ordonnance* (as when one states: *ordonnance* in the art of building) seems to us to express this art of properly disposing according to the purpose of the building: 1) the elevations, volumes, construction parts, columns, solids and voids; 2) the plan, entries, passages, transition spaces, and the relationship between different rooms; but only at a larger scale, for the details in this part depend on what is known as *distribution*. (See this word).

When the word ORDONNANCE does not apply to architecture, but rather designates one of her operations, or a particular building, it signifies the manner in which the architect ordered the volumes, the parts, and the details considered in their ensemble, in their effect, in the impression that their appearance produces, and also in the proper character of the building. Thus the *ordonnance* of a building may be called noble, grand, simple or common, shabby and fragmented. In this respect, the *ordonnance* of an edifice must be in accordance not only with its dimensions but also with its use. The *ordonnance* of a vast palace may have little correspondence with its dimensions, while yet another *ordonnance* may be too large for the smallness of the building.

Thus, *ordonnance* is to *order*, considered as a quality of architecture, what the effect is to the cause; that is to say, *order* put into practice.

As to *order*, understood in the language of art as an assemblage of relations, of forms and proportions, where each kind of column is the indicator and the type, one might say that there are as many *ordonnances* and there are *orders* of columns. One therefore gives the name *ordonnance* to a disposition of columns belonging to each of the orders; and each of these *ordonnances* will adopt the name of each of the orders. Therefore, there are Doric, Ionic and Corinthian *ordonnances*.

Such are the names given, not only to each of the manners in which each of the three orders is implemented by the architect, in the plan and the elevation of a building, but these names are also given to the building mass that displays no columns in its elevation, as long as the components of this elevation exhibit spaces which are proportioned according to the rules of such and such an order, and the moulding details or profiles, that recall the taste and the character of details assigned to these orders.

One also distinguishes among five kinds of *ordonnances*, which are based –concerning the disposition of columns in the front peristyles of temples– on the number of columns forming the front of these peristyles, ranging from the temple that has only two columns at the corners, and progressively to the temple that has ten, or the decastyle.

ORNAMENT In the entry *decoration*, we referred the reader to the present article regarding matters that relate to *ornament* properly speaking, in other words, what is specifically designated by this term in the language of architecture.

In this article, *ornament* is certainly understood to be a part of decoration, but as such it cannot be a true synonym of the word to which we dedicated a lengthy article. Decoration, as we said earlier, embraces the general idea of the art of embellishing monuments of all kinds, in all their parts, and with all the means that belong to the arts of design. We saw that if the resources of painting form the largest part of the means of decoration, especially in interiors, then sculpture's share is particularly concerned with the exterior.

This article will not include the productions of the art of sculpture such as colossi, statues, or bas-reliefs, whether they be placed in squares, in niches, in pediments, or in the historical or allegorical compositions which are applied to the walls, thus rivalling those of painting. All of this is more particularly comprised in the idea of decoration.

Technically speaking, *ornament* comprises this secondary embellishment that one observes in the arabesque. In fact, there are no objects of *ornament* that painting cannot depict, for all these objects fall within the means of painting. One also speaks of *ornamental* painting; and we have seen that the arabesque genre can reproduce all the ornamental details sculpture uses to embellish

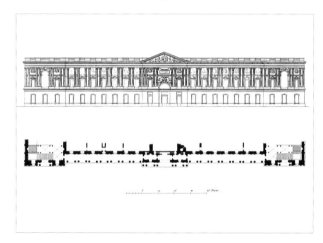

Fig 64. Colonnade of the Louvre, Cl. Perrault.
From: A. C. Quatremère de Quincy, *Histoire de la vie et des ouvrages des plus célèbres architectes*, J. Renouard, Paris, 1830

architecture. However, the word *ornament* is more especially appropriate to the art whose help architecture relies on, and this art is sculpture.

This is why we are considering *ornament* here, only from the perspective of its intimate relationship with the execution of architecture.

As we stated above, from the standpoint of material execution architecture is naught but sculpture. She owes the forms that embody her existence to the mechanical work of the chisel. But outside of what is purely mechanical in stone cutting, or in the articulation of other materials, the art of sculpture is entrusted with guiding the more or less difficult or delicate work that completes the impressions of various signs – so to speak. This work becomes complementary to sculpture – considered as a kind of writing – thus making it increasingly intelligible to the eye and the mind. It is *ornament*, properly speaking, that renders these subtle nuances tangible.

Thus, every kind of order has its *ornaments* whose character corresponds to the character of its forms. Everyone knows that the order that expresses strength and simplicity, the Doric, comprises in its column flutings, in the contours of its capital, in the triglyphs and the metopes of its frieze, in the mutules and the profiles of its cornice certain *ornamental* parts that partake in the general type of heaviness and severity of proportions.

The Ionic, being a middle order between the Doric and the Corinthian, by virtue of its proportions, its forms and profiles, comprises *ornaments*

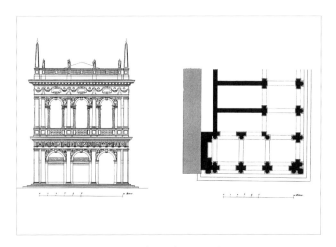

Fig. 65. St. Mark's Library, J. Sansovino.
From: A. C. Quatremère de Quincy, *Histoire de la vie et de ouvrages des plus célèbres architectes*, J. Renouard, Paris, 1830

that are lighter and more varied in its flutings, its base, its capital, and the profiles of its entablature. The Corinthian, through the more abundant and diversified use of *ornamental* details in its base, its shaft, its capital and all the parts of the ordonnance, establishes an accordance between its proportions and its forms that allows it to express the qualities of magnificence, richness and lightness, etc. It is well known that those who tried to push this expression even further in the so-called *composite* order, did so only by changing the *ornamental* details of all the members of the Corinthian order, in such a way that no smooth surface remained.

Everyone knows, at least in general, the principal *ornaments* with which sculpture decorates

architectural members. Suffice it to mention here the denticules, ovolos, leaves, chaplets, pearls, palmettes, foliage, stalks, caulicules, volutes, acanthus leaves, and scrolls, that the architect distributes depending on the ordonnance. We shall not describe these details whose nomenclature we have recalled only to well establish the idea of what is especially known as *ornament* in the execution of architecture.

Nor shall we linger on the origin or the kind of etymology behind each of these details. We have often indicated and demonstrated their source in the analogies that the artist discovered by chance; in the plants that adhere to buildings; in the elements borrowed from women's head-dresses; in the offerings made in sacred places; in the uses of allegory; or in man's instinctive habit to ornament his products.

We shall limit ourselves here to discussing *ornament* as being simply the means in the hands of the architect to add a clearer significance to that of the character of an edifice; this character having already been established by its style, its forms, and its proportions.

The first point to note consists of correct distribution. This word includes above all the idea of measure regarding the *ornament* that connects either the order or the edifices of the same order, to the character that must be expressed; because each order (as we saw in the entry of that name) occupies a principal hue in the scale of architectural variety, and can offer varied nuances and tones depending on its use.

Thus the Doric order, whose character is strength and simplicity, can manifest these two qualities through the different proportions that it can admit; and the architect can distribute a certain number of *ornaments* that may give this ordonnance some Ionic characteristics. For example, many ancient Greek Doric capitals exhibit such light motifs in the neck. Some more significant *ornaments* still, figure in the metopes, and the Doric Temple of Minerva in Athens [Parthenon] has carved palmettes in the acroteria. Let us also note that the proportions of this Doric temple are somewhat more elegant than those of most edifices of the same order, according to the ancient

Greek system. Since then, the moderns have elongated the proportions of the Doric order, and they even put ovolos in the echinus, as well as profiles and filets in the abacus.

The second point to note with respect to the use of *ornaments*, is the choice to be made from their different kinds. Just as the difference between the highest and lowest degrees in the distribution of *ornaments* contributes to the expression of simplicity, elegance or richness, so the manner of each kind of *ornament* has also the ability to lend itself to this expression, to reinforce it, and render it tangible to the eye and the mind.

Of the great number of objects that sculpture acquires for architecture, there are those that produce effects that are solemn or happy, simple or varied, gracious or severe; and already each order, depending on its character, appropriates the gravest or the lightest profiles, or the most articulate and undulating *ornamental* motifs. Following a judicious choice of flower-work or foliage of oak, rose, laurel or cypress, there is no festoon, no garland, that does not present one idea or another, or an effect that is more or less analogous to the style of the monument.

Thus considered, architecture's moderate use of *ornament* becomes the expression of the degree of richness that each edifice receives depending on its character; that is to say, the use to which it is dedicated. Between the use that excludes any kind of *ornament* (like a prison, for example), and that which admits the largest abundance of *ornament*, such as a temple, a palace, or a theatre, there are many degrees, each of which must also be impressed by the choice of object that becomes its ornamental motif.

Following the distribution and the choice of *ornaments*, we shall mention, as the third point to note, the execution of objects that the architect entrusts to the sculptor's chisel.

Ornament, according to the specific meaning that we have given it, is especially composed of objects that are carved in mouldings and profiles, and are applied to the principal surfaces of architectural forms. Therefore, the execution of these kinds of *ornaments* can modify the effect of architecture, for *ornaments* are a class of signs whose impressions are made tangible by sculpture. It lies within the province of this art to fashion *ornaments* by varying their projection, depth, sharp contours, and to enhance their figuration in a lively way. Now, whatever the differences between their effects, they also contribute in some measure to the expression of the building's character.

One need not repeat that the dimensions of edifices as well as the distance between the eye and the observed building, have to be taken into account in the execution of *ornaments*. There are manners of treating foliage that are gentle and light, severe and elaborate, abrupt, or accomplished and stylized; because in execution, architecture appropriates the practical qualities and procedures of sculpture. The same applies to the execution of *ornaments* regarding their effect in an edifice, and to the manner of treating statues depending on their proportions, or on the distance from which one is compelled to view them.

However, one would form a very incomplete idea of the sculptural applications of *ornament* in architecture, if one were to be limited to the details of profiles and the elements of columns.

Edifices are not solely composed of columns and entablatures. Wall surfaces and elevations in all their forms are also apt to receive many of those running *ornamental* motifs which sometimes interrupt the uniformity of smooth surfaces while, at other times, they explain the purpose of the edifice through the use of allegorical signs. Hence these continuous string-courses, on the interior or the exterior, adorned with intertwined bands and scrolls and diverse symbols that vary with the context.

In this view, *ornament* becomes the object of the most ingenious compositions, because there are few edifices which one cannot endow with their proper significance through the use of symbols or attributes that correspond to their purpose.

Having limited the idea of *ornament* to what is generally understood by the imitation and the use of all the objects that the word *ornament* designates in the plural, it remains for us to indicate the ways of naming these *ornaments* depending on their use or their execution.

Thus we have:

Running ornaments. Such are the *ornaments* sculpted on friezes, string-courses, plinths, beads, etc., which continuously repeat the same object, such as ovolos, astragals, knot-work, and foliage.

Corner ornaments. Such *ornaments* are placed at the corners of casings, around doors, windows, or in the returns of frames or cornices. These *ornaments* are in single or double arrangements.

Ornaments in relief. These *ornaments* (beads, astragals, ovolos, shells, heart-shaped leaves) are carved in projecting relief upon smooth surfaces such as friezes or string-courses.

Sunken ornaments. Such *ornaments* are either simply carved lines presenting only contours, or carved within the thickness of the material without projecting from the surface, like Egyptian hieroglyphic signs.

Nautical ornaments. This appellation is given to certain edifices having a hydraulic purpose, such as grottoes, fountains, reservoirs, etc. They ordinarily represent all the objects that relate to water such as shells, fish, nautical rush, reeds, icicles, lapidifications, etc.

PAINTING In this Dictionary, we shall consider *painting* from two points of view, that of the kind of composition and that of the paint itself, which are the only common points between the art of *painting* and that of building.

We shall first discuss the use, or the misuse, of the means available to the painter in their application to the interior decoration of edifices.

Secondly, we shall consider the architect's use of colour and coating in the interior and exterior.

§ I To consider the practice of *painting*, that is to say, the subjects of imitation that are proper to this art, as part of the means of decoration in architecture, requires the extended theoretical development of a treatise.

In order to fit the subject within the narrow confines of this article, we shall posit in principle that when *painting* is called to decorate an edifice, it cannot be practised with all the independence that the genius of the composition allows. Consequently, we shall maintain that the architect shall never cease to be the organizer and the manager of all the necessary accessories that should properly conform to the principal object of the building. (We except from this theory the use of isolated and removable paintings.)

Thus, the architect must determine: 1° the nature and the kind of composition; 2° the space and the proportion of *paintings*; and 3° the manner and the effect of their execution.

Regarding the kind of subject and the nature of the composition, it would be superfluous to linger too much here in order to prove that the paintings that decorate each edifice must hold a corresponding relationship with that edifice's proper purpose; and that the treated subjects are chosen either from historical facts, from allegorical ideas, or from the capricious region of arabesque inventions. When it is used with

Fig. 66. Galerie des Carraches, Palazzo Farnese, Rome. From: Julien Guadet, *Élements et théorie de l'architecture,* Librairie de la construction moderne, 1909

discernment, decorative *painting* becomes an effective means of specifying the character of each monument and for conveying its use.

But it is of great importance for the architect to establish the space and the proportion of compositions, as well as the figures from which they are formed. Here, too, it is useless to dwell too long to explain the obvious, which is that the general harmony of the whole results mostly from the rapport of proportions between the objects of decoration and the volumes of construction. Nothing appears more ridiculous to the simple judgment of the senses, not to mention the mind, than the application of these small objects and these small arabesque motifs to the imposing masses of edifices whose purpose demands a heavy and serious character. Often certain compositions that are overly weighted with figures of large dimensions tend to diminish the effect of architecture by giving its masses and its forms an excess of disagreeable heaviness.

The manner and the execution of decorative *painting* produce also a kind of harmony that should fall under the special direction of the architect. An execution that is free, easy, and contrary to the effect of the building may suit the large dimensions of certain interiors as well as certain subjects, which, like large ceilings, only allow us to consider their sheer mass. An execution that is refined, light, stylized, and designed to be seen close to, will suit the small spaces and elements of a delicate architecture where the refinement of the brush enhances that of the material execution of sculptural ornaments and profiles.

There is another indispensable propriety in the compositions of decorative *painting*, according to which the painter has to keep these compositions within the space prescribed by the architect.

Many are the examples, especially in Italy, of this sort trespassing on the part of *painting* into the domain of another art. Some painters have occupied all the spaces of a building; they have utilized all its surfaces as a vast canvas and, in so doing, have destroyed all the architectural members with the illusions of colour; they have broken all the architectural projections with figures; and brought cloud formations to the point of infringing upon the constitutive parts of the ordonnance; even the building form itself has disappeared because of the usurpations of *painting*.

Yet, simple common sense tells us that *painting* should be admitted in an edifice only as an auxiliary ornament. Architecture offers fields or compartments, but under certain conditions. By offering the entire space of a dome or a ceiling without the slightest indication of a structural member, architecture grants the painter the freedom to assume that this is an empty space through which one perceives the sky, or any other fictive figure and object seemingly supported by clouds.

There are other surfaces that the architect can leave for the decorator's brush that can be seen as openings whose appearance does not affect the feeling or the effect of solidity. In these cases, the architectural members and masses serve as frames for the fictive voids of *painting*. The painter should keep to the limits prescribed by the architect, for in vain would the painter claim that these voids are but fictitious. The retort to this claim would be that it is not enough for architecture to be solid; it must appear to be so.

§ II *Painting* is united with architecture in another area, related more particularly to the processes of the painter of ornament, in other words, the coating with coloured substances and the variety of their uses in the interior as well as the exterior of edifices.

Such processes are quite numerous, and it seems that they were more so among the ancients than among the moderns.

It is well known and established today, as a great number of ancient temples in Italy and Sicily have shown, that their exterior columns, as well as all their parts, received a light coating in stucco which, on the one hand gave an agreeable polish that the materials themselves did not have, and, on the other, simulated the most beautiful marbles. All the Doric temples of Sicily were coloured in this way. The *painting* was applied in different hues in the metopes, the mutules, and the details of profiles. (See COLOUR).

In truth, the use of marble in architecture was so common among the ancients that an edifice with an exterior of ordinary stone would have seemed indecorously poor, especially a temple. Not only did the ancients imitate the appearance of marble with colour, but they also knew how to change the colour of marble. Pliny tells us that a simple white marble could be transformed into Numidian marble by the introduction of veins and tints. With greater propriety, *paint* was used to colour the coating of brick columns like the ones that we observe in great numbers in the ruins of Pompeii. All of them still display the stucco coating and the well preserved tints that were used to cover it.

There is no doubt that *paint* was used on the exterior of many ancient houses. This practice is still preserved today in many a city in Italy; and Genoa has taken this luxury in the exterior of buildings to the point of introducing gilding in many of its palaces.

In general, the taste and the practice of ornamenting the exterior of edifices and houses depend on the nature and the quality of available materials. The finest materials for this work are the revetments where there is a mixture of marble and lime powder, and the coating known as stucco. Lime itself becomes the very preparation where colours are painted.

But in countries where there is considerable use of wood in construction, where this material constitutes not only the framing, but also the partitions and their panels, architects must of necessity use coloured coatings on the interior as well as the exterior of buildings. Such are the façades of private residences in China and Constantinople, which are usually painted in many colours, thus producing an agreeable effect according to travellers.

There is no need to repeat here that *painting* forms a large part of the ornament of almost all the interiors of palaces and houses. Nowadays, and in our [European] countries, colours and their varied applications are used only when they are demanded.

A few words regarding the different procedures of *painting* in its technical relation to the art of building and various decorations.

Monochrome painting. This is a kind of *painting* where only one or two colours are used on a background of a different colour, which is sometimes gilded. It is known as *grisaille* when it consists of a grey colour.

Painting in chiaro scuro. This is a kind of *painting* where only black and white colours are used, producing figures or bas-reliefs that imitate white marble or stone.

Distemper-painting. This appellation is given to the kind of *painting* that uses colours that are diluted with water and mixed with small amounts of gum and glue. It is used on plaster, wood, skins, canvas and paper. This is how the decorations in theatres and public ceremonies are painted.

Painting in fresco. This appellation is given to the *painting* that is executed on walls that are freshly coated with a mortar made of lime and sand, and with water-soaked colours. This kind of *painting* is one of the most solid, and is even used in places where it is exposed to the air.

Painting in oils. This kind of *painting* uses colours that have been ground and mixed with the most siccative oils. This *painting* is more frequently used in interiors, on wood panelling, etc.

It does not seem necessry for us to mention other kinds of *painting* in this article, such as *enamel*, *pastel*, or *miniatures*, etc., which, as their names indicate, are totally foreign to architecture.

PERSPECTIVE One distinguishes between *linear perspective* and *aerial perspective*, and the former alone pertains to architecture.

As a science, *linear perspective* forms part of mathematics, and as such it is subject to principles that are rigorously demonstrated. It teaches the manner in which the lines that circumscribe objects are seen by the eye of the observer, depending on the eye's location and its distance from these objects.

It has been incorrectly assumed that the ancients lacked the science of *linear perspective*; and what particularly validated this error, is the apparent violation of the rules and the most simple elements of not only the science, but also the appearance of *perspective* in many bas-reliefs, especially those of Trajan's column, where it was impossible and even unwise to practise it. This opinion was also based on the ignorance displayed by most of the decorators who painted the arabesques at Herculanum and Pompeii, although there are certain architectural subjects that prove the contrary. It must be said regarding this matter that, even today, there are painters who do not know the processes of *linear perspective*, and that there is a certain art of drawing lines following one's feelings, or one's eye, rather than following principles and rules. Now, we believe that many painters in antiquity were satisfied with this approximation, and all the painters of *decoration* who drew and coloured all the arabesque fantasies on the interior of houses at Pompeii were among them. These examples do not prove that the ancients did not know the rules of *perspective*;

or that they did not use it in their most important buildings, especially in the decoration of theatres, which demanded a strict application.

In truth, the ancients practised the art of painting architectural *perspectives* on walls as successfully as the moderns, and it is impossible to admit that buildings such as theatres, where *perspectives* were judged by the eyes of a multitude of people, contained errors in *perspective* that would have shocked even the least informed spectator; for whereas knowledge is needed to correctly draw the lines of a feigned architecture, instinct alone suffices to be revolted by its errors. In the theatre of Claudius Pulcher was a painted decoration that was executed with such realism and such illusion, according to Pliny, that the crows collided with it, for they were fooled by the imitation of roof tiles. One should look at such narratives as the figurative expression of the perfection of the imitative means employed.

But of what use are these authorities and similar examples recounted by writers, if Vitruvius himself tells us explicitly when and who invented the art of linear perspective? According to this architect, who is certainly knowledgeable in this area, the practice of *perspective* goes back to the century of Aeschylus where Agatharcus had admiringly applied it in the theatre at Athens. He was succeeded by his two students, Anaxagoras and Democritus, who wrote down and published his precepts. Thus, we observe that in architecture, as well all the other arts, practice precedes theory. As an attentive observer of nature, the painter first imitated objects as they presented themselves to his eye. Later, geometry demonstrated the reason behind this perception, and the ways to reproduce it without recourse to a model.

Therefore, the practice and the science of *perspective* preceded the era of Pericles and had by that time already been reduced to rules. The following passage from Vitruvius deserves to be quoted in its entirety:

Namque primum Agatarchus Athenis, Eschylo docente tragediam, scenam fecit, et de ea commentarium reliquit. Ex eo moniti Democritus et Anaxagoras de eadem re scripserunt, quemadmodum opporteat ad aciemoculorum radiorumque extensionem, certo loco centro constituto, ad lineas ratione naturali respondere, uti de incerta re incertae imagines aedificiorum, in scenarum picturis redderent speciem, et quae in directis planisque frontibus sint figurata, alia abcedentia, alia praeminentia esse videantur. (Pref. Bk. VII).

"In the first place Agatharcus, in Athens when Aeschylus was bringing out a tragedy, painted a scene and left a commentary on it. This led Democritus and Anaxagoras to write on the same subject, showing how, given a centre in a definite place, the lines should naturally correspond with due regard to the point of sight and the divergence of the visual rays, so that by this deception a faithful representation of the appearance of buildings might be given in painted scenery, and so that, though all is drawn on a flat, vertical façade, some parts may seem to be withdrawing into the background, and others to be standing out in front."[31]

The reasoned practice of *perspective* amongst the Greeks did not remain confined to the enclosure of theatres, for it was introduced in the schools of painting as a necessary requirement for painting as well as decoration. The painter Pamphilos, who started the most celebrated school of drawing at Sicyon, used to teach perspective publicly. He claimed that painting could not achieve anything perfectly without geometry. *Omnibus litters eruditus, praecipue arithmeticae et geometriae, sine quibus negabat artem perfici posse.*

Thus, before Apelles, who was the student of Pamphilos; before Protogenos and the most renowned painters of Greece, *perspective* was being taught and practised as in modern times, where it was already known and practised before the sixteenth century, as we see in the compositions in the cemetery at Pisa, in the paintings of Perugino, Masaccio, Giovanni Bellini and others.

Information regarding the study of *perspective* will not be found in this article, for this matter needs to be demonstrated with figures, and we therefore refer the reader to works that are dedicated to teaching the methods of *perspective*.

Feigned perspective. This appellation is given to paintings on walls that represent architectural decorations, monuments and landscapes, which are sometimes placed on gable-ends in order to hide their deformity, or to portray some distant scenes.

This practice comes within the domain of *feigned architecture* which we have treated before. This kind of painting was especially developed in Bologna, and practised by skilled painters who produced models of remarkable perfection in composition as well as in the charm of the execution or the illusion. Regarding this matter, the reader may consult Algarotti who has gathered the most curious facts on this kind of work.

PRACTICE In the arts of design, this word expresses the use of material means, instruments and procedures employed by the artist in technical operations, pertaining especially to the domain of execution.

It is in this sense that the word and idea of *practice* are contrasted to the word and idea of *theory*. In fact, the latter expresses a knowledge of the reasons and principles upon which the rules that must direct *practice* are founded.

Every art, therefore, has a *practice* that befits it, since the arts produce their own inventions through means that are as distinct or diverse as the elements of their natures, that is to say their proper model, and the faculties of the organs and the senses to which their imitation pertains, as well as the processes through which this imitation makes its effects tangible.

Accordingly, in the entries *art* and *architecture*, we tried to define and clarify the principle – which is at once abstract and tangible – upon which architecture is founded, and from which architectural theory derives. As to *practice*, we must first of all state that this word and its idea comprise two notions; that is to say, that in architecture, as in every art, there are two categories of *practice*, or two kinds of *practice* that are easily distinguished through the natural division of the objects to which each applies.

Indeed, from the standpoint of teaching or speculative knowledge, every theory comprises more than one division, and includes two classes of notions that pertain either to the moral side of each art, to what is designated by the words *genius, invention, taste, judgment*, etc., or to the material aspect of art, to its instruments, its mechanical means, its execution.

The same applies to *practice*. It comprises two parts, especially in architecture. One of these parts belongs to the field of science, the other can be classified within the purely artisanal domain.

What I would call *learned practice*, Vitruvius has already well defined (as we saw in the entry ARCHITECT). According to him, "practice is the continuous and regular exercise of employment where manual work is done with any necessary material according to the design of a drawing."[32] Thus, the use of materials that will embody the architect's invention requires a profound *practical* experience deriving from very broad knowledge.

For example, one must have good knowledge of the different materials available for the art of building in each country, of the properties that a multitude of causes impress on these materials, and the relationship between the required solidity and the required expense.

To this fundamental knowledge must be added the even more skilled *practice* of the use of materials that must obey and lend themselves to the numberless configurations in buildings, especially in the vaults, cintres and stairs, and a multitude of local constraints and particular needs. The result of this sort of *practice* is known as stereotomy or the science of stone cutting, which becomes especially necessary to the art of building as the accumulation of needs or the taste for change demand forms which are more and more complicated. Thus, a more complicated *practice*, aided by geometry and calculus, devises new means to execute and render more solid the combinations of stone and materials in the most difficult projects. We indicate here only the spirit and goal of this *practical science*, which is treated in the various articles on construction included in this Dictionary.

Within the *practical* knowledge required of his architect, Vitruvius – as we have seen in the entry ARCHITECT – includes many sciences that are scarcely mentioned here, owing to their very indirect relationship to architecture. However, we believe that the *practical* knowledge of perspective is one that the architect cannot afford to omit from the circle of studies that we have called the learned *practice* of architecture.

The second part of the *practice* of this art, is one that must be called *manual practice*. Such an appellation bears its own definition. It is well known that the good or poor quality of all the kinds of materials of which buildings are composed, and the more or less intelligent manipulation of the procedures that enter their use, can contribute either to their durability or hasten their ruin. And it is further understood, without insisting on the subject, that each of these mechanical divisions, as in all kinds of trades and industries, holds secrets that *practice* alone can reveal. Thus, we affirm, as did Vitruvius with respect to the great knowledge that he recommended to his architect, that it is not necessary for one destined for architecture to undergo an apprenticeship in the lesser degrees of manual work and their counterparts, but rather to have personal manual experience only in the most important of these *practical* works. And so the fundamental work of the young student in architecture must include the cutting of stone in the field, the knowledge of the practical procedures of carpentry, as well as many other procedures, in order to prevent all kinds of fraudulence and bad workmanship that could compromise the durability of monuments.

PRACTICE One gladly accepts this word in a less technical meaning, giving it a less material significance, if in examining or appreciating works of art by subjecting them to the critique of feeling and taste, one judges them to be either the result of an original inspiration or of a routine operation depending on either examples or rules.

Thus, when many works are said to be just the result of *practice*, one designates an all too common defect that can be explained in many ways.

In fact, in every art of imitation, there are procedures of execution that can be quite promptly transmitted to students through a certain routine instruction. Observing the master at work communicates much more readily to the hand that which intellectual teaching transmits to the mind.

Generally, there is a tendency, as if instinctive, that makes one disposed to be the follower of some master by copying his works, his manner, and preferentially borrowing his defects. A very ordinary misconception makes it such that the idea of imitation is confused with that of copying. In such a misconception, the man or the work taken as a master, distracts from learning from the veritable master, which is nature. Imperceptibly, the work degenerates owing to the artist's failure to draw from the source of the true and the beautiful. The operative part of the work, which is but the body, claims to replace the spirit which it banished. It is then that one observes the multiplication of works called facts of *practice*, because one no longer discovers an immediate transmission of truth, beauty, or quality emanating from the great model, but rather a simple repetition of the works of others, and the trace of operations whose sole guide was routine.

The word *practice* thus changes acceptation without actually changing in meaning. It always signifies an execution that is more or less dependent on the exterior senses or on the hand; and the artist is always advised to study it. In fact, whoever lacks *practice* will also lack, in every art, the means to express ideas, to give them existence, and to render their impressions tangible. The artist must therefore acquire *practice*, that is to say, that he must have experience in all the parts – mechanical and material – upon which rests the reality of the images, forms, and compositions that his genius helps him conceive.

But from this necessity of *practice*, often derives a troublesome misunderstanding in the artist's studies and the public's judgment. After all, that which is known as execution regarding the arts of design, is the only thing that can be taught in a material manner, because it partakes in the nature and properties of procedures which are those of the mechanical arts, and which are imparted only through examples or the repetition of copies. Nothing outside of this operative part can be submitted to a regular teaching method. All that derives from feeling, all that partakes in the faculty of imagination, cannot be communicated. Thus, in the schools of the most famous masters, we generally observe their students skilfully acquiring their manner or the exterior qualities of their talent, and becoming their copyists instead of their imitators.

In the public schools of fine arts, it is even more natural to find the *practical* or operative part prevail over the intellectual part, or that of taste and invention. In fact, the need for concurrence between the mind and the hand tells us that if it is easy to direct the hand through the intermediary of the eye or the examples that address the eye, it is all the more difficult to convey to the mind the abstract notions of the true, the beautiful, the proper, etc.

We would add that the natural effect of the large number of works or master works that are placed in front of the students' eyes is to contrast the free acts of each – in other words their originality – with a kind of obligation to follow already carved paths and regulate one's steps upon those of others. From here derives the habit of no longer thinking for oneself, of no longer seeing with one's own eyes, and of not seeing beyond the distance already travelled. *Practice* then becomes a kind of wide road where all meet and all follow each other.

PRINCIPLE One reads in more than one lexicon that such is the appellation given to the rules or the laws that one must observe in every art. It seems to us, however, that the word *principle* comprises yet another definition, which, grammatically or theoretically speaking, does not permit it to become a simple synonym of *rule* or *law*.

Principle (Latin *principium*), in the proper sense of the word, indicates something that must be given prominence, and which should be considered as signifying *origin, primary cause*. Thus, we hold that in every theory – and especially in that of the fine arts – the word *principle* does not designate every rule and every law, but rather every general and fundamental truth from which other, secondary truths derive; that the word *principle* designates a primary or basic notion, from which notions of a lesser order are deduced, thereby becoming what one calls rules. (*See* RULE).

Thus for example, the following axioms in ethics (*do unto others as you would have them do unto you.*), and in physics (*nothing comes from nothing; nothing returns to nothing*), are not called rules, but rather *principles* with fertile consequences, from which emanate the notions that govern jurisprudence, or those that explain the operations of nature.

Every art has in its theory *principles* from which emerge the ensemble of rules, which, in order to have authority, need to rest on universally recognized truths. These truths compel common sense to conform to the sound logic deduced from them.

More than any other art, architecture needs to base its rules on *principles* such as those that have just been defined. Lacking a real and obvious model, which forces the eyes to compare the imitated object with the imitating one, this art operates by way of analogy rather than similitude, that is, it imitates nature not in her positive work but rather in the reasons behind this work; in other words, by appropriating the *principles* that guide nature's action.

Consequently, architecture's imitative quality rests on a judgment by virtue of which the architect – examining the works of nature, and scrutinizing the reasons or the causes for her effects on our understanding or our mind – endeavours to reproduce the same effects on us through similar combinations.

For example, one observes that nature makes nothing that is not useful, nothing that does not have an aim; and she develops means that are proportionate to the achievement of this aim. From here, one deduces the principle that, since every work of architecture has an intended purpose, then *every detail must be congruent with this purpose*; that is, *it must be useful*. In studying nature, one is convinced that this *useful*, to which everything must lead, is accompanied by the *agreeable* or the *pleasurable* in such a way that only thought can isolate them, by subordinating the latter to the former. Hence the *principle* that the useful and the agreeable must be united, but in such a manner that the second must derive from the first.

In a large number of entries, we have explained the various *principles* from which the effects and the impressions of architecture emanate. We shall not repeat them here, for the present article has no other objective than to elucidate the value or the propriety of a *principle* in architecture, by considering it, in point of fact, as a *simple truth* from which one can deduce many *composite truths*.

Unity, for example, (*sit quod vis simplex duntaxat et unum*) is an elementary *principle* of all the arts, and consequently of architecture. Now this principle will necessarily beget another, such as this one: *the whole must have a rapport with its parts*, and consequently, *every part must be in harmony with the whole*; because without this, there would no longer be unity. From here it follows, in a particular application, *that a large whole must have large parts*.

Thus, what one calls *principle*, irrespective of its proper level, is like the declaration of a fact which is recognized and corroborated by experience, or like a truth, which is at once intellectual and material, and about which there is no disputation, because it enjoys universal approbation.

Now, since the rules that can be deduced from these principles are such that they can apply to a great number of details and circumstances, one is compelled to acknowledge that they will not have the same authority. *Principles* are indisputable, while rules comprise exceptions, for many local reasons resist their rigorous application. Taste, for example, being necessarily dependent on feelings, will also have its own *principles* which are independent of the rigours of reason or reasoning. From here derives the arbitrary part that taste introduces in many rules, in order to attenuate their severity. (*See* TASTE) Therefore, it is under the rubric of these exceptions that abuses and vices enter into the rational system of architecture.

For example, there is certainly no principle more accepted, nor a more invariable rule, than the *principle* and the rule that assert that *the weak is carried by the strong*. However, one finds in certain generally accepted forms an exception to this application that practice admits, and against which neither taste nor reason can lay claim. Such

is the case, for example, of the forms used for brackets [console], and busts [terme]. Brackets, in fact, may be considered as the ornament in an entablature, or as inconsequential caprices when they support busts. The form of the bust, which has no other use in decoration, seems to solicit the same right for an exception, even when it serves (as in many cases) as an accessory to a retable or a pediment. But, to conclude from these licences which are tolerated by taste that one could use isolated busts as real supports for entablatures and pediments would be an intolerable aberration.

PROPORTION This word generally designates the relationship between size or weight, quantities or numbers.

The word used by the Greeks to express this idea was *synmetria*, which aptly designates the effect of *proportion*, whose property it is to establish a relationship of reciprocity between the whole and its parts.

In fact, there is a frequent mistake regarding the meaning of the word *proportion* in its application not only to works of art, but also to those of nature. Applied to any object, the word *proportion* does not mean that there are some measures within the constitutive parts that are indeterminate or independent from any permanent law. In this case, the word *dimension* must be used. The idea of *proportion* contains that of fixed and necessary relationships that are constantly the same, and are reciprocal between parts which have a determined goal.

Thus, it is evident that all the creations of nature have their dimensions, but all do not have *proportions*. A multitude of plants exhibit such disparate measures, so numerous and so evident, that it would be impossible, for example, to determine with precision, the reciprocal measure between the branch of a tree and the tree itself.

It is particularly in the animal kingdom, or that of organisms, that one can form a correct idea of *proportion*. It is here that the idea acquires all its manifestness, especially when one consults the organization of the human body. If in their bodily structure, individuals exhibit a permanent system of *proportions*, as well as varieties that prevent one from considering them as if cast of the same mould, the same must apply to art's imitation of nature.

Now, this last consideration is addressed to those who, by failing to recognize or refusing any regulating *principle* to architecture, pretend to deny the existence of *proportions* in architecture on the basis that its system is not subjected to the rigour of mathematical precision. But how could anyone fail to see that this art acts like nature herself; how could anyone fail to recognize the geometric uniformity in the works of architecture?

What is most important to confront within the opinions of many, is the already mentioned confusion between the idea of *proportion* and that of

Now such is the property of the Greek system of architecture, as we have demonstrated in more than one article. But in addition, we wish to demonstrate here that Greek architecture alone deserves the privilege of this property.

That which prevents many from recognizing this privilege is the frequent habit, especially in parlance, of confusing some simple relationships of measure or dimension in buildings – like those of scale, volume, height, size, which are easy to judge – with the complicated relations of *proportions*. As to the impressions that one receives from simple dimensional relationships, no one fails to be moved by human stature, or by the interior or the exterior of a building, if it offers some very evident contrasts between the parts. Now, in all

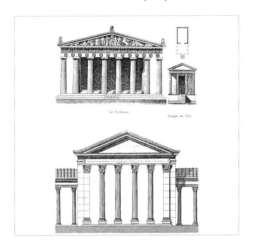

Fig. 67. Parthenon, Temple at Cori; and Portico of Octavia.
From: Julien Guadet, *Éléments et théorie de l'architecture*,
Librairie de la construction moderne, Paris, 1909

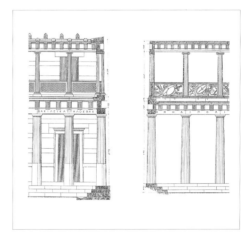

Fig. 68. *left*, Stoa at Athens; *right*, Stoa at Pergamon.
From: Josef Durm, *Die Baukunst der Grieschen*,
A. Kröner Verlag, Leipzig, 1910

dimension, by proving that the former rests on a system which is necessarily and invariably correlative between the whole and its parts.

Indeed, for an architecture to be endowed with a proportional virtue, it is not enough that the parts of an ordonnance[33] be in any incidental relationship with the whole, and that the whole bears any casual correlation to the parts. This is precisely the opposite of a proportional system. In this system, each of the constitutive parts of an ordonnance bears a fixed and necessary dependence on its whole, and *vice versa*; in such a manner that each member, as in nature, accounts for the exact measure of the body, as this measure accounts for the precise dimension of each member.

the works of all architectures, there could be either an accordance or a discordance between these relationships and their effects; one that I would call *instinctive*.

To mention a few examples, there are, in certain Gothic churches, some general relationships of measure, as in size, width, and height; there are also some more particular ones that are betoken by simple instinct, as in the correlation between a thrusted mass and the support that carries it, both of which are inspired by need, and that the eye is forced to accept. It is also certain that one perceives in the frontispieces of Egyptian temples, pylons, propylons, and pyramids, some right relations of dimension between their parts, whose execution took place by virtue of invariable rules.

However, it is not possible to attribute, either to the Egyptians or to the Goths, that which ought to be called a system of *proportions*, or systematic *proportions*.

A true system of proportions does not rest solely on general relationships of measure, as for example those of the height of a body with respect to its volume, or the length of a hand with respect to that of the arm; but on a reciprocal and immutable connection of the principal, the subordinate, and the lesser parts. Now, this connection is such that each part taken by itself, is apt to show solely by its measure, not only the measure of every other part, but also that of the whole; and that through its own measure this whole can reciprocally account for that of each part.

Such a system does not exist and is not evident in the art of building of the Egyptians nor in that of the Goths; it will also be useless to search for it in some other architecture. And such is the undeniable prerogative of Greek architecture.

We have already demonstrated in more than one article (*See* ARCHITECTURE), how, and through which confluence of causes, Greek art was able to acquire this system. We shall repeat here only some abbreviated notions.

By all accounts, the concrete principle from which the system of Greek architecture emerged was the primitive construction in wood; and especially this genre of construction which is at once simple and solid, and composed of parts that combine and link with each other in a manner most fitting to unity and variety. Some have exaggerated the influence of a similar model on the first works of the art of building, by attributing to it the virtue and the properties of nature. No, nature never intended to offer this art a model to follow in the first constructions based on necessity; but amongst the local varieties of primitive habitation, there could have been one whose form and constitutive elements accommodated and lent themselves more successfully to the association of ideas of proportion and imitative taste. And we are forced to recognize that such an encounter and such an association must have given birth in Greece to the primitive constructions in wood.

We have expanded on this notion elsewhere (*See* WOOD, HUT), and demonstrated that the use of stone, for example, considered as an element or a primitive means of construction, could have suggested neither the diverse combinations, nor the varied forms of wood, nor especially these numerous and necessary relations between the constitutive parts of a whole that coordinates them with a regulative principle from which issues a beginning of *proportion*, in the sense that this word ought to be understood.

The idea of *proportion* and that of *harmony*, bear an affinity with each other. Now harmony signifies *connection*; and the idea of connection includes, whatever the circumstance, that of necessary relations. But, in construction, the most necessary relations are those dictated by the nature of things, which, in this case, is the materials employed. No other matter lends itself to more necessary relations, requiring at once their increase and consequently their tangibility, where the connection between the parts produces a more necessary and more evident continuity with the whole.

Such is the first cause of this system of *proportion* that originated in Greece along with the art of building; where it slowly developed under the influence of a process of construction that complies with necessary relationships, and where it changed in response to the progress brought by time. Indeed, when prosperity and a more daring knowledge rendered the use of stone customary, work in this material substituted itself to that of wood, and must have repeated the combinations. Lastly, as the genius of architecture concluded its own development, all that was left was to apply to its work the laws of proportion which nature herself follows, and whose study or imitation of the human body and through the other arts of design combined to render its expression familiar to the mind and the eyes.

The habit of seeing and understanding the result of this study, especially in the images of sculpture, could not but exercise an active influence on the works, the combinations, and the effects of architecture. If all the arts of design share a common link, it is particularly the imitation of the body, whose model is under the artist's eyes. Only, architecture cannot acquire this imitative faculty save through the indirect influence, and if one may say it, through the transposition of the examples furnished by the imitation of the human body into her works. Thus, one observes that wherever the true and reasoned imitation of the body and its *proportions* were unknown, architecture knew no proportional system.

As soon as this imitation was perfected in Greece, it became obvious for everyone that its value consisted in the evidence of the relations of measure between all the components; and the measure that each part is required to have with the whole, as the whole has with every part. Hence, a practical science developed, by virtue of which one could determine – in all the fixed relations of art, as in nature – the length of a finger from a finger-nail; and from a finger, that of the hand; from the measure of the hand, that of the face or the head; and, reciprocally, the total measure of the body revealed that of the smallest part. One could determine the number of times that each part entered within the whole.

How could the art of architecture not acquire this science? How could this art, associated as it is to the works of sculpture in buildings, remain a stranger to the principle of beauty evident in the works of sculpture? How could the idea of taking the body's organization as a model, and establishing between all the parts of construction a module that regulates all relations, not be promptly applied to a combination of circumstances that the calculations of carpentry already prepared for such an assimilation?

But should this be in doubt? Is the matter not as certain, as evident in the formation of the Greek orders, as it is in the structure of their statues? Is a building that is constructed according to the principle of this architecture, in the reciprocal measure of all the parts of its composition, not endowed with the same property of regular correspondence between its members as in the parts of the human body?

Let the other known modes of architecture be investigated, one will not find the proportions exhibited by Greek architecture. Outside certain

relationships – of the sort mentioned above, and which we called pure results of instinct – one would search in vain to prove, for example, that the parts which constitute either the columns, or the entablatures, or the frontispieces in the monuments of Egypt, are qualified throughout by permanent relations of reciprocal measures with their whole. Thus, the same column, compared in two buildings, will have the same height, the same diameter; but its capital will sometimes vary by half its height. The same capital on top of the same genre of column, will not only be two or three times higher on one column than on the other, but it is sometimes composed of three forms of capitals, the one on top of the other. Hence, neither is the column able to inform us as to its capital, nor the capital about the measure of the column to which it belongs. The same applies to all that concerns the parts of Egyptian constructions. Furthermore, it could not be otherwise in an architecture composed of such few parts, and whose elementary principle seems to be uniformity.

More useless still would be the search for what must be called a system of proportion in Gothic architecture, which, concerning the orders, the forms, and the details of ornament, was but an incoherent compilation of all that was transmitted to it by the degenerate taste of the Lower Empire. The Gothic, placed at the extreme opposite of Egyptian architecture, had such a multiplicity of details and divisions, that the diversity which makes its character, could only prevent these combinations – which are the result of a simple type – from becoming a system. In vain, may one attempt to deduce the measure of the capital from that of the column; or reciprocally from the diameter of the column to the measure of the intercolumniation; from the dimension of the support to that of an interior; or from the supporting to the supported mass, etc.

We affirm indeed that *proportion,* in the sense that it must be understood, that is to say, an imitation of that *proportion* which nature imposed on organisms, cannot be the necessary result of the art of building in every country. The human mind is not necessarily led there. Certain pre-existing conditions which do not and could not be universally encountered, converged among the Greeks to give birth to this genre of imitation. First, having adopted as a rule the representation in stone of all the aggregate parts of primitive carpentry construction, architecture initially possessed a fixed point that protected her from the indefinite vagueness of all fantasies. There, she found a kind of model that was able to naturally fix the relations of the height and thickness of the column shaft. The forms, the divisions, and the necessary relationships between the pieces of wood had naturally produced the large and small parts of the stone building, from the base to the entablature, and from the basement to the pediment. From this imitation, which was purely instinctive at first, derived the advantage that no other architecture had: it was to base all the details and their respective relations on something that recalled or indicated a necessity of being, and of being such. The same can be said of all the ornaments where one finds, as in the works of nature, that pleasure always derives from necessity.

Architecture, then, having to take hold of an ensemble that was built on a constitution similar to the human body, had only to regularize in a more permanent proportional system, that which the imitative instinct had already adumbrated. Nothing, therefore, was easier or more natural than to submit the whole to a module whose divisions and subdivisions became, as the foot or the head is for the human body, the regulator of all the parts as well as their smallest fractions.

The effect of such a system on the composition of buildings was to produce a result which in its genre resembles that of nature, as the works of sculpture clearly demonstrate. One knows that every member, every fraction of a statue executed with regularity, no matter how small, allows us to determine with the utmost precision, the size and volume of all the members, of all the divisions and subdivisions, and even the smallest part whose measure may be unknown. Likewise, if the whole ensemble is known to us through a narrative, we would still be able to determine without error the measure of each of its fragments.

Now, the same applies to an ordonnance of Greek architecture. The only remaining triglyph of the temple of Olympian Jupiter in Agrigento, prior to the recent discoveries, enabled us to recover the measurements of the whole monument, just as the measurements of its whole would have informed us about those of the triglyph. One single dentil in a cornice informs us as to the size of the whole entablature; and once known, the entablature makes known the kind, the order, and consequently the dimensions of columns, and so on and so forth.

Such is the veritable and undeniable imitation of nature that must be recognized in Greek architecture; an imitation which one cannot find nor surmise in another architecture. It is this correlation with the constitution of bodies that gave Greek architecture an unquestionable superiority over all other methods of building.

Once introduced into the art of building, the power of this principle of harmony compels everything to experience its influence. Indeed, as soon as this system of imitation was inspired by the proportions of the body, it progressively impelled the artist to draw new analogies from the same source. Among these analogies were the three modes called *orders*, that represent the three expressions within which nature's action is ordinarily contained, to wit, the higher, the lower and the middle term. When Vitruvius sees in the imitation of the male and female bodies, the type of the Doric and Ionic orders, and takes this comparison to the level of exaggerated details, we should only consider this manner of seeing as a very natural misuse of a truth which itself is already metaphorical. To bring this notion towards a more plausible explanation, one may propose that in all probability the science of proportions of the human body must have instructed architecture in the secret of varying the character and the physiognomy of the orders, in the same measure and manner in which nature acts, depending on the degrees of force, refinement, or size that one distinguishes when comparing individuals of the same species.

But this may lead us away from the theory that has been the object of this article.

We did not set out, as we mentioned at the beginning, to give the many details of *proportion* in every part of architecture and her compositions. Our only goal has been to consider *proportion* from its general point of view; to define its elementary idea; to develop its theoretical nature in its application to architecture; to show that one often confuses the relationships of simple dimension with those of proportion; that certain simple relationships, like those of size, height, and the expanse of masses, could, without art and without system, belong to all buildings of all architectures, as to a multitude of industrial objects; but that as a permanent system of necessary and reciprocal relations between the whole and the parts, *proportion*, belongs and could only belong to Greek architecture; that she first owed this privilege to the original principle of her genre of construction in wood, and later to the study of the human body, which was developed and perfected by the arts of design, and whose principle and results she was able to appropriate.

PROPRIETY The idea that this word expresses falls in many ways under that of aptness (See this term). Indeed, that which *fits well*, seems to strongly resemble that which is *convenient*.[34]

If it was only a question of indicating the nuance that separates these two expressions in the morals and the language of a society, then one would perhaps not be encumbered to determine to which order of sensibility their meanings belonged. Perhaps one could suggest, without too much misapprehension, that the idea of *aptness* relates more to morals, and that of *propriety*, to manners or customs. Thus the figures of a work of art will offend *aptness* by the obscenity of the postures, whereas others will shock *propriety* by the incorrectness of costumes.

It is not as easy to distinguish between the meaning of these two words when it comes to their use in architecture.

If we believe Vitruvius, the ancients may have had only one word to designate that which we are expressing by aptness and *propriety*. This word was *decor* or *decorum*, and derived from the

verb *deceo, decet*: that which is convenient. (See the word *aptness*, where the three kinds of qualities which it designates were developed. These qualities referred, the one to the very nature of edifices, or those to whom they are destined; the other to the accordance between the parts of an edifice and the edifice itself; and the third to the locality required by the monument.)

Vitruvius ascribes the idea of that which we nowadays call *propriety* in particular, to the observance of the conditions required by each edifice. The same subsequently applies to the respect for the practice consecrated by custom, in the elementary types of architecture. "... if dentils be carved in the cornice of the Doric entablature or triglyphs represented in the Ionic entablature

Fig. 69. Théâtre de Bordeaux, section.
From: Julien Guadet, *Éléments et théorie de l'architecture*, Librairie de la construction moderne, Paris, 1909

over the cushion-shaped capitals of the columns, the effect will be spoilt by the transfer of the peculiarities of the one order of the building to the other, the usage in each class having been fixed long ago."

This last reason that Vitruvius gives, no matter how simple, seems to us the most suitable to define the idea of *propriety*. Thus, in society, the observance or the contempt towards an inherited practice reveals he who is civil and he who is coarse. To scoff at established practice is injurious to *propriety*. Well, such is the case as regards any practice of architecture which rests on the nature of things; on the authority of time; and on the inherited examples and suffrage of a considerable number of centuries.

We shall also add that in this art the observance of *propriety* will not result in blind and routine use, but rather in a reasoned respect towards all that has been consecrated by custom. It is particularly to the domain of sensibility that belongs the act of discerning the modifications that many causes and cases introduce to inherited practice. Now, what a sensibility enlightened by experience prescribes before all else is not to offend custom without a necessary reason or a plausible motive; it is not to innovate in the received and accredited things, without this change being justified by necessity and the added effect of approval.

For example, never have the ancients in their works offended the general principles of a cornice's outline.[35] However, the known exceptions are only varieties in proportion, justified by an evident reason. Thus, when the Greeks place one order on top of another in the interior of a temple, one observes that they omit from the entablature of the lower order those parts known as the frieze and the cornice, while leaving only the architrave. This omission is precisely one of those derogations of custom, which far from being an unsuitableness (*disconvenance*), becomes instead, in this case, a new homage to the rationality of the custom, and consequently to *propriety*. Indeed, two superimposed orders of columns imply two levels, and when applied to buildings of more than one level, each will receive a complete entablature. But this is inadmissible in the interior of a Greek *naos*. Therefore, not to add the elements which represent beams and rafters to the lower Doric architrave, was an act of genuine *propriety* .

What we have just related, seems to us sufficient to explain in what sense and to what extent *propriety* implies the respect of what has been established and accredited by practice, and the manner in which it authorizes changes, when they are grounded in reason or in considerations of utility. But the sensibility for *propriety* is so intimately tied to what one calls taste in all the arts, that one despairs of communicating it to whomever did not receive from nature the intellectual organ to which this sensibility corresponds.

There is even less hope of communicating this to one whose unmanageable mind, made for jumbling everything and inept at discerning the nuances comprised by rules, admits no truth of an intellectual order but the negation of all that cannot be demonstrated physically, and believes that nothing can be proven because everything cannot be demonstrated. For such minds, there is no *propriety* but arbitrariness.

The word *propriety* is sometimes held in architecture to have a meaning close to the word *convention*, as when propriety in architecture is said to require that we accept some compromises such as those that exist between all the arts and their models in order for them to fulfil their purpose and produce their effect. (*See* CONVENTION)

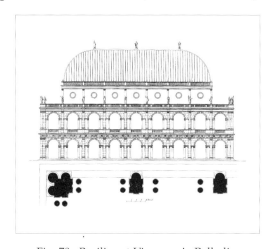

Fig. 70. Basilica at Vicenza, A. Palladio.
From: A. C. Quatremère de Quincy, *Histoire de la vie et des ouvrages des plus célèbres architectes*, J. Renouard, Paris, 1830

PUBLIC EDIFICES Although the etymology of this word (*œdes*, house) seems to solely designate habitations, usage has given it a more elevated meaning. A *building* designates ordinary constructions, whereas an *edifice* comprises the idea of a *monument*, especially if it is understood under the general rubric of *public edifices*, which is the meaning used in this article.

The character of *public edifices*, artistically considered, does not necessarily derive from the public function of a building. Of course, the buildings constructed with public funds and intended for general use are known as such. Only in architectural parlance, the same appellation is not given to the palaces of great and notable persons that are distinguished from ordinary habitations by the grandeur of their massing and the richness of their elevations.

Public edifices must first be distinguished by their solidity. That which is built by the public realm must be durable. Any evidence to the contrary betrays weakness or lack of vision. The monuments erected by the public realm reveal its character and genius. Consequently, *public edifices* must employ the most refined and select materials. This kind of luxury never provokes censure; only scarcity is tolerated by a malevolent mind. The individual's interest in good construction and excellence in *public edifices* is of two sorts. One of these interests derives from the fact that since each individual contributes to their expense, then that individual has a right to

richness that it reached. Thus, every nation has a stake in the correspondence between the construction of its *public edifices* and the principles that must have contributed to their erection. Therefore, it is important for builders of public works to feel and understand the moral interest that is associated with their endeavours.

However, one must not imagine that the character that befits *public edifices* derives only from great expense. The merit of art can compensate for the lack of funds more than one thinks. When economic concerns reduce the expanse and the grandeur of an edifice, there is another grandeur that replaces that of dimension: it is that of invention, taste and style. Baldassare Peruzzi, the architect of the palazzo Massimi in Rome,

Fig. 71. Ste. Geneviève (Pantheon), J.-G. Soufflot.
From: A. C. Quatremère de Quincy, *Histoire de la vie et des ouvrages des plus célèbres architectes*, J. Renouard, Paris, 1830

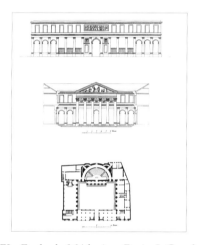

Fig. 72. Ecole de Médecine, Paris, J. Gondouin.
From: A.C. Quatremère de Quincy, *Histoire de la vie et des ouvrages des plus célèbres architectes*, J. Renouard, Paris, 1830

demand from the builders the best use of the sums with which they are entrusted. Every individual wants what is raised at everyone's expense to be built as if he had constructed it himself. Now, everyone wishes to build solidly when the means are available, in order not to be exposed to the ruinous expenses of renovation and reparations.

The other interest is that of self esteem. *Public edifices* are signs that allow the eye to read the history of each era. And each individual wishes to leave remembrances of his passage on earth that recall his existence and the causes that enriched its course.

Finally, *public edifices* represent the nation itself, as they attest to the degree of taste, skill and

demonstrated in this building, as well as other buildings of moderate budgets which he endowed with the character of *public edifices*, that there is an art of producing the grand while using the small, and to appear rich while being economical. The Medical School in Paris is a small edifice built with a moderate budget, but the architect gave it an air of great importance. Few monuments, even the largest ones, have as noble an appearance.

No other nation built more kinds of public edifices with such grandeur, opulence and magnificence as the Roman nation. This nation is usually taken as a model, but this seems to be a false belief, for we can admire this nation but not pretend to imitate her.

In speaking of the Roman people, one forgets that this people did not form one nation, but that it became the centre of all nations. It is evident that a necessary relation must be established between the causes for grandeur, power and the population of a nation, and the means available to erect her monuments. Such are the criteria to be considered before a building enterprise. When one examines the causes that produced these great edifices that we admire among different peoples of antiquity, one is persuaded that, in general, they were the result of certain circumstances that must be seen as exceptional in comparison to the present time.

It is well known that the Egyptians condemned to forced labour the peoples that they subjugated. Their conquests gave them slaves, who in turn became manual labourers.

The temple of Ephesus was built with contributions from the Greek republics and Asian kings.

The greatest and most beautiful monuments of Athens were constructed by Pericles not only from Attic funds, but also from the contributions given to him by the diverse peoples of Greece for their common defence, which he skilfully diverted for the benefit of his city.

When Rome was left to her own means alone, she had poor edifices; but Augustus said that he found a city of clay and left a city of marble, for during his time, and even before, the riches of all the conquered nations found their way to Rome.

It would be an exaggeration today to pretend to use such a comparison, since the greatness and the opulence of *public edifices* must always be proportionate to those of the nation. Doubtless, linear grandeur forms a part of architectural beauty, but this grandeur occupies a lower level than the colossal and the gigantic. There is always an element of grandeur that accompanies the beautiful; and the beautiful is within the resources of all nations. In fact, what made the monuments of Pericles particularly recommendable was less their large dimensions or their opulence than a certain distinctive beauty. One could still find, even after many centuries, a kind of youthful vitality that makes one think that they have not aged at all.

Thus, the magnificence of *public edifices* depends on the grandeur and the richness of compositions and ideas as much as on the dimensions of volumes and the sumptuousness of materials. But there is also another condition which is indispensable to the value of *public edifices* and the effect that they must produce. This condition rests on the observance of a kind of scale of moral proportion in each building; depending on the nature of its purpose and the character of the idea that it invokes in the public's mind.

When some modest buildings in a city display a certain mediocrity, architecture easily finds ways to make the *public edifices* shine, and to endow them with their proper rank through a tangible gradation, and without great expense. Architecture is a language whose signs are either natural and tangible, or conventional; but these signs lose their proper meaning as soon as practice not only permits but also operates and thus mandates their confusion.

In the laws of Charondas, we read an article that will revive, if not the material interest, then certainly the moral interest in the spirit of architecture.

"He (says the legislator of the *Thurion*) who erects a house more beautiful than the temples of the gods or the edifices destined for public service, far from deserving esteem, merits only infamy. No private edifice should insult public monuments by its own magnificence."

RESTITUTION There is an important distinction to be made between the idea, the work and the application that this word designates, and the application comprised in the words *restore* and *restoration*. One *restores* a dilapidated or partially destroyed work of art, based on the surviving remains that allow, more or less, the repetition of what is missing; one *restitutes* a work or a monument that has entirely disappeared based on the authority of descriptions, or sometimes based on indications furnished by other works of the same kind.

In devoting oneself in *restitutions* to a kind of research whose nature – that always includes some element of instinctive foresight – is at once attractive and hazardous, one must not shut one's eyes to relevant reservations in order to avoid the dangers that surround this work. Before all else, the general theory of imitation must teach us to distinguish between the works of art described by writers – those that find counterparts amid existing works, or where the narrative transmits an authentic image – from those whose ensemble and details elude all forms of language.

The description of a painting, for example, precisely because it is minutely detailed, will be most inadequate to allow conjecture as to its composition, for it will be an ensemble that analysis destroys. But such is not the case with a monument, especially if the writer has added measurements to the described parts that help to reassemble them in their true relations.

An architectural ensemble is generally a composite of identically similar parts. Sometimes, there is but one column in an edifice that displays the largest number of columns; and likewise, there is but one capital in a colonnade. The same applies to ornamental details. The description of a Greek edifice is highly precise when it indicates the type, the order and the measurements, especially for one who has the knowledge of similar works. One must admit however, that there is a beauty that no narrative, or better still, no copy could transmit. But it would be unfair to require from a *restitution*, that which is not even required from a drawing made after the original.

Besides, if such *restitutions* do not increase the number of original architectural models for artists and students, they will always offer the advantage of expanding the knowledge that pertains to this art; enlighten its taste with a large number of parallels; facilitate the understanding of texts; furnish authentic facts to the history of art; and offer diverse materials for criticism, which, without this research would remain unknown, and, so to speak, lost.

The *restitution* of monuments based on the descriptions of writers, is therefore not a fruitless task or a simple curiosity, even if these descriptions do not permit reproducing with complete faithfulness the totality of the true relations or the qualities that made the merit of the originals.

We should add, therefore, that there have always been men desirous of thus repairing the losses of beautiful works. Raphael himself drew on two descriptions from Lucian for the subjects of two of his most ingenious paintings, which represent, the one, the wedding of Alexander and Roxane, the other, the beautiful allegory of the Delation, as imagined by Apelles.

Towards the middle of the last century, that is to say, at a time when there was little knowledge of Greek ruins, the Marquis Poleni attempted quite a successful *restitution* of the temple of Ephesus based on the incomplete material provided by Pliny, and on the information furnished in various passages scattered among other authors.

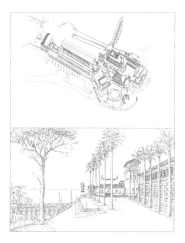

Fig. 73. Villa Laurentum, Léon Krier.
From: Léon Krier, *Architecture, Choice or Fate*,
A. Papadakis Publisher, London, 1998

Based on passages from authors, the monument of Mausolus occupied many an architect, and their scholarship can only acquire a greater soundness as travellers expand the knowledge of the remains of antiquity.

Doubtless, Mr. de Caylus lacked the resources of factual knowledge when he tried to *restitute* two very uncommon monuments described by Diodorus of Sicily: the funeral-pyre of Hephaestion, and the hearse that transported the body of Alexander from Babylon to Alexandria. Also, he may not have been sufficiently familiar with the particular meaning of the texts.

Indeed, it is important, in order to succeed at such *restitutions*, that the same man be at once the translator and the artist. When the double operation of translating and drawing combines within the activity of one intelligence, then, the translation and the drawing exchange reciprocal influences. The clear and precise intuition of the proper forms of the described object is of marvellous help for the meaning of the words that designate it; and in its turn, the form of the object to be discovered, will emerge more faithfully from the pencil of the artist who appropriated the knowledge of the words and the precise meaning of the description.

It is for having personally lacked the union of these means, that Mr. de Caylus gave but an ill-formed and insignificant idea of the two monuments described by Diodorus. Proceeding in accordance with our own means, but in the manner that has just been described, we tried to reproduce the two monuments in drawing form, which one can find in Tome IV of the *Mémoires de l'Institut* (Classe d'histoire et de littérature anciennes; and, better still, in our book: the *Monuments restitués*, etc.)

We expanded on the subject of this article in order to explain the usefulness of the *restitution* of antique monuments based on the description of writers, and the manner in which it is important to proceed for this kind of work to gain the interest that it deserves.

RESTORE This word is more frequently used with regard to sculpture rather than architecture; it is considered not in a purely mechanical sense, but in its rapport with the reintegration of ancient works and monuments degraded by time or by all sorts of accidents to which they were exposed.

The word *restore* has become quite common since the time when the arts flourished anew, especially in Italy, toward the fifteenth and sixteenth centuries. It was then that began the search, among the ruins of ancient Rome and other cities, for the remains of defaced statues that successive upheavals had buried under the débris of buildings which they had once adorned. Since most of these works were of marble, artists exerted themselves at recuperating the integrity of their first form, by resculpting the dilapidated parts and the missing members, using the same

material. Of the infinite number of statues recovered from destruction and barbarity, there were very few that needed no *restoration*, at least in part. The art of *restoring* requires a special talent that is not common, because skilled and renowned artists have rarely practised it. One can cite, however, some antique statues, whose missing parts were resculpted by Michelangelo and Bernini. Since the time when the style of antiquity had become more familiar, skilled men appeared who could, if not imitate, then at least feign in their restorations, the manner, or one might say, the physiognomy of the antique.

The idea of *restoration* as well as the work and the operations that it designates, was also applied to ancient architecture and a large number of her

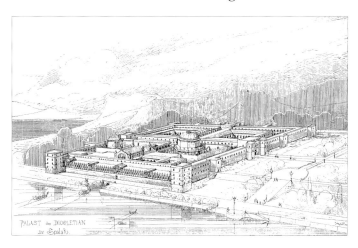

Fig. 74. Palace of Diocletian, Spalato.
From: Josef Durm, *Die Baukunst der Etrusker und Römer*,
A. Kröner Verlag, Stuttgart, 1905

monuments. As to this art and its works, one must say that the difficulties and the drawbacks of the processes of restoration are of a lesser consequence. Perhaps, until the present time, we have been erroneously applying the disadvantages of the *restoration* of statues to the more or less dilapidated constructions of antiquity. I speak of this excess of respect which can only hasten or complete the decay of many a monument.

Architecture, in fact, is necessarily composed of similar parts that can be identically copied or reproduced by means of an exact observation of measures. Talent does not figure in such an operation, which can be reduced to the simplest mechanism. One can imagine the difficulty, and perhaps the impossibility, of matching the top or bottom half of an Apollo or a Venus, to the other, missing half. But one cannot understand the danger to a mutilated building, if its peristyle were to be completed, for example, with one or several columns, built in the likeness of their model, and in the same materials and measures. Such is, in many cases, the nature of the art of building, that similar additions could be made to a half ruined building, without altering the preserved part in the slightest.

Consider the peristyle in the Pantheon of Rome, which was *restored* by replacing the granite corner column, and by the reconstruction of the entablature in this same part, without this operation harming the rest of the composition, and without the slightest depreciation as to opinion. In fact, who prefers to see this beautiful ensemble degraded by an unfortunate mutilation? On the contrary, who does not prefer to enjoy the totality of its composition, especially when the restoration in question induces no one into error? How many antique monuments would be preserved if only the care was taken to put back in place the fallen materials, or to replace a stone by another stone?

A ridiculous prejudice has prevailed over this subject for a long time. This is owing to the kind of mania that was engendered by the so-called picturesque system, of the genre of irregular gardens, which by excluding from its compositions all buildings or complete constructions, seems to admit only ruined buildings in its landscapes, or those that appear to be so. Painting had also previously made fashionable the genre called *of ruins*. (*See* RUINS) Since then, any project of restoring a ruined antique monument was subject to the disapproval of the followers of the picturesque.

However, we acknowledge that there is a middle ground to be kept in the restoration of antique edifices which are more or less in ruins.

Firstly, one must *restore* the extant remains, only in view of preserving that which is likely to offer some valuable examples to the art of models or to the science of antiquity. Thus, the measure of these restorations must depend on their pertaining interest, and the degree of dilapidation of the monument. A prop is quite often the only

thing needed by a monument, in order for it to be assured of many more centuries of existence.

Secondly, if the building in question is composed of columns, with entablatures and friezes ornamented with sculpted foliage or filled with other figures hewn and cut by the ancient chisel, then it should suffice to bring back the missing parts in their ensemble, and treat their details in such a manner that the observer is not mistaken between the ancient work and the work that was brought solely to complete the ensemble.

What we are proposing here has recently occurred in Rome with respect to the famous triumphal arch of Titus, which has fortunately been extricated from all that obstructed it, and whose defaced parts have also been very wisely restored, precisely in the manner and the measure that has just been described.

RUINS In its singular form and its ordinary sense, this word designates the state of dilapidation or destruction which threatens a building or in which it is found. An edifice is said to be in danger of falling into *ruins*, and the *ruination* of a house is said to be impending. The use of this term in the plural designates a state of complete *ruin*. For example, an accident is said to have caused the *ruin* of a building, whereas a certain site is said to be in *ruins*.

If the question at hand concerns the considerable remains of monuments, or vast ruined edifices, or those of ancient cities whose vestiges time has not yet erased, one speaks the *ruins* of Palmyra, or Spalato. Thus, one is said to consult the *ruins* of the Coliseum in Rome or to visit the *ruins* of the Parthenon in Athens.

Although one could use the name *ruin* – and one does – to designate modern destructions, it is certain, however, that this appellation does not arouse the same general interest as when it is applied to the remains of antiquity. The more they age, the more importance they seem to accrue; hence the need for their preservation.

The *ruins* of ancient monuments have become the object of special studies, research and imitation in architecture, as well as in a certain genre of painting which we shall discuss below.

In fact, Greek architecture outlived herself and her authors, less because of traditions that were long interrupted and more because of the *ruins* of her monuments. It was there that the examples that revived the processes of great constructions, as well as the initial concepts of architecture and the rules of taste, were rediscovered, during the renaissance of the arts. Thus, Greek architecture owes her introduction to modern peoples to the influence of documents concerned with the *ruins* of antiquity. From these *ruins* emerged all these treatises on the elements of architecture where each of the most famous modern architects endeavoured to renew the broken link with forgotten traditions, and to find the principles and the rules of proportions. These *ruins* facilitated the

Fig. 75. Acropolis Ruins.
From: Stuart & Revett's *Antiquities of Athens*,
Reprint, B. Bloom, New York, 1968

establishment of parallels on the various parts of each order, as well as their general proportions and their particular details. Enlightened by these parallels, taste was able to deduce the correct adjustments that establish the measures of order – which are always a guaranty against the deviations of an ill-regulated imagination – without being inflexible in all their applications.

One must say, however, that the knowledge of ancient art, studied in its *ruins*, was initially very incomplete; for its main object and all its materials were solely constituted from the vestiges of ancient Rome. Only chance had decided on their loss or their preservation; and it is probable that most of the best preserved remains belonged to the latter periods.

But additional fields of *ruins* must be opened for the exploration and comparison that benefit the history and the theory of art. Chronology must shed light upon objects that have heretofore been confused under a single denomination common to all; and it must methodically classify the innumerable works that emerge from *ruins*, according to periods, nations and schools.

In fact, it so happened that travellers visited and traversed all the regions of the ancient world. Southern Italy brought to light the *ruins* of Greek architecture. Sicily, in her many temples in varying degrees of ruination, furnished some definite dates regarding the style of the Greek Doric order. Greece preserved many of her most beautiful monuments, and the locations of all her most ancient cities have been found and ascertained based on their extant *ruins*. Asia Minor has been traversed in all directions, and the remains of her most ancient cities have exhibited numerous models of the Ionic Order.

Egypt, still standing in her eternal *ruins*, has furnished historical learning with much authoritative information that carries the knowledge of her unchanging taste, and her ever uniform buildings back three thousand years. Eager travellers, going beyond Egypt, have also conquered remote countries that were either under her rule or under that of her arts. Thus, the exploration of Egyptian *ruins* has been pushed several hundred leagues beyond the cataracts.

In the North of Italy, and in other regions of Europe, the exploration and the study of ancient *ruins* has been no less active nor less fruitful. The writing and the language of ancient Etruria, having become more or less legible or intelligible, reveal to us that this ancient country was more or less affiliated with the art of early Greece, and that she also propagated agriculture and culture among the early Romans. There is no city in Italy that did not display the noble ambition of finding her genealogical descendence within her ancient *ruins*. France, in many of her provinces, and especially those of the South, has exploited a soil rich in remains of Roman magnificence, and we observe a similar zeal on the part of other European nations, where all sorts of ancient *ruins* emerge daily as testimonies to Rome's power, and the practice of her arts.

Thus, the treasures of ancient *ruins* grow and expand daily in scholarly collections. In multiplying and spreading their useful influence, which is rich in valuable lessons for all the arts, these collections, if they do not entirely protect the arts from the corrupting effect of the spirit of innovation, then they bring them back to the path of the principles of the true, the beautiful, and the great.

We mentioned earlier that *ruins* in general, and particularly those of ancient architecture, had a special rapport with painting.

The *ruins* of ancient edifices have for a long time occupied the painter's brush. We observe in the story of Raphael's life that, in order to fulfil the wishes of Leo X, this great artist not only restituted with drawings the remains of the principal monuments that still existed in his time, but that he most probably painted them; that is to say, he painted what is known as tableaux of *ruins*.

As the art of landscape painting developed and became a separate genre, it became difficult for Rome, this city whose views owe so much to the famous *ruins* that she contains, not to inspire the idea of adorning the background of painted compositions; and many are the landscapes that were enriched with the more or less free representation of some ancient *ruins*.

But, in this genre as in others, the representation of *ruins* became a somewhat isolated and distinct part; in other words, there were painters who painted only ancient *ruins*. Some of these painters produced images that were so faithful to the ruined monuments that they can be profitably consulted by the architects themselves. Among those painters was the famous *Pannini*, who composed the objects of his paintings and executed them so correctly only because he reconciled the knowledge of the architect with the judgment and the talent of the painter. There is a picturesque way to compose paintings of *ruins*, to correctly imitate the effects of light on the materials, and to reproduce the effects of decay with all the accidents of chance. This picturesque manner demands some very special studies, but which are exclusively in the domain of painting.

Limiting ourselves to what concerns architecture, we would also mention the *ruins*, ancient or not so ancient, used in the compositions of irregular gardens. Those who compose such gardens, often include simulacra of ancient ruined monuments consisting of an elevated hillock, broken columns, scattered stones, or sections of dilapidated walls, and fragments of entablatures or capitals.

RULE Speech has borrowed both the word and the idea of *rule*, which apply to all kinds of intellectual operations, from the material instrument used in a large number of mechanical operations to draw straight lines. Theory uses this word especially in regard to those precepts dictated by experience, which serve to guide those who practise the fine arts and lead them to perfection by the most direct path.

Rules, therefore, are to the realm of the works and operations of the mind what they are to the domain of the works and operations of the hand; and they occupy the same role, which is to direct and shorten operations.

We saw elsewhere (*See* PRINCIPLE), that there was a distinction to be made between principles and *rules*. We said that the word *principle*, as its etymology indicates, expresses the idea of *origin*, of *source* from which consequences derive, and these consequences are the *rules*. In their respective domains, principles of all sorts are either ancient conventions, or general theses whose existence, legitimacy or evidence is not contested; and which serve as a foundation to the laws that are deduced from them.

Principles are general truths, *rules* are their particular applications.

Principles are simple by their very nature, otherwise, they would not be principles. *Rules* are necessarily composite: firstly, because they often derive from more than one source; secondly, because they also relate to varied ends.

Being *simple*, the principles that are grounded in unity or universality are immutable; they can neither be modified nor be compromised with any consideration. It is with them that everything else must be co-ordinated. Being composite or derivative, *rules* are often variable in their details.

Depending on time, place and circumstance, necessity and propriety require many modifications, which one calls exceptions or licences.

Lastly, principles are small in number, and one cannot discover new ones; while *rules*, on the contrary, are numerous. Now, there are principles that are extremely fertile in deductions, and which are often the very concise expression of a large number of insights and subtle relations; because in this domain, as in all matters of intelligence, there are no limits. Thus, it is always possible that a new insight, which emanates from a fundamental truth, gives birth to some new *rule*.

As a result, there must be various classes of *rules* that could appear more or less imperious, depending on whether they emanate from a more

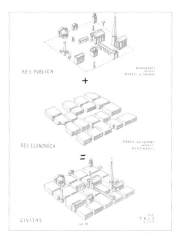

Fig. 76. Civitas, Léon Krier,
From: Léon Krier, *Architecture, Choice or Fate*,
A. Papadakis Publisher, London, 1998

or less restrictive principle, or whether they are its more or less direct and necessary consequences. Indeed, lacking the benefit of this observation, it often happens that one gives or considers as a principal and rigorous *rule* that which is but the indirect conclusion of another *rule*. Also, one often observes how the confusion of ideas in this regard could transform into a *rule* the very exception of this *rule*.

In applying the elements of this theory to architecture, it seemed to us that the *rules* of this art could be classified into four divisions. There are indeed *rules* based on the principles of reason and the very nature of things. There are *rules* that have as a principle the constitution of our mind and the laws of our senses. There is a kind of *rules*

that has only custom and the authority of reason as a principle. Finally, there are rules that derive only from habit, and even some prejudice.

§ I To the first class, correspond those sorts of *rules* that one finds established everywhere. Such are, in particular, those of solidity, unity, and simplicity, whose goal is to satisfy necessity and to produce the useful.

Reason alone, or the nature of things, guarantees the implementation of these *rules*, and compels the recognition of their authority. These are the *rules* that form the practical code of construction; that compel the builder to proportion the masses of an edifice, and the weight of these masses with respect to their point of support; that teach the just balance between solids and voids; that determine the manner in which the use of materials conforms to the general design; that teach the relationship of distance, of height and of span between objects. These are the *rules* that establish with mathematical certainty the extent to which boldness can go without compromising solidity; that determine the proportions that depend on equilibrium and balance, and the resistance of volumes, forces and thrusts. All these *rules* are sometimes the result of experience, which is often a substitute for calculation; and sometimes the result of calculations, grounded in the laws of physics and mechanics, which dispense with the lessons of experience.

Such is, in effect, the advantage of these rules: allowing the architect to enjoy the results of centuries of accumulated science, shortening his labours, and assuredly enabling him to proceed with infallible means. Also, these sorts of *rules* have few gainsayers among them; no one contests their usefulness. Since they can always be brought back to mathematical demonstrations, the only disputation about them is one of degree; for as the objects to which they are applied are not always the same, these *rules* are adverse to a rigorous and mathematical uniformity.

Enough said about the authority and the agency of *rules* in that part of architecture known as the art of building.

§ II It is in the nature of the second class of *rules* to experience many more contradictions. These are the *rules*, we have said, that are based on the principles of our sensations and on the nature of our mind, the *rules* that one may call of sentiment, of taste. Well, it is immediately apparent how and why they are subject to more controversy. This, however, does not imply that their basis is less certain; because this certitude is moral and, as such, it is not the kind of material evidence that strikes the senses.

Still, moral truths have no less of an effect on us than physical truths; only, they need to be perceived and appreciated through their corresponding organs. If the *rules* of solidity contain a truth that strikes everyone's senses with unimpeachable and material evidence, there is also another kind of evidence that appeals to intelligence, to feeling, and to taste. Therefore, there are rules that teach the ways and the means through which all can experience the impressions resulting from the accord between works of art and the moral faculties that must judge them.

Additionally, we observe that all works of art endowed with this property are capable of producing the same impressions at all times and in all countries. This is because the moral laws of intelligence are as universally recognized as the laws of physical equilibrium, for example. The faculties of our mind, made to appreciate moral truth and beauty, are no less able to judge measures and numbers than the properties of physical organs. Yet, through an aberration of judgment, it may happen that the kind of critique that recognizes only that which can be measured or calculated, finds itself applied to the *rules* of sensibility and taste. There is nothing to conclude from this, however, save that the blind man who denies the existence of light, proves only that he has no eyes. The same applies to those who lack the moral capacity to recognize intellectual matters. But there has always been, at all times, a common consent to recognize *rules*.

Indeed, there has always been and there will always be some certain and invariable *rules* of sensibility and taste; for they are founded on the nature of our minds.

These are the *rules* that teach how to observe the just relations of symmetry and eurythmy, whose effect is to manifest for the eyes the visual harmony of lines or forms, in a manner similar to the *rules* of musical harmony, which perform for the ear an ensemble of pleasing sounds.

These are the *rules* that teach how to transform a building into a work where the whole and the parts, as in an organism, correspond to each other in such an order and accuracy of reciprocal measures that the whole can indicate the dimension of every part, and the smallest part can reveal the dimension of the whole.

Now, these *rules*, known as the *rules* of proportion, having their principle and their cause in the imitation of the very works of nature, cannot be contested. He who would contest their effect and influence on us fails to recognize the very principle of the cause of delight that we receive from the harmonies of nature.

The same must be said of all the *rules* of architecture, for they derive from the source of sensations that the works of nature produce in us; and, as such, they are naught but a transposition of the same causes, applied in their effects to works of architecture. Such are the *rules* that depend on the principle of this unity whose effects nature manifests for us everywhere and in everything. She has so constituted the perceptual faculties of our mind to feel and judge, that in order to obtain agreeable impressions from an object, we require that it present itself in simple relationships that facilitate its perception. Thus, every *rule* that is founded on the principle of unity will be as secure in its domain as those that depend on the judgment of the physical senses. No one can deny that the incoherence and the proliferation of parts produce confusion, thus annulling in us the feeling of pleasure caused by the perception of an ordered whole. Therefore, the *rules* of unity in the composition of a plan, the *rules* of unity in ordering its elevation, and the *rules* of unity in the distribution of the details of its decoration, have nothing arbitrary, nothing questionable about them. Nature herself laid down these *rules* in the totality of her works. Man did not make them, and the artist did not imagine them; he only recognized and transferred them to the productions of his genius and his work.

The same may be said of the *rules* applicable to the theory of character. Who does not know that nature imparted a way of being to each of her productions; a special physiognomy that serves to identify them without uncertainty, and which is itself an obvious indication of its qualities and properties? Man cannot help but follow this sort of model in the conformation of a certain number of his works; because, in being assigned to a particular purpose, they obtain the more or less formal obligation to identify in their forms, the kind of need to which they correspond. One cannot enumerate how many objects of craft observe this *rule* in the realm of worldly necessities; unless the accident of caprice diverts their form from corresponding to their use.

Therefore there is a *rule* for sensibility and taste that is dictated by nature, which prescribes to each kind of building the character that it must have, in order to answer as clearly as possible to the kind of need or use to which it is intended. By adopting this *rule*, art imitates nature in her works, and in the kind of instinct for mechanical industry within a multitude of objects whose form or type are dictated by natural necessity.

If this instinct is a law of nature, then the *rules* that derive from it cannot be regarded as arbitrary; therefore, to counterpose some infractions of a more or less direct nature is not an objection against these *rules*. Indeed, there is no law of wisdom, of morals or justice that cannot be challenged under the pretext that there are insane, immoral or unjust men or acts.

There is another law of nature that architecture appropriated, or whose consequences she appropriated in order to form one of her *rules*; this law decrees that in architecture – considered in her works as well as in those of the great model from which she borrows the spirit – the agreeable always proceeds from the useful. Nature, in her wisdom, took care of joining pleasure to the satisfaction of every need, and architecture adopted the same law; likewise, she willed that the necessary parts, or the details of construction, became at once objects of need and

pleasure. Architecture then, established as a *rule* that every ornament, proceeding more or less directly from a necessary use or utility, is bound to manifest its origin, thus becoming enabled to satisfy at once reason and imagination.

This is the order of *rules* where one encounters the most contradictions. Without a doubt, the decorative part of architecture is subject to a considerable number of conventions that offer a vast field of arbitrariness. However, it is undeniable that after scrutinizing the origins of all ornaments, one finds that most of them seem to be based on some utilitarian reason, or are likely to be brought back to a rational system. Consequently, it is for this kind of ornament to legislate the arbitrary one. Simple common sense suggests that if there must be exceptions to the *rule*, the *rule* does not give way to the exceptions.

We have just surveyed within a very general theory, the two classes of *rules* in architecture that must be seen as based on evident facts, on intellectual or physical authorities, and whose existence and reality cannot be denied. The same does not exactly apply to the other two classes of *rules* that remain to be discussed.

§ III There is a third category of *rules* that recognizes no other principle than that of customs and examples; and those who observe these *rules* are not few. While the preceding *rules* are written in this great book of nature, which very few are able to read, these *rules* form the object and the matter of nearly all didactic treatises. In fact, these treatises offer us only the analysis of separated parts of buildings according to each of the orders that enters their aggregate; as well as their inventory of forms, great and small. The outcome of these *rules* is to teach the relative measures of each of these details, following a certain concordance of examples borrowed either from antiquity or from modern times.

As architecture would cease to be one of the fine arts if one were to fix her measures and her harmony of relations in an arithmetical manner, one must regard what is prescribed in these treatises only as a somewhat moderate advice on practice. These treatises, in their domain, are like grammars whose *rules* teach more about what we must refrain from in order to avoid errors than about what must be done to produce beauty.

It is obvious that these sorts of *rules* have no effect save on that section of architecture that one may call technical or methodical. These *rules* are also subject to a double hazard: first, on the part of those who treat architecture solely as a pure trade, but, even more, on the part of those minds that have no patience for any kind of constraint, and who deny theoretical truths because they cannot be subjected to material or mathematical evidence.

§ IV Now we arrive at the last class of *rules* that we termed of *habit* and *prejudice*; and this is where their blind and scrupulously careful respect leads. If indeed architecture has for some time given herself up to the madness of innovation and to all the games of caprice as a consequence of the contempt for rules, and if she often finds herself exposed to the dangers of untried systems, one could, for the most part, attribute this effect to the insipid monotony of these servile minds who know only how to trail behind their predecessors. This servile herd of copyists induces that false independence which attributes to *rules* that which is due only to the faulty manner of interpreting and following them.

Then, some will exclaim, *rules* were made only after masterpieces and, having preceded the *rules*, these masterpieces are now useless.

But there is confusion and misapprehension about the idea that one forms, and the use that one makes here of the word *rule*. It is obvious that one is referring only to those *rules* written or deduced in detail following treatises, that is, *didactic rules*. Yet, did the architects after whom these *rules* were written not act in accordance with the *rules* of a superior order, written in the great book of nature? Were the relationships of accuracy, truth, and harmony the results of intellectual labours and of a genius that imitates the works of nature? Were they not general *rules* before they were particularized into methods whose value is often discredited by the routine mind and by prejudice?

It is therefore uniquely against the written *rules* – based on the works of artists and not that of nature – that the innovating mind who despises the past, addresses its contempt. While acknowledging that he who only knows written *rules*, without tracing the principles from which they are deduced, runs the risk of being naught but a reproducer of the works of others, we contend that the misuse to which these *rules* may be subjected – especially on account of limited study – is no reason to condemn their use. One cannot concede, in fact, that the practical lessons that teach the secrets of the art and the genius of the great masters – thus assuming the authority of their examples – could become useless according to some, and harmful obstacles to the production of masterpieces according to others.

We repeat that under the common name of *rules*, the developments of great principles that regulate genius are confused with grammatical analyses, which are to the science of architecture what scholastic rudiments are to rhetoric and poetry. As we have already stated, these *rules*, which are deduced from the best works, are not useless or harmful, although they can induce in many the habits of routine that dispense with having to search for higher lessons and models. Thus, the misuse that a matter may undergo, is not always a reason to prohibit its application.

However, as the innovators in art and especially in architecture, continue to object, *rules*, whatever they may be, do not produce genius. Undoubtedly, we would answer that if they were to produce it, then genius would only be a matter of *rules*; consequently genius would no longer exist, for there would only be a mechanical procedure, and masterpieces would be made as easily as one draws a straight line.

No, written *rules* do not create genius; but who could deny their usefulness in guiding the artist in the study of the laws of nature, in the observation of relations, of properties, and the qualities from which result the impressions of the beautiful and true. *Rules* do not create genius, because nature alone is capable of that; but could certain *rules* not enlighten the recipient of this gift by guiding him more surely?

No, *rules* do not create genius but there is no work of genius outside these *rules*; since we observe that it is uniquely to men of genius that we owe the examples that constitute written *rules*.

No, *rules* alone do not create masterpieces, but they spare many trials and gropings, they prevent many errors, and protect from the blunders that the imagination may cause one to fall into.

Those *rules* that do not emanate from the great principles of a lofty theory reside within the subordinate realm of simple practice; but they do not fail to be considered as signs that guide the artist through the regions of invention, without however preventing him from proceeding according to his will, or to carve other paths, as long as they attain the goal by a surer and shorter way.

SCULPTURE (*The art of sculpting*) If this art is considered, according to its own theory and its own means of imitating nature, as an art that is independent of architecture, then it seems that it has no place in this Dictionary.

Yet, we included *sculpture* for the same reasons that we included painting, in other words, solely in their relationship with the art of building. Now, I find three principal relationships which are of great importance for the architect.

The first consists in the uses of *sculpture* in architecture; the second, in the value that a well reasoned use of *sculpture* adds to architecture; the third, in the accordance that must exist between the style and the taste of the sculptor, and the style and the taste of the monument where his *sculpture* will figure. We shall limit the discussion in this article to these three points.

On the uses of sculpture in edifices

In searching for the principle that links *sculpture* with architecture within the very nature of things, it suffices to consider the kind of resemblance between these two arts and the materials from which they are made. Works of *sculpture* present themselves to the eye only through the mediation of materials; and architecture acquires consistency only through the materials that she uses, to such a point that if she were to be

reduced to the simple idea of mechanical execution, she would be unable to realize her conceptions save by utilizing most of the procedures and practical means that she shares with the art of sculpting.

Since the art of the sculptor entered the material elaboration of edifices as early as the origins of architecture, it was quite natural that the two arts became intimately associated in the invention of ornaments, in setting forth the character of different expressions, in the multiplication of forms, as well as in composition and the production of effect.

For example, the art of the sculptor became indispensable for the architect to establish this variety that gives each of the orders it proper

Fig. 77. Porte St. Denis, Paris, F. Blondel.
From: A. C. Quatremère de Quincy, *Histoire de la vie et des ouvrages des plus célèbres architectes*, J. Renouard, Paris, 1830

character. Thus, each kind of ordonnance, and the proportions of its constitutive forms, acquired a new virtue still and a more assured influence on the senses and on the mind, as soon as a measure and a choice of ornaments of diverse gradations were found to be in a relationship of harmony with the impressions that derive from their characteristic type. Accordingly, the Doric order, which expresses strength and solidity, did not demand from *sculpture* the elegance and the luxury that suit the other orders. The intervals between triglyphs – the triglyph being a commemorative representation of primitive construction in wood, excluding any other decoration in the frieze – were the only spaces that the sculptor filled; whereas the profiles of the capital and the entablature were left smooth, and there are hardly any exceptions to this rule in antiquity. Contrariwise, the Ionic order owed the elegance of its capital, and the varied details of its frieze, its mutules, its torii without base, and all the mouldings of its entablature to *sculpture*. *Sculpture*, in all the energy of its means, was also utilized to endow the Corinthian order with the highest character of richness. It suffices to mention the Corinthian capital in order to illustrate the intimate relationship between *sculpture* and architecture, and the value that ornament adds to that of proportions.

Further developments in this matter are ineffectual. It is obvious that the art of sculpting is, in reality, a necessary part of architecture, endowing her with the most energetic means of her language by strongly manifesting her ideas, rendering them intelligible and reinforcing their impressions.

But in addition to this necessary use, who could enumerate all the debts that architecture owes to *sculpture*? It suffices to recall that ornament is the least part of the art of *sculpture*, which comprises two major divisions: that of bas-reliefs, and that of statues.

The use of bas-reliefs offers to buildings not only the irreplaceable art of decoration, but also the easiest means to convey their purpose.

Who could enumerate all the contexts and the parts of edifices where the ancients used *sculpture* in its bas-relief form? It may be easier, and certainly shorter, to name the parts that seem to have never received figures in bas-relief. We are speaking, here, of Greek architecture, for it is well known that it was a general practice in Egypt to cover all buildings and all their individual parts with hieroglyphic *sculptures* in bas-relief.

One must recognize that Egyptian *sculptures* in bas-relief were veritable inscriptions, and one must add that such is the function to which this art must naturally confine itself when powerful causes prevent the development of imitation. Still, one observes that the bas-reliefs in Greece – where *sculpture*, even in its early beginnings, did not experience the same obstacles as in Egypt – were initially a kind of writing. Even though the art of imitation progressed, it must be realized

that, while being perfected, sculptural figures never deviated from the system that considered them as conventional signs; as characters of a mode of writing and of marking out ideas and figures on backgrounds that suited the demands of architecture.

In fact the use of *sculpture* in bas-relief never deviated from the sphere of architectural propriety. I shall explain. It is well known that sculptors in modern times executed bas-reliefs as if they were paintings, in other words, independently from any fixed purpose, especially on the exterior of edifices. Hence this picturesque genre that one observes even in works from the fifteenth century, where perspectival views give the impression of distant spaces that visually destroy the appearance of the real background, which is the surface upon which these figures are attached. Ancient *sculpture* never presented this kind of bas-relief; and whether the ancients had a reasoned system, or whether individual sculptors were ignorant of the procedures of linear perspective, no trace of such a bas-relief exists.

I am quite convinced that this was due, in large part, to the general and varied use of *sculpture* in bas-relief in architecture. In fact, the infinite number of objects like vases, tripods, candelabra, altars, funerary cippii, sepulchral urns, etc., from which derives that multitude of ancient bas-reliefs that today are separated from the monuments for which they were destined, must be considered as works of architecture.

This explains the spirit in which ancient architecture conceived *sculpture* in bas-relief. And this seems to us to be the simple common sense use of bas-relief in friezes, around enclosing walls, around vases and on any surface that does not accept the idea of a receding background.

Unless there is a special case where *sculpture* in bas-relief is called upon to replace painting in a given context that is independent of the construction of a monument, the task granted to *sculpture* by the very nature of things must be constantly reduced to a kind of figurative writing; that is to say, that the figures, the acts and the things that it represents must, for its own interest as well as that of architecture, be developed in such a manner that no surface, no member, or any other part of the edifice is altered, nor appear to be so.

As to statuary *sculpture*, its diverse uses and embellishments are known in architecture, whether statues occur at the crowning of buildings, whether they adorn walls, occupy the intervals between columns, or fill the niches for which they were made.

The more accurate knowledge of Greek temples made available to us by travellers, reveals a more frequent use of statues than was earlier thought. I refer to the statues placed in the tympana of pediments. The figures that were displaced from the temple of Minerva at Athens [The Parthenon] and transported to London, reveal that these tympana were occupied, on each side of the temple, by twenty statues that could be isolated, and where the parts that were against the tympanum were as finished as the parts that faced the observer. Such was also the use of statues in the pediments of the temple at Egina. These well known facts gave rise to the assumption that certain series of ancient statues, such as those of the Niobe family, occupied similar spaces. However, this hitherto unknown use of statues in edifices should not exclude that of *sculpture* in bas-relief in pediments. One may even assume that the pronounced projection of statues could occur only because of the depth of the receiving pediment, and this depth was a natural outcome of the considerable projection of the members and the profiles of the Doric order.

On the value that sculpture gives to edifices

When one considers the many ways in which *sculpture* is used in architecture, it is easy to imagine the value that architecture gains from *sculpture* for the pleasure of the eye as well as that of the mind. How many surfaces and spaces that answer many constructional needs would remain insignificant and devoid of effect if *sculpture* and its varied ornaments were not to break their monotony and frigidity. Considering works of *sculpture* from this angle, one is compelled to recognize that even their very absence contributes to

endow buildings with character. If some buildings owe their merit to the luxury and the abundance of ornamental *sculptures*, others owe their effect and their beauty precisely to the total absence of these accessories. Let us imagine a nation where architecture, without the collaboration of *sculpture*, is reduced to the uniformity of materials and to the varieties of forms and proportions; it is not difficult to predict the indifference that such a state of affairs would produce in the minds of most people.

Sculpture contributes varied effects to edifices: it seems to endow them with life; it diversifies them; it creates needs that become pleasures; its objects allow us to better appreciate distances, proportions, scales and measures.

Is it necessary to indicate the extent to which the subjects that the architect demands of the sculptor, within the spaces determined by the architect, contribute to satisfy the mind of the observer, whether by conveying the purpose of the place, or evoking its memories, or awakening in him ideas that join the charm of moral impressions to the pleasure of physical sensations? Does the observer not appreciate this happy effect of moral harmony between all the parts and the whole, that make the useful and the agreeable serve the same goal through the judicious or ingenious choice of historical, poetical or allegorical objects carved by the sculptor's chisel?

If such are the advantages that architecture gains from her union with *sculpture*, then it is clear how important it is for the very value of buildings that the different kinds of ornament that the chisel produces do not become, as is usually the case, a kind of commonplace that means nothing in any place, because it is found everywhere. Doubtless, the architect sometimes needs to fill certain voids, to engage the eye of the observer, to conceal a few irregularities, or to establish certain points of symmetry. There are numerous commonplace objects and inventions that painlessly receive the routine work of the decorator. But the taste displayed by the architect will be evident in the choice of these objects. There are no ornaments from this great repertory – which are often mindlessly repeated – that cannot recover a meaningful value through expressive accessories and new adornments.

On the accordance of style between sculpture and architecture

Despite the value and the advantages that buildings gain from works of *sculpture*, there are some drawbacks, as we have seen, that must be avoided. Misuse always derives from practice; and it is in the nature of every practice that sometimes one loses sight of its purpose. As routine familiarizes the eye with certain objects, the mind grows accustomed to not asking for their meaning. Even the architect often uses signs and images of objects like a man who uses the characters of writing without knowing their meaning. Such misuse will occur especially if the architect ceases to be the organizer of the whole building enterprise in its smallest details, and allows the sculptor the free will to choose the ornament, the style and the manner of objects that are associated with his architecture, be they bas-reliefs or statues. This accordance of style between the two arts is more important than one thinks.

What is known as *style* or *manner* in the arts of design is a quality that can be understood, felt or defined in many ways. But of the different ideas that describe style or manner, the most tangible is that which results from their effect, for it is easily grasped by the eye. According to this idea, style is that which gives works of art a particular physiognomy which is so distinct that there is no mistaking it. Thus, there is no way of confusing ancient *sculpture*, for example, with that of Bernini, nor the statues composed and executed with a simple principle and in postures that are often rectilinear, with those where an ill-regulated desire for variety introduces picturesque effects, contrasting postures, and movements that are out of plumb.

Now, the question is to determine which of these two systems of *sculpture* better suits architecture. But, in admitting statues in its decoration, this art can only offer them a position whose forms are more or less regular and with straight lines in the elevations. Thus, the sole feeling for the accord or the harmony of lines will indicate that if nude or draped statues, with postures and attire that we shall call *à l'antique* (in order to define them with one word), are placed between columns, or in niches, they will produce a better effect than those whose movements, members, and flying draperies will stand in contrast with the neighbouring forms.

The same with decorative statues that surmount ridges or the tops of monuments. Some critics have disapproved of the use of statues in such locations under the pretext that statues ought not occur in places where humans are not supposed to be. This erroneous idea is but one of the numerous modern mistakes regarding the conventions of imitation which is confused with

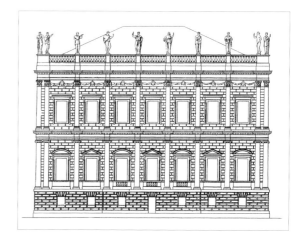

Fig. 78. Whitehall Palace, I. Jones.
From: A.C. Quatremère de Quincy, *Histoire de la vie et des ouvrages des plus célèbres architectes*, J. Renouard, Paris, 1830

illusion whose characteristic is to [mis]take the image for a reality.

It is doubtful that the ancients had ever understood the imitation that is proper to *sculpture* in such a way, where the absence of natural colours is an unsurpassable obstacle to this deception that may be regarded as the aim or the masterpiece of art. But regardless of the sculptor's understanding and the degree to which he intends his imitation to impress the observer's senses, the architect must consider the matter from a different angle. He must never intend to use statues as if they were living beings. For him, statues should only be statues; and *sculpture*, whether in bas-relief or in the round, in its true rapport with architecture, is but a means to adorn buildings, to explain their purpose, and to endow them with new interest.

Nevertheless, it is clear that the two arts act in concert, use common instruments, and, in general, use the same materials. For this reason, it is indispensable that they share a common manner, and a common way of articulating materials. Depending on the scale of edifices, on the order used, on the heavy, rich, or graceful varieties of character, the sculptor's chisel endows his works with varying degrees of freedom and severity, boldness and precision, projection or smoothness; as well as that necessary harmony of character in the ornaments and the *sculptures* that are engaged to the walls. This harmony is no less significant in the execution of statues, although it is of lesser importance for construction.

This theory concerns only the use of statues in the architect's compositions, whether in their role in decoration, or in the role assigned to them by the building's purpose. There are numerous reasons that will prevent these reflections from applying to the choice of statues, for they are surely subject to all sorts of modifications and compromises.

SIMPLE, SIMPLICITY The adjective *simple*, is often used substantively, and one distinguishes between the words *simple* and *compound*.

Simple, or *simplicity*, is an essential quality in all the arts, and one of the most active and tangible principles behind the pleasure that we obtain from them.

Indeed, whether the work of art in question addresses the intelligence, the imagination, the feelings, or any other faculty of our mind, and whether it addresses these faculties through the mediation of one of the senses, these faculties and the senses that serve them demand a facility of conception, figuration and delight.

Thus, our mind requires that ideas and images present themselves in a clear order, and in forms that can be grasped without confusion. Such a state of ideas, forms, lines, and their figures, we call *simplicity*.

Simplicity and unity can easily be confused with regard to their natures and their effects; but they are two distinct notions. When Horace said:

...sit quodvis simplex duntaxat et unum, he probably did not see these words as perfect synonyms, or as redundant expressions of the same notion. Although it is true that the effects of these two qualities are often found together, that the principle of unity that impresses a building is perhaps the result of the spirit of *simplicity*, and that the merit of *simplicity* occurs reciprocally where there is unity, the intellectual analysis, however, assigns a different character to each.

Unity, especially in the arts of imitation, consists in connecting all the parts to the whole, in bringing all the details back to a fixed point, in making each object display a necessary composition from which nothing can be removed without destroying the whole. (See UNITY)

Fig. 79. Palazzo Pandolfini, Florence, R. Sanzio.
From: A.C. Quatremère de Quincy, *Histoire de la vie et des ouvrages des plus célèbres architectes*, J. Renouard, Paris, 1830

It is clear that such a quality must truly be congruent with the effects to be expected from *simplicity*.

Yet, *simplicity*, with respect to the arts of imitation, consists in establishing the most natural order within the elements that compose each object; in organizing its ideas and its images in a manner akin to this economy that nature displays, wherein the principal aim is never obscured by the accessories, and where all the details are hierarchically distributed, thus making the whole shine.

The theoretical developments of these two qualities have such diverse applications that numerous volumes will not exhaust the matter. The same holds true for *simplicity* as for unity. A building must have unity in its first conception; in its plan, its aim, and its means of execution.

The same applies to *simplicity*; and as all the arts are held together by a common point, there is no precept that applies to rhetoric, to poetry, to music, and painting that is foreign to architecture.

The work of the architect comprises three kinds of *simplicity*. The *simplicity* of conception in the general plan; the *simplicity* of general effect which must express the aim of an edifice; and the *simplicity* in the means of execution.

Simplicity must reign above all else in the first conception, or the general plan. By conception and plan, I designate the fundamental idea that rests on the monument's purpose.

Every work of architecture is an assemblage of parts that the architect creates. In this very abstract view, there is, within the domain of the architect's genius, an art of assembling these parts for the benefit of the greatest pleasure. But since architecture fundamentally exists only through and for the needs of society, the architect would fall short of his obligation were he to limit his art and the merits of *simplicity*, in plan and conception, to a design whose regularity, uniformity, and symmetry produce a commendable building, but one that is outside the dictates of reason. Antiquity bequeathed to us many building types which are models of *simplicity* that the architect must always imitate. However, we shall add that the architect should adopt the spirit of this *simplicity* rather than its reality. Modern social customs, more complicated needs, and different institutions have established considerable differences between monuments dedicated to the same use by the ancients and the moderns; their dispositions can no longer admit perfect resemblance.

Accordingly, the Greek temple type is simple in all respects because the open air practice of religious ceremonies did not constrain the architect. But the diversity of climates places many more constraints on the interiors of many monuments. Without a doubt, all these causes added a multiplicity of objects and details to the conception of the plan among the moderns. But *simplicity*, properly understood, and far from its reduction to the lowest mathematical expression, would

shine with further merit and brilliance in the composition of a monument that answers to complicated and numerous demands. A very large number of rooms can be distributed with clarity over a vast expanse of land, and can be connected by a sequence of passages without presenting the image of a labyrinth.

It is nature, or the purpose of an edifice, that inspires the architect with the general idea that must serve as the type for his invention; for there is no monument whose use is not subject to a simple datum that becomes the first regulator of its composition. No matter how diverse and numerous are the details of a building's programme, *simplicity* could always be found, if the architect was able to subordinate all the constitutive parts to a general motif that explains them. This general motif is the same for architecture as it is for poetical compositions. The longest poem of the most varied cantos can also be based on a subject of a *simple* nature and thus admit various developments which never detract from the principal aim, numerous though they may be. Such is the advantage of *simplicity* in the principal conception of a work of art.

The second kind of *simplicity* in a monument is that of its effect. By the word *effect*, I designate the impression that a work of art makes on us. In architecture, this impression derives especially from the elevation, which constitutes the essential part of a monument, in a manner akin to the relationship between the face and the body. Doubtless, there is a natural connection between the plan and the elevation; but their effect is understood by the few. Also, it often happens that a faulty and complicated elevation with over-elaborate details, is built atop a simple and judiciously organized plan.

The *simplicity* of effect, then, requires that the general organization of an elevation be developed with lines having few interruptions. Projections should be built only if based on a tangible need. And in the *simplest* architectural parti, and in the most uniform use of the orders and their accessories, there are always enough details that will prevent a building's effect from falling into monotony. To imagine mixtilinear elevations in order to introduce useless variety, is to transform architecture into a truly infantile game. It is to degrade this art by replacing the idea of the useful and the necessary, which must always be present in order to satisfy reason, with that of caprice and arbitrariness that will transform the edifice into an object of fashion, which is a kind of taste that belongs only to the productions of an ephemeral luxury.

The *simplicity* of effect derives also from the judicious and moderate use of ornament. It is an error in architecture, as in all the other arts, to assume that richness depends on lavishness in matters of ornament. What becomes overly abundant becomes base. An excess of ornament will unfailingly depreciate the value of architecture, and the resulting confusion of this exaggeration will destroy the desired impression for the mind as well as the eye. *Simplicity* is not the principle, but the true means of the art of ornamenting, that is to say, to give value to ornament. If ornament lacks this value, then it has failed to reach its goal. But what is a means that does not produce its effect? All the products of the mind, the poet's inventions, the orator's or the writer's compositions, always and everywhere demonstrate that the abuse of images, and the ceaseless use of figures and ornaments, impoverish the language and cause disgust or indifference towards the richness that is lavished upon it. Now consider the effect of one of these peristyles, these frontispieces of monuments, where a well ordered succession of parts, members, profiles, orders, capitals, and ornamental details are seen against smooth backgrounds, where everything is distributed with an economy that permits the eye to observe with ease, and the mind to grasp the reason with facility, and to embrace the whole and the details and admire the link that unites them. Compare this impression to that of the monuments of India with their variegated compositions of a multitude of denticulated forms, or the frontispieces of these Gothic churches that are overloaded with innumerable sculptures offering no respite for the eye, and where the confusion of details impacts the mind with the same effect as that of a crowd in which no single

individual can be distinguished. In this comparison, one gains a clearer idea of the quality known as *simplicity* of effect in architecture, and the confusion that is its opposite.

The third kind of *simplicity* that characterizes the work of the architect in a fundamental way is that of the means of execution.

What is understood here by means of execution comprises a more encompassing idea than the sole procedures of construction. It is not that *simplicity* in its procedures does not form one of the material elements of the quality of which we speak. Actually, in the first constructions built by a less developed art of building, one observes that a great *simplicity* always reigned in the conceptions, the plans and elevations. Little by little, and with the help of various instruments that permitted more variety in the use of materials, arches came to replace flat arches, volumes were superimposed with more boldness, ceilings and roofs were built higher, and every kind of material was bent to fit the contours of the building's forms.

It is in the nature of man and that of all his inventions, that they never end. Novelty has its limits, but the desire for the new has none, and more novelty is demanded even when it has been depleted. Yet, this is how the bizarre and the extravagant are considered, and one must admit that there is no end to this kind of novelty. The *simple*, like the true, is a unity. The complex is like falsehood, its varieties are infinite. Who could enumerate the varieties of poor taste in architecture, once the corrupt use of the science of construction inculcated its difficulties, its problems, its solutions, its overhangs, its trifles, its tours de force?

I have said enough to convey how a superfluous *simplicity* in the means of execution can constrain or halt the full play of genius in architecture, and how the misuse of diversity in the processes of construction allows capriciousness to enter, thus degrading architecture. *Simplicity* in execution, then, holds a middle point between these two excesses. It does not oppose grandeur, boldness, or propitious moves in plan and in elevation; but it requires that whatever is produced by art, or even science, shows clearly the ways in which the building is constructed, that not only is the building solid, but that it appears so, even to the untrained eye.

Simplicity in execution, or the system of construction, has a double influence. I speak of an intellectual influence, and that of taste. We have already treated, in many an entry, the question of the imitative system of primitive construction in wood that became the type of Greek architecture, and we have shown how of all the models based on local needs and instincts, wood construction (or the hut) gave to architecture this happy mean that unites variety and *simplicity*.

Thus, in the system of construction that emanates from the imitation of which we speak, it is clear that the more the architect remains faithful to the primitive type in his constructional processes, the more *simplicity* the general form of his building will acquire. We have demonstrated elsewhere, that having abandoned this originating principle, architecture found herself devoid of any rule, and fell into the chaos of eccentricities where it was no longer possible to find an end to the deviations from reason, because it was impossible to find a principle.

The superiority of Greek architecture most certainly derives from the nature of her principle which is at once *simple* and varied. It is within this principle, considered as a means of execution, that construction finds the solidity that rests on *simplicity*. It is within this principle that composition is obliged to respect this alliance between necessity and pleasure, which is but the union of reason and taste in the forms that art bestows on edifices.

This principle exerts the same influence on what is known as decoration, or the art of ornamenting architecture. How could the taste for ornament and its inventions be given a limit, how could one put a halt to the caprices and the confusion of all decorative elements, if the constitutive principle of architecture does not intervene as a regulator? *Simplicity*, being an essential quality of what constitutes ornament in architecture, finds, within the *simplicity* of the system of construction or execution, its principle, its rules, and the model for this happy mean beyond which there is luxury, and short of which there is poverty.

SOLIDITY *Solidity* is an essential quality of the art of building, upon which depends the duration of edifices, and which, more than one thinks, forms an important part of their beauty. Moreover, delight, commodity, and richness will soon loose their value without the merit of *solidity*.

It is in the nature of man to admire and search for whatever will make his works durable. Since he has an indomitable feeling within that urges him to prolong the duration of his existence, whether on the physical level, through the means of preserving health and reproduction, or on the intellectual level, through the desire to perpetuate his memory and his name, this feeling can only exert an equal influence upon his manual work. Now, of all the arts, architecture is one

Fig. 80. Palazzo Medici-Ricardi, Michelozzo.
From: A. C. Quatremère de Quincy, *Histoire de la vie et des ouvrages des plus célèbres architectes*, J. Renouard, Paris, 1830

that most aptly satisfies this desire for perpetuity, which is the characteristic of nations as well as individuals.

Ancient peoples have left us some memorable examples of this passion, and of the means used to satisfy it by the art of building. The numerous remains of their edifices, ruined though they may be, testify to the care that they took in insuring their durability by the *solidity* of materials, and the ways of using them. The state of destruction of most of these monuments does not contradict this statement. In fact, all human efforts put together cannot produce anything eternal. The idea of immortality, with regard to the productions of the individual, is but a hyperbole of language. Time is their natural enemy, and everything falls prey to its influence. Add to this, the innumerable causes that accelerate destruction such as natural disasters, wars, revolutions, and the political vicissitudes that change the faces of empires. But far from attributing the state of degradation of the most ancient buildings to their lack of *solidity*, one observes, on the contrary, the most convincing proof that the ancients had perfected this value to a high degree, since all the elements of destruction combined did not succeed in making their buildings disappear.

This value is clearer still in those monuments that owe their preservation to chance or to some particular cause that relates to their purpose. Many of the monuments still existing in Rome, and other places, are nearly two thousand years old, and bear no trace of decay save that of a darkened hue, even though they have not benefited from the slightest care. Yet, in spite of all the accidents that may have damaged them, they are sure to better transmit the lessons of *solidity* to future centuries than modern buildings have been able to transmit to us.

This proclivity towards *solidity* seems to have been on the wane since ancient times. The edifices of the middle ages do not compare with those of the preceding centuries; and if we except some of the edifices built during the first two centuries since the renewal of the arts, where the customs, opinions and taste of particular individuals brought back the luxury of *solidity* to the building of palaces, we cannot predict a long durability to most of the constructions of the present age.

What would the taste of our time be, if one were to examine it from the point of view of opinions and customs that exert such a particular influence on the means from which *solidity* derives? One cannot deny that a well understood *solidity* can at times be economical and at other times expensive, depending on the different aims that a building may have. *Solidity* is economical in buildings that are destined for a long duration, for it renders needless the reparations, remodellings, and modifications that weak constructions necessitate after a small number of years, by delaying as much as possible their need for reconstruction. Therefore, *solidity* economizes for

the future; but, for this reason, it is expensive for the present. Thus, one builds with or without *solidity* depending on the prevalent customs and opinions; and a more or less selfish principle would either limit *solidity* to the pleasure of the moment, or extend the enterprises of the art of building into the future.

The absence of *solidity* that results from the search for economical means, depends also on certain causes such as the lack of materials that nature does not distribute equally everywhere; or this great partition of fortunes among individuals who prescribe to everyone an economy of materials and procedures; or the spirit of commerce or industry that only calculates the income that derives from renting buildings; or systems of government from which derives this kind of apparent equality that is more easily manifest in the exterior and visible economy of buildings.

Now, all these causes, and many others, react equally on the construction of public monuments, because it is very natural that what is known as the public spirit of a people be composed of individual customs and opinions. When the feeling that drives customs is concentrated within personal pleasure, and that of the moment, then, public expenditure, which is solely raised from individual contributions, soon experiences the effects of the computation of interest which places economic considerations above all else. The first consideration on the part of builders is that of expense. Therefore, the first condition that is imposed on the architect is not to build what is best, but rather what is least costly. Yet, grandeur, this principal quality in monuments, cannot occur without costly foundations, or the use of choice materials, or prolonged processes that demand considerable time and a great confluence of means. Thus, the spirit of economy finds it more expedient to opt for projects of lesser dimensions. Hence the reduction of all compositions, and the diminishing of all that guarantees a long life to edifices that perpetuate the glory of a nation.

With these thoughts, we wished only to explain the intellectual value of *solidity* in architecture and its relation to politics.

We exempt ourselves from making technical and material recommendations, and the reader should not expect to find here a treatise on the laws of *solidity*, and is referred to the entries on construction in this dictionary.

In this entry, we shall limit our succinct exposé to the principal and practical elements of *solidity*.

First among these elements is the good quality of foundations. This is where any economy is detrimental. Being the carriers of constructions, foundations themselves must be carried by a stable soil, and one must continue excavations until one finds this quality, or else one must compensate for it by the use of solid platforms or pilings.

Generally speaking, any expense that is added to the foundations is an economy for the future of the edifice, even if it is not visible, and even if it seems to be made for the moment; for it is the principal guarantee for a stability that will spare those future restorations whose expense may equal that of construction.

Given that every edifice is a composite assemblage of parts, the principle of *solidity* compels that the parts be considered individually at first, and then in their composition or in their links.

Individually considered, the parts of an edifice are its materials. It is upon their choice that the *solidity* of construction depends.

This choice has two objects: the first is the kind of materials; the second is their quality. When the nature of physical causes or intellectual considerations permit the architect to choose from all materials, then marble and stone would certainly be the preferred ones; and the choice among stones is usually for ones that offer the most durability. Obviously, it is the quality of stone that allowed the integral remains of three thousand year old edifices to come down to us, which proves that their ruined state has a cause other than the defects of stone.

Brick occupies a second place after stone with respect to the *solidity* of materials. Brick is a kind of artificial stone qualified by a great consistency when it is well made. When it is used with good mortar, it may even form a more compact whole than one could obtain from stone, and it has the advantage of lightness, facility of execution and durability in the construction of arches. Indeed, there are many half destroyed arcades in brick, where the other half has remained suspended in mid air for a considerable number of years without showing the least disintegration.

After brick, comes quarry-stone, those small veneer stones built on solid blocking. The Romans have built some very solid constructions of this kind that Vitruvius described. Wood comes last among the materials that give *solidity* to buildings; not that this material is not used in ordinary houses and in many countries to produce durable works, but as we are treating *solidity* here only in its rapport with the art of architecture, that is to say the edifices that fall in the domain of this art, wood only enters the considerations that usually concern roofs, thus requiring this good choice of material that contributes to the long duration of monuments. (See WOOD)

If *solidity* depends above all else on the choice of materials and their quality, then the second task of the architect is to have the best composition, that is to say the relationship between the parts.

Regarding this last point, the principles of *solidity* can be divided into two classes: the first consists of the simple notions that result from common sense and experience; the second comprises the mathematical knowledge upon which the science of construction is founded.

The art of building comprises two classes of edifices: the first are simple in their plans, their elevations and in their whole; the others are composed of quite varied elements that answer either to more complicated needs or to the most sophisticated taste.

The edifices of the first class have their models in the building enterprises of Egypt and in a considerable number of Greek temples which were built, in general, according to a uniform type that required only straight lines, simple plans, and interiors that do not necessitate vaulting and lateral thrusts. The *solidity* of such monuments was the very result of their simplicity. Common sense taught architects that the effect of durability in their constructions depended on the art of uniting all the parts and all the materials; that this union produced a right equilibrium of forces;

that one member could not operate independently of another, or support itself without offering support to another member; that a force cannot operate without an opposing resistance. The same instinct for *solidity* taught that the fewer the parts of construction, the fewer are the possibilities for disjunction, which is the first agent of destruction. We also observe, in most nations, that the most ancient edifices are constructed with stone blocks of considerable dimensions. Now, simple common sense and experience demonstrate that it is important for the *solidity* of edifices that the quantity of their materials be reduced as much as possible by enlarging their volumes as much as nature permits.

Whereas the above rule applies uniquely to stone construction, it also pertains to walls made of brick or of uncoursed rubble, because the perfection of this procedure requires that buildings constitute an indivisible whole. The same applies to certain kinds of masonry made of volcanic scoriae that resemble sponges, but have the hardness of iron, and offer an infinite number of pores or small holes into which the mortar enters thus incorporating itself into the material.

Thus, one of the great means of *solidity*, irrespective of the nature of the building, is that of the cohesion of materials. The most customary means to achieve this cohesion is the composition of mortar, especially in stone, rubble or brick construction. Tooled ashlar, depending on its hardness, also accepts some mortar in the joints. But the ancients have left us numerous examples of stones linked together by metal cramps, especially in bronze. The ruins of Egypt show the use of wooden tenons between stones, while iron is the preferred metal among the moderns.

The means of the *solidity* that we have discussed pertain especially to a construction considered within a simple system, that is to say without recourse to what is known as *science*. There is no doubt that more complicated uses and requirements, that buildings that satisfy new purposes, and that the orientation of minds and studies towards mathematical sciences, have all introduced into architecture certain compositions whose execution could not take place without the computation of forces, and the knowledge of mechanics and geometric operations that demonstrate the virtue of the different sorts of curves used in vaults. With the help of this science, the moderns were able to erect buildings whose dimensions surpass in boldness all that the ancients had done. The art of building vaults of all kinds offered new compositions to architecture that brought with them the love for the marvellous and the taste for the difficult. One is perhaps permitted to believe that in sacrificing simple ideas and forms in favour of complicated and difficult inventions, architecture has only replaced one kind of grandeur with another, and exchanged the easy delight that results from admiration for the often painful and always less durable feeling of astonishment.

In fact, more than one thinks, it is important for the principle of *solidity*, in its rapport with the sensations that architecture produces, to be clearly evident. Every artifice that disguises this principle goes directly against the spirit of architecture, and against this instinct for reason that compels us to place the useful above all else in the works that are especially based on necessity. Now, as *solidity* is the foremost necessity in edifices, and as the durability upon which it depends is its principal result, we not only require edifices to be solid, but we demand to know it; and in order to know it, most of us want to see it evident so that we can judge on the basis of our own feelings and not solely on the practitioner's guaranty.

What allows judgment with certainty in this matter is the constant observation of the principle which states that *the strong carries the weak*. This is why pyramidal masses have always been admired, for one cannot help but see *solidity* taken to the greatest excess by the very nature of these constructions, since the conditions are such that the *solidity* of the supporting structure augments as the supported weight diminishes. When, in an opposite system of construction such as that of the pendentive, despite the artifice that assures its *solidity*, we observe that the supporting force diminishes as the supported mass increases and this contradiction shocks our senses. This method of building must be used only when it is warranted by a pressing necessity. It is not that our mind does not appreciate and admire the difficult solely because it is difficult. But these tours de force belong especially to periods where the ideas of antiquity were forgotten, and where every sensible theory was unknown. Consequently, the beautiful was confused with the extraordinary, and grandeur with exaggeration, richness with lavishness, and *solidity* with a multitude of artificial means and extraneous reinforcements, buttresses and flying buttresses, which, in exposing the flaws of boldness itself, may momentarily astonish the eye.

STYLE The etymology of this word, whose use in French has deviated from its original meaning, is the Latin word *stylus*, or the Greek word *stylos* . In each of these two languages the word designated either a round body such as a column, or an engraver's point, round like a pencil, sharp on one end and flattened on the other, which was utilized to write on wax-coated sheets. The sharp end served to trace characters on the sheet, while the flat end served to erase. *Style*, as one observes, and as the paintings of many a monument in Herculanum demonstrate, was considered in certain cases to be a pen or a pencil; but sometimes it was also quite a deadly weapon, and ancient history tells of many an example of the use or abuse of the *stylus*, either for defence in case of an attack, or for suicide. Now, this dangerous use is still confirmed by the name *stylet*,[36] given to a kind of dagger which is known in modern times.

Consequently, to arrive with any certainty at the origin of the idea which was once, and still is nowadays, more particularly associated with the word *style*, whether in literature or in the arts of design, it is easy to see, and this certainly does not require long proofs, that the moral notion of this word was, as with many others, a necessary derivation of its material notion. The idea of the mechanical operation of the hand or the instrument that traces signs was applied by metonymy to the operation of the mind, in the art of expressing one's thoughts with the signs of writing. Indeed, in order to render the notions of intelligence more evident, man is always compelled to borrow their expressions from the senses and from material images. Thus, the same word, *style*, meant that which is least material, that is the conception of ideas and the art of developing them according to a certain order; it also signified that which is least intellectual, that is to say, the malleable tool, which by means of graphic signs, gave *colour and form to thought*.

Such a transposition occurs also in our language (and I think in every language as well) with respect to other notions and instruments. Thus, we speak (without leaving the subject of this article) not only of the writer as a calligrapher, but also of the writer as a man of genius, as having a *beautiful pen*, a *pen* that is *bold, brilliant*, and *clever*. The same word *writer*, applied to these two men, shows us, very naturally, how the sharp instrument used to trace letters gave its name to the talent of rendering thought through the use of words and their signs.

The word *style*, then, was and has always continued to be applied to this talent in literature. It is to the works and the dictionaries that treat this vast area of the mind that we shall now refer the reader who wishes to understand all the nuances of this notion, and its consequent borrowing by the arts of design.

However, it is important, in order to properly judge the link that unites the graphic arts with those of rhetoric, to indicate that that which is known as *style* in literature is considered under two principal bearings.

The first designates particularly the form that a writer gives to the ensemble of his ideas, according to the nature of the subject that he is treating, the effects that he wants to produce, and the accord between this means and the goal at which he aims. There is no treatise on oratory or rhetoric that has not enumerated and explained through attributive epithets all sorts of *styles* and their relationship to all the genres of prosaic literatures, whether poetic, historic, philosophic, didactic, etc., or to all the different gifts of reason, of imagination, of the mind, of feelings, of taste and all the other qualities of each writer.

According to the second point of view, the word *style* designates, in a much more general meaning, this typical and characteristic form that some very general causes impress on the productions of the mind, depending on the differences in climate, physical impressions, habits, mores, the actions of governments and political or moral institutions.

In the latter sense, when *style* is applied to the idea of the form that each person gives to the expressions of his thoughts, depending on the property of his particular faculties, depending on the nature of the subjects that he treats, on the various kinds of productions, or the influence of physical, political or moral causes in different countries, *style*, we say, becomes synonymous with *character*, or the proper manner, the distinctive physiognomy that belongs to each work of art, to each author, to each genre, each school, each country, each century, etc.

Thus, one recognizes how the acceptation of the word *style* was naturally suited to literary works, or the art of expressing through rhetoric the ideas or images of things, and how it also entered the vocabulary of the arts of design. Indeed, these arts should be considered as a language and as a manner of writing that employs forms and materials, especially to express in evident form intellectual relations and moral affections, and to produce, by other means, those effects that fall in the province of the imagination, of the intelligence, and of taste.

Without any doubt, it is from literature that the moral use of the word *style* passed into the language of theory in the fine arts. It would be very easy, if such a parallel would not uselessly lengthen this article, to review all the nuances of taste that have provided literary criticism with the multitude of epithets through which all genres of style are distinguished. We would have explained that *style* designations such as *sublime, pompous, energetic, brilliant, moderate, agreeable, light, prosaic, historic, clear, confused, regular, dis--ordered, noble, vulgar, natural, artificial*, etc., apply with the same precision to the arts of design, and are founded on the same principles, based on the same examples, and we would find among all educated people the same accord of views, opinions and feelings.

Thus, in the critique of these arts, the word *style* is used in the same manner and in the same measure to appreciate the different ways of seeing, understanding and sensing the natural objects imitated by artists; to determine the manifold genres of form, composition, proportion and harmony, which must have a rapport with the diverse kinds of subjects that emerge out of each art, according to the rank that each subject occupies within the class of physical beings, or within the creative sphere of poetry and imagination.

This same critique of art, as in the case of literary critique, distinguishes also between notable differences of *style* that natural causes of climate and moral causes of customs or political institutions impress on works of art, and their influence on each artist as well as that of the century in which he lived.

Style, then, with respect to the arts of design, their works, the subjects of these works, and the manifold modifications of the faculties of each artist expresses also a characteristic state that identifies and distinguishes them, in the manner in which nature endows every nation, every country, every individual with a particular physiognomy.

This is how an eye endowed with some enlightenment can distinguish at first sight the art productions of each century, its most brilliant masters, and the distinct practices of each school.

Thus we see the connoisseur of antiquities discern without hesitation between the *style* of the ancient Attic school, the *style* of the new one, the *style* of the Helladic school, the *style* of the school at Sicyon, the school of Egina, the school of Corinth, etc. Thus was the *style* of each period of art clearly manifested. And nowadays still, the knowledge of the artist and the archaeologist enables them to distinguish the great varieties of *style* that separate the productions of distant ages.

In the language of the arts of design, *style* is very often a synonym of *manner*; and in order to distinguish between the two, one could perhaps say that *manner* comprises an idea which is more especially applicable to the execution of a work or to the practical talent of the artist; whereas the word *style* designates rather the use of the moral qualities that determine *manner*, and also the result of general qualities that influence the taste of each century, each country, each school, each genre.

According to this distinction, if one speaks of the works of Raphael, for example, one would say that he had three *manners* rather than three *styles*. It is because his productions are often compared according to a certain technical rapport, which is made evident to the eye by the execution. But if one were to compare the same master according to the ensemble of qualities, which include conception, composition, nobility of forms, characters, and adjustments, with Michelangelo, then one would conclude, I believe, that the latter had a more skilful drawing *manner*, and more bold a *manner*, but that Raphael surpassed him in *style*.

Following this same distinction, if one were to compare the Venetian school to the Roman one, the former, while superior in the *manner* of painting and colouring, yields to the latter when it comes to the nobility and the grandeur of *style*.

This brings me to remark that one never uses the word *style* with respect to colour and the harmony of hues. One says the drawing *style*, the *style* of composition, draperies, etc., and one does not say the *style* of colour, the *style* of harmony, but rather the *manner* of colouring, the *manner* of the chiaro-scuro, etc.

What we have just said of the arts of imitation of a corporeal nature seems to us to equally suit works of architecture. The word *style* in this art, in so far as it indicates the differences of system, of taste and physiognomy, whether between peoples, or between centuries, or artists within the same period, assumes the same acceptations and receives the same distinctions.

Style, in the monuments of the art of building, indicates that which forms the characteristic trait of the local taste of each country; which implies that almost no one should be mistaken as to what it denotes. Thus, the Egyptian *style* is recognizable by the uniformity in massing, the monotony of its details, the simplicity of its lines, and its great pursuit of solidity; whereas the Arab or Gothic *style*, being completely opposed to the Egyptian *style*, has a physiognomy that permits no one to mistake it at first sight.

We shall not deal here with the *style* of Greek architecture, because it is not the object of this article to analyze all the *styles*, but only to analyze the notion, the meaning and the acceptations of the word *style*. We shall therefore simply remark that this word applies to the many varieties that the art of building of the Greeks underwent through the ages. Architects also, distinguish in their monuments and in the variations of their tastes, many a diversity of *style*.

One recognizes the ancient Greek *style* in the forms and the proportions of the Doric order without base.

One recognizes the *style* of the following periods by the very elongation of forms and proportions of the Doric, by the more common use of the more ornamented orders, especially in the preference given to the Corinthian among the Romans, and one must also say, by the use and the excess of opulence, the profusion of decorative resources, and the abandonment of the fundamental types or principles that form the constitution of this art.

Finally, one calls the *style* of the latter period of Greek architecture, or the Graeco-Roman, the one that is distinguished by an ignorance of the reasons that assigned each form its place, each use its form, and each purpose its physiognomy. One recognizes this period by a disordered mixture, caused by the very habit of using the débris of ancient buildings in new ones, from which resulted the confusion of types and the forgetting of any order.

Architects also use the word *style* to designate the issue of taste in the arrangement of all the parts which constitute the whole of architecture. They recognize a *style* of forms and proportions, a *style* of profile and details, a *style* of decoration and ornament.

Thus, of all the arts of design, architecture, while ostensibly having the least in common with what is known as the *art of writing* or literature, has nonetheless adopted the sort of metonymy which once associated the intellectual expression of ideas with the notion of the instrument that was initially only intended to trace their signs. And why should this metaphor not justly apply to architecture, if it is true that this art, in accordance with the spirit which constitutes its genre of imitation, through this or that choice of forms and proportions, renders intelligible to the eye this or that abstract conception, this or that intellectual combination; if it is true that this art, through the diversely modified use of parts, members, details and ornaments, awakens in us resolute ideas and positive judgments of the objects it creates, as do the signs of writing; if it is true that through the modulated harmonies that it produces, it knows how to arouse in us the impressions of all the moral qualities which belong to its imitative domain.

In ending this article, where in showing the origin and the use of the word *style*, we aimed only at demonstrating the appropriateness and the scope of its application to all the arts, it remains to be said that in the arts of design, this word is still used in a vague manner which is not well understood save by the artists who teach, or by the pupils who study; as when it is said of a work that *it has style*, or that *it has no style*, or composition, or that the drapery lacks *style*.

It seems to us that in this expression, where no epithet specifies the genre or the nuance of the *style* of which we speak, this word should be understood as *style* par excellence – like that of sculpture in antiquity, or that of the greatest painters in history – unless this expression could still be interpreted by the one used in other cases, as when a man or a work is said to be without physiognomy, without character, that is to say, as lacking these traits that particularize objects, or individuals, and render them easily recognizable among all the others.

SYMMETRY In EURYTHMY, we referred the reader to the article SYMMETRY in order to give a full account of the notions that seem to us appropriate to elucidate the particular idea of the first of these two words, through a comparison between their actual differences, which fundamentally belong to the nature and the meaning of each notion.

To begin by considering the word *symmetry*, we maintain that it is the same as the Latin *symetria* and the Greek *synmetria* whose composition

suffices to explain its relationship to the works of nature or art, where it signifies *correlative measures*.

This idea, which is clearly expressed in the Greek word, was consequently translated by the Latin people in the language of architecture through the word *proportio*, or proportion, which is now generally accepted in French, not just to express any relationship between the measures of two objects, but rather a system of correlation through which one single part indicates the whole, as the whole indicates the measure of each part. (*See* PROPORTION).

The word *proportion*, having prevailed in French over the word *symmetry*, the latter word, following the customs of ordinary language, came to be limited to signify only a relationship

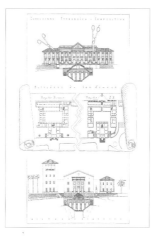

Fig. 81. Belvedere di San Leucio, Léon Krier.
From: Léon Krier, *Architecture, Choice or Fate*,
A. Papadakis Publisher, London, 1998

of exact conformity between two measures, two objects, two buildings, or two coequal masses on both sides of the same building. (*See at the end of this article*, SYMMETRY *understood in the technical meaning of identical correspondence.*).

If the question is, as it is in theory, to consider the parallel between the word *symmetry* and the word *eurythmy*, then we could refer the reader to the word *proportion*, which is the translation and the exact correlation of *symmetry*. Nevertheless, we shall repeat here that its elementary composition, which is the word *syn*, (with), and *metron*, (measure), necessarily indicates, clearly and precisely, the general expression of a measure in relationship to other measures; that is to say, a measure that could serve as a *matrix* to others which seem to derive from it; a property which becomes or can become reciprocal between all the parts of a whole.

Having developed this theory at length in the word *proportion*, we shall not linger further over this obvious explanation, and the applications offered to us by the works of nature and art. We recalled this notion only because it is apt, firstly to enable one to perceive through its proper meaning the unequivocal idea to which it is connected; and, secondly, to establish solely through the difference of words and their composition, the difference that exists between *symmetry* and the word *eurythmy* with which it is usually confused. Nowhere in modern writings does one find an analysis that gives a clear idea of these two words with respect to their relationship to architecture.

Nevertheless, we find in Vitruvius (Bk. I, Ch. 2, and Bk. VI, Ch. 2) a brief development of the use and definition of the word *eurythmia*, but the interpretation that he gives, having been rendered unclear owing to a lack of examples and applications, and having remained vague and abstract, justify one in questioning the simple acceptation of the word; and also in searching first, in the word's composition, for what it cannot signify, and later, for what it seems to express.

This word, through which Vitruvius, as we shall see in the passage quoted below, pretends to explain one of the qualities and the beauties of architecture, being composed of the adverb *ev*, *good* or *beautiful*, and of the substantive *rythmos*, *rhythm*, can only mean *beautiful rhythm* or *beauty of rhythm*. We have given above the etymology of the word *symetria* but to acquire a precise idea of the difference between the two qualities expressed by *symmetry* and *eurythmy*; it seems appropriate to me, to search for their distinction in the words *meter* and *rhythm*.

Now, it is known that *meter* (*metron* in Greek) signifies *measure*, and that *rhythm* (*rythmos* in Greek) signifies *number*.

These two notions appear to correspond. However, it is evident that the word *meter* applies to the appraisement of the dimensions of objects, while the word *rhythm*, which signifies *number*, applies to the measure of quantities and that of time.

Since there are two words, then, that derive from two different elements, it must be within these two varieties of etymology that resides the difference that language applies to each of these ideas.

But let us define *rhythm* more positively, in its special applications in music and poetry. What is rhythm in these two arts? It is a measure of duration in time, that is to say, a measure that fixes the alternation of the slowness or rapidity of movements in an instrument or a voice, in the expression of sounds or words. This is what determines long and brief verses in poetry, or the length and brevity of sounds in music, or the order of their successions and the duration of their intervals.

Thus, we already perceive the difference between rhythm and meter in poetry. Verses can be at once rhythmic and metric, and they can be metric without being rhythmic. They can be at once one or the other; until an order, a principle, a certain convention, regulates the slowness and the rapidity of pronunciation in each syllable of a language, and later determines the measure of the verse by that of the [metric] foot or the syllables which constitute its length.

If such is on the one hand, the nature of rhythm in versification, and on the other, that of meter, then it is evident that the notion of rhythm which regulates the order and the succession of sounds and their intervals, is distinct from that of meter, which only determines the measure of verse, by the [metric] feet that compose it.

As to rhythm in music, one must realize that it derives from a certain order, by virtue of which the musician, according to what he intends to express, accelerates or reduces the duration of sounds, and modifies their inflections by a succession of varied movements.

Now, if architecture's use of the same word teaches us that the idea of rhythm has been borrowed from music, then one must search for the kind of resemblance that could, in theory, reconcile the effects of the forms which address the eye, with some of the effects through which sounds please the ear.

Now, it seems to us that the diverse uses of forms in architecture, the varied combinations of their dimensions and the intervals between their parts, the more or less alternating mixture of their projections, the effects of their repetitions or their contrasts, the smoothness or the roughness of their contours or their lines, and many other impressions induced by simplicity or multiplicity, as well as the very distinct impressions of symmetry (or proportion) are apt to correspond through their influence on the eye, to the varied effects that musical and poetic rhythms produce in the ear.

Is this not what Vitruvius specified as among the properties of architecture, in the article where he defines eurythmy in its relationship with this art? These are his words:

"Eurythmia est uenustas species commodusque in compositionibus membrorum aspectus. Hec efficitur cum membra operis conuenientia sunt altitudinis ad latitudinem, latitudinis ad longitudinem, et ad summam omnia respondent suae symmetriae."

"Eurythmy is beauty and fitness in the adjustments of the members. This is found when the members of a work are of a height suited to their breadth, of a breadth suited to their length, and, in a word, when they all correspond symmetrically."[37]

To explain the difference between eurythmy and symmetry, this is what follows in Vitruvius:

"Item symmetria est ex ipsius operis membris conueniens consensus ex partibusque separatis ad uniuersae figurae specimen ratae partis responsus. Vti in hominis corpore e cubito, pede, palmo, digito ceterisque particulis symmetros est eurythmiae qualitas. sic est in operum perfectionibus. Et primum in aedibus sacris aut e columnarum crassitudinibus aut triglypho, etc.."

"Symmetry is a proper agreement between the members of the work itself, and relation between the different parts and the whole general scheme, in accordance with a certain part selected as standard. Thus in the human body there is a kind of symmetrical harmony between forearm, foot, palm,

finger, and other small parts; and so it is with perfect buildings. In the case of temples, symmetry may be calculated from the thickness of a column, from a triglyph, etc."[38]

Let us first observe that these two articles are consecutive in the Vitruvian text, which is a proof that he did not regard the two words as containing the same notion. Consequently, their definition presents us with very distinct ideas.

In fact, *symetria* or proportion, as explained by Vitruvius, and as the defined by the word itself, finds in nature a precise type, a permanent regulator whose evidence should not be ignored. Such a regulator governs with a reciprocal correspondence every part of an ordonnance with respect to its *whole*, in such a way that the part indicates the measure of the *whole* as the *whole* indicates the measure of each part.

But eurythmy, as Vitruvius and as the word in itself imply, being simply an agreeable relation of measures, spaces and intervals between the parts of a work, does not have in nature a type which can be positively applied to the order which it must follow.

In a word, we say that the compass can judge the accuracy of the relations which constitute *symetria* (or proportion). But as to the accuracy of *rhythmic* relations, the eye, poised in judgment, possesses only taste and the sentiment for beauty; and this is what the word itself indicates, namely, *beauty of number or rhythm.*

Actually, every *rhythm* is not necessarily beautiful. In music, there are good and bad rhythms; that is to say, it is possible to have a good and a faulty use of melody as well as prosody, or long and brief intervals of sounds, and a succession of lively or slow movements from which will result agreeable or disagreeable effects. Similarly, in architecture, certain distributions of lines and spaces, certain divisions of parts and ornaments, certain successions of members or profiles will produce impressions which are more or less agreeable. But, as we saw, Vitruvius proposes neither an example nor a regulative function in this matter. In reality, there is no substitute for the experience of our senses in our knowledge of the effects of the various combinations that we discover in the works of nature and art.

Eurythmy remains therefore in the domain of the theory of taste. But such is not the case with *symmetry* or proportion, considered in its elementary notion. The assimilation of reciprocal relations with respect to the whole and the part in the human body presents a fixed idea, an evident rule of what a work of art can be in order to please us in the same manner as a work of nature. There is no clearer idea or more distinct a notion.

From where then, comes the confusion between the two words? It must be said that it is because the notion of rhythm, an essential and positive notion in music and poetry, is, properly speaking, but a metaphor for architecture; it is because the idea of order, of interval, of the succession of sounds, or the slowness or rapidity of movements for the ear, has been transposed into the idea of order, space, and successive intervals of forms for the eyes, and for the visual faculty.

But this rhythmic effect exists no less in architecture, even if a borrowed word is used to designate it. Taste and feeling will not fail to recognize it.

Is there, in fact, a similar effect in the use of forms, lines, contours, spaces, projections or recesses, ornaments, and all the ancillary details of architecture? Is there, in their continuity or their interruption, in their repetition or their succession, in their more or less periodic return, an array of means capable of procuring for the eyes the variety that they need? Is there, as a result of all these combinations, some kind of varied means, whose effect on the eye is equivalent in its genre to the effect exerted on the ear and the mind by the means proper to poetic and musical rhythm? Well, admittedly, it would be quite natural to transpose to the art of forms the expression proper to the art of sounds. And depending on whether the effect of this transposition succeeded in being agreeable, it would have also been called *beautiful*, or *excellent*. Lastly, through metaphor, architecture received its *eurythmy*; a quality that is clearly very distinct from *symmetry* or proportion.

It is, therefore, *the just correspondence of height, width, and length between all the parts of a building,* *and the architectural execution of the orders,*[39] which, in the words of Vitruvius, formed architectural eurythmy. Here too, as in music and poetry, all the parts, all the details of the execution, could admit a gradation, a more or less agreeable succession to the eyes. Thus, the torii, and the profiles which constitute the divisions of a column base, for example, and those of a capital, of a pediment, or an entablature, have relations of height and width, not only with each other, but also with the large spaces that receive them, and where their more or less successful distribution can exhibit a character of heaviness or lightness, monotony or variety.

Certainly also, eurythmy – understood in a larger scale and over larger spaces, and always consisting, according to Vitruvius, in the most agreeable correspondence of height, width and length – applies in the same way to large scale relations of buildings and their general dispositions; that is to say, to the correlation between the large exterior or interior masses, as well as to the harmony of their measures in height, width and length. One could thus survey all that is included in the compositions of architecture, such as porches, arcades, vaults, niches, and doors; in a word, solids and voids, and one may find that there could be a more or less successful relationship in the measures, distance or proximity between all objects. Hence, one would realize that the more or less successful or agreeable relations between all the parts, considered by themselves or with respect to their whole, could quite naturally be compared to the delight in musical rhythm, considered in the succession of sounds, in the measures of time and the accuracy of movements.

All of this should explain the difference of means and effects between *symmetry* and *eurythmy*. Their very names suffice for this explanation.

Symmetry, as defined by its name alone, as an ensemble of parts through which one part indicates the measure of the whole, and through which the whole reveals the measure of each part, is actually and perhaps exclusively applicable to what one must call the *system* of architecture, understood in the use of different orders of columns, of their proportions, their profiles, and all their ancillary parts.

One must realize, that in borrowing from the forms of poetic and musical language, *eurythmy* does not present us with something as clear, as precise, and that could be submitted to a positive calculation. From here derives the usual confusion between the properties of the one or the other of these two qualities.

But in matters of art theory and taste, no notion exists without having some aspect adjoin that of another notion, or without borrowing something from it. Indeed, there is no quality (as in ethics), no virtue, which even if possessing its proper character, does not more or less partake in the character of another. Thus, force and moderation, wisdom and courage, are quite distinct virtues; however, there is no true force without moderation, nor true moderation without force. It is the same with all the qualities in the arts and, consequently, those that constitute the value of architecture.

The pleasure that results from eurythmy, depends, then, in certain cases, on the properties of the system of *symmetry*. Our eyes and minds are at once captivated by an ensemble of relationships which, although emanating from a different source, do not fail to affect us in a similar manner. Indeed, it seems that one could compare the virtue of eurythmy and *symmetry* in architecture to that of melody and harmony in music. One knows that although these two properties are different by their very nature, they are sometimes drawn together by their effects, to the point that one often confuses them because of the manner in which they are enjoyed and appreciated.

If in this article we have expanded more on the word eurythmy than the word *symmetry*; it is first because, in the article that relates to the latter we found it easier to establish the parallel between the two notions that distinguish them; and second, in the word PROPORTION, which in French is a synonym of *symmetry*, we have treated quite lengthily the meaning and the use of the term. (*See* PROPORTION). It remains for us to treat the word *symmetry*, which we shall consider more briefly as indicating in French a relationship of identical repetition between two objects or two parts of the same work.

SYMMETRY This word has, in French, a common meaning recognized by everyone, the explanation of which is not worth dwelling on. If, however, we devote a few lines to it, it would be to enunciate a few abbreviated reflections on the cause of pleasure which we find in *symmetry* as it is commonly understood.

Therefore, *symmetry* in architecture and her works is often this exact correspondence of similar parts which are repeated on one side and the other of a building or site, either in dimension, in the composition of the masses, or in the entire conformity of details.

If we were to search for the principle of this division of a given whole into two similar and uniform parts, it seems to us that we would find it in this feeling which makes us admire many of the works of nature, and invites us to transpose its imitation to the productions of our arts. It must be stated, indeed, that nature took care of assigning *symmetry*, particularly and without exception, to the exterior organization of living or animated creatures.

From here derives that sort of instinct that induces man to give to every work which he intends to endow with the value of unity, this property upon which depends the most apparent character of unity of plan, of means and ends. If the human body, for example, instead of presenting on each side the identical repetition of the same parts, found itself unequally equipped with members in one fashion on the right and another on the left, would it not seem that there is more than one being inside the same being?

Now, then, it is evident that the same exterior effect should take place in a building where each of its two halves exhibit *unsymmetrical* measures, parts and details. It would no longer appear as a single building, but rather a composite of many.

The identical repetition of the same elements and the principle of *symmetry*, are so inherent to the nature of architecture that the longest colonnade is composed of a single, repeated column. If one were to try, as in the examples found among certain peoples, to diversify the types and the measures of columns, then the building would appear as if composed of fragments from many buildings. The easy pleasure of unity, would be replaced by the painful feeling of disparity.

However, one observes that while nature has fixed an exact *symmetry* in the exterior of bodies, she followed yet another system concerning the parts of their interior organization, which is not revealed naturally on the outside. So it is with architecture. The *symmetry* that we require in the façades of a great number of edifices, like palaces, would become a trifling constraint if the interior is not subjected to the unity of aspect. Many customs and needs would be opposed to an identical repetition which, in many cases, cannot be understood by the eye or the mind.

SYSTEM This word is formed from two Greek terms, the preposition *syn*, and the verb *istemi*, together signifying what is expressed by *ensemble*, and *composition*.

A *system*, no matter the art in question, is an assemblage of many things forming a whole. It is not in the scope of this Dictionary to survey the many applications of this word, nor to enter into the diverse meanings that it comprises, nor to treat the good or faulty use of what is known as the *spirit of system*.

Limiting ourselves here to explaining the meaning in which the word *system* is used in architecture, we maintain that it is ordinarily employed to designate the theory of the original principle from which this art is born, and the primary causes that impressed on it its special character, as well as the conditions needed in order to satisfy the unity of its principle.

What we call *system* in architecture precedes rules. Rules only determine for the artist the best means in which to be faithful to the original types that constitute the *system* of architecture. (*See* ARCHITECTURE)

In order to better explain what we mean by *system* in architecture, we must return to some notions. Although we considered Greek architecture to be the only true art, we did not, however, fail to recognize other ways of building that derived from different causes and original elements among other peoples, in other times and places. We have also demonstrated that having

no factual model to imitate in nature, architecture could in truth only accept certain causes, certain needs given by nature as an alternative; that as these causes and needs varied and differed depending on place and climate, they in turn were endowed by nature with different means of imitation; that from these local causes derived some local *systems* of construction, order, and embellishment; that among these *systems*, there was one more fertile than all the others, more apt to unite different principles of unity and variety, solidity and delight, to offer the fortunate combination of need and pleasure, that is to say, that which could at once satisfy reason, the senses and the imagination; and this is what seemed to us to constitute the superiority of the Greek *system* of architecture over other architectures.

One concludes from this that the idea of *system* is applicable to more than one kind of architecture; and that each architecture can have her own *system*. But it does not follow that every *system* – although inspired by the diverse causes that one might call *physical* or *material* – is equally beautiful, and that there is no preferable one. Nature herself produced edifices or different forms of building in different countries, as she produced different species of animals or plants which are real and immediate productions of her will and her power; but this should not lead one to conclude that being works of nature, these modes or *systems* of building had an equal merit; that there should not be a hierarchy among them; and that intelligence, reason, and taste should be forbidden to recognize the pre-eminence of one over the other. Actions towards all the productions of nature, towards all created beings, can all the more apply to works which are indirect consequences of natural causes.

This is why – having demonstrated in different articles what seemed to us to be the natural causes that exerted a more or less necessary influence on the diverse *systems* of architecture among all known peoples – it seemed to us that the Greek *system* was more of a *system* than all the others; for it is the more complete combination of elements that can form a whole; where every part finds a necessary reason that is subordinated to the dominant reason of the whole; where every part explains its own condition and location; where each detail is at once the consequence and the principle of another detail; and finally, where nothing can be added without it being superfluous, and where nothing can be removed without destroying the whole. Now, this seems to me, to be quite a satisfactory definition of the word *system*.

TASTE Among the diverse acceptations of this word in the practice of the fine arts, the most general is the one that designates it as an instrument of the mind rather than genius.

In this respect, we shall first consider *taste*, defined as a *sense of propriety*. Next, we shall examine it under another of its acceptations, applied to the *manner of seeing and imitating* nature. Finally we shall explain it from a third point of view, as a synonym of *distinctive character*.

§. I *Taste as a sense of propriety.*
There is no doubt that the word which expresses the general idea of *taste* in its application to the products of the mind and imitation – borrowed as it is from the physical senses' property of appreciating the savour of food – signifies, in a moral sense, the faculty of discerning the qualities of objects and works of art.

To appreciate the value and the nature of this faculty in the sense that we are outlining here, one must recognize the qualities of the objects and works, of which taste is the special judge.

Experience and theory teach us that in all things and among all objects of imitation in the fine arts, there are certain light and delicate relations, whose observance does not constitute the essential merit of a certain work, but rather its complementary and accessory value, and adds to the delight that one receives from it.

For example, what in ordinary parlance constitutes a *man of taste* in society, consists in manners with respect to behaviour, in being to the point as to conversation, in wittiness as to charm, and in easy and pleasing forms as to exterior appearance.

Likewise, in all that relates to imitation in the fine arts, and which no analysis can demonstrate, the faculty known as *taste* applies principally to

agreeable qualities, to the choice of a certain way of doing things, or acting in a way understood only by sentiment.

Thus, in design, *taste* does not teach the regularity of forms or their appreciation; but it is *taste* that more often makes or justifies the exceptions to rules, softens their rigour and tempers their severity through a kind of charm.

In a composition, *taste* does not make one discover the great partis of the ordonnance, or those fortunate lines, those imposing masses that capture at once the mind and the eye; but it is *taste* that often blends with these combinations, the charm of easiness from which results the appearance of a spontaneous creation.

In colour and in execution, *taste* is incapable of producing these great effects, this brilliant harmony, this prestige of truth, this boldness in making, which, as everyone knows, belongs to another faculty, another moral region. But the influence of its counsel is no less useful, whether it moderates the play of the imagination, or whether it suggests a fortunate choice of varied resources, or whether it adds to the value of work certain charms that hide the imprint of effort.

Thus, after genius completes its productions, *taste* endows them with charm.

In architecture, the effect of *taste* is no less evident, nor less important. This art, being the one most susceptible to arbitrariness, is perhaps the more in need of the justification of *taste*.

It is *taste* that assigns to each monument the measure and manner that constitute its character; it is *taste* that chooses among the varied nuances of different styles that which is proper to the general expression. It is *taste* in particular that decides on the wealth that architecture has at her disposal, on the distribution of her uses, and the choice of ornaments in rapport with the general purpose of the building, and the effect of each of its parts.

In searching for the influence of *taste* in architecture, and for understanding its effect, one is persuaded that what discloses and manifests its influence everywhere is not difficult to discern; but what constitutes this influence consists neither in the magnitude of the invention, nor in the power of reasoning, the vigour of the execution, or the effect of truth. This influence is rendered evident by virtue of a certain accord with one or the other of these qualities; it regulates their course, and decides and fixes their propriety with respect to each subject and its components. Thus, *taste* is defined with a great deal of correctness, as the *sense of propriety*.

Considered under the preceding definition, *taste* is therefore a necessary quality to the complement or the perfection of other qualities. Although it operates in the realm of things that appear to be less important, it is from its operation or cooperation that results the fullness of the merit and the agreeableness of every work of art. However, one should beware of allowing it too much influence, for its misunderstood purpose can lead to excess; and if is not contained within sound limits, it will manage to spoil that which it was meant to embellish, and end by destroying itself. There are numerous examples of this excess.

§. II *Taste as a manner of seeing and imitating nature*. The word *taste* has a second meaning which is used in the language of art in association with an epithet like *grand, shabby, correct, pure, depraved*, etc. It seems then that *taste* must signify for the artist a *manner of seeing and imitating nature*.

To define here all the ways of seeing from which result all the diversities of *taste*, amounts to repeating the critical notions found in the articles whose words characterize each different way. But we should not omit the most ordinary and common notion, which is the one designated by the words *good* or *bad taste*, and about which there is much disputation. This notion assumes that among all the manners of seeing and imitating nature, there is one recognized as the most preferable. Now, on this point, there have been many disputes in which the familiar proverb, *one does not argue about taste*, has frequently been cited without thinking that this proverb applies only to *physical taste*, about which any argument is ridiculous. On the contrary, it is about the reason for *taste,* understood morally, that disputation is not only natural, but necessary.

In expanding the question of *taste* to all countries, all ages, and consequently to all the diverse

manners of seeing, some held that rules for *taste* were determined by number and scope, while others believed that because of these very diversities, no *taste* was better than another.

We do not intend here to enter the very core of this debate, which is the same as the one between *regular and irregular* taste (*See* IRREGULAR); we shall confine ourselves to demonstrating that the word *taste* admits a very vague interpretation, and that the vagueness of this idea was more responsible than one thinks for the divergence of opinions.

If, according to the meaning that should be given to the words *good taste*, these words indeed signify the best ways of seeing and imitating nature, then there is a contrasting view of *taste* within which reside two questions that one often forgets to take into account. The first point is to ascertain if these nations and people which we include in the comparison of *the manner of seeing and imitating nature* had really seen her, and had ever really considered imitating her; the second and more important point consists in examining if the nations and people of these ages were and are still capable of seeing this nature, of studying her, and consequently of knowing her.

We have demonstrated elsewhere (see IRREGULAR), that in comparing the different *tastes* that prevailed or still prevail in different ages and countries, with the one that we recognize as being the only *good taste*, that one should not be counting votes, anymore than one should be evaluating the merit of every single work in a more limited circle, since the largest number is necessarily that of ignorant people.

Any genre of *taste* which results solely from the mechanism of instinct, or from the irregular influence of local or temporary causes, is not based on the study of nature, and thus cannot be compared with the one we call *good taste*; for, inasmuch as it is certain that the first genre of *taste* in the arts of imitation does not derive from any study, so are we sure that the one termed *good taste* was born in the nation most apt at imitating nature, in the country where its study was favoured by all sorts of circumstances which put the artists in the necessity of probing deeply into the great principles of their model, and thereby profiting from all the results.

As one of the manners of *seeing and imitating nature, taste* can only succeed in answering this question and in becoming the best of these manners by the most perfect knowledge of the principles of this imitation. Now, as these principles are constant and invariable – though frequently misunderstood – it always happens that what is termed *good taste*, reappears and regains its influence as soon as there are sufficiently enlightened times and people who feel the need to return to principles. And, in reappearing, this *taste* reveals itself as always the same, whereas false and *bad taste* will multiply under a hundred different forms; this is so because it lacks a principle, or if it has one, then it does not recognize it.

§. III *Taste as physiognomy or distinctive character*. To complete the explanation of the principal varieties of the word *taste* in its relation to the language of the arts, it must be said that this word is also used in a nearly similar meaning to that of manner and physiognomy, whether it is applied to the centuries or the nations that cultivated or still cultivate the fine arts successfully, or to the artists of diverse schools and their productions.

It is most certainly and uniquely of *manner* and *method*, that one speaks of an *Italian, Florentine, Venitian, French,* or *Flemish taste, etc.* These diversities of manner are but the varieties of the same *taste*; and they are fundamentally, so to speak, dialects of the same language. All schools are unified by a community of principles; but each, having cultivated one part in preference to other parts, distinguishes itself either by its superiority in one genre, or by its inferiority in another.

The word *taste*, inasmuch as it signifies a distinctive character in the works of each master, displays still another nuance of meaning. Properly speaking, one could pretend that there are as many *tastes* as there are artists. *Taste* then will signify individual physiognomy, personal variety, or each person's individual manner.

Thus, one speaks of the *particular taste* of each artist in order to express his inclination towards a certain area of art, and the preference that he gives to one kind of subject over another. This *taste* is sometimes called natural, for it appears to be innate and comes from the proclivity that one seems to have received from nature.

It is clear that all these notions are applicable to architecture as well as the other arts. Indeed, one distinguishes between different styles of architecture by giving them also the name of *taste*. One speaks of the architectural *taste* of the Greeks, the Romans, or the moderns; or the Gothic *taste*, the Egyptian *taste*. This word, then, is sometimes a synonym of principle, sometimes of manner, and sometimes of caprice.

In general, no other art is more easily subject to what is known as *taste*, understood as a manner that derives from personal or local inclinations. Also, the establishment of maxims for *taste* that do not become a game of caprice is one of the difficult tasks of theory.

How could an art that is condemned to lending itself to the variable needs of societies, an art whose true model resides within the intelligence of the moral laws of nature, and whose compositions cannot be measured against a materially evident type, not be exposed to becoming a game for the fantasies of the imagination, or the paradoxes of the spirit of system, and the mobility of the spirit of innovation?

THEORY The idea of *theory*, contrasted to that of practice, implies an intellectual or a spiritual activity which reasons and combines; it is different from the physical or manual activity that shapes and executes, and comprises varied levels of teaching.

In the entry PRACTICE, we proposed that the province of execution, especially in architecture, be divided into two parts: the one called *learned practice*, the other designated *manual practice*.

Here, we believe that in giving the word *theory* its customary meaning, in other words, that which comprises the knowledge of an art that is acquired by study or teaching, we can distinguish between three levels of theoretical study or instruction.

We believe in distinguishing between the *theory* of facts and examples, called *practical theory*; the *theory* of rules and precepts, called *didactic theory*;

and the *theory* of principles or the reasons upon which rules are based, called *metaphysical theory*.

In applying this distinction to architecture, it is clear regarding the first kind of theory, that it is possible, following a narrow instruction, to reproduce what has been already done. One can teach students to follow the inventions and works of predecessors, to adopt the work of such and such a master or such and such a monument as models; to consider as constant objects of imitation the forms, compositions, the decorations of the whole or the details that shape the manner, style and taste of predecessors, without asking for the reasons why one should proceed in such a way. This kind of practical and routinist *theory* has very often reigned in different countries and centuries; and if it has some imitators or continuators of varying success – depending on the merit and the talent of certain great men, or heads of famous schools – many, however, have been the servile copyists who have perpetuated the failings and defects of those that brought them into honour. The routinist *theory* of which we speak, the one that teaches only through facts and examples, is so obvious that it requires no oral lesson to convey it; whilst the influence of a master has often more strength than all the doctrines contained in books and treatises.

Next comes the *theory* of rules and precepts, or *didactic theory*, which instructs through special study or through the lessons of a master or a school, how to discern certain common points in works of art where their authors concurred; it also teaches how to make observations regarding the effects of these works, how to compare them, and consult the examples of the past, as well as that approbation of general opinion that suits most aptly as a guide for individual judgment. This kind of *theory* characterizes a large number of treatises composed by the most skilful architects. Having analyzed all the components of architecture, and made them conform to the authority of examples in numerous parallels, they sought to establish the best relations between forms and the most appropriate proportions for the special character of each kind of ordonnance; the most congruent divisions

conformable to the visual faculty, and the ornamental details agreed upon by the most authoritative artists. From this agreement on works or observations on works, or successive approbations, derived the rules which succeeded even in antiquity to establish architecture and make a system out of her processes. These rules, and the precepts that derived from them, formed the material of all the didactic *theories* of the moderns, and the daily teaching in schools.

Yet, it is easy to perceive that above this *theory*, there must be a higher level of teaching; a critique of a much subtler nature. It is not the one that confers rules, but rather the one that goes back to the sources from which these rules emanate. It is not the one that writes the laws, but rather the one that scrutinizes and penetrates their spirit. It is not the one that derives its principles from particular works, but rather the one that bestows the principles of our very nature on these works; as well as the causes of the impressions that we experience, and the ways through which art touches us, moves and pleases us. This *theory* develops the reasons that serve as a basis for these rules. It recognizes that certain beauties are applicable to all architectures; but far from establishing an equality among them, as some minds would like to believe, this *theory* leads us to recognize that only one of them deserves the name *art*. Satisfying all the needs, and fulfilling all the conditions of utility, this *theory* offers to genius the most numerous resources, because it was the product of a primitive model that united at once the simple and the composite, unity and variety; because it alone appropriated an imitative system which consists, much less than one thinks in the transposition into stone of the forms of carpentry long used in construction, but rather in the assimilation made by fortunate combinations of the laws of proportion, given by the works of nature to the manual works of man.

These three stages of *theory* have been the subject of so many entries in this Dictionary that we cannot reference here all the words where they are treated. We dare flatter ourselves, regarding the last kind of *theory*, that nowhere else can one find developments that are so numerous and so complete.

TREE In the entry Wood, we shall demonstrate – as an undeniable fact warranted by the nature of things, by the imperative requirements of all nascent societies (with very few exceptions), and especially by the extant evidence of all kinds of known architectures that have legibly conserved the proofs – that wood was the material that furnished the first necessary shelters, as well as the large and embellished dwellings of the early ages of an already advanced civilization. Accordingly, we will show that it was not only natural but necessary that this material – which is still used everywhere as an indispensable means of construction, even in stone edifices, having been for a long time the unique material of early dwellings – became either the adumbration, or the type, or the more or less material or more or less fictive model upon which the art of more advanced societies based and regulated the characteristic forms, the elementary combinations, the general proportions, and the disposition of members in stone architecture.

In fact, we encounter everywhere the historical proof of this descendence from Greek architecture. The two verses from Ovid that express the metamorphosis of the house of Philemon and Baucis are the most appropriate epigraph for this theory.

Illa vetus dominis quondam casa parva duobus
Vertitur in templum, furcas subiere columnæ.

Yes, such is the truest expression of the real metamorphosis that architecture underwent; and this is how *trees* became columns.

However, we must understand one another regarding the mode of imitation that occurred between the *tree* and the column. Many writers fell prey to a ridiculous misunderstanding in this regard in failing to account for the degrees that this imitation had to necessarily traverse.

It is agreed that the more or less primitive, early societies, generally found their first shelters and their first materials within forests, and built for themselves huts of varying solidity with the branches of *trees*. One can easily imagine the development that must have taken place. Larger houses demanded more solid materials and higher supports. *Tree* trunks, used in a rough manner and without art, must have supported roofs made out of hewn but non-fashioned branches. This is where the period of tools and sharp instruments begins.

We shall not trace the development of this expansion of buildings resulting from increases in population and industry, which everyone can imagine and assess. But we have said enough about this subject in order to demonstrate that many systematic minds either run rapidly past the intervals of this development or bring together in the most unlikely manner the periods that witnessed only coarse adumbrations of columns with much later periods when the *tree* was converted into a column; and better still, when the column of fashioned wood was substituted for the *tree*. Furthermore, it was only after a certain time had elapsed that the stone column, having to replace the wooden column, became its perfected imitation.

It is evident, then, that if the column passes for an imitation of the *tree*, and for having at least recalled the idea – especially in the diminution of its shaft, as Vitruvius observes – this purely analogical imitation has nearly no material element left in it. Having understood what was originally its principle, one must recognize that what is left of this principle, in the stone column fashioned by the art of architecture, is no longer but a resemblance in the third or fourth degree.

TUSCAN We cannot precisely estimate the degree to which the ancients had developed what we call a systematic theory in architecture. The only ancient book on architecture that survived is that of Vitruvius, who composed it during the time of Augustus. As to the Greeks, we have no knowledge of their writings save their mention in the preface of the seventh book of Vitruvius. There he tells us that he drew the principal ideas of his book from their writings, and endeavoured to give them a coherent whole. The list of writers he cites is numerous, and is divided into two classes: those who are renowned, and those less famous.

Most of the works of the first class dealt with some famous monument. Some works treated proportions in general, while other works treated the proportions of a particular order. Silenus wrote a treatise on Doric proportions, *De symetriis doricum*. Theodorus wrote on the Doric temple at Samos; Chersiphron and Metagenes on the Ionic temple of Diana at Ephesus, and that of Minerva at Priene, which is also Ionic; Ictinus and Carpion on the Doric temple of the citadel of Athens; Theodorus on the round building at Delphi; Philo on the proportions of temples, and on the arsenal of Piraeus; Hermogenes on the Ionic temple of Diana at Magnesia, and the pseudo-dipteral temple of Bacchus at Teos; Arcesius on Corinthian proportions, and on the Ionic temple of Aesculapius at Tralles.

The more numerous writers of the second class wrote treatises on proportions and mechanics. I omit their names.

I extracted this enumeration of Greek writers from Vitruvius only in order to differentiate their treatises from those of famous architects of modern times, and to deduce some probable consequences regarding the modern theory of the five orders. It seems that no ancient writer treated the orders in a systematic manner. One of them wrote on Corinthian proportions, *De symetriis Corinthiis*, while others who chose an Ionic monument wrote on the rules of proportion of this order. It is not known whether treatises on proportion in general (*praecepta symetriarum*) enlarged on the subject, or whether they were simply limited to establishing the proportions of the orders. In any case, the extracts from Vitruvius demonstrate that the Greeks knew only three orders.

Vitruvius's treatise, which was composed from the works of his predecessors, must have also borrowed their spirit and their method. We see no evidence that he discussed more than three orders. Although the proportions that he assigned to each order did not form part of a coherent theory, since he developed the subject in different chapters and under different headings, he still gathered material, under the same title, regarding the invention and the diversity of kinds of columns, which he limited to Doric, Ionic and Corinthian. It is only after having described the origin of the Corinthian capital

(Bk. IV, Ch. I) that he mentioned the different kinds of capitals, with different names, that could be placed on the column; but it cannot be inferred whether these were new kinds of columns.

Nothing better explains that a difference in the composition and the ornaments of the Corinthian capital does not constitute a distinct order. And yet, based on remaining fragments of some Corinthian capitals, which were composed differently from that of Callimachus, some modern authors imagined that there was a fifth order known under the name *composite*. We have already refuted this error in another entry (*See* COMPOSITE); and we only repeat it here in order to draw a similar conclusion with respect to the so-called *Tuscan* order.

However, the moderns felt well authorized since they cited the authority of Vitruvius and even that of monuments. We propose to confront this double authority.

In the article on Etruscan architecture, we expanded on the subject of the origin and the system of the art of building among the Tuscans. We showed with a considerable degree of evidence based on historical facts and monuments, that all the arts of the Etruscans, as well as their mythology, their institutions, their language and their writing, were in perfect correspondence with those of the Greeks. It was apparent that some very ancient communications existed between the two regions, and that one could not but recognize the greatest similarity between the Etruscan system of construction in wood and the one that served as a model for the Greek. Therefore, one question remained: did the Greeks borrow from the Etruscans or did the Etruscans borrow from the Greeks their common system of building? We shall not repeat here the reasons that compel us to believe that the true origin of this system was in Greece.

In the article ORDER, we developed the theory of order at length and we demonstrated that one does not make a new order by adding, changing, or omitting one of the three principal parts that constitute its essence. As we are only repeating these reflections, we shall recall that what is known as the *Tuscan order* is naught but the Doric order divested of triglyphs and with an added base, according to Vitruvius's detailed description of the column in the *Tuscan* temple that existed in Rome during his time.

In fact, it is good to note that the use of wood in the construction of temples – which, as we have said many a time, was the origin of architecture in stone – may have never ceased in Greece, and spread not only to Etruria but also to Rome until the reign of Augustus. We have the example of the temple of Capitoline Jupiter that was burned under Vitellus. Tacitus, in describing the cause of the fire (*Hist.*, Bk. III, Ch. LXXI), tells of the fire having reached the roofs of houses that came up to the level of the temple's ground floor, thus attaining the old wooden structure, which

Fig. 82. Tuscan Temple.
From: Josef Durm, *Die Baukunst der Grieschen*,
A. Kröner Verlag, Stuttgart, 1905

he called *acquilas*, that supported the ridge-piece. Now, regardless of how one translates the word *acquilas*, whether it is the word *pediment* that corresponds to the Greek word *aetoi*, or whether it designates the *eagles* that were sculpted at the ends of rafters and supported the *fastigium*, it is certain that wood formed part of the composition of not only the roof, but also parts of the pediment as well as the entablature.

But the description of the *Tuscan* temple by Vitruvius tells us that, during his time, temples in the Etruscan manner were built of wood and masonry. Now, it is in describing this temple that he discusses the column, the proportions and the details. Pliny, in a very short article (Bk. XXXVI, Ch. XXIII), copied Vitruvius, and summarized this

architect's disparate notions in two lines, in which he tells us there were four kinds of columns: *genera earum quatuor*; that Doric columns were six diameters in height, and that the Ionic and Corinthian were nine, while the *Tuscan* were seven. *Quae sextam partem altitudinis in crassitudine ima habent doricae vocantur, quae nonam ionicae, quae septinam tuscanicae. Corinthiis eadem ratio quae ionicis.*

Such are, in fact, the proportions that Vitruvius gave to his four kinds of columns.

Based on this information, modern architects included the *Tuscan* column among the architectural orders. More than any system, it was the very nature of things that gave rise in Greece to what the moderns designated by the name of *order*. Vitruvius conceived of a scheme, following some sort of speculative theory, according to which the Doric order derived analogically from the body of a man, and the Ionic from that of a woman. These were simple witticisms and allusions that were based on some vague comparisons between objects that have nothing in common. It seems much simpler to look for the varieties of character, forms and proportion not only in each kind of column (because the column by itself does not constitute the order), but also in each mode of architecture that an order expresses within the natural demands of this art, thus manifesting the principal qualities within its domain through the accordance of lines, forms and materials, relations and proportions, as well as ornaments. Thus, the idea of solidity and consequently simplicity, and the ideas of elegance and also richness, formed two opposing characters, in between which was naturally a middle point. Here, as in all matters, there are two limits and a middle point. Such is the simple origin of the Greek orders. We have already remarked that to build in a more solid and more simple manner than the Doric would be to produce the heavy or the poor; and to build in a more elegant and rich manner than the Corinthian would be to produce the thin and the laden.

However, this is what the moderns did by adding to the richness of the Corinthian with the so-called Composite, and to the severity of the Doric with the so-called *Tuscan*.

Having misunderstood the passage from Vitruvius in its true sense, that is to say, as uniquely concerning the *Tuscan* temple and not a system for the orders, the first modern architects who wrote about architecture felt authorized in their treatises to produce an order that in reality was only a modification of the Greek Doric.

But they were also induced by a certain number of Roman monuments that are still preserved today, where many half-columns of taller proportions than the Doric are found in arcades and porches, without offering the slightest characteristic details of this order in their entablatures. It is well known that the Doric order underwent some substantial changes in Rome, especially in its proportions which were considerably elongated to attain more than eight diameters. Therefore, it seems quite probable that the Doric accommodated various changes in the use and the economy of its frieze, once it was engaged to piers. Thus, what is considered to be *Tuscan* is actually a distorted Doric.

We shall not comment here about the rules that modern treatises established regarding their so-called *Tuscan* order. All were based on a progressive system of height in what they called the five orders. Now, whilst the column of the *Tuscan* temple according to Vitruvius had seven diameters and the Doric six, modern architects, in their wish to follow the new system that places the *Tuscan* on the last step of their proportional scale, gave it six diameters. This system of progressive augmentations has the Composite as its highest point. Now it is obvious that despite its concordance, this system has no authority either in Vitruvius or in Roman monuments.

The question remains to know if today's *Tuscan* was that of the past. But what is out of the question is that the Greeks never knew more than three orders, and that the so-called *Tuscan*, like the so-called Composite are but parasitic, and as such useless and flawed orders, that good taste in architecture will repel, if simple reason will not repudiate them first.

TYPE *Type* derives from the Greek word *typos*, a word which according to general acceptance, and consequently applicable to many nuances or varieties of the same idea, expresses what is understood by *model, matrix, impression, mould, figure in relief* or in *bas-relief*.

There is no doubt that the Greek writers often expressed through the words *epi typon*, what we designate as *bas-reliefs* of varying projections.

It is within these compound words that the word *typos* expresses certain varieties of sculpture. Thus, the word *entypos* must have designated the idea of hollowing [sunk carving] as applied to figures, either in moulded or cast works, or thrust in a hole in the earth, or formed in a bronze or plaster mould. It may have also been reduced to denote stone carved figures for stamps etc. The word *ectypos* seems to designate a production made from a hollow mould, from which one extracts the sample which has been impressed. The word *prostypos* clearly signifies the figure which stands out against a flat background, or what is known as raised relief [*alto-rilievo*.]. But since many different variations entered the use of these words – because of the ignorance of the particular character of each kind of work, which was common in the days of old as well as nowadays – who could say that, notwithstanding the composition of these words, many a writer could not have used the one for the other, especially in descriptions made after other descriptions.

Moreover, one can affirm that wherever Pausanias has used the word *typos* regarding sculpture, whether he indicates materials – for example when he says that a sculpture is of white marble – or whether he uses the word to designate works of sculpture in metal, he always designates by this appellation those works that we call *bas-reliefs*.

The use of the word *type* in French is less often technical and more often metaphorical. This is not to say that it is not applied to some mechanical arts; witness the word *typography*. It is also used as a synonym of the word model, although there is between them a difference which is easy to understand. The word *type* presents less the image of a thing to copy or imitate completely, than the idea of an element which must itself serve as a rule for the model. Thus, one will not say – or at least it would be wrong to say – that a statue, a composition of a finished painting [*rendu*], has served as a *type* for the copy that was made of it; but rather that one fragment, one esquisse, one thought of a master, one more or less vague description, gave birth to a work of art within an artist's imagination, whose *type* was supplied by such and such an idea, such and such a motif, or such and such an intention. The model, understood in the sense of practical execution, is an object that should be repeated as it is; contrariwise, the *type* is an object after which each artist can conceive works that bear no resemblance to each other. All is precise and given when it comes to the model, while all is more or less vague when it comes to the *type*. Concomitantly, we see that there is nothing in the imitation of *types* that sensibility and the mind cannot recognize, and nothing that cannot be contested by prejudice and ignorance. This is what happened for example in architecture.

In every country, the orderly art of building was born from a pre-existing seed. Everything must have an antecedent; nothing whatsoever comes from nothing, and this cannot but apply to all human inventions. We observe also how all inventions, in spite of subsequent changes, have conserved their elementary principle in a manner that is always visible, and always evident to feeling and reason. This elementary principle is like a sort of nucleus around which are assembled, and with which are consequently coordinated, all the developments and the variations of form to which the object was susceptible. Thus did a thousand things of all sorts reach us; and in order to understand their reasons, one of the principal occupations of science and philosophy is to search for their origin and primitive cause. This is what ought to be called *type* in architecture as in every other area of human invention and institution.

There is more than one path that leads back to the original principle and to the formative *type* in the architecture of different countries. The main paths are evident in the nature of every region, in historical notions, and in the very monuments of a developed art. Thus, in going back to the origins of societies which had a beginning of civilization, one sees the art of building emerging from causes and with means which are sufficiently uniform everywhere. Cut stone never formed part of early buildings; and everywhere we observe, except in Egypt and India, wood lending itself with much more appropriateness to the modest needs of men or families gathered under the same roof. The slightest knowledge of the narratives of travellers to these countries inhabited by primitives renders this fact incontestable. Thus, once that kind of combination, to which the use of wood is susceptible, is adopted in each country, and – depending on the demands of construction – becomes a *type* that is perpetuated by custom, perfected by taste, and accredited by immemorial usage, it ultimately passes into enterprises in stone. Such is the antecedent that – in many articles of this Dictionary – we named as the *type* for more than one kind of architecture; as the principle after which an art that is perfected in its rules and in its practices, was modelled.

Nevertheless, this theory, which is based on the nature of things, on historical notions, on the most ancient opinions, on the most constant facts and on the most evident testimony of every architecture has often had two adversaries.

Given that architecture cannot be, nor can she render the image of any of the creations of physical or material nature, some could conceive of no kind of imitation other than that which relates to palpable objects, and pretended that in this art, everything is, and must be submitted, to caprice or chance. Imagining no other imitation than the one whose model is obvious to the eye, they fail to recognize all the degrees of moral imitation; that is, the imitation by analogy, by intellectual relationships, by application of principles, by the appropriation of manners, combinations, reasons, systems, etc. Hence, they deny everything that is based on metaphorical imitation in architecture, and they deny it because this imitation is not materially necessary. They confuse the idea of *type* (the originating reason of a thing), which cannot command nor furnish the motif or the means of an exact similitude, with the idea of model (the complete thing), which compels a formal resemblance. Since the *type* is not susceptible to that precision which is demonstrable by measures, they reject it as chimerical speculation. Thus, in abandoning architecture, without a regulating guide, to the vagueness of all the fantasies to which her forms and lines are susceptible, they reduce her to a game whose conditions are dictated by every individual. This resulted in the most complete anarchy in the ensemble and the details of all compositions.

There are other adversaries whose shortsightedness and limited mind can understand only that which is positive in the realm of imitation. They admit the idea of *type*, but they admit it only under the form and with the obligatory condition of the imperious model. They recognize that a

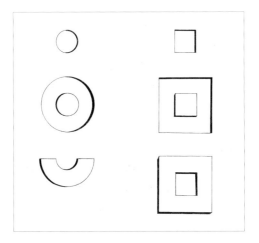

Fig. 83. Types, based on diagrams by Carroll William Westfall. From: R. Van-Pelt and C.W. Westfall, *Architectural Principles in the Age of Historicism*, Yale University Press, New Haven, 1991

system of wood construction, in a tradition of constantly ameliorated and modified assimilations, must have finally been transposed into stone construction. They observe how stone construction conserved this tradition's principal motifs, thereby saving architecture from the eccentricities of chance and fantasy by leading the mind back to the origin of things in order to delight it with a semblance of imitation; but from this they conclude that it is not permitted to deviate from any of the details of the model which they want to endow with an inflexible reality. According to them, columns must continue to look like trees, and capitals like the branches of a tree. The pediment's tympanum should be eliminated; and all the parts of the roofing must be

servilely copied in the gable. They admit no convention between wood construction and its translation into stone.

Thus, in confounding the idea of *type*, the imaginative model, with the material idea of a positive model, which will deprive the *type* of all its value, two adversaries, by two opposing routes, agree on distorting the whole of architecture; the first by emptying it absolutely of any imitative system and freeing it from any rule, from any constraint; the other by chaining and repressing this art within the bonds of an imitative servility that would destroy both the feeling and the spirit of imitation.

We have undertaken this discussion in order to better explain the value of the word *type* in its metaphorical use within a variety of works, and the error of those who either fail to recognize it because it is not a model, or misinterpret it by imposing on it the rigour of a model that carries with it the meaning of an identical copy.

The word type is also used in architecture to designate certain general forms which are characteristic of the building that receives them. This application fits perfectly with the intention and the spirit of the preceding theory. Moreover, one may also cite many uses belonging to certain mechanical arts that may serve as examples. No one is unaware that a multitude of pieces of furniture, tools, seats, and clothes have their necessary *type* in their uses and the natural customs for which they are intended. Each of these objects finds its very *type* – and not its model – within the demands of necessity and within nature. In spite of what the peculiarly industrial mind tries to innovate in these objects, opposing even the simplest instinct, who does not prefer in a vase the circular form to the polygonal? Who does not think that the form of a man's back ought to be the *type* of a chair's back, or that the rounded form should not be the only reasonable *type* for a hair arrangement?

The same is true of a great number of buildings in architecture. One cannot deny that many owed their constantly characteristic form to the primitive *type* that them gave birth. We have proven this point regarding tombs and sepulchres under the entries PYRAMID and TUMULUS. We also refer the reader to the article CHARACTER.

UNIFORMITY The very composition of the word *uniform* or *uniformity*, comprises its fundamental meaning. This word indicates that each object, or each building, presents either the same form in its ensemble, or repeats a single and same manner in the details of its individual parts.

Even though – in a very similar composition in Greek – *monotony* expresses with respect to sound an idea that is entirely analogous to the one expressed by *uniformity* in forms, there is a considerable difference in their meanings. Most words are ordinarily formed and composed from a simple idea. These words are subsequently used, when there is a lack of other words, to express ideas or the modifications of ideas that no longer bear an exact relationship with their original sense.

Such is the reason for the different modifications of the words *uniformity* and *monotony* in the language and in the mind of their users. Furthermore, the word *monotony*, whether it is applied to the art of sounds, or whether it is metaphorically transposed to the other arts, expresses nothing but a defect, a disagreeable effect. But the same does not apply to the word *uniformity*, or to its use in many circumstances, or to the idea assigned to it by custom in many situations.

No one is unaware that in many a situation this word expresses the idea of praise. In this sense, regarding people's behaviour, one speaks of the *uniformity* between their conduct and actions, and their doctrines and principles. Similarly, in a material sense and in the physical order of things, one praises the *uniformity* of a plan, the disposition of a garden, a square, or a façade. For, in this case, the idea of *uniformity* partakes in the idea of unity, which is always highly considered, and is a principal quality in all works of art. (*See* UNITY) But since unity does not exclude variety; and since it is, on the contrary, a complete quality, and is completely praiseworthy only because of the temperateness that makes all its value, then the same applies to *uniformity*. *Uniformity* ceases to be agreeable and loses some of its value as soon as the mind or the eye realize that what should be a necessary link between the whole and its parts – an indispensable condition for a building's structure, a result of the need to see without confusion – has degenerated into a sameness that removes even the desire to look. Then the mind and the eye will be affected only by the painful feeling of a repetition that is either useless or excessive. In such a way, *uniformity* becomes a defect.

Uniformity is praiseworthy when it is a rapport of equality between parts that need to be so disposed in order to produce the effect of a whole; but when it is a purposeless repetition of the same forms, the same parts, and where the same motif is repeated endlessly, it produces boredom, and thus becomes a defect.

If a writer, for example, uses the same sentence structure in his style, the same form of discourse, or the same words; if this repetition evinces the need to fix the attention; if this return to the same means purports to produce a more profound impression, then, *uniformity* in these cases is not only admissible, but is also beauty. It becomes a flaw when it is the evident result of the author's sterility or lack of ideas and poverty of resources.

Similarly, in architecture, there is a certain *uniformity* that is particular to this art, which employs but a small number of characters in its compositions, such as columns, capitals, and other members whose repetition is fundamentally necessary. But if they were to be used differently in every building or part of a building which itself forms a whole, then the architect will no longer be producing the idea of unity and variety, but that of multiplicity; no longer variety, but mixture. Still, in certain cases, *uniformity* is not only a pleasure, it is a need.

But should this entail that in other applications where interior diversity is a necessity – like the interior disposition of a vast palace for example – the art of architecture is supposed to have a single design for each separate volume, and a single order for each detached part? No, without a doubt. There will be parts in these buildings that face each other like the façades of a large interior court, thus requiring a rapport of general symmetry, and the *uniformity* of the same lines that compose their masses. However, many a variety could occur in the details of an otherwise *uniform* ensemble. All the more reason for the architect to be free not to observe *uniformity* in the separate courts of the same palace, or in the parts of a large volume that are not brought together within the same perspective.

In this regard, it is even permitted to say that the inviolable observance of the most complete *uniformity*, applied to this last case – even if it proceeds from a good principle, and even if the architect is not reproacheable – is, however, capable of producing an impression that teaches us that (in matters of taste) there can be some excess even in the good, and that on this point, taste can also exercise a similar judgment.

To illustrate this I would like to give the example of the great and magnificent palace of the king of Naples, built at Caserta by Vanvitelli. Of all known palaces (we speak of the greatest ones) there is no palace that approaches that of Caserta or could be compared to it in size, the unity of plan, and the symmetry of all the façades; as well as the *uniformity* of ordnnance, of aspect, of ensemble, of parts and details. This *uniformity* produces the most perfect resemblance between each of the four great interior courts that divide the ingenious plan in the form of a cross, as if they were independent of each other. Anyone who traverses this vast plan, on the ground floor, will not experience the disagreeable sense that results from an identical similarity, or that useless repetition that is as tiresome for the eye as for the mind. However, although a scrupulous observer of *uniformity*, Vanvitelli permitted himself to embellish the principal façade of his palace which faces the gardens with columns and pilasters, while the other façades were deprived of this decoration; and, most certainly, no one finds here a defect of *uniformity*.

The architect is free to depart from *uniformity* in the interior distribution of all the rooms that compose the ensemble of a large palace. He will not restrict himself to rendering a similar plan for all of them. On the contrary, he will take pleasure in producing a diversity of lines and forms, that will delight the eye of the observer. A large apartment will offer a succession of chambers, halls, small rooms, and galleries, where, without affectation, all the varieties of dimensions and forms will be found, and where circular forms follow quadrangular and polygonal ones.

The same applies to the elevations of all the interior divisions. Certainly, nothing is more tedious in each of these parts than the continual repetition of the same order, the same profiles, the same motifs of decoration.

In the exterior of a large number of buildings, the architect will take equal care in accommodating the principal correlations of similitude, symmetry and regularity required by *uniformity*, with the use of details that diversify the building's

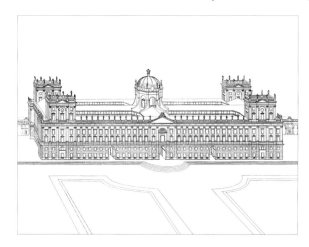

Fig. 84. Caserta Palace, L. Vanvitelli.
From: A. C. Quatremère de Quincy, *Histoire de la vie et des ouvrages des plus célèbres architectes*, J. Renouard, Paris, 1830

appearance without altering the principle of unity. It would be ridiculous if the windows of a palace were not organized on a parallel line, and did not display equal intervals, or did not follow a similar kind of ornamentation. However, in the most beautiful buildings of the greatest masters, one observes with delight that the windows of the same floor – and whose casings are of equal form and proportion – are alternately crowned either with triangular or with segmental pediments.

The exterior of a building often comprises the application of several orders of columns or pilasters, superimposed the ones on top of the others. These façades show that the architect took pleasure in repeating the same orders in the decoration of different floors. This, without a doubt, is *uniformity*. But, as no necessity, no apparent need justified this repetition, the observer will not be grateful to the architect for a repetition that exhibits three times the same thing in one elevation, which, in bringing together the three orders, could have allowed the observer to experience the pleasure of comparing three different impressions made available by the varieties of proportion, style and detail.

Generally speaking, we do not ascertain enough the reasons for the pleasure that architecture especially brings to us. This art is a composite array of correlations; and its genius resides in finding and determining the most agreeable correlations to draw pleasure out of the very necessity to which it is subject. Failing to recognize necessity as the first principle of pleasure in architecture amounts to failing to recognize the essence of this art. Hence the double mistake on the part of those who exercise it, and those who judge it. If in the system of the art of building need was made to predominate over pleasure, it may go as far as destroying any impression and any sentiment of pleasure. From an alleged unity, understood in a very material sense, the building will fall into *uniformity*, and necessarily into its excesses, that is to say: *sameness* and *monotony*. In wishing everything to be based on reasoning, one can go as far as banishing reason itself; for it is truly irrational to pretend that architecture no longer has varied correlations, or a diversity of proportion, forms, and ornaments; and that the eye as well as the mind have nothing to cling to, nothing to compare, nothing to imagine. If, on the other hand, pleasure in variety is given too much authority over the reason for necessity, then architecture – having become independent of any rule and any convention – will fall into the unlimited fields of caprice and disorder. When the excess of *uniformity* deprives our eye and our mind of the pleasure of comparing, because sameness destroyed all matter for comparison, it so happens, as a result of the contrary excess of disorder, that the eye and the mind will find themselves unable to appraise these relations that derive from chance and which present but the image of confusion, or that of a game without rules.

Consequently, what is known as *uniformity* in architecture (this art which is by nature subject to *uniformity* more than any other art) becomes a merit or a defect, depending on the application to particular parts, and on the measure brought to them by reason and taste; and finally, if *uniformity* partakes to a certain extent in unity, with which it should not be confused, perhaps it is so only because it is tempered by variety, without which *unity* itself would cease to be the foremost among all the qualities in the fine arts.

UNITY This quality is foremost in all works of art; that is to say, it is the foundation of all the others, for it is the most necessary. It is the most necessary only because its principle and its effects result essentially from the nature of our being and depend on our faculties; in other words, on the means that we possess to conceive the ideas behind objects, to receive and remember their images, and judge their impressions.

Unity is the principal condition of every work of art only because its principle resides in the very unity of our *mind.*

Now, this *unity* of our mind is one of those truths in fact as well as theory, of which we find within us the easiest demonstration. It reveals and manifests itself at any instant by that *unity* of action whose most simple correlations are clearly evident to our senses.

Thus, each of our senses, for example, tells us that it cannot equally receive simultaneous impressions from many objects at once. In fact, everyone knows from personal experience that no two of our senses can be *actively* employed at the same time, and that no one sense can be *strongly* affected by more than one sensation at the same moment. We say *actively* and *strongly* because, in truth, each of our senses is endowed with an active faculty and a passive one; and it is through the effect of this double property that we are able to see conjointly two separate objects. But there is a great difference in vision for each of them. There is intuition for only one of the two. I can look at only one of them at a time. I can hear many songs, many conversations simultaneously, but I can listen to only one. There is a similar difference of action and meaning between what one calls *smell* and what one calls *scent*, or between the words *touch* and *feel*.

Herein clearly resides the principle of the essence of *unity*, and of its necessity in works of art and imitation; for the word necessity in the arts applies to their need to please; a condition without which they will produce no impression at all, save a vague, confused and complicated one. Hence, it is evident that in order to enjoy works of art, the mind's first need is to receive their impressions clearly, to easily discern their ensemble and their harmony of relations, and to judge without encumbrance the end and the means used to please. Now, in order for the mind to be so affected, it cannot be encumbered, nor distracted by a diversity of fleeting impressions, which, in their inopportune competition, can address only the passive property of our senses and not their active faculty.

Everything that tends to prove our mind's *unity* of action in the judgment and the enjoyment of the works submitted to its consideration, everything that demonstrates how physically impossible it is for the mind to be divided in order to give equal consideration to two concurrent sensations, tends also to prove the need for *unity* in works of art; that is to say, that every work must be conceived, composed, and executed, according to the principle of *unity*.

Now, it is important, first of all, to understand the meaning given to this word, as well as the spirit of the *unity* in question. It seems to me to be of little use to caution that this word ought not to be taken in a material or arithmetical sense (which would be *non-sensical*), or that *unity* should imply the absence of divisions within a work credited with *oneness*. On the contrary, it is precisely from the parts that compose a work of art that results the merit of *unity*, in such a way that the greater the merit, the greater the number of parts.

The *unity* amongst the constitutive parts of a work of art is akin to the *unity* of action between a multitude of facts and circumstances. The *unity* of action is not an individual action, or the action of one; on the contrary, it is a collective action, irrespective of the number of participants who,

through an ordered concurrence, produce such an effect that it appears to be the work of one. The same applies to beings or bodies, where *unity* does not consist in a uniformity of action in every part, but rather in a diversity of their uses, which is subject to a driving principle that converges the different functions of each member or each organ towards the same end.

Thus, in all works of art, *unity* is neither that uniformity of forms, of facts, and situations, nor that identical likeness of persons, objects, actions, language, figures, physiognomies, and aspects, which can only be *sameness*. An assemblage of numerous figures held to the same line, to the same level, the one next to the other, would present figures that are *gathered* without being *united*; and such a composition would be precisely the one farthest removed from *unity* as it is understood morally, because it would be limited, as it were, to a material and arithmetical *unity*. This is not true *unity* because it exhibits no parts, since it would only offer in the spirit and fact of a composition a multitude of individualities re-stated in one singular and same motif. Let us add that, relative to the principal end of this art, which is to please the mind through the impressions that it experiences and by the action that it brings, the end has been bypassed, since the resulting outcome for the mind is nothing but the disgust that accompanies monotony or the lack of effect and action.

The multiplicity or the complication of objects, as we have explained, is another means – although in the opposite sense – to destroy the *unity* of a work of art. There is no one who does not feel compelled by the mere instinct for truth to admit that *unity* is violated when many arts quarrel over the conception, composition and the process of execution within the same work by encroaching on each other's domain. That same *unity* is violated if two subjects of composition were to occupy the same painting; if there was more than one point of sight within a perspective; if the same personage in a drama had more than one character; or if a poem rested on more than one principal event. Everyone understands, then, that the mind finds itself in the painful situation of listening to many sources at once; that being divided between situations and sensations that fight for its attention, it receives only broken and incoherent impressions; that being obliged to pass more or less promptly from one object to the other, it can neither experience integral effects, nor complete sensations. This is an effect that everyone experiences before those collections of paintings, which, pressing the one against the other, do not permit us to be strongly influenced by any of them, because our attention is divided, as when it beholds a crowd where no one person is noticed because everyone is seen at once.

What is *unity* then, understood as a moral principle for the perfection of works of art, and as an active cause for their effects, as well as the delight that the mind experiences? We affirm that *unity* is the *link* that produces a whole; that is to say, the accord of the parts with each other and with an ensemble; that its object is such that all the details and all the subsidiary parts of a work of art could be brought together and coordinated with respect to one point that becomes, at it were, the centre; that its activity consists particularly in establishing among all the objects a combination that is and appears to be necessary, where nothing could be removed nor added.

Such is in effect the property of this quality, in that it compels us to assemble within us the representation of the most numerous objects, not in an isolated manner, but so that they depend on each other, thus preventing us from seeing the part as something entire and complete.

The principal aim of *unity*, when the artist realizes it in a work, is such that it leaves us nothing to desire and nothing to subtract. *Unity* or its effect, could be found lacking in a work of art in two manners: either by the absence of that which is necessary, or by the presence of that which is superfluous. *Unity* will disappear, either when a work lacks those elements that could explain or constitute its nature, or when a work displays elements that are foreign to its proper nature.

Indeed, the nature of an object, properly speaking, is the foundation and the base for its *unity*, because it is really within this nature that one discovers the reason for each part, and the

place that it must occupy; and because the nature of this object would be different if one of these parts either did not exist, or existed differently.

Thus, when an architect is commissioned to construct a building, his first task is to form a clear and precise idea as to its nature and its purpose. Then, he will invent and dispose the various parts in such a manner that from their union arises a building that is precisely what it must be. Likewise, the fundamental *unity* in a painting results, above all else, from the clear and precise idea of the subject to be represented, and the idea that forms its nature; and subsequently from the necessary relations between each part, each figure, and each subsidiary element, and this idea.

Whenever we are unable to form the slightest idea of an object's *unity*, when we do not feel that the diverse parts that we behold with our eyes and our mind befit each other and form an ensemble, these parts, seen separately and considered in isolation, could well delight us, but the same may not be said of the object seen or considered in its entirety. It follows from this, that when each separate part of a work does not befit the idea of the whole, and when it bears no relationship to other parts, it is consequently opposed to *unity*, and hence it is a disagreeable imperfection.

Now, we said earlier that the discord between the parts, or between one part and the whole, can contradict the nature of an object and rupture its *unity*, either because it is lacking or superfluous, or because it is like an excess or a deficiency. Everyone understands, for example, that every narration, every discussion that is foreign to the discourse on a given subject and that distracts the mind of the listener from the aim at hand, destroys *unity*. The same applies to the nature of a subject that an orator intends to prove or demonstrate, while an important point is lacking. Episodes in a poem that are too numerous or too foreign to the core of the subject; redundant characters in a drama; figures that overload the composition of a painting; the repetition of useless members in a building's composition, all violate by their redundance the nature and thus the fundamental *unity* of a work of art, just as much as omissions, lacunas, or the absence of necessary constitutive parts.

Since in the representations that we observe there is either one or the other of two manners of contradicting *unity*, we are necessarily affected by a painful and disagreeable feeling. The artist bent on producing a perfect work must always have in mind this maxim that has always been recommended to the orator: *to utter all that is necessary, and to utter naught but the necessary*. What is recommended to the artist in practice must be equally necessary in theory, in the judgments extended upon his work. If one does not know what forms the nature of works of art, then one is also fundamentally unaware of the laws of their *unity*, and one will never know nor perceive their perfection. This is why there are such differences of judgment on this matter. One frequently observes people who admire the beauty of a discourse, a play, or a painting, because they have been impressed by the merit of some passages, some situations, or details, whereas these same works produce in others a disagreeable impression. It is because the former know only how to see the parts within a whole, while the latter see only the whole through its parts. Now the pleasure experienced by the first group is, properly speaking, one of instinct, and is available to many; whereas that experienced by the second group is only within the reach of those whose senses have been perfected by study and knowledge.

It is obviously much easier to analyze the idea of *unity* in the fine arts; to demonstrate that which it consists of, that which produces it, and that which destroys it, than to develop its principal notions and teach the practical means of its implementation. Such is the fate of ideas and abstract notions, they can only address themselves to sensibility. Thus, nothing is more difficult in this respect than to didactically teach the artist the means to implement the precepts of theory. *Unity*, if we have defined it well, and in the only manner proper to a definition (that is to say, to contain the most notions possible in the least number of words), *unity* is the link that unites and brings together at one point all the parts of a work of art, and coordinates them in

such a way, that nothing can be added or subtracted. It seems to us that the artist will find the secret of this moral and intellectual link, only by constantly keeping in mind, and by discerning that which constitutes the proper nature of the object or the subject to which it applies, and by recognizing, on the one hand, that which is necessary, and on the other, that which is useless for the development and the effects of this link and all the parts that compose it.

It is evident that the abstract theory of *unity* could attain much greater clarity if one were to transform it through practical examples into applications that are particular to each case, to all particular circumstances, and to all secondary facts, which would comprise varied observations

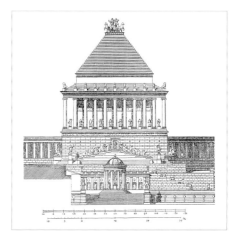

Fig. 85.   Temple of Mausolus at Halicarnassus.
From: Josef Durm, *Die Baukunst der Grieschen*,
A. Kröner Verlag, Leipzig, 1910

in each technical division of every art, dependent though they may be on the same principle. There could perhaps be no wider subject, one that would be completely out of scale with the available space of an article on theory; it would constitute the material for a massive book.

In fact, the complete merit of *unity* in each work of art, as well as art itself, results from the observation of many *unities* that one could, theoretically speaking, consider as secondary. In the work of the painter for example, in addition to the first *unity* of conception, one could count a *unity* of composition, a *unity* of action, a *unity* of manner and style, a *unity* of forms or design, a *unity* of adjustment, a *unity* of character, a *unity* of colour, and a *unity* of execution. Without doubt, it is from the more or less complete ensemble of all these *unities* that will arise the more or less evident effect of that abstract *unity*, a general quality that produces the fortunate link that makes a whole out of disparate parts. But how numerous are the detailed observations required by the analysis of all the means and procedures through which each of these *unities* is produced, and all the defects that oppose their production.

Bringing these notions back to the art of architecture, we shall lightly touch on the practical theory relative to the means that produce the different kinds of partial *unities* from which results a building's general *unity*. We shall call these *unities*:

Unity of system and principle
Unity of conception and composition
Unity in plan
Unity in elevation
Unity in decoration and ornament
Unity of style and taste

On the unity of system and principle. The unity known by this name consists in not confusing within the same building certain varieties – which among different nations are the product of a particular original principle – with certain types that are based on models with no mutual rapport. There is no better explanation of this *unity* of system or type than the very frequent examples of restored or added parts to Gothic buildings, according to the system and the types of Greek architecture. Nothing can better give the contrary idea of *unity*, that is to say, that of duplicity or of two buildings in one. But without going to such a striking extreme, one knows that there are a large number of practices in the art of building that offer a contradiction between systems and principles. Such is the one that owes its cause to the very destruction of ancient monuments during the Lower Empire. I am speaking of arcades built on top of free standing columns, which is a kind of dissonance whose misuse is exposed by the system of Greek architecture. As a matter of principle, *unity* cannot be more tangibly violated than by a mixture presenting the use of two mutually exclusive manners of building at once. It is a sin

against *unity* to associate pointed arches with Greek orders; to place the capitals of one order on top of the columns of another; to multiply the pediments where there is but one roof; to establish many storeys of columns, entablatures, and consequently floors, on the outside of a building that has no levels on the interior, etc.

On the unity of conception and composition. The *unity* of intention and of views that must become the common link between all the parts depends on the conception of a monument. A monument should also emanate from a single intelligence which organizes its totality in such a manner that one cannot remove anything, add or change anything, without altering its harmony. It is on this primary thought that its *unity* depends. A very large number of buildings, and some of the most famous ones, display the original intention of their creator. Formed at first according to another plan and for another purpose, new intentions organize the building's expansion either by new architects or during succeeding periods. A building then becomes an admixture of additions or modifications, in the midst of which even the trace of the original intention disappears, and with it the idea of a link that subjects its parts to the law of *unity*. One would be at pains to cite a more striking example of the lack of *unity* in conception and composition than the Tuileries palace in Paris, a work where a large number of architects laboured during a long succession of years, at building, dismantling, and rebuilding, to the point that nowadays one barely perceives the conception of the first author. No other monument exhibits such a proliferation of conjoined pieces. A totally opposite example is the one already mentioned in the article on UNIFORMITY (see this word), the palace of Caserta, which was conceived, composed, executed and completed in a short time by the same architect.

On unity in plan. From the *unity* in plan, which is the basis and the essential principle of a building's constitution, will derive, more than one can say, the effect of the link or the accord of the whole with its parts, as well as that great reason for order and harmony that defines *unity* and renders its precepts evident. Determining the exterior massing, as well as the interior distributions, the plan's principle of *unity* rests first on the clearest possible idea of the nature of the building; that is to say, on the reason for each part, and the reason for its relation to the whole. Enough said about the *unity* of plan, considered in the sense of an abstract theory. As to the more practical sense of a plan's composition, in view of pleasing the mind and the eyes, *unity* will chiefly result from the use of simple lines and regular contours, and from the correspondence between easily understood parts. Symmetry, in general, is a quality and a congruity in a plan, for the reason that, more than any other combination, it offers the idea of a completed and entire whole, and that it particularly simplifies the work of the mind in its search to understand the architect's conception. However, *unity* is not harmed by certain dispositions which oppose different forms and diverse outlines. A *unity* that needs variety, accommodates itself to certain contrasts in plan, as much as it rejects the affectation of broken part or mixtilineal outlines, which seem to have been under the renderer's pencil nothing but a game of fancy whose puerile abuse must be relegated by common sense and good taste to the inconsequential fantasies imagined by a mercantile luxury in order to diversify its products.

On unity in elevation. What particularly constitutes *unity* in elevation is a correspondence between the exterior massing and the interior that ensures that the eye and the mind perceive the principle of order and the necessary links that determined this *unity*. The principal aim of a façade or a building's elevation is not to offer combinations and compartmentalized forms for the amusement of the eye. Here, as elsewhere, if the pleasure that results from seeing does not originate from a necessity or a reason of utility, then far from being a source of value and beauty, this elevation will be nothing but a brilliant defect. But here, as elsewhere, most people fall into error while transposing ideas, that is to say, in subordinating necessity to pleasure. Hence this

multitude of building elevations, whose forms, combinations, dispositions, ordonnances, and ornaments, contradict the principle of *unity*, which is founded on the proper nature of each thing. What is important then to the *unity* of which we speak is not that an elevation exhibits more or less parts, more or less ornaments; it is that the elevation must fit the type, the nature and the purpose of a building; that it corresponds to the reasons, intents and needs which order its interior disposition; that the exterior of the building be unified by the visible link of *unity* in accordance with the demands of the interior.

If, then, the task is to examine the effects of *unity* in elevation, in the sense of delight or pleasure in a decorative ensemble, it seems that one could propose that these effects are principally caused by the use of one order of columns, by an equal spacing of columns, or by their alignment, without projections, back or fore parts. If the building has many storeys, as in a palace, the *unity* in elevation would be much better served by subordinating each storey to the same disposition of openings by a distribution of solids and voids in such a way that the solid dominates the void, by providing large spaces between storeys, by subjecting the entire massing to a uniform entablature, and by producing as few divisions as possible.

Generally, the intellectual *unity* in the elevation of buildings, more than any other perhaps, partakes in what one may call material or arithmetical *unity*. There is perhaps no art that is exposed more than architecture to the repetition of objects and forms, and to the multiplicity of needs and uses which tend to introduce into compositions the idea, the appearance, and often the reality of what one may call a plurality of objects within the same object, or elevations within the same elevation. Such is obviously the obligatory condition in church elevations on whose naves one observes – above the roof and the pediments that should terminate the building – a new building, bearing little relation of form or even proportion to the one that it surmounts. I am speaking of most churches with cupolas. This is not to claim that there is no way to subject this double elevation to the moral principle of *unity*, nor to suggest that this problem is insoluble; on the contrary, the great basilica of Saint Peter in Rome seems to us to be the one to have best approached this solution. It is most certainly the one where this *unity* of massing and order is most successful, thus producing for the eye and the mind the least disparity between the two elevations. However, most other churches of this genre seem to me more suitable to demonstrate the lack of *unity* in a building, and especially in its elevation.

On unity in decoration and ornament. What is known as decoration or ornament in architecture is the part that is necessarily the most arbitrary and the least subject to fixed rules. Consequently, it seems to have been the part that escaped the theoretical or practical laws of *unity* the most. However, such is the nature of *unity* – morally understood, and in the manner that we have defined it – that nothing exists in the domain of nature, and in that of the arts that imitate her, to which one cannot apply the consequences of a principle which, being a principle of order, must regulate all the combinations and all the inventions of the mind. Now, since by its nature, decoration rests on the most fleeting elements, it is even more important to protect it from a disorder that could destroy its effects. Thus, it is to *unity* that the compositions of decoration must be brought back, but within a proper measure.

As with any other part of architecture, the principal need answered by decoration is pleasure, since therein resides its primary object and its essential goal. Now, either the genius of decoration employs the great resources of painting and historical or poetic sculpture in buildings, or it is content to use their graphic characters which can be applied, under the name of *ornament*, to all sorts of members and standard parts of the general composition. Thus, it is not difficult to see how these works could be subject to the two conditions of *unity*. The first is the one that will establish their link with their subject, and with the ensemble where they will figure; the second, which is common to other works of art, concerns more especially execution.

Under the first of these conditions, decorative *unity* consists, above all else, in the choice of subjects congruous with the building's purpose. History and allegory make available to the genius of decoration some inexhaustible sources of inventions and compositions which are apt to give character to the monument, and complete its harmony. This harmony consists in a correct combination, and an accord with surfaces and placements, such that the very body of architecture does not disappear under its accessory elements, that its members are not altered nor broken, and that it is not hidden by ornament. This *unity* of harmony consists also in a use that is so moderate and that exhibits such an understanding of the means of decoration that a succession of ornamented and smooth parts will display a transition apt to make their effect salient. The excess of decoration destroys its impression; and intellectual *unity* , which is a link between various relations, also finds itself cancelled as soon as any idea of rapport, and consequently accord, disappears.

As to the particular *unity* of every *decoration*, considered in itself and aside from its rapport with architecture, there is nothing to say about it here, since it enters in the general theory of all the arts.

On the unity of style and taste. This kind of *unity* is listed among others that pertain to the perfection of the works of architecture, only because it is easier and more common to find its deficiency within this art than in all the others. Indeed, style and taste in a building depend without a doubt on those of the architect; it is he who, through his projects and their realization, endows the building with a particular character. But his art is the only art that needs to use the hands of others, the only one whose management and completion depend on circumstances that the architect does not control. When one considers the many causes for alterations, and for repairs and variations that tend to modify large building enterprises, one is compelled to conclude that even the most famous buildings display anomalies in taste and style that remove the valuable character of *unity* that would otherwise have made them accomplished works.

To this lack of *unity*, one could add the lack of *unity* in execution, and this subject could also offer to our present critique many considerations, which, being too close to the technicalities of material procedures, seem to be out of the spirit of a theory whose object it was to establish some ideas about one of the moral or intellectual qualities of architecture that architects and those who judge their works fail to recognize.

There is no doubt that this analysis of the nature and the effects of *unity* does not constitute part of the initial studies that the architect undertakes. There is also no doubt that the feeling for the true and the beautiful lead him, often without his knowledge, through the same paths to the same goal. But such is not the case with the majority of people who judge his works, nor even the small number of those who are called to direct them, and it is particularly to them that such considerations may be of use.

VARIETY *Variety* in works of art is a quality that theory can define only by comparing it either to an opposite quality, which is *uniformity* – understood here as a misuse of unity – or to what frequently passes for its synonym, namely *adversity*.

As we have already explained, unity (*See* UNITY) is an important quality in all works of art. It is that which makes a whole out of all the parts that compose a work of art. In binding all these parts as nature binds an organism, unity grants the mind and the eye the pleasure to understand with ease, to see clearly, to grasp without effort the goal desired by the artist as well as the compelling reasons behind the means that he employed, and to judge the merit of each invention.

But this quality known as *unity* has dangers that must be avoided and against which the undertakings of many a writer and artist have come to grief.

Nothing is easier than to fall from unity into uniformity. The latter has the following effect. Out of fear that the mind and the eye will experience too much trouble and difficulty in seeing and judging, uniformity everywhere establishes sameness, symmetrical similitude, complete repetition of all parts, details, and forms, in such a way that the mind and the eye have nothing left

to do since the whole can be seen in a single part. But if our mind refuses to rejoice in whatever offers it difficulty, trouble, or complication, if it abhors tiredness, it is no less an enemy of prolonged languor and rest. The mind needs a certain degree of action and movement; and rest pleases the mind inasmuch as it is not forced. The middle point, which is the secret of the pleasure that our mind experiences in each art, exists between the tiredness that results from activity, and the boredom that results from inertia.

If the notion of unity were to be so constrained as to make it approach that of sameness, then the result would be the reduction of every art and every work of art to this nullity of means and effects, leaving the mind no hold to exert its action, and rendering such action utterly useless. For the mind delights in bringing together and comparing the objects that it perceives, and it will have nothing left to do where these two conditions do not exist.

Understood in this context, uniformity hardly resembles and totally differs from unity. The mind desires and delights in unity because it demands, above all else, that that which it is required to see and hear, be heard and seen with enough clarity for it to be understood without much difficulty. Disorder and confusion make the mind weary, while simplicity, which is the customary companion of unity (*See* SIMPLICITY), facilitates the actions of discernment, comparison and judgment through the mediation of an established order.

But does this mean that the mind demands that painting should have only figures that are organized in straight lines, or architecture only façades without divisions and details, or rhetoric only discourse without movement, or music chords that are played only in unison; or poetry drama without action, narratives without fiction, and compositions without episodes. On the contrary, the mind summons *variety* with the help of unity. *Variety* is to unity what the seasoning that awakens and supports the appetite, is to the body.

If *variety* is defined by sensibility when compared to the notion of uniformity, which is its opposite, it also finds no less tangible an explanation in the difference of meaning and idea of the word diversity, which is very often used as a synonym of *variety*. It is not my purpose here to establish grammatical exactitude in our appreciation of the two terms. However, it seems to me that the word diversity applies more particularly to the idea of genre, whilst *variety* concerns the idea of kind. One speaks of the diversity of colours, climates, characters, nations and mores. The word *variety*, however, designates shades of the same colour, irregularities within the same climate, the unevenness of a character, the disparities in the customs of the same nation or in the taste of the same man. One speaks of a diversity of beliefs and a *variety* of opinions.

If this is true, then diversity is much less befitting than *variety* to the characteristics that are compatible with unity.

These characteristics must prevent unity from falling into uniformity without altering the principles of the former. Thus, *variety* will never attack the foundations of things, or the bases for invention, or the principal forms of a building, or the laws that govern or regulate its general composition and ordonnance. Only when these large objects have been determined according to the demands of unity, does *variety* intervene in all the details, by introducing within the general parti of the composition and its massing some modifications of forms, effect, design and character, thus giving the building a new appeal without changing its plan or its intentions, and exciting the mind and the eye to behold objects which are at once the same but dissimilar. In such a way, *variety* multiplies artistic creations in imitation of nature who produces an infinity of dissimilarities based on the same type.

Such is the idea of *variety* that we gain from the works of the great masters in all the arts. In painting, for example, nothing is more apt to produce a unity of composition in some subjects than a certain semblance of symmetry between the corresponding masses on either side of a picture. Raphael often used this method; and certain critics remarked that this kind of symmetry is agreeable to the observer, for it offers a whole in two equal parts, and facilitates the means to behold and enjoy the totality of the conception. We expect the same effect from each edifice that observes symmetry by generally repeating on one side of its elevation the design of the other. However, Raphael knew how to maintain unity in a symmetrical composition without falling into uniformity. If there was an appearance of uniformity in the general parti, he very astutely anticipated this difficulty by a skilful and ingenious *variety* of lines, forms, attitudes, groupings, adjustments and motifs, thus offering the mind and the eye that special pleasure that one experiences when beauty emerges from what could have otherwise been a defect.

Since *variety* makes for the charm of unity, it must be recognized that *variety* could not occur without the principle of unity. These are two correlated properties, where one does not exist save under the other's conditions; and this is what distinguishes *variety* from diversity, which corresponds to uniformity. Thus, both are opposing flaws. Yet, we do not oppose *variety*, in itself, to uniformity; and we consider the first to be less a contrariety and more a rectification of the second.

Of all the arts, architecture is perhaps the one that is most disposed, by the very nature of things, towards uniformity. In the entry of that name (*See* UNIFORMITY), we even suggested that this word comprises two different meanings: the first expresses a defect (as a misuse or an excess of unity), while the second signifies a natural identity between building forms; and architecture cannot dispense with this second kind of uniformity. However, the more one recognizes its importance for the existence of this art, the more one is compelled to admit that, as with the other arts and perhaps even more, architecture needs to introduce *variety* into her works.

Thus, even in the necessary uniformity of the symmetrical volumes of a façade, the architect could introduce some variety by virtue of certain movements in lines, in projections, and in the combinations of their details. The architect could correct an excess of uniformity in a plan by opposing certain relationships between different parts, which is an artifice of architecture that aims at disguising a very substantial symmetry. He could introduce *variety* against a forced uniformity in elevation by a skilful combination of solids and voids, or a succession of smooth and articulated parts, and the use of the different characters of the orders. But the infinite variations of decorations, ornaments, materials, colours, and all the substances available to architecture, offer the architect an infinite set of resources which, far from breaking the unity of the whole, will actually further enhance its effect.

One must reiterate that *variety* is but the opposite or the enemy of uniformity, which is the abuse of unity. On the contrary, *variety* serves unity; and without the former, the latter will fall into a sort of uniformity which is synonymous with monotony.

VISUAL ANGLE The visual *angle* should be consulted in architecture in order to determine the relationships of size. One observes that the height has limits that are necessarily determined by the need to commodiously see from the bottom to the top when the visual radius forms a forty five degree angle with the horizontal line. When this *angle* is increased to seventy degrees, it begins to place elevated objects at a distance inconvenient to sight. And if this same *angle* increases further, it will render the distance so bothersome that it would be impossible to look without twisting one's neck. Therefore, assuming that at forty-five degrees, the visual *angle* is the middle term; and that seventy degrees is the extreme *angle* for the tallest height possible; then at twenty degrees, the *angle* will be the other extreme for the smallest height possible, because there is the same progress in descending from forty-five to twenty as in ascending from forty-five to seventy.

Consequently, one can establish, as a principle, that each architectural part of a certain height will appear too low if the visual *angle* is less than twenty degrees, and too high if this *angle* is more than seventy degrees. (*See* PROPORTION)

Since objects appear greater or smaller, depending on the visual lines, there are some cases when the architect can change the customary proportions of different architectural elements. Antiquity offers us some examples and

Vitruvius gives some precepts in the second chapter of his sixth book. Nevertheless, one must remark that these changes should be small in number and be used only with great caution. Many architects think that even these changes of proportion should never occur, for this would amount to substituting a real illusion for one that is apparent only through the eye's habit of evaluating distances and comparing objects with respect to their remoteness.

It is generally known that there are two things that help judge the distance of objects, namely, size and colour. These are factors that diminish and weaken in direct measure with the remoteness of objects. The diminution of colour is caused by the increase of the interposed quantity of air; size is also diminished by the narrowing of *angles* formed by lines that extend from the outlines of objects, making a sharper *angle* when they project from a distant object than when they come from one that is close. But even though images of distant objects effectively appear smaller to the eye, it cannot be said that the eye fails to judge their size, for it understands their distance.

Thus, without thinking of the rules of perspective, and without our imagination explicitly examining the reasons and the different effects of distance – which depend on the narrowing of *angles* formed by visual lines – common sense rarely fails to notice these circumstances. If by chance it did fail, as when painting or perspective deceive us, then this is a sure sign that it does not usually falter.

In order that the precautions required by Vitruvius against the distance and the obliqueness of objects are rendered indispensable, one must assume that all that belongs to sight depends on the eye, which is not true. Sight uses experience, the other senses, as well as the judgment that corrects it; and this judgment never fails it; otherwise, painting and perspective would always deceive, for there is no more reason to mistake a circle for an oval when it is seen obliquely, than there is to take an oval for a circle, when the oval is painted to appear circular. (*See* PROPORTION).

WOOD In the entry *architecture*, we treated the subject of *wood* – in the primitive use that the Greeks applied to their constructions – as having been the model for forms, for disposition, and for the system of relationships, as well as the proportions and the orders that constituted their architecture, which later became that of all nations. We explained in that entry, as we have in the entry *hut* and others, the manner in which this sort of imitation should be understood; the point to which deductions based on this principle ought to be taken; and the spirit that once directed the taste of the Greeks in this assimilation that is at once material and metaphorical. We shall limit ourselves here to demonstrating that it was and still is necessary for man to give to his architecture a more or less tangible model, to which – depending on the development of the human mind – new imitative combinations derived from a more elevated and more abstract order of ideas are applied; in other words, the general laws of nature and the moral faculties of our intelligence.

Reason cannot admit that early people at the beginning of civilization – following a more or less primitive or uncultivated period of life, having found themselves already joined together in societies, and having need of larger and more solid constructions – imagined, in an a priori manner and without an instinct determined by a previous habit, the creation of an ensemble of reasoned and reciprocal combinations using cut stone. Reason also has little grounds to admit what is known as the action of chance, which sometimes produces those singular encounters, those partial accidents of the aggregation of forms in which one can amusedly see a game of nature; but that chance begets an ensemble of imitative combinations, where every object has its reason and can be accounted for, this, can never exist.

Early societies, in their infancies, did not owe the first combinations in the formation of shelters that nature suggested to them, to the simple action of an unknown principle. To the contrary, wherever there were forests, it was a necessity – as we have demonstrated (*See* ARCHITECTURE) – to use *wood* in the first constructions that answered to need. But it is in the nature of this material to lend itself to the exigencies and the progress of societies, with varying means or instruments, expense or economy. The Greeks, in their first state of civilization, could not help but augment, ameliorate, and reduce to a more determined form, the first trials that satisfied necessity. Thus, depending on the propriety dictated to them by necessity, they gradually fashioned the rustic work made of coarsely hewn trees or beams, as well as coarse habits.

There is nothing arbitrary in this. Nor is this a fiction. It is a kind of history written following nature. Therefore, there was nothing fortuitous in the elements of the first art of building among the Greeks; it was simply a succession of natural effects, deriving from the most natural principle of the most simple art of building.

The first constructions to be endowed with more art, necessarily became those that recalled most faithfully their model; thus carpentry must have been the customary construction for a long time. Since the art of fashioning *wood* requires numerous stages in its applications, one knows not how long it took the Greeks to refine the plans, forms, and proportions of their temples, for example; and to fashion in *wood*, the columns and their capitals, the entablatures, roofs or porticoes.

Nor can one determine the precise period when stone came to replace *wood* in buildings. This theory neither demands nor requires any chronological authority. What can be said – as shown by history – is that long after stone replaced *wood*, it was quite possible and even probable that the work in stone remained united to the work in *wood* for a long time afterwards; and we learn from Vitruvius that this was practised among the Etruscans.

We have dealt lightly here with the original causes of Greek architecture, only in order to show the role that *wood* must have played, and that the primitive works of the art of building in this material among the Greeks were and could not help but be the models for stone architecture.

For a lack of certainty in information about the traditions of diverse other nations, separated from us by the distance of time and place, we are left with this truth that applies to everything: that man creates nothing in the true sense of the word; that the *ex nihilo nihil* is for him an irrevocable stopping point; and that in his works, he always needs an antecedent whose existence is very often lost in the mists of time. Thus, since we cannot generalize and apply our theory to all architectures, we shall merely cite for its support, the large edifices of the architecture called *Gothic*.

In considering the churches and other monuments of the Middle Ages, their naves, the multiple jets of ribs that intersect on the surface of vaults, seemingly imitating the ramification of trees, one cannot say how many ridiculous hypotheses had been warranted by these haphazard resemblances between the procedures of construction and the productions of nature. Some pretended that the art of building of the Middle Ages found it models in forests; some saw in the height of Gothic vaults and the inflections of their cintres, the copy of an avenue of trees whose branches cross and intertwine. These are vain comparisons, having perhaps derived – unperceivingly – from the ancient Greek doctrine so well ascertained by facts and by tradition, that is to say, from the influence exerted by construction in *wood* on its imitation in stone.

Well, what modern critics did not perceive regarding the system of building and vaulting by architects called Gothic (one knows not why), is that almost the same sort of imitative process operated within this system.

We have enlarged upon this system, on its historical notions and the authorities that confirm them, in the entry GOTHIC . Here, in a few words, we shall merely indicate that it was *wood* that gave to this architecture her elements, her processes, and the models for her reality. Yes, *wood*, but not that in the forests as some want to believe,

but the *wood* that has been hewn, fashioned and modified in previous constructions. In one word, it was carpentry, it was the art of felling, cutting, assembling *wood* to shape pillars, lintels, rafters, king-posts, etc.; an art that constituted then, and still constitutes today in most of Europe, the component of all buildings great and small; and of houses, palaces, and especially churches.

As we saw in the entry GOTHIC, these vaults, whose models are believed by some to be in forests, are naught else but timber works that formed ancient churches, and of which, there are still extant examples; in other words, *wood* assemblies whose intervals were filled with masonry. It is evident that if one were to mentally omit these intervals, one would find this skeleton of timber work as it is practised today; but in the thirteenth, fourteenth and fifteenth centuries, people built in stone what had previously been made of *wood*.

We shall finish this article by observing that beyond the advantageous properties that wood has over stone, one must note, in particular, wood's ability to lend itself to the most simple as well as the most complicated ideas. Stone very rarely furnishes long pieces without risk of breaking; its handling is expensive, its transport is difficult, and its hoisting requires machinery. *Wood* suits the largest as well as the smallest spacings; it is adaptable to any contour, any configuration. In a country that offers only stone for building, the use of arches enters with difficulty, or at least in very late developments. This is perhaps the reason that best explains the absence of any cintred part, of any circular form, of any arch, in the monuments of Egypt. Contrariwise, nothing was easier in timber work than to curve pieces of *wood*, and join them together in order to form arcades and arches. Yes, the arch must have derived from processes belonging to work in *wood*.

NOTES

1   A Hermes designates a torso or half-human male figure supported by a pedestal, in lieu of a column. To be differentiated from an Atlante, which is a full male figure standing in lieu of a column, and supporting an entablature in the manner of caryatids. e.g. the Atlantes at the Temple of Olympian Zeus in Agrigento, Sicily. *Trans.*
2   From the French *terme*, the Italian *termine* and the old English *terminus*; designates a male or female torso surmounting a pedestal and supporting an entablature. *Trans.*

3   Quatremère uses the word moral in two senses: the first designates the intellectual, as opposed to the material realm, while the second designates ethical concerns. *Trans.*
4   In quoting this passage from Morgan's Vitruvius, (I, II, 5,6) I have substituted the word *aptness* to Morgan's word: propriety. This is because of Quatremère's differentiation between *bienséance* and *convenance*, which I have translated, respectively, as aptness and propriety. *Trans.*

5   Quatremère quotes Vitruvius out of order. For the integral text, see *De architectura*, I,1, 2 and 3. The present quotes and all the following ones from Vitruvius are from M.H. Morgan's translation, Dover, New York, 1960. *Trans.*

6   *Ibid*, Introduction to Book VI. *Trans.*

7   Read, *artistic* truth. *Trans.*

8   Book III, 1,1, Morgan, p. 72.

9   Quatremère's use of the word paradox is understood here in the sense of contrariness. *Trans.*

10 Book VI, 2, Morgan. p. 174.

11 In providing these extracts, Quatremère considerably edited and paraphrased Perrault's text. For Perrault's integral argument, see the *Ordonnance* pp. 96-112, and the recent translation by I. Kagis McEwen pp. 154-166. For the purposes of the present book, I have translated the text as it occurs in the *Historical Dictionary of Architecture*. *Trans.*

12 Perrault uses the term "aspect" to designate the varying perspective views of a building. I have translated "aspect" as "view." *Trans.*

13 This refers to a design by Antonio Labaco for the cupola of St. Peter's. *Trans.*

14 This refers to La Halle de Blé de Paris by N. Le Camus de Mézières. *Trans.*

15 Book VIII, p. 198. Morgan.

16 In Quatremère's text, the next six paragraphs very closely paraphrase Perrault's *Ordonnance*, Part One, Chap. VIII, pp. 20-21. Yet there are no quotation marks. It is possible that this was a printing error. As indicated in the entry CHANGE OF PROPORTIONS, I have translated Quatremère's text as it appears in the *Historical Dictionary of Architecture*. *Trans.*

17 Quatremère is referring to Chapter VIII of Part V. One of the *Ordonnance*, "De la diminution et du renflement des colonnes," pp. 20-2. *Trans.*

18 See the *Ordonnance for the Five Kinds of Columns after the Method of the Ancients*, Introduction by Alberto Pérez-Gómez, Translation by Indra Kagis McEwen. © The Getty Center for the History of Art and the Humanities, Santa Monica, CA, p. 83. *Trans.*

19 Here, too, in this paragraph, Quatremère uses Perrault's text without quotation marks. See Kagis McEwen, *Ibid*, p. 84. *Trans.*

20 Vitruvius lists six fundamental principles of architecture in I,2,1: *ordinatio, dispositio, eurythmia, symmetria, decor* and *distributio*. The mentioning of five principles here is perhaps an indication that Quatremère was using Claude Perrault's translation of Vitruvius. Perrault reduces Vitruvius's six principles to five, by using the word proportion to designate both *eurythmia* and *symmetria*. Perrault's text reads: "L'Architecture consiste en cinq choses: savoir, l'Ordonnance, qui est appelée *Taxis* les Grecs; la Disposition, qui est ce qu'ils nomment *Diathesis*; l'*Eurythmie*, ou *Proportion*; la *Bienséance*, & la Distribution, qui en Grec est appelée *Oeconomia*." *Les Dix Livres d'Architecture de Vitruve*. Pierre Mardaga, éditeur. Liège, 1988. p. 9. *Trans.*

21 This translation of de Mézières' text is from: *The Genius of Architecture; or The Analogy of That Art with Our Sensations*. Nicolas Le Camus de Mézières. Introduction by Robin Middleton, translation by David Britt, © 1992 The Getty Center for the History of Art and the Humanities, Santa Monica, CA, pp. 102-4. *Trans.*

22 Book IV, Chapter 1, p. 102. Morgan.

23 *Ibid*, p. 109.

24 *Ibid*, p. 104.

25 *Ibid*, p. 109.

26 *Ibid*, p. 110.

27 *Ibid*, p. 109.

28 *Ibid*, p. 86.

29 Four hundred kilometres, *Trans.*

30 Quatremère uses the word metaphysical to designate the realm of essences, and the source of rules in art. See note 19, Introduction.

31 Morgan, p. 198

32 *Ibid*, p. 5.

33 Ordonnance, here, is synonymous with composition. On the distinction between *order* and *ordonnance*, see these articles. *Trans.*

34 From the French verb *convenir*, to suit. Hence *convenance* or propriety, suitability, aptness. *Trans.*

35 Quatremère, uses the word *modénature*, from the Italian *modenatura*, or cornice outline. *Trans.*

36 Stiletto or stylet. *Trans.*

37 Morgan, p. 14.

38 *Ibid*.

39 *Ibid*, Book I, Chap. 2, 1. *Ordinatio est modica membrorum operis commoditas separatim uniuerseque proportionis ad symmetriam comparatio. Trans.*